THE ASTROTWINS

SUPERCOUPLE

Authors: Tali Edut, Ophira Edut
Editor: James Kerti
Book Design: Rosie Dienhart
Contributing Editors: Jen Beattie, Matthew Swann
Copy Editor: Vanessa Montgomery
Production Design & Illustration: Will Dudley

*Thank you to the talented and generous Astrostyle team for
flowing, growing and pivoting in the Year of the Water Tiger,
creating this book in divine collaboration and super-friendship
with us! We dedicate this book to you.*
Ophi & Tali

CONTENTS

Introduction

Supercouple Astrology

Your Supercouple Chart by Planet

supercouple *(def.)*

NOUN

The third entity created when two people align their energy to become a force greater than the sum of their parts;

In astrology, the blending of two individual's astrology charts or zodiac signs into a "Composite" or combined chart;

A celebrity couple who intrigue and fascinate the public; also referred to as a "power couple," sometimes by a portmanteau that combines their names (e.g., Bennifer, Kimye, Brangelina, Billary)

VERB

To combine two people's astrology charts and form a third chart, called the Composite midpoint, which inspires them to become something greater than their individual identities.

supercouples
THE NEW RELATIONSHIP
ASTROLOGY

Picture this: It's an idyllic, cloudless afternoon on the California coast. High wedding season. The Sun hovers above the placid Pacific as the last notes of "Pachelbel's Canon" waft into the briny air. You shift in your folding chair for a better view of your friends who are holding hands under a resplendent arch.

The officiant clears their throat and begins:

> *We are gathered here today to legalize the stressful, disappointing and monotonous future of Hunter and Jamie. To recognize the death of their hope and the crushing reality that life will not live up to what they're dreaming it will be. Hunter and Jamie, do you take each other as partners and co-pilots, driving down this road together blindfolded? To blame and berate...take for granted and neglect...to resent and regret, 'til disgust or divorce do you part?"*

Outrageous as it sounds, so many modern relationships devolve into a version of this. When life inevitably serves us the tough stuff, we feel lost in the middle of a stormy ocean without a map or a clue. So we keep soldiering through, hoping it will get better, while the magic slowly dissipates.

Here's the thing: You don't choose a partner to have an average or boring life.

No way. No thanks. Your hopes are infinitely higher than that.

You pair up to make magic—to achieve the #couplegoals that keep your connection alive as you face life together as a team. You do it to feel sexy and magnetic and happy for years to come. Maybe even to become that enviable, inspiring duo that makes everyone wonder how your spark is still blazing after all these years.

Create your own Supercouple Chart at **SUPERCOUPLE.COM**

You want to beat the statistics, not become one.

You want to be...a Supercouple.

A Supercouple is created when two people blend their energy and the alignments give them new superpowers that they didn't possess on their own. They don't "become one" or water down their personalities. Rather, a third entity forms.

A Supercouple is a thing unto itself—a fusion, a hybrid, something greater than the sum of its parts. As our friend Matthew says, it's when "1+1=3." Magic.

Don't we all want more of THAT in our relationships?

We started to notice this desire in our clients, who would ask us to read their astrological charts—then, with a sheepish tone and a slight pleading look in their eyes—wondered if we might just take a teensy peek at their partner's chart too.

From there, the truth serum poured out: The embarrassing issue they couldn't get past. The fear of ending up with the wrong person, being unsure if they were settling or if they were expecting too much. The frustration of having the same argument again and again and...again.

Lucky for all of us, astrology has a special tool called the Composite Chart, which blends any two birth charts and turns them into a greater super-entity, which you've probably figured out by now we call the Supercouple.

Sometimes, getting past stubborn relationship blocks isn't about "I want this" and "they want that." Compromise fails because one or both of you can't bend on a core value—not that you should. Because what happens if you do? Resentment, distancing, contempt and all the relationship killers take hold. Couple goals: canceled.

What if, instead of trying to speak each other's languages, you had a third dialect that both of you learned? A level playing field, where neither one of you had an advantage because you were both mastering the steps to a whole new dance.

Good news: You'll find this new relationship approach in the Composite Chart.

The Composite Chart—AKA the Supercouple Chart—is the instruction manual to your relationship. It literally reveals who you and a partner can become together.

As astrologers and matchmakers for three decades, we've used the Composite Chart to help our clients navigate the stormy plot twists, to keep the spark sizzling, to get through communication meltdowns, affairs, midlife crises and wild uncertainty.

If you're considering a commitment and wondering about its potential, the Supercouple Chart can be SO empowering. After all, wouldn't it be nice to answer, "What am I getting myself into?" before you tumble completely head over heels down the relationship rabbit hole?

We discovered how powerful a Composite Chart can be back in 2003, thanks to...Beyonce.

Here's the story: We were backstage at the Las Vegas MGM Grand Hotel, doing astrology chart readings for a parade of celebrities. Slated to perform at the Billboard Music Awards, these megastars were trotted through a lavish swag room, treated to luxury merch and pampered between rehearsals.

A doe-eyed singer in jeans and a sweatshirt sat at our table and introduced herself: Beyonce, a Virgo. It was her first astrology reading, and she was extremely curious. Beyonce was still part of Destiny's Child and had just done a couple of breakout hits with Jay-Z, "03 Bonnie and Clyde" and "Crazy In Love." Rumors swirled that the two had chemistry outside of the music studio, too.

After telling Beyonce all about HER chart, Tali winked and asked, "Would you like us to do a compatibility chart for you and...a certain someone?"

A guilty grin spread across her face: "Yes!" After Beyonce called her mom and Jay-Z to collect birth times, we made her a Composite Chart—a 60-page document eked out on our portable printer—and explained the highlights of her Supercouple connection with that Sagittarius "rocafella." The next day, Beyonce gushed that she stayed up late reading her Composite Chart and found it "fascinating."

Now we're not taking credit for Blue Ivy Carter or the Lemonade visual album or anything that happened after that moment. But we CAN attest to witnessing Beyonce's relief and excitement when she learned there was a map to help her decide whether dating that edgy guy from the Brooklyn projects was a good idea for a wholesome Houston girl like her.

Fear not: Supercoupling doesn't require celebrity status or a portmanteau like Bennifer or Billary or Brangelina. It's a state of mind, not just a status. It starts with the willingness to explore a higher-octave energy than you can individually emit, to enter that "third space" where your energies lock into place.

Supercouples can be twin flames, lovelorn soulmates, people who live happily ever after. Supercouples also break up, cheat on each other or become platonic after years of being romantic.

Human drama happens. Life forces you to evolve. You might be together for a reason, a season or a lifetime. But when a Supercouple IS united and doing what they do best, they're a spiritual force of nature.

There's no "right" way to be a Supercouple. There's only a desire to tap into the cosmic code of your connection.

Every single one of us has Supercouple potential. It's activated when we come together around a common goal. Business partners can be Supercouples. Family members can be Supercouples (as twins, we know this well). Friends and creative collaborators can too.

Being a Supercouple simply means allowing the chemical compound of your shared energy to take shape. As you learn about every single planet in your Composite Chart through this book, you'll understand your shared mission and superpowers, and how you can play to their strengths.

If so many of us WANT to have an extraordinary "relationship unlike any other," then why do long-term couples have such a relatively low success rate?

Maybe we've just been using the wrong equation to measure relationship "success."

Maybe we need permission to finally stop shoehorning ourselves into a "one-size-fits-all" cookie cutter relationship model. ("One size fits none" is more accurate...)

With this handbook to your Composite Chart, you have new tools and techniques at your fingertips. You can recalibrate after a fight and even after a betrayal. Supercouples can find "new relationship energy" long after your nest has emptied, or you pee with the door open, or you sleep in separate rooms because one of you snores.

Think about it: We've got tools to enhance every other part of our lives. We biohack our health with supplements and stem cells. We raise our spiritual vibration by meditating and manifesting and microdosing. Our homes hum with "smart" devices.

Supercoupling is the silicon chip that can bring your relationship into the Information Age. When you have your Supercouple Code, you can dial into it anytime.

Let's start now.

Ophi & Tali

Ophira & Tali Edut
The AstroTwins

> Note: In this book, we'll refer to the **Composite Chart** by several names: your **Supercouple Chart**, your **blended or combined sign**, and as many variations as we can think of to keep the writing interesting without confusing you.

A QUICK GUIDE TO GETTING THE MOST OUT OF THIS BOOK

LEARN: **Supercouple Astrology**

1. Do your Supercouple Chart at Supercouple.com

2. Explore each planet in your chart with this book. Working on a specific issue? Use the cheatsheet below.

3. Download our bonus resources at Supercouple.com and start putting what you learn into practice

SUPERCOUPLE TOOLBOX

Get free tools to guide you through the book at SUPERCOUPLE.COM

CHEATSHEET: YOUR SUPERCOUPLE PLANETS

Planet	Role It Plays in Your Relationship
SUN	Your relationship's personality
MOON	How you feel secure and express emotion
ASCENDANT	Your outward expression as a pair
MERCURY	Your communication style
VENUS	Date planning and seduction
MARS	Sexual chemistry & compatibility
JUPITER	Where you'll grow and be lucky
SATURN	Structures and boundaries you need
URANUS	Where you'll rebel together
NEPTUNE	Dreams and fantasies to explore
PLUTO	Your shadow work as a couple
LUNAR NODES	Your past lives, shared karma & destiny

THE SUPERCOUPLE SYSTEM:
MIND, BODY, SPIRIT

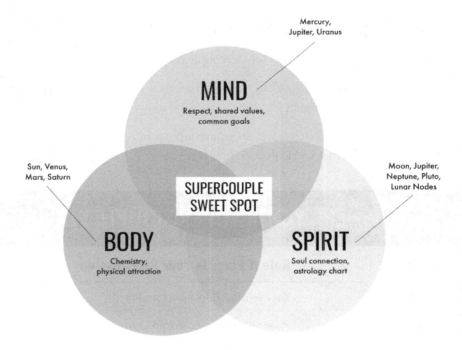

To activate your Supercouple superpowers,
you must attune to each other in three key areas:

MIND: Respect for one another, a shared mission, common goals—because if you don't want the same things in life, why bother?

BODY: Yes, physical chemistry matters! We're spiritual beings having a human experience. Attraction can be fostered, but not forced.

SPIRIT: Are your souls in sync? Here's where astrology steps in! Use your Supercouple Chart to understand your shared cosmic code (see page 25 to learn what every planet rules). Plug into that energy and experience the divine love encoded in your connection!

Create your own Supercouple Chart at **SUPERCOUPLE.COM**

THE 4 SUPERCOUPLE SEASONS:
YOUR RELATIONSHIP ROADMAP

Even the strongest Supercouples will go through seasons when it's not exactly smooth sailing. After all, you're two individual souls on a shared journey, and there will inevitably be times when you're out of sync.

The planets in our solar system are always moving. As they travel through the heavens, they create astrological moments of challenge and opportunity. We can't escape those cosmic crossroads, but we CAN prepare for them, knowing when one is due to arrive.

Throughout your lifetime, there will be key moments when the planets in the sky intersect with those in your birth chart, unleashing potent forces. These cycles can send most of us scattering in new directions that we're wildly unprepared to handle. Even strong Supercouples can find themselves at a crisis point, becoming a house divided.

How do we get through these times and, if necessary, recover? As the planets test your commitment, they demand that you build new emotional muscles or communication skills. From midlife crises to the stresses of bills or parenting, these seasons are scripted in the stars.

To help you navigate and plan ahead, we've created the Supercouple Seasons Relationship Roadmap.

SEASON 1: Ready for Adulting

Ages: 26-32

Astrological Cycles: Saturn Return (and lead-up)

What Happens: Adulthood officially begins, with new responsibilities and a desire for life direction. You're "ready to be ready" for big decisions like marriage, kids, a stable career, but not quite ready to give up the fun and youthfulness either.

Your Journey: How can you start building a more serious commitment or life with someone while also figuring out who you are? Is this the right person? Are you ready?

GET IN SYNC WITH YOUR SEASON

Grab your *FREE* Supercouple Seasons Relationship Roadmap at SUPERCOUPLE.COM

SEASON 2: The Clock Is Ticking

Age: 33-45

Astrological Cycles: Jupiter Return, North Node Return, Uranus Opposition, Neptune Square, Saturn Opposition, Pluto Square

What Happens: A series of intense planetary alignments force you to figure out the right balance between "me" and "we." How much can you compromise for the good of the partnership without feeling like you're sacrificing your needs or your identity? This is the most intense of the four seasons, with time-sensitive decisions around money, marriage, fertility and career that can max out pressure and stress. It also includes the "astrological midlife crisis" and cosmic cycles that coincide with key hormonal shifts. Dueling desires for security and freedom compete.

Your Journey: To create a stable relationship without losing your autonomy, and to navigate desires that will be at odds with the "rules" of traditional relationships.

SEASON 3: Midlife Makeover

Age: 46-56

Astrological Cycles: North Node Opposition and Return, Chiron Return

What Happens: Priorities change as the main fertility cycle ends and attention shifts toward long-term security and enjoying the second half of your life. Deep healing and reinvention can occur as you seek a sense of purpose.

Your Journey: Do you and your partner still share the same goals and values? Do you still want what you signed up for, and if not, what does change look like?

GET IN SYNC WITH YOUR SEASON

Grab your *FREE* Supercouple Seasons Relationship Roadmap at SUPERCOUPLE.COM

SEASON 4: Wisdom & Wonder

Age: 57+

Astrological Cycles: Second Saturn Return

What Happens: The arc of adulthood that began at 29-30 during your first Saturn Return completes, starting the next major 30-year cycle of life. Saturn rules aging and maturity, and you may face these issues, through your own life cycle, elderly parents or children becoming full-fledged adults—perhaps going through their own Saturn Returns!

Your Journey: What does an impactful life well-lived look for you individually and with a partner? Where can you find meaning and make a difference? How can you age gracefully and into mature love?

Head to Supercouple.com to unlock our exclusive bonus secrets to thriving in every Supercouple Season!

SUPERCOUPLES: A REASON, A SEASON OR A LIFETIME?

Do all Supercouples last forever? If they did, the entire celebrity gossip business would die. No matter how much science and technology advance, relationships remain an unsolved mystery. The heart defies logic and algorithms and it can't be altered in a lab.

We've come to accept that as part of the human condition. Still, it hasn't stopped us from spending over three decades trying to hack relationships, to take some of the sting out and encourage people to keep pursuing love, while defining commitment on their own terms.

You might be reading this and wondering why one of your most epic relationships ended. "Were we really a Supercouple if we broke up or fought all the time or got divorced?"

The simple answer is: Yes. Any two people can become a Supercouple when they decide to blend their energy. Every person you've "Supercoupled" with is, at the very least, a teacher. There was a reason you came into each other's lives, no matter how long you were there.

The best way to use this book is NOT to say, "Are we or aren't we a Supercouple?" Rather, we encourage you to run a Composite (Supercouple) chart and discover the potential and possibility you can unlock. Do you like the essential energy this relationship will create—or is not going to satisfy you? That's where YOU get to choose.

The Supercouple Chart empowers you with free will and conscious choice. It can help you create closure and make peace with relationships that didn't last forever, or explain the times when you and a partner got out of sync. Use it as a tool, not a rule—then go forth and design the relationship that satisfies you best.

Create your own Supercouple Chart at **SUPERCOUPLE.COM**

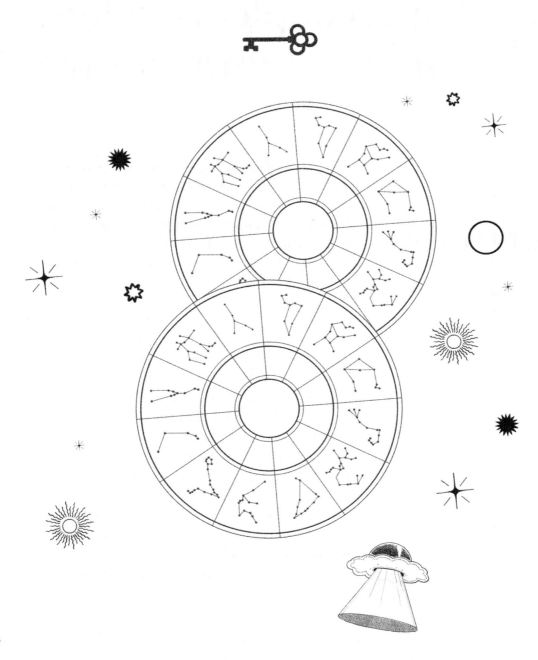

Supercouple Astrology
101: MEET YOUR COMPOSITE CHART

GET YOUR CHART

Do a free Composite
(Supercouple) chart
at SUPERCOUPLE.COM

Every relationship has a personality of its own, a unique third entity that gets created by your shared energy. Of course, you'll both have individual personalities and needs. But this book is about the "us" that emerges when two people unite, and how the energy of your connection brings out different sides of each of you.

Well, guess what? It just so happens that there is a unique astrological chart for every relationship. It's called a Composite Chart in proper astrology-speak, and it's derived by taking two birth charts and calculating the midpoints between each planet. Your Sun sign and their Sun sign, your moon sign and their moon sign, your Venus sign and their Venus sign, and so on. To simplify this technical term, we call it the Supercouple Chart—or just the Superchart.

The Superchart reveals the personality of your relationship. It also sheds light on what it would look like if you two met each other exactly in the middle! It's a guide to finding a perfect compromise in just about any situation. A lofty goal? Certainly. But how awesome is it that you can astrologically map this ideal state of co-existence? That's one reason we love Supercharts so much. They are the "cosmic care and feeding manual" that every relationship needs!

Supercharts are also an amazing tool for reviewing past relationships. Why WERE you so insanely attracted to each other for that brief but passionate spell? Is there a reason the two you "just knew" you were soulmates? How did you interact with each other in a past life—and what is your shared destiny in this incarnation? These answers and more can be found in the Superchart.

The chapters that follow are meant to help you discover divine harmony in any relationship—whether you found each other for a reason, a season or a lifetime.

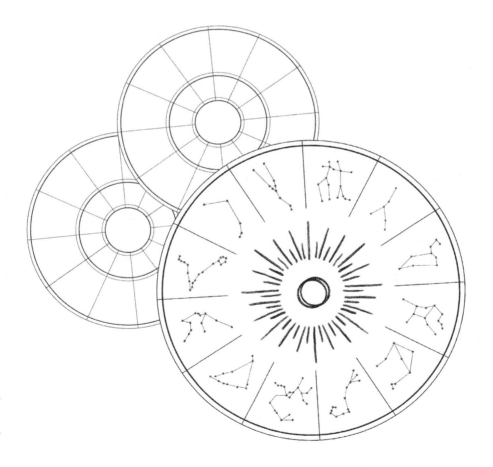

Step 1: Make Your Supercouple Chart

DO YOUR RELATIONSHIP'S SUPERCHART

Ready to calculate a chart for YOUR relationship? We've got you covered. To create a Superchart with our cosmic calculator go to:

SUPERCOUPLE.COM

To calculate your astrology birth chart, you'll need the time, date and place of birth for both people. Some people don't know their birth time. If you can't find it on your birth certificate, you can try contacting the Vital Records office in your state or area of birth (if you were born in the United States). And if that still doesn't work, make as close of an estimate as you can or enter 12:00 noon.

Without a birth time, you won't be able to accurately learn your rising sign, also known as your ascendant. Nor will you correctly know which houses the planets in your chart fall in. But there is still a LOT of data you can glean by entering your date and location of birth—so don't let that stop you from checking out your astrology natal chart.

Step 2: Find Out What It Means

INTERPRET YOUR SUPERCOUPLE CHART

Now that you have your Superchart calculated, you can jump ahead to the planet chapters and start reading all about your relationship! If you have the birth time for both people, lucky you! For each planet, you can read interpretations for both the zodiac signs and the houses.

CHEATSHEETS

Get free planetary cheatsheets for your Superchart at SUPERCOUPLE.COM

An important thing to note: The zodiac sign and house may bring two different energies to each planet in your Superchart. For example, your Composite Sun may be in the zodiac sign of outgoing, showstopping Leo. But if it falls in the mysterious eighth house, some of those shiny rays may be directed toward private pursuits rather than public ones. As a couple, you may be as introverted as you are extroverted.

Astrology is an interpretive dance. It's important to use this book as a guide to discovery, not the law—a tool, rather than the rule. Every relationship is unique. There's not one single way to interpret a planetary placement. What you read in *Supercouple* is meant to get the wheels turning. The rest of the journey is up to you.

Want to dive deeper into your astro-geeking? The next few sections of this book go into greater detail about the "three-part puzzle" that makes up a chart: the planets, zodiac signs and houses. If you want to understand what these cosmic terms are all about, we've got you covered. And we promise that even a beginner can learn!

Step 3: Balance "Me" and "We"

COMPARE YOUR INDIVIDUAL PLANETS TO THE SUPERCHART PLANETS

GET YOUR CHART

Do a free Composite (Supercouple) chart at SUPERCOUPLE.COM

Simply understanding your Superchart is not enough. Both you and your partner will have to adjust if you're going to meet each other in this mutual "third space." And guess what? You might not want to do that all the time.

This demand for flexibility and compromise is the reason they say relationships take work. To succeed as a couple sometimes means fighting against natural tendencies as individuals. "Knowing thyself" is a crucial part of the equation! That's why we recommend that you also calculate individual birth charts for you and your partner. And yes, we've got you covered again here. You can do any birth chart for free on our website at:

astrostyle.com/birthchart

From there, flip to the last pages of every planet section in this book, the "Compatibility" sections. We've spelled out the adjustments you'll each need to make in order to achieve Superchart nirvana. It will support you in addressing the ways in which your relationship might be pulling you out of your comfort zone or creating tension that you don't know how to work through.

COMPOSITE MIDPOINT VERSUS DAVISON CHARTS

You may have heard about the Davison Chart, which is similar to the Composite and also a very cool tool, however, we are not using that system in *Supercouple.* The main difference is this:

> ***Composite Charts*** take two individual charts and find the midpoint on the zodiac wheel between every planet. This is the system we call the Superchart.

> ***Davison Charts*** find the midpoint of your birth dates and birth locations, then draw up a third chart that gives your relationship an actual birthday and birth location.

You won't learn about Davison Charts here, but they're certainly fascinating! As anyone who begins exploring astrology knows, there is always more to discover.

The 3 Key Parts of the Supercouple Chart

PLANETS, ZODIAC SIGNS + HOUSES

Every astrology chart is composed of three key components: The planets, the zodiac signs and the houses. If your relationship was a movie, each piece of this "three-part puzzle" would have a specific purpose in the film:

Planets: The actors

Zodiac Signs: The roles they play

Houses: The stages where the scenes take place

Create your own Supercouple Chart at **SUPERCOUPLE.COM**

1

Planets:
THE PLAYERS IN YOUR LOVE STORY

In the "movie of your relationship," the planets are ***the actors.***

Each planet (or Superplanet, in the case of your blended chart) governs a specific aspect of your relationship's character or identity.

For example, Jupiter is the happy-go-lucky nomad in the cast. Saturn is the wise oracle who keeps you motivated and working hard toward your shared goals. Mercury is your communications coach, while Venus wings in like a love fairy to set the stage for seduction. As you read *Supercouple*, you'll learn how to **work with** this entire ethereal ensemble, one planet at a time!

2

Zodiac Signs:
WHAT ARE YOU TWO LIKE TOGETHER?

*The zodiac signs determine **the roles the actors (planets) play, or the costumes they wear.***

In every astrology chart, the planets land in a specific zodiac sign—for example "Mercury in Scorpio" or "the moon in Virgo." In the Composite Chart, this sign is derived by finding the midpoint between the zodiac signs in your individual natal charts.

Zodiac signs "modify" the planets, adding nuance to their character. They give each planet its script. For example, let's say

Jupiter was Bradley Cooper. In Pisces, Jupiter would be Cooper as the romance-and-booze-addicted Jackson Maine of *A Star Is Born*. In big-mouthed Sagittarius, Jupiter would hearken Cooper's comedically obnoxious role as Phil in *The Hangover*.

3

Houses:

WHERE YOUR LOVE STORY TAKES PLACE

*The houses are **the "movie sets" where the scenes of your relationship take place.***

The 12 houses of the zodiac all represent different parts of your life together, from work to home to relationships to career. The houses follow the progression of the zodiac signs—for example, the first house shares traits with Aries, the zodiac's first sign. The seventh house mirrors Libra, the zodiac's seventh sign, and so on.

The planets in your Superchart are the "residents" of these houses, traveling through each in their journey around the Sun. To keep this metaphor going, the 4th house (like Cancer) would be the scene of your home. The 10th house (like Capricorn) might be your place of work or the VIP room of an elite club.

The Planets in Your Supercouple Chart

In the "movie of your relationship," the planets are ***the actors.*** And each planet plays a different role in shaping the way you blend your lives. In *Supercouple*, we guide you through every planet to help you understand the entire "cosmic cast" of your relationship. To get you started, here's an at-a-glance overview of every planet's role in your Superchart.

THE INNER PLANETS:

The inner planets are the smaller, rocky (terrestrial) planets that are closest to the Sun: Mercury, Venus and Mars. In astrology, we include the Sun and moon as inner "planets," since we track them in relation to our position on Earth. In the Superchart, they are the planets that govern your day-to-day interpersonal dynamics in the relationship.

> *Sun:* Your Relationship's Personality
> *Moon:* Your Relationship's Emotional Nature
> *Mercury:* Your Relationship's Love Language
> *Venus:* Your Relationship's Romantic Style
> *Mars:* Your Relationship's Erotic Fire

THE OUTER PLANETS:

The "gas giants"—Jupiter, Saturn, Uranus and Neptune—are called the outer planets. Astrologers include Pluto, which is an "icy dwarf" in technical terms, as one of the outer planets. In the Superchart, they reveal how you operate together in the external world, as well as the psychological dynamics of your relationship.

GET YOUR CHART

Do a free Composite (Supercouple) chart at SUPERCOUPLE.COM

> *Jupiter:* Where You'll Expand Together
> *Saturn:* Where You Need Boundaries
> *Uranus:* Where You're Experimental Together
> *Neptune:* Your Relationship's Fantasy Factor
> *Pluto:* Where You'll Project On Each Other

SPECIAL CHART POINTS:

There are many special points that astrologers look at beyond the planets, including the ascendant, a number of asteroids, fixed stars, and nodes. In *Supercouple*, we cover two important Composite points that are essential for any couple to understand.

> *Ascendant/Rising Sign:* Your Relationship's Image
> *Lunar Nodes:* Your Shared Karma & Destiny

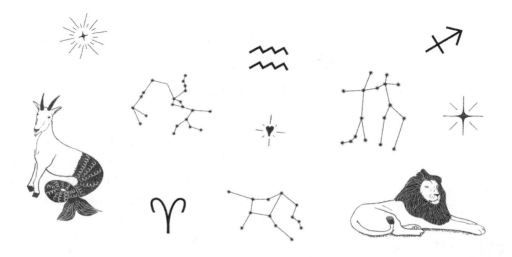

The 12 Zodiac Signs in Your Supercouple Chart

The zodiac signs determine *the roles the actors (planets) play, or the costumes they wear.*

There are 12 zodiac signs, which evolve in a very specific order from Aries to Pisces. The order of the zodiac signs represents the movement from birth (Aries) to elderhood (Pisces), or self (Aries) to spirituality (Pisces), or beginnings (Aries) to endings (Pisces). No matter what signs are in your Superchart, learning to work with the energy of all 12 signs offers you access to the entire universe!

Wherever a planet lands in your Superchart, it takes on the role of that particular zodiac sign. This will color your approach to amour. We describe this in depth in the chapters that follow, but here is a quick guide to the traits of all 12 zodiac signs.

WHAT DOES IT MEAN THAT A PLANET IS "IN A SIGN?"

GET YOUR CHART

Do a free Composite (Supercouple) chart at SUPERCOUPLE.COM

The zodiac wheel looks a lot like a clock. It's a circle divided into 12 equal parts, each one associated with a different zodiac sign. As planets make their circular orbit, they are always traveling through the realm of one of the 12 zodiac signs. For example, if Mercury is in the Aries part of the sky, we say, "Mercury is in Aries." If Pluto is in the Scorpio part of the sky, we say, "Pluto is in Scorpio."

In ancient days, there were constellations that aligned with each of the 12 slices; however, the constellations have shifted. In Western astrology (the method we use here) that does not change the zodiac signs. (Contrary to the false rumors of a 13th sign spurred by NASA several years ago!) Western astrology measures the zodiac geometrically and by the seasons.

In your individual natal chart, we do a freeze-frame of the sky at your exact moment of birth. Wherever the planets are in that "clock" (AKA the zodiac wheel) will determine the cosmic makeup of your chart.

Supercharts are calculated differently. Here, we take two natal charts and find the midpoints of every planet on the zodiac wheel. For example, say you have Venus in Aries and your partner has Venus in Sagittarius. In the Superchart, your Venus sign is likely to be smack-dab in the middle, nestled in the sign of Leo.

When you have a Supercouple Planet in this sign, it brings out these traits in you...

ARIES ♈

Daring, attentive, impulsive, lusty, physical, exciting, passionate, fresh, original, temperamental, bossy

TAURUS ♉

Stable, traditional, indulgent, sensual, slow-burning, persistent, loyal, tenacious, affectionate, possessive, demanding

GEMINI ♊

Dynamic, talkative, strategic, opinionated, curious, flirtatious, unpredictable, innovative, cultured, impulsive, noncommittal

CANCER ♋

Nurturing, emotional, domestic, sensitive, family-oriented, private, creative, caretaking, aloof, artistic, insecure, passive-aggressive

LEO ♌

Bold, generous, loyal, protective, decadent, playful, courageous, expressive, entertaining, demanding, energetic

VIRGO ♍

Supportive, tactile, analytical, practical, engaging, dedicated, selective, wise, resourceful, perfectionistic

LIBRA ♎

Charming, romantic, cultured, luxuriating, beauty-loving, fair-minded, stylish, indecisive, decadent, demanding

SCORPIO ♏

Magnetic, loyal, protective, deep-feeling, intuitive, erotic, intense, artistic, dedicated, jealous, secretive, complex

SAGITTARIUS ♐

Adventurous, worldly, wise, free-spirited, optimistic, outspoken, idealistic, impulsive, comedic, temperamental, changeable

CAPRICORN ♑

Structured, serious, family-minded, lusty, ambitious, dedicated, traditional, value-driven, goal-oriented, status-conscious, reserved

AQUARIUS ♒

Unconventional, open-minded, rebellious, hilarious, community-oriented, idealistic, active, rational, scientific, cool, experimental, best friends

PISCES ♓

Dreamy, intuitive, visionary, soulful, ultrasensitive, isolating, intuitive, compassionate, deceptive, sacrificial, destructive, escapist, unrealistic

THE 4 ELEMENTS OF THE ZODIAC

The zodiac signs are divided into four groups of three zodiac signs that are associated with an element in nature

FIRE Signs are creative initiators:
ARIES, LEO, SAGITTARIUS

EARTH Signs are builders who create legacies:
TAURUS, VIRGO, CAPRICORN

AIR Signs are communicators who spread ideas:
GEMINI, LIBRA, AQUARIUS

WATER Signs are emotional and family-oriented:
CANCER, SCORPIO, PISCES

THE 3 MODALITIES OF THE ZODIAC

The zodiac signs are also divided into three groups of four zodiac signs that share a common expression and core drive

CARDINAL Signs are leaders and trailblazers
ARIES, CANCER, LIBRA, CAPRICORN

FIXED Signs are stabilizers and traditionalists
TAURUS, LEO, SCORPIO, AQUARIUS

MUTABLE Signs are social, interactive and expressive
GEMINI, VIRGO, SAGITTARIUS, PISCES

Create your own Supercouple Chart at **SUPERCOUPLE.COM**

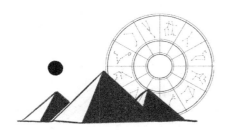

The 12 Houses in Your Supercouple Chart

*The houses are **the "movie sets" where the scenes of your relationship take place.***

The zodiac wheel is a 360-degree circle, divided into 12 segments, or houses. Each segment, or house, represents a different essential aspect of our lives. In the "movie of your relationship," the houses are like the different sets or stages where the planets ("actors") play out their roles (given by the zodiac signs).

CHEATSHEETS

Get free planetary cheatsheets for your Superchart at SUPERCOUPLE.COM

WHAT DOES IT MEAN THAT A PLANET IS IN A HOUSE?

The circular wheel of the astrology chart is divided into 12 for the zodiac signs—but that's not all! If you know your time of birth, you can divide the wheel a second time, into the 12 houses.

There are many different house systems that exist, but the one we use is the Placidus system. Every astrologer has their preference, but this has proven most accurate for us after viewing thousands of charts.

In your individual natal chart, we do a freeze-frame of the sky at your exact moment of birth. The planets will be moving through one of the 12 houses, which locks in their location. For example, you might say, "I was born with my moon in the 9th house." And from there, you can explore how the intuitive moon works its magic in the cosmic zone of travel, adventure and abundance! (AKA the 9th house).

Supercharts are calculated differently. Here, we take two natal charts and find the midpoints of every planet on the zodiac wheel. For example, you have Mars in the 1st house and your partner has Mars in the 3rd house. In the Superchart, your Mars sign will be right in between them, most likely winding up in the 2nd house. However, this depends on how equally sized the houses are in your chart!

The first house begins at what would be 9:00 on a clock. From the first house's "cusp" (or beginning border), we travel around the zodiac wheel in a counter-clockwise direction. This counter-clockwise journey represents our relationship's evolution, from the individual (1st house) to the collective, greater society (12th house).

GET YOUR CHART

Do a free Composite (Supercouple) chart at SUPERCOUPLE.COM

HOUSES 1-6: THE PERSONAL HOUSES

The first six houses are called the "personal" houses. They rule our private and immediate lives and our day-to-day interactions with peers and family. How we earn our income and take care of our bodies also falls in this grouping of houses. A Superchart with lots of planets in the first six houses may put the couple's focus on home, family and traditions.

HOUSES 7-12: THE INTERPERSONAL HOUSES

The 7th through the 12th houses are the "interpersonal" houses. They govern contractual relationships, joint ventures, travel, career, society, spirituality and even our "transition" at the end of life. A Superchart with a lot of planets in the later houses tends to put the couple's focus on external experiences, like career achievement, traveling, spiritual exploration and leaving a public mark.

THE 12 HOUSES IN YOUR SUPERCOUPLE CHART

1st House

Associated with: Identity, initiative, individuality, daring moves

In Your Superchart: What first impression do you make as a pair? The 1st house begins the zodiac, and covers all the "firsts" in your relationship: the impact you make as a couple, leadership, new initiatives, fresh starts and beginnings. The sign on the cusp, or starting edge, of this house, is referred to as your rising sign or ascendant. Planets in the 1st house of your Superchart direct how you appear to the world. They also reveal your willingness to take a chance or fight for yourselves.

2nd House

Associated with: Values, material resources, basic routines, foundations

In Your Superchart: How secure are you as a pair? The 2nd house of your Superchart covers all matters related to your immediate material and physical environment—taste, smells, sound, touch, sights. It also rules income and the way you manage money as a couple. This house is the "pleasure palace" of luxury, sophistication, the arts, and sensual touches like candles, a good bottle of wine, and music. Planets in the 2nd house of your Superchart will definitely have a say in how disciplined or decadent you are when it comes to your finances.

3rd House

Associated with: Communication, cooperation, peer relationships

In Your Superchart: How do you communicate with each other? Planets in the 3rd house of your Superchart guide all forms of interaction, from how you socialize as a couple to the ways you converse through dialogue and text. This is the "local zone" where day-to-day activities take place and you mingle close to home. As the peer center of the horoscope wheel, it is the realm of siblings, coworkers, neighbors and your shared friend circle. Look to the 3rd house for clues on date planning, day trips and playful activities you can enjoy in the evenings at home.

GET YOUR CHART

Do a free Composite (Supercouple) chart at SUPERCOUPLE.COM

4th House

Associated with: Family, nurturing figures (the mother), financial security, home

In Your Superchart: How can the two of you create an ideal home life? The 4th house sits at the very bottom of the zodiac wheel, and thus, rules the "foundation" of your relationship. This includes your home, privacy, and the nest egg you save. Parents and children live here—including your own inner children! The emotional matters ruled by the 4th house come with a strong trigger alert. How do you nourish yourselves? What's your approach to family and parenting? These matters are influenced by any planets in the 4th house of your Superchart.

5th House

Associated with: Creative expression, fertility, romance, fame, fashion

In Your Superchart: How do you romance each other? Since the 5th house governs creative expression, drama, fun and play, planets here have a lot to say on the matter. Since this is the zone of fertility and pregnancy, any planets in the 5th house of your Superchart may direct how easy (or difficult) it is to conceive. Childlike energy and raw emotion, such as joy, come from here—and so does being bold, assertive, passionate and glamorous. When it's time to dress up for a high-profile date or sexy photo shoot, the 5th house of your Superchart is definitely activated!

6th House

Associated with: Health, fitness, data, details, analysis, organization

In Your Superchart: Is it time to make a plan? Turn to the 6th house of your Superchart, which is the domain of efficiency, health and service. This realm rules schedules, systems and the everyday management of your lives together. Activities like diet and exercise, budgeting, cleaning and volunteer activities are all affected by any planets in this zone. Need some helping hands? The 6th house rules service providers such as babysitters, nannies, gardeners, and housekeepers. Since it's also the house associated with pets, planets in this realm of your Superchart might indicate if you'll adopt a cat, dog or goldfish.

7th House

Associated with: Committed partnerships, socializing, fairness and equality

In Your Superchart: What are your favorite couple-time activities? The 7th house is the sector of committed relationships, negotiation and togetherness. Planets in the 7th house of your Superchart reveal your favorite bonding activities—namely, the kinds that are fun, pleasurable and luxurious like fancy vacations, epic concerts and all-night excursions. Contracts, marriage, and business deals live in this realm. Look to your 7th house when you're taking on a long-term project together. Planets here provide clues on how to best cooperate and play to each other's strengths.

GET YOUR CHART

Do a free Composite (Supercouple) chart at SUPERCOUPLE.COM

8th House

Associated with: Sexuality, shared resources, spirituality, the "shadow self"

In Your Superchart: Feeling that urge to merge? The 8th house of the Superchart is the zone of joint ventures, particularly ones involving a property, long-term investments or shared resources. If you open up a bank account or buy a home together, you're in 8th house terrain. Real estate inheritances, taxes and loans also live here—any larger, lump-sum of cash that arrives all at once. Planets in the 8th house don't simply govern your finances though! This is also the house of birth, death, sex, transformation, mysteries, and bonding at the deepest level. It's the space where "I" becomes "we" and two entities merge into a greater whole.

9th House

Associated with: Wisdom, travel, global relations, diversity, higher education

In Your Superchart: How adventurous are you as a pair? The 9th house is the global zone of the zodiac wheel and planets here reveal how you travel, study and broaden your horizons together. Your risk tolerance is regulated by any planets in this exploratory realm: Are you free-spirited gamblers or cautious types who only take calculated chances? This philosophical center governs your shared religious beliefs, spiritual philosophies, morals and ethics. Will you follow traditional wisdom or will your relationship draw you down a more unconventional path? Planets in the 9th house of your Superchart will have a say on this matter!

10th House

Associated with: Careers, provider figures (the father), structure, long-term goals, legacies

In Your Superchart: What are your shining achievements as a couple? The 10th house sits at the very top and most public part of the chart. Planets in this zone of your Superchart direct your career ambitions (and how to support each other's professional aspirations), long-term goals, structures, and master plans. This disciplined realm rules authority figures, providers and parents (particularly the father). The cusp, or border, of the 10th house is also called the midheaven, and it clues astrologers in to the worldly accomplishments you'll crush together.

11th House

Associated with: Idealism, community, groups, society, technology, teams

In Your Superchart: What will the two of you stand for—and who are your people? The 11th house is the zone of society, groups and humanitarian action. When planets land here in the Superchart, they direct your community activities as a couple. This rebellious, experimental house also rules the future. What do you hope and wish for together? Planets in the 11th house can reveal your idealism and help you tap into group resources to bring your vision to life.

GET YOUR CHART

Do a free Composite (Supercouple) chart at SUPERCOUPLE.COM

12th House

Associated with: Surrender, the dream state, illusions, transitions, spirituality

In Your Superchart: Let it go, let it flow! The zodiac completes with the 12th and final house, which rules endings, closure and healing. Planets in the 12th house reveal how willing you are to surrender and have faith in the universe. This is also the zone of dreams, illusion and escape. Do you go into denial together? What vices and addictions might you share as a pair? Planets in the 12th house show where you can be self-destructive together or make sacrifices that drain your shared resources. Imagination, spirituality and esoteric activity live here. In this boundless house, you can dream up the best ideas together. But lines can get blurry and you must be careful not to become codependent or enabling of each other's vices.

Your Supercouple Chart

SUPERCOUPLE

SUN

our "relationship sign"

Use Your Supercouple Sun to Understand:

- Your blended personalities
- Your "identity" as a couple
- The way you shine when you're together
- How generous to be, both with one another and the people in your world
- Energy levels—how to get pumped up and where to tone it down
- Your worldly focus as a pair
- How much attention to give each other

WHAT'S THE PERSONALITY OF YOUR RELATIONSHIP?

In your birth chart, the Sun is the essence of who you are as an individual—the self you show to the world. It's the light you shine, the energy you give off, the "personal brand" that comes to mind for people when they think of you.

In that spirit, the Supercouple Sun is the personality of your relationship. It's how people remember you as a couple. ("Oh they're so fun to be around!" or "Well, that's an intense combination.")

Since the Supercouple Sun is the midpoint of your individual Sun signs, the way you operate as a couple might mix into a wildly different cocktail. For example, blending a Sagittarius and a Pisces, two squirmy and commitment-shy mutable signs, could produce a

Supercouple Sun in committed, serious Capricorn. Suddenly, your free-spirited Sagittarius "runaway bride" friend is happily putting a ring on it, and your player-ific Pisces pal is suddenly obsessing about 30-year mortgages—well, blame it on the solar flare of their Supercouple Sun.

If you're the kind of person who's afraid to lose yourself in a relationship (a valid concern), or you and your partner polarize into your individual stances every time you disagree, the Supercouple Sun offers a fresh portal into common ground.

Maybe you'll never understand their Gemini tics and they'll think you're just a Leo drama queen...but if you focus on the path of your Supercouple Cancer Sun (home, family, sentimental moments), the mental noise around that dissonance dies down. Try it!

When you slip into a dry spell together, think of the Supercouple Sun as your fueling station. Energy is always banked here; a readily available resource for couples to siphon for pleasure and excitement. (If only you'd remember that when your minds start wandering elsewhere! Well, IYKYK and now you do!)

Supercouple Sun in Leo? Recharge with a royal superdate. Roll out the red carpet with side-by-side massages, slip into your fanciest 'fits and head to a place with luxury amenities and endless photo opps. Are you an Aries Supercouple? Hit the tennis courts and work out some stress with competitive physical exercise.

Bottom line: The Sun is the brightest spot in your blended chart, so use it liberally! Those solar flares can be the saving grace of your bond if you remember this simple maxim: The couple that plays together, slays together.

Supercouple SUN
IN THE ZODIAC SIGNS

In the Sign of	Makes Us	Strengths	Challenges
ARIES	Feisty	Adventurous, innovative, positive	Competitive, selfish, impatient
TAURUS	Steadfast	Traditional, secure, patient, affectionate	Stubborn, stagnant, demanding
GEMINI	Dynamic	Social, curious, collaborative, experimental	Gossipy, indecisive, scattered
CANCER	Comfortable	Creative, nurturing, deep emotional connection	Codependent, self-indulgent, moody
LEO	Extravagant	Joyful, playful, enthusiastic, strong leaders, decadent	Ego-driven, prideful, needy, exhausting
VIRGO	Sensible	Insightful, supportive, healthy, strategic	Critical, picky, overanalyzing, perfectionistic
LIBRA	Elegant	Peaceful, affectionate, charming, attractive	Avoidant, passive-aggressive, superficial, vain
SCORPIO	Intense	Magnetic, intuitive, passionate, shrewd	Jealous, punishing, unforgiving, possessive
SAGITTARIUS	Adventurous	Enthusiastic, wise, optimistic, exploratory	Tactless, insatiable, gluttonous, arrogant
CAPRICORN	Ambitious	Driven, committed, down-to-earth, responsible	Pessimistic, work-focused, austere, harsh
AQUARIUS	Futuristic	Authentic, community-building, social, innovative	Avoidant, rebellious, contrarian, distant
PISCES	Enchanting	Empathic, healing, compassionate, imaginative	Codependent, escapist, unrealistic, adrift

Create your own Supercouple Chart at **SUPERCOUPLE.COM**

SUPERCOUPLE SUN

ARIES ✳ ♈

OR THE 1ST HOUSE

We feel most confident & united when we are:

- Going on an adventure
- Trying new things
- Doing something physical
- Sharing novel discoveries
- Showing off our shared talents
- Challenging each other
- Enjoying a friendly competition
- Sharing an inspiring one-on-one experience
- Spoiling (or even babying) each other

Supercouple Style: NOVELTY SEEKERS

Look before you leap? Oh, what's the fun in that? Adrenaline-junkie Aries is the zodiac's first sign, and this fiery Sun guarantees a relationship full of thrills. As a duo, you'll blaze trails on an eternal hunt for novelty. When tackling new experiences, you'll spur each other on, chasing adventure and climbing to new heights. While you may take disappointment hard, you bounce back quickly. Life becomes an eternal exploration when you're together. You've gotta keep on keeping on. Those bumps and bruises? They're just valuable lessons you learn along the road to mastery.

But guess what's NOT an option? Quitting. Although you can be an impulsive pair, once the two of you finally commit, you are in it to win it. Aries is ruled by Mars, the fiery red planet of energy and drive making you quite the competitive tag team. In mythology, Mars is the god of war and aggression. Highly impatient and combative, you boast this planet's fighting spirit when you come together. First place, first prize, first to market: together you become trendsetters and groundbreakers who love being number-one.

Aries rules the head, which may explain why you're such a, well, headstrong pair. When pursuing a shared goal, you may literally "ram" your way through barriers to create breakthrough results. Aries is one of the four cardinal signs that start the seasons (along with Cancer, Libra and Capricorn). Together, you are initiators who lead the pack! Starting is easy for you two. Finishing? Not quite so much. Your shared space quickly fills with half-done projects that you'll get back to "someday." Pro tip: Don't leave them lying about unless you're both comfortable living in utter chaos. Fact is, no couple may be more in need of a savvy storage system than you two!

Aries is the first of the zodiac's three fire signs (including Leo and Sagittarius). Sharing this Sun is certain to turn you into a spotlight-stealing pair—even if on your own, you'd rather fly under the radar. Originality is your shared calling card—you just bring out the innovative side in one another. And while you're often imitated, your power couple magic will never be duplicated. Mutual friends will follow you two, as you lead them on one boundary-pushing adventure after another. It's anyone's guess what you'll cook up together! What's unique about your bond, however, is how you manage to blend your talents without morphing into a two-headed being. Since Aries is the sign of autonomy, this relationship thrives when each of you is pursuing independent passions while pouring plenty of energy into your co-created ventures.

Here's the trick to mastering an Aries Sun relationship: Give each other lots of space when you need it, but be ready to shift back into "I'm paying rapt attention to you, my love" mode at a moment's

Create your own Supercouple Chart at **SUPERCOUPLE.COM**

notice. Keep each other updated on your projects. When one of you hits a snag, the other will eagerly rush in for the save. You also love to cheer each other on and brag about the other's achievements. Because you inspire each other to take chances, there will be lots of highs and lows—but that's part of what makes this so exhilarating!

Entitled much? Your ego-boosting Aries Sun teaches you both to expect the best. Wielding such confidence is what helps you shatter glass ceilings, and that's a remarkable trait. But when unchecked, your "Team Us" vibe can get downright diva-like; aggressive, even. To avoid being cast as villains, channel your shared competitive streak into supporting each other's career goals.

Power struggles may erupt between the two of you, especially when a heated disagreement polarizes you from each other. Be warned: with fiery Aries at the helm, conflict can ignite at a moment's notice, turning a peaceful discussion into a dumpster fire. (And oh how tempers can flare in this union!) Since Aries is the zodiac's first sign, it's technically the "baby" of the wheel. In this relationship, you may find yourselves devolving into childish reactions, staging tantrums, throwing objects, stomping your feet. To avert destruction, you may have to take turns being in charge. Moreover, learn when to surrender control instead of fighting for "my way or the highway." Being right isn't always worth it!

No matter how many ups and downs life brings, this relationship has solid survival instincts. Once any stormy feelings pass, you two have a remarkable ability to see the bright side of most situations. And when you're in a positive state of mind together, you could light up a stadium with your effortless charm!

Famous Aries Supercouples: Prince William & Kate Middleton, Sarah Jessica Parker & Matthew Broderick, Glennon Doyle & Abby Wambach, Queen Elizabeth II & Prince Philip, Katherine Hepburn & Spencer Tracy, Courtney Love & Kurt Cobain, Adam Levine & Behati Prinsloo, Sonny & Cher

SUPERCOUPLE SUN
TAURUS ✳ ♉
OR THE 2ND HOUSE

We feel most confident & united when we are:

- Indulging in decadent meals
- Pampering ourselves and being affectionate
- Spending time in nature
- Celebrating traditions
- Dressing up for a formal event
- Enjoying cultural activities
- Curating a beautiful home environment
- Saving up for the future
- Taking long naps and sleeping in

Supercouple Style: SENSUAL SECURITY

They say that good things come to those who wait—and this patient, process-loving partnership is here to prove it. The Taurus Supercouple relationship blossoms at a slow and steady pace, getting richer with each passing year. When you met, you may have had a knowing feeling of "this could be my person." Yet the actual courtship was likely drawn out. The reason? Taurus is the first of the three methodical earth signs (along with Virgo and Capricorn). Like crops in a garden, everything in your relationship must be cultivated according to natural rhythms.

Create your own Supercouple Chart at **SUPERCOUPLE.COM**

Rushing, as you'll both quickly learn, takes the pleasure out of an otherwise decadent plan. Taurus is ruled by Venus, the planet of beauty, luxury and romance. Being together will keep your five senses in perpetual high gear. A gourmet dinner, vintage wine, and boom...you're relaxing into a luxurious 14-hour slumber in each other's arms. At its core, this connection cherishes comfort, value and practical luxury. That said, you're a down-to-earth duo and you work hard to pay for your indulgences.

Symbolized by the persistent and plodding Bull, Taurus has two speeds. With your shared Sun in Taurus you're either contented like a couple of steers luxuriating in a verdant pasture or hyped-up and ready to charge. *Toro, toro!* This isn't a lazy relationship by any stretch of the imagination, but it does come with a built-in energy conservation program. Together you will patiently assess whether something is worth the investment of time and resources. Then if the green light flashes, it's all systems go!

Taurus is one of the zodiac's four fixed signs (along with Leo, Scorpio and Aquarius), located in the middle of every season. Your shared role is to hold down the fort and make sure the work gets done between the planting and the harvest cycles. Even while charging ahead, this relationship requires routines and due process. (Cue the "mechanical Bull.") Work is broken into simple steps, and you two thrive when you take daily action that inevitably manifests concrete results for your diligent efforts.

On a good day, you'll show up together as patient, organized, supportive, romantic, careful, and dedicated. When you're content and in the groove, you're in your happy place. You know what you like as a couple, and that's that. You stick with your preferences, and you rarely change unless there's a really good reason.

Stubbornness can be an Achilles heel of your relationship—
especially when you both dig your heels in and refuse to budge.
On the upside, this union has a lot of staying power. You bring out
each other's loyalty and dependability. Beware, however: The safety
zone can turn into a deep rut if you never move out of it, and the
two of you can fall into spells of inertia. To combat this, you must
intentionally push yourselves to take a chance and try something
new. Maybe you hit a new location periodically for your date nights
instead of always auto piloting to "our favorite."

If you happen to live in a culinary hotspot, lucky you! This
relationship inspires an appreciation of fine food and wine, so
why not make a game out of sampling one new restaurant a week
or month? You could also bring this into your own kitchen by
experimenting with a cuisine from a different region—which,
naturally, you'll pair with the appropriate wine. Since Taurus is the
zodiac's arts lover, tickets to a live theater production or special
museum exhibit can give you both lots to talk about. When you need
to unwind together, opt for gentle outdoor activities like long bike
rides and trail hikes.

On a larger scale, change and calculated risk brings the progress
you need to ensure that your bond doesn't stagnate. Sometimes,
it's good for the two of you to shake things up in a big way too, like
moving to a new city or selling off some stocks to invest in crypto.
You won't make these decisions lightly, however.

Taurus is the sign of values and ethics and people may look to the
two of you as their role models. Within your shared circle, you may
be the ones to plan the holidays, organize vacations and basically
be the family rocks. This level of responsibility can feel like both a

privilege and a burden for you two. Burnout is especially dangerous territory for a Taurus Sun relationship since you may turn on each other when your circuits are fried. Learning to say no, without guilt, will be something the two of you have to work toward as a pair.

You prefer to keep the peace within this relationship, but when you're pushed past your limit, watch out! When one of you is worked up about something, steam pours out of your ears. We'll see you pacing, muttering the same thing over and over, clenching your fists and looking like Bulls ready to charge! Moments like these can be highly tenuous—and if you don't learn how to deescalate, majorly destructive. Just like the Toro plowing, horns down, toward its target, you can lose all perspective when you're fired up. In those moments, you may each say or do things that you'll live to regret. So learn quickly to NOT wave the red cape when your partner seems to be spoiling for a fight. Go to your corners ASAP!

One surefire way to soothe tension? Touch each other often. The combined Taurus Sun is highly affectionate and even a long hug becomes somatic therapy for you both. Going to bed early can keep your bond strong, whether you indulge in hours of deep lounging or sensual boudoir play. You heal your partnership when you're physically connected. In fact, you're a highly imaginative couple in that arena! For best results, activate all of your senses. Maximize the bedroom experience with sexy playlists, warming massage oils, silky sheets, scented candles and of course, mood lighting. You might even keep a refrigerator in the room so you can feed each other in bed, using each other's bodies as silver platters.

Famous Taurus Supercouples: Victoria & David Beckham, Megan Fox & Machine Gun Kelly, Lisa Bonet & Lenny Kravitz, Mick Jagger & Jerry Hall, Warren Beatty & Annette Bening

SUPERCOUPLE SUN
GEMINI ✳ ♊
OR THE 3RD HOUSE

We feel most confident & united when we are:

- Diving into deep metaphysical discussions
- Socializing with inspiring people
- Inventing something new together
- Exchanging witty banter, memes and long texts
- Discovering cutting-edge artists and thought leaders
- Playing games and exploring culture
- Gossiping about common enemies

Supercouple Style: MIRROR, MIRROR

Wordplay is foreplay in the Gemini Supercouple Sun relationship, and no subject is off limits here! Gemini is one of the three social air signs along with Libra and Aquarius. Conversations get lively fast, whether you're debating the evening news or bantering about your summer concert schedules. Clever and quick-witted, you'll stay looped in on the juiciest gossip; in fact, you may be the regular subject of it yourselves. What can you say? The dynamic duo vibes you exude leave people curious, even envious.

Gemini is represented by the Twins, which can make you inseparable. In each other you've found a kindred spirit who wants to hear your thoughts and actually understand them. Attraction may begin as a meeting of the minds. "We couldn't stop talking," you may both report back to friends after your first encounter.

Create your own Supercouple Chart at **SUPERCOUPLE.COM**

The downside of twinning? You two feel like soulmates one day and siblings the next. But relax! These platonic spells are not proof that the magic is gone. Sharing a foundation of friendship is the gift of a blended Gemini Sun. Truth is, you're as much "in like" with each other as you are in love. But there's a reason they say absence makes the heart grow fonder. To stoke the embers, pull yourselves away from each other and develop autonomous interests. Curiosity is an aphrodisiac for this match.

Mobile Gemini is ruled by Mercury, the winged messenger. As a couple, your energy circulates in a quick and frenetic way. Moving around together is a must. Since interests change on a dime for the two of you, it's anyone's guess where your shared GPS will lead.. One winter, you're obsessed with snowboarding, hitting the powder every weekend in matching weatherproof onesies. The next year, you fly south as snowbirds, Instagramming your way through the tropics as you live your best digital nomad lives. No matter the destination, you quickly charm the locals, scoring invites to the hottest parties and events.

Being part of your shared friend circle has definite benefits! Well, for as long as the good vibes last. Gemini is one of the four ever-changing mutable signs, along with Virgo, Sagittarius and Pisces. These signs finish every season, preparing us all for a shift in the weather. Sharing a Gemini Sun can make you quite a mercurial couple! While the relationship's can't-stop-won't-stop pace guarantees excitement, friends may struggle to keep up with you, much less track you down.

Commitment can be challenging within this relationship, too. Since feelings run hot and cold between you, it's possible that you'll break up and get back together multiple times before finally settling in. Or you may get locked in the pursuer-distancer dance, picking petty fights to create distance when the other gets close. (And then blaming it on the other one's attachment style.) The secret to breaking this "come here, now go away" pattern? Devote yourselves to a shared pursuit that will sustain mutual interest for more than, oh, six weeks. Engage in the process rather than fixating on the end goal: collect data, track each other's progress and talk each other through the challenging moments.

The hands, arms and lungs are the body parts ruled by Gemini. Notably, these all come in twos, like twins. There's a lot of gesturing when you're communicating and you may literally enjoy making things by hand. When you're feeling excited in one another's company, you may get so hyped up that you forget to pause for air between statements. Simple breath work exercises can help you two recenter and gather your thoughts, especially if you find yourself talking just to fill the space instead of thinking through your responses.

Part of the fun (and curse) of the Gemini Supercouple Sun is that you inspire such range in one another that your desires vary wildly from day to day. Will you be the vivacious jokesters, or the snarky critics? Your duality as a couple can be confusing—and nearly impossible to put a label on sometimes. As this relationship matures, you two may realize that "relationship anarchists" is the best-suited title for your undefinable bond. As a couple, every decision may be fraught with a bit of back and forth. Waiting before you make any binding decisions will be your saving grace. "Let me get back to you on that" will be words to live by. Then go reflect, research and wait until every mood has a chance to ebb and flow before you act.

Famous Gemini Supercouples: Marilyn Monroe & John F. Kennedy, Neil Patrick Harris & David Burkta, Kylie Jenner & Travis Scott, Reese Witherspoon & Ryan Phillippe

SUPERCOUPLE SUN
CANCER ✳ ♋

OR THE 4TH HOUSE

We feel most confident & united when we are:

- Co-hosting a dinner party or a family celebration
- Working on a creative project together
- Enjoying the arts
- Bonding with relatives
- Sharing cozy moments at home
- Spending time near water
- Taking beach vacations
- Decorating the house
- Taking care of our people

Supercouple Style: EMOTION OCEAN

How sweet it is! There's a whole lotta feeling in the Cancer Supercouple relationship. As one of the zodiac's three emo water signs (along with Scorpio and Pisces), Cancer brings out the soulful, sentimental side of you both. Even if, separately, you are both nomadic, this relationship is sure to activate your nesting instincts. Follow the pull to settle down and you will quickly learn the joys of domestic life, complete with copper-bottomed pans, snuggly pets—and possibly kids that you'll nurture with love.

Cancer is one of the zodiac's four cardinal signs (along with Aries, Libra and Capricorn), the signs that begin every season. These are significant points on the chart, much like the NSEW points on a compass. Cancer represents our foundational security and roots and is symbolized by the Crab, with its impenetrable outer shell and vulnerable underside.

Just as the Crab carries its home on its back, you two set up a cozy space wherever you go with framed photos, handmade art objects, and lots of soft places to sit. Home, in fact, may be the place you feel truly comfortable together, dropping your guards and emoting freely. Returning to a safe space together is essential to keeping the peace. If you have children together, you'll make excellent co-parents, creating a safe harbor of family life for them to bask in.

Whether they share your DNA or are "chosen family," the Cancer Sun relationship centers around caring for others. From kids to pets to less-fortunate neighbors, having people to look after gives you a sense of shared purpose. But look out! Relationships get codependent fast if you confuse "being supportive" with taking on other people's problems as your own. Encourage people to dry their tears and face their fears—then build that same resilience within yourselves!

Since Cancer is associated with the archetypal mother, the parental figures in your lives shape this relationship in profound ways. Exploring childhood memories will be an essential part of the "getting to know you" process. If you experienced trauma when young, for example, this relationship can help you break that family pattern. Just don't expect that process to happen overnight. Before you can create a new narrative, you may trigger one another, watching ancient habits that you thought you'd outgrown flare up.

Did you have an idyllic childhood? You may set up home near your family of origin to keep the good vibes flowing.

Just as a crab's claws grip, this Composite Sun sign energy may lead you two to cling to comforts. Security is everything in this pairing, perhaps to a fault. Financially, you are shrewd and practical together, saving your pennies for a rainy day. But when the seas are stormy, you may soothe with unhealthy vices, polishing off bottles of wine or stuffing down "scary" emotions with unhealthy snacks or energy-depleting meals. Retail therapy can also be a vice, but resist overspending! Without an ample cushion, you may become nervous or ruled by your feelings.

While the two of you may become masters of "going with the flow," Cancer is ruled by the ever-shifting moon. Get ready for smooth sailing some days and choppy seas the next. Like luna herself, the energy between you can wax and wane by the hour. Emotions, in fact, are quintessential "first responders" in this union, although they may not be the most reliable gauge of what's actually happening. Within this relationship, you can be prone to unpredictable moods swings that catch each other off guard. Along with tears, you'll walk on eggshells around each other without coping techniques. Learn to self-soothe so you can step away and get centered when emotions arise rather than snapping at each other, or worse, having public meltdowns.

Cancer is associated with the chest and stomach, so when you come together you often "go with your guts," even when this flies in the face of logic. When you two get a strong feeling, it may be accompanied by a flutter in your chests or butterflies in your tummies. Learn to listen to those sensations and find healthy ways to share about them with one another. Shadow work can be profoundly healing for you two, especially if you have a nurturing couple's therapist, coach or support group to guide you through the process.

On a good day, your instinctual bonds provides deep empathy for your connection. You two can sense an oncoming current, then ride that wave to a mutually beneficial outcome. During stressful times, however, you're like sponges who subconsciously absorb each other's energy. And without a mature level of emotional regulation, you may feel like you're aboard a tiny vessel that's crashing around in deep waters. The trick to navigating stormy seas? Learn to successfully surf your own emotional landscapes, then create shared coping techniques when the riptides roll in.

Here's a great place to begin: During rough moments, ask each other this one fundamental question: "How do you feel about that?" But it doesn't stop there. You must both learn to actively listen to the answer, without rushing to soothe, judge, coach or correct one another.

The next magic words? "I understand why you would feel that way." You don't have to agree; in fact, faking alignment can damage your bond. Validating each other's feelings, however, is the secret to success in a Cancer Supercouple relationship.

Famous Cancer Supercouples: Zendaya & Tom Holland, Faith Hill & Tim McGraw, Angelina Jolie & Billy Bob Thornton, John F. Kennedy & Jackie Onassis Kennedy,

Create your own Supercouple Chart at **SUPERCOUPLE.COM**

SUPERCOUPLE SUN

LEO ✳ ♌

OR THE 5TH HOUSE

We feel most confident and united when we are:

- Entertaining the crowds by dancing/singing/throwing epic parties
- Celebrating special moments like anniversaries
- Pampering ourselves with luxury
- Giving each other gifts
- Watching an artistic performance
- Co-leading a project or organization as a sexy power couple
- Looking at old photos (or having a photoshoot!)
- Building a shared legacy and life

Supercouple Style: ROYAL ROMANCE

Ready the thrones! With regal Leo as your Supercouple Sun sign, this relationship has "power couple" written all over it. Like palace royalty, you'll dazzle the world as a pair with your showstopping style and unparalleled creativity. When you channel that fierceness into a shared mission, people sit up and take notice. Not that you two have to work that hard to attract attention! Since you amplify each other's shine, even a simple errand run can draw admiring stares.

Leo is symbolized by the proud and passionate Lion, and your relationship is about achievement, whether you're captivating an audience, building a family or breaking the Internet as a dynamic (even controversial) duo. You love turning mundane moments into "launches," celebrations or any excuse to treat yourselves. When together, you're like giant kids who just want to play. There's rarely a dull moment when in this relationship, but make sure to get some rest! Every date doesn't have to be an epic, five-venue journey—although we're not saying there's anything wrong with that.

Since Leo is associated with fertility, couples with this Supercouple sign might begin picking out baby names early on in the dating process. Active parents, you'll get down on the floor to play educational games or take the little ones on field trips to science museums and amusement parks. (Hey, it's fine if you guys enjoy the outing even more than they do!) Of course, sharing a Leo Sun doesn't necessarily mean you'll create a dynastic family together. But your bond may involve "birthing" something, like producing a local talent show, recording music together or flipping houses and turning them into posh vacation rentals.

Huge-doses of praise and appreciation keep you both high, but warning: if you get hooked on each other's validation, you may give your power away in the process. It's understandable: Leo is ruled by the Sun, the center of our solar system. That great ball of fire heats everything up with sexy passion, but when the Sun sets, it's ice, ice baby. At times you may feel obligated to keep one another happy and shining...or else. Bottom line: Your egos are not your amigos in this somewhat self-centered bond. Build up inner fortitude and make sure you each have other sources of encouraging support outside of the relationship.

Create your own Supercouple Chart at **SUPERCOUPLE.COM**

When in the company of others, be mindful! When together, you easily upstage friends and family, creating a competitive energy among your crew. Even if you've adopted a "selfless" identity as a couple, generosity may come back to bite you when others are unable to reciprocate in kind—or a sister-in-law wants to host Christmas dinner for a change. While your shared moral code is strong, you can get hung up on what's "right" and "good." And when that's challenged, the claws come out as you defend your fierce shared ideals. As you two mature, you become aware of the impact your supersized energy has on others in the room. Direct your flair for powerful leadership and invite everyone to discover their spot in the sunshine. Used properly, your shared energy leaves others awakened and revitalized in an empowering way.

Leo is one of the four fixed signs along with Taurus, Scorpio and Aquarius, which fall in the middle of every season. Your role as a couple is to hold down the fort and make sure the work gets done between the planting and the harvest cycles. This pragmatic placement is a saving grace for your relationship's indulgently hedonistic Sun sign, teaching you the art of delayed gratification. Note: Saving bottle service and stretch Hummers for a special occasion is not the same as "depriving yourselves." Before you start production on anything from a home reno to an engagement party, map out a project plan together, including timeline and budget. This gives your brilliant ideas a fighting chance of becoming the epic legends you know they're supposed to be.

That said, when you're both lit up about an idea, your enthusiasm is infectious. Leo is one of the three fire signs along with Aries and Sagittarius. One spark of genius can quickly blaze into a three-ring circus. Nothing wrong with that, as long as you two don't burn through cash and resources before you've built the metaphoric tent. (A very real issue when you both become zealously optimistic!) Try to swing into the process like a pair of graceful trapeze artists instead of shooting yourselves out of a cannon and accidentally landing in a cage with white tigers.

The heart and upper back are the body parts associated with Leo. Stand up tall and proud together but don't forget the difference between "lionhearted" and "coldhearted." Ruthless aggression can overtake you two at times when you allow your pride (the name for a group of lions, in fact) to trump your loving nature.

Truth is, you'll both love being there to spoil, pamper and protect each other—and the people you love. So what if your appetites are huge? Your combined energy may be hard for others to match. Try to remember that people express love in different ways. Not everyone can show it with your level of magnanimity. But it's never boring to be part of your glamorous world, so let your stars shine. Somebody's gotta rule, and it might as well be you two!

Famous Leo Supercouples: Jennifer Lopez & Ben Affleck (Bennifer), Kim Kardashian & Kanye West (Kimye), Tom Hanks & Rita Wilson, Paul & Linda McCartney, Gwen Stefani & Blake Shelton, Katy Perry & Russell Brand, Kevin Bacon & Kyra Sedgwick, Gisele Bundchen & Tom Brady

SUPERCOUPLE SUN

VIRGO ✳ ♍

OR THE 6TH HOUSE

> ### We feel most confident & united when we are:
>
> - Enjoying wellness routines and working out together
> - Humbly supporting each other's passions
> - Spending time outside in nature
> - Setting up a green and sustainable home and lifestyle
> - Organizing our shared space
> - Having analytical conversations
> - Critiquing everything from pop culture to our mutual friends
> - Doing charitable service work
> - Cleaning and gardening
> - Supporting each other's achievements and growth

Supercouple Style: HAPPY HELPMATES

Order, order! With a Supercouple Sun in Virgo, your relationship centers around structure and efficiency. Even if your individual lives are chaotic, once you come together, things start getting cleaned up—and fast! Since Virgo is the sign of service, you're a naturally helpful couple who may occasionally slip into coaching or nagging each other. The intention behind this is pure. You want to have a positive impact on each other's lives! (And you definitely do.) Routines that would normally fall by the wayside, like morning workouts and cooking healthy meals, become part of your relationship's daily fabric.

Mercury, the winged messenger, is the ruling planet of Virgo, making you a thoughtful, communicative pair. The details matter to you two! You'll analyze everything from a neighbor's questionably placed lawn furniture to the day's headline news stories. Knowing each other's preferences is a must; in fact, you'll thrill at the opportunity to surprise the other with a carefully researched gift. While together, you may spend a good deal of time absorbing, dissecting and sharing information. What you don't already know, you'll quickly ferret out, finding that needle in the haystack that others impatiently overlook.

Virgo is one of the zodiac's three earth signs along with Taurus and Capricorn. Time outdoors can do wonders for your intimacy, whether you're taking a moonlit stroll or planing for a marathon bike trip. Some couples who share a Virgo Sun may strive to live back-to-earth lifestyles. For others, this may show up as a shared hunger for material luxury, like couture clothing, limited-edition art and fine home goods. While you're not a flashy pair, you two can make minimalism look incredibly chic.

You'll love designing systems together, which comes in handy if you share a home. It begins with exhaustive research as you scour for high-quality materials at the most economical price or study the practices of multiple masters. When you come together and emerge with a solution, you don't just change your own lives, you set templates for the rest of the world to follow.

Virgo rules the digestive system, so it makes sense that one of your shared gifts is helping each other digest information—even the stuff that would be otherwise difficult to stomach. When one of you is nervous, the other picks up on their anxiety, making it hard to keep food down. Conversations about bodily functions can be downright intimate between you! (But does everyone need to hear that you haven't had a normal bowel movement for days?) Clean eating and regular exercise are sanity savers, pulling you both out of the "overthinking" trap.

Since Virgo is symbolized by the Virgin (or Maiden) you can be a pair of purists...though not necessarily puritanical. You just operate as the quality-control department when together. Is it organic, non-GMO and ethically sourced? What is the thread-count of those sheets? This matters to the two of you. Besides that, taking great care of your bodies keeps the erotic fires burning! It's all good as long as you don't veer into Virgo's tricky territory of perfectionism. Want the best for each other, but stop short of pointing out "flaws" and offering unsolicited critiques. Channel these nitpicky tendencies into a relaxing project like solving a crossword puzzle together or even cleaning the house! The Virgo Supercouple gets turned on by a sparkling atmosphere...which might even be an aphrodisiac for you two!

Because your shared opinions together are well-formed (hey, you've only spent 100 hours talking them through!), you two know what's best. But look out! You may come across as preachy or judgmental to mutual friends. Cultivate patience for people who are still "in their process." Each of you were once there too, after all, and no matter how many data studies you've emailed, save your energy and adopt this mantra: When the student is ready, the teacher will come.

While Virgo has a reputation for being a neat freak, that's not always the case. You two may have a perfectly color-coded bookshelf in one room and a disaster zone of a workshop in the basement. The reason for this split? This relationship is one of the zodiac's four mutable signs, along with Virgo, Sagittarius and Pisces. These are the signs and houses that finish every season, preparing us for a transformation. This metaphor is appropriate:

As the leaves fall off the trees, they scatter around the yard. When the snow thaws it turns everything into a muddy disaster.

While deep in your discovery process together, it might look like a storm blew through your shared space. And when you finally notice your overflowing inboxes or piles of "sourcing materials"... anxiety! Hiring a cleaning service or space organizer can be a game-changer, so treat yourselves to that peace of mind instead of trying to DIY it all.

Famous Virgo Supercouples: Will Smith & Jada Pinkett-Smith, Prince Harry & Meghan Markle, Bill Clinton & Hillary Rodham Clinton, Prince Charles & Princess Diana, Prince Charles & Camilla Parker Bowles, Heidi & Spencer Pratt, Jessica Simpson & Nick Lachey

SUPERCOUPLE SUN
LIBRA ✴ ♎
OR THE 7TH HOUSE

We feel most confident & united when we are:

- Indulging in luxury experiences
- Listening to live music
- Co-hosting epic parties and events
- Sharing deep and philosophical conversations
- Balancing mind and body through meditation and yoga
- Fighting for justice or a cause we both believe in
- Shopping for runway-chic outfits...then hitting the town!
- Getting side-by-side spa treatments

Supercouple Style: BALANCING ACT

Peace, love, and harmony! That's the ultimate trifecta for relationships with a Supercouple Sun in Libra. Symbolized by the Scales, a Libra connection may feel like a constant balancing act. As you weigh every option judiciously or attempt to find a middle ground, it's important that you don't tip from sweetness to sacrifice. That said, you may bring out each other's diplomatic nature, which can be a true positive. As a couple, you'll uncover win-wins where others only see dead-ends.

Libra is one of the zodiac's three articulate air signs, along with Gemini and Aquarius. The two of you can move mountains with words alone. The Supercouple Libra Sun makes you a philosophical pair who loves turning every topic over to weigh it from different angles. And oh, what a pair of charmers you can be! Set you two free at a networking event together and you'll own the space. Watch the clock though! That "five-minute conversation" can morph into a three-hour discourse before you know it.

Ruled by gentle, beauty-loving Venus, Libra is the zodiac's harmonizer, which will float you along in a bliss bubble for long stretches of time. When it's time to address a pink elephant in the room, you may detour into "pleasantries" or suddenly become busy and distant. Or you may focus sharply on "the positive" indulging yourself with feel-good activities like shopping, eating and partying.

But this pull for consensus can be a double-edged sword, posing a challenge when it's time to tackle tougher topics. Conflict avoidance is a genuine trouble spot for a Libra Supercouple. Alas, if you pretend everything's "fine!" you may tip the scales to the opposite direction, as resentment boils over into anger. In Italy, there's an expression known as *la bella figura,* in which Italians not only dress to impress but also exhibit their brightest, best personalities when in the company of others. But take it too far and your relationship will be stuck in the superficial. Or worse, problems may spiral out of control, creating huge, expensive messes for you to clean up together later. Learn the art of conflict negotiation—and practice until you perfect it! This will go a long way to keep your union authentic.

Libra is ruled by gentle Venus, the sign of beauty, which blesses your bond with a strong aesthetic sensibility. A feast for your eyes will be a surefire aphrodisiac, whether you're trying on couture on the Champs-Élysées or checking out a special exhibit at The Met. You may cultivate a style together that is curated and colorful, expressing yourselves through fashion and artistry. The Composite Libra Sun will turn you into culture-vultures who know a sonata from a "so not a musical masterpiece" that's climbing the pop charts. As you develop this mutual love for luxury labels, fine food and art, you two can come across as snobbish—but you're probably just crowing about the masterpiece you've been savvy enough to discover.

But what makes you two happiest as a pair? Love, sweet love—particularly the honeymoon phase, which should never end as far as this relationship is concerned. The glyph for Libra is the setting sun, representing that magical hour before everything goes dark. Who could blame you for wanting to prolong such a moment? But don't forget that the starry night sky brings its own enchantment. Once you let go and allow this relationship to deepen, together you'll discover incredible dimensions of amour—ones that don't require you to be "camera ready."

Libra is one of the zodiac's four cardinal signs (along with Aries, Cancer and Capricorn), the signs that begin every season. These are significant points on the chart, much like the NSEW points on a compass. This reveals your relationship style from how you two "do" partnerships to the qualities to seek in others when you need a complementary force. While you're natural partners, you're also strong leaders who may butt heads while defending your tastes. Where best to use your cardinal authority together? By building a long-lasting, harmonious partnership. With the Sun shining here, you two have good reason to feel confident about this relationship's longevity. This part of your life together is blessed with el Sol's energetic, courageous beams. So even if a not-so-dynamic duo knocked either of you off your center in the past, you've dusted yourself off and tried again.

Libra rules the lower back, AKA the booty, which is why it's so important to get off of yours regularly. Although both of you hate to be rushed, a sedentary lifestyle is no good for you. Here's where the magic of two comes to the rescue again. Teaming up as workout buddies or accountability partners keeps you in motion. And if that involves a little pat and squeeze between bench presses, we promise that we're not judging!

Famous Libra Supercouples: Beyonce & Jay-Z, Blake Lively & Ryan Reynolds, Tom Cruise & Katie Holmes, Michael Douglas & Catherine Zeta-Jones, Diego Rivera & Frida Kahlo, Sophia Vergara & Joe Manganiello, David Bowie & Iman, Kristen Bell & Dax Shepherd

SUPERCOUPLE SUN

SCORPIO ✳ ♏

OR THE 8TH HOUSE

We feel most confident & united when we are:

- Treasure-hunting for rare finds from vinyl to vintage wines
- Co-creating a passion project
- Attracting people with our quiet mystique
- Laughing at wickedly funny inside jokes
- Stepping out like a sexy power couple
- Connecting to our physicality through movement, sex or healing touch
- Bonding over a common enemy
- Providing for the people we love
- Hiding out in our love nest

Supercouple Style: MAGNETIC MYSTERY

Can you feel the energy? The Supercouple Sun in Scorpio charges your relationship with a sexy intensity that's so palpable, we're betting you're not the only two who can feel it. Smoldering and mysterious, your combined magnetism is unmatched. Even when trying to fly under the radar, you two draw attention and leave people wondering, "Who were they?" No surprise there! This transformational sign rules everything from sex to investments to death. There's nothing light and fluffy going on in this connection, which is part of its seductive magic. When you come together you'll plunge deep into the shadows, exploring life's hidden dimensions.

A highly intuitive pair, you pick up each other's unspoken signals and could make a sport out of reading each other's minds. Like a pair of panthers stalking their prey, you may have quietly circled each for years before working up the nerve to initiate contact. The truth? This relationship is as much about observation as it is about interaction. Even after years as a couple, you'll enjoy some form of cat and mouse game, surprising each other with a new look or unexpected plan. It may have taken you a bit of time to express interest in one another. But once you did, you felt that scorching passion. Skilled and generous lovers, you help one another explore your darker emotions and sexuality, guiding each other through fifty-plus shades of irresistible and soul-communing experiences.

Warning: possessiveness and jealousy can become issues in this relationship. Scorpio governs the reproductive organs, making sex both an essential bonding agent and an oft-triggering topic for you two. No matter how wildly experimental you were before meeting each other, in this relationship, you'll prefer fierce devotion to one another. Merging your energies makes you both stronger.

This locked-and-loaded bonding style applies to both romance and finance, in fact. As a couple, you may build wealth through a diversified portfolio of real estate, stocks, crypto and other savvy investments. But here's the deal: Joining your lives doesn't mean splitting everything 50/50. You'd be wiser to play to each person's strengths. Also, carve out independent turf that you each can rule over without stepping on the other one's toes. Otherwise, power struggles can erupt...along with a hot mess of control issues, childhood wounds and other painful stores that would be best left un-messed with.

Intense Scorpio is ruled by Pluto, the planet of power and control, which may explain the guarded energy that's common in this relationship. Before a word is uttered, you may pierce one another with your gazes. Or you may each become so secretive and enigmatic, that you can't figure the other one out fast enough for this union to catch fire. In mythology Pluto was the god of the underworld. Your Supercouple Scorpio Sun may draw you toward darker subject matter, even the taboo. Playing with this energy comes with a warning label; however, since there may be more than the usual level of jealousy between you two.

Trust takes time to build in the Scorpio Supercouple relationship. But once you both get there, your bond grows serious, fast. That said, even a minor betrayal can be a dealbreaker for you two. Like scorpions, you're more than capable of delivering painful stings. Revenge is a dish you serve ice cold, catching the other one off guard. Even if you're generally laid-back as individuals, you'll take perceived slights especially hard in this union. It can take years for you to forgive each other for (possibly innocent) disappointments. Scorpio is one of the zodiac's emotional three water signs (along with Cancer and Pisces). You can't help but feel everything so deeply as a pair!

There are actually four incarnations of Scorpio: the first is the venomous, possessive scorpion itself; the second is the slippery, charming-yet-deadly snake; the third is the soaring eagle whose piercing gaze sharply observes the landscape (and its prey) below; and the final version is the ever-burning, all-seeing phoenix that rises up from the ashes into eternal rebirth. Under the sign of life, death and resurrection, this relationship's energy embraces these life cycles and continually transforms and reinvents itself.

Vulnerability is so not Scorpio's jam, but push past the fears of opening up and you'll discover the healing salve that transforms you from scorpion to phoenix. Rather than holding on to hurt, seek healthy outlets for processing the tsunami of feelings your interactions are sure to stir up. Talk therapy and private, offline support groups can do wonders. Study methods like Nonviolent Communication which teach you compassionate conflict negotiation. Anything that keeps you two from slipping into vengefulness is a positive!

To fortify this complex union, try working alongside one another. Here is where you become reliable, predictable and a steady force. Scorpio is one of the zodiac's four fixed signs, along with Taurus, Leo and Aquarius. Your shared role is to hold down the fort and make sure the work gets done between the planting and the harvest cycles. Many trust-building exchanges emerge from time spent in the trenches, hustling toward a common goal. You just have to remember to be patient with the process!

Famous Scorpio Supercouples: Barack & Michelle Obama, Mila Kunis & Ashton Kutcher, Nick & Vanessa Lachey, Cardi B & Offset, Humphrey Bogart & Lauren Bacall, Lucille Ball & Desi Arnaz

SUPERCOUPLE SUN
SAGITTARIUS ✳ ♐

OR THE 9TH HOUSE

We feel most confident & united when we are:

- Traveling and exploring new terrain together
- Cutting loose on the dance floor or at karaoke
- Cracking jokes with random strangers and becoming fast friends
- Attending spiritual circles and self-development workshops
- Developing an entrepreneurial business
- Going on outdoorsy adventures
- Throwing dinner parties
- Laughing until our sides hurt

Supercouple Style: ADVENTURE MATES

Send in the clowns! Relationships with the Supercouple Sun in Sagittarius are sure to tickle the funny bone, bringing out the entertainers and satirists in you both. Together you spot the absurdity of human nature, turning it into comic material for your inside jokes (and maybe the wider world). Yet, this shared Sun makes you a wise and philosophical pair, who enlightens the world with their perspectives. Talk about a paradox! Sagittarius is one of the "split personality" signs of the zodiac, half horse and half human, which may explain why you two are a dichotomy of a duo.

Sagittarius is one of the zodiac's three trailblazing, expansive fire signs along with Aries and Leo. You'll take everything bigger, stronger and faster, please. Passion heats up quickly for you two, igniting a "crazy idea" into a full-scale project in record time. Even if you're cautious as individuals, this Supercouple Sun increases your risk appetite. (Sagittarius is the sign of the gambler.) While your ideas spread like wildfire, you may lose control of the blazes in your zeal to push forward on an accelerated timeline. Soon, your maximized vision has gone over budget, forcing you to scale back or start over. Once you stop "building the plane while in the air"—and start honing your planning powers—you two greatly increase your chance of success.

Fortunately, Sagittarius is ruled by abundant, benevolent Jupiter, the largest planet in the solar system. No wonder Sagittarius relationships are blessed with so much good fortune! People are attracted to the bright energy you exude when in each other's company. Refreshingly optimistic, this relationship inspires you to scan the horizon for opportunities. Even when you "fail," your combined sense of hope won't allow circumstances to sink your spirits for long. You'll chalk it up as a life lesson and inspire everyone with tales of your experience. Besides, the fickle finger of fate always seems to point you two toward the next bright opportunity—even if you have to reinvent your shared journey a few times over.

In moments when life does feel dark and hopeless, get out and mingle. A random night at the karaoke bar could make you stars for the night, and you never know! Your duet of "Islands In The Stream" could break the ice with an applauding stranger...who becomes a business partner three weeks later.

Your ruler, Jupiter, is also the planet of global expansion. You become the ultimate free spirits together: optimistic, open-minded and ambitious. You're both happiest in wide-open spaces with plenty of adventure and excitement—especially if you can connect across cultures. Treat every day like a journey, when you're camping under the stars or playing urban explorers in a bustling new city. Sagittarius is one of the four mutable signs, along with Gemini, Virgo and Pisces. These are the signs that finish every season, preparing us for a transformation. This explains your shared comfort with change. And often, all that's required to move that needle is a dose of outside inspiration!

Sagittarius is symbolized by the Centaur, a half-human, half-horse mythical creature. From the waist up, you knowledge-seekers are reaching for the highest truth. As straight-shooting Archers, you sling arrows that pierce the veil of inauthenticity. You two love to "tell it like it is," especially when it makes people laugh. However, your brutal honesty has been known to devastate feelings—especially each other's! Cultivate patience, and be careful not to come off as know-it-alls. Instead, use your wisdom to empower each other to keep moving forward, trusting that you'll discover the right answers on your own.

From the waist down...it's all animal instinct and restless hooves. It's not easy having a Sun sign that rules ethics and the hips and thighs, the body parts associated with Sagittarius! While this can be a monogamous relationship with deep loyalty, your coming together is about exploration. Risk-taking is a hallmark of this connection, and together you love to take on dares—which can make commitment rocky in moments.

As busy bees, together you have a million friends, projects and irons in the fire. As a result, you two may not be the most reliable day-to-day allies, for one another. But if one of you has a five-alarm crisis, you'll rush in for an epic save. Time and distance are irrelevant—if you have a connection, that's all that matters. Good thing, since the traveling nature of your Supercouple Sagittarius Sun may send you to opposite corners of the world at times! But hey, who says you can't meet for a balloon ride...in Cappadocia?

Famous Sagittarius Supercouples: John Lennon & Yoko Ono, Jared Kushner & Ivanka Trump, John Legend & Chrissy Teigen, RuPaul & Georges LeBar, Katy Perry & Orlando Bloom, Lily Tomlin & Jane Wagner, Frank Sinatra & Ava Gardner

SUPERCOUPLE SUN
CAPRICORN ✳ ♑

OR THE 10TH HOUSE

We feel most confident & united when we are:

- Pushing ourselves with a new challenge
- Getting public recognition for our hard work
- Impressing the world with our power-couple achievements
- Mingling with the VIP influencers and making them our friend group
- Attending exclusive and invite-only events
- Staying active with outdoor sports (skiing, mountain biking, hiking)
- Providing for our family
- Introducing each other to relatives and childhood friends

Supercouple Style: DETERMINED DUO

Eyes on the prize! The Supercouple Sun in Capricorn blesses you two with tireless focus. Once you've set your sights on a shared goal you work steadily toward the finish line. Flexibility may not be your relationship's strongest suit, but achievement (as you both define it) certainly is. When you set your mind to something, you are committed! You may become so fixated on reaching the end point, in fact, that you forget to enjoy the actual journey. But that's one of the biggest mistakes the two of you can make. The trek to the summit is filled with opportunities to learn each other's strengths, gifts and quirks. After all, getting to know each other's full-bodied personalities is what intimacy is all about!

Of course, discovering that might be the real journey for you two. Serious Capricorn is ruled by Saturn, the planet of tough lessons and wisdom. Accustomed to regular butt-kickings from taskmaster Saturn, you often see life as an uphill battle, with the ultimate reward arriving only through suffering and sacrifice. You'll both skip the good stuff today if it means getting the reward tomorrow. Maybe that explains why you two have more trophies and loyal friends than most people. When either of you gets moody, let your family, closest friends, and partner be there for you—just as you always are for them.

Ambitious Capricorn is symbolized by the Sea Goat, with the head of a goat and the tail of a mermaid. Picture this creature climbing up a rocky hill, taking one cautious step at a time. And that's exactly how you two like to do everything. Legend has it that this sign ages in reverse, and in a sense, you may both feel like Benjamin Buttons, despite all the gravity-defying projects you take on. Once you realize together that life doesn't have to be a struggle, you both suddenly learn what it feels like to be young and carefree.

Here's where that mermaid tail of the Sea Goat comes in to play. While you can be a couple of straight-arrows as a pair, you're both magical and outrageous in plenty of other ways. With the wry, humor the shared Capricorn Sun can bring, the two of you know how to hit each other straight in the funny bone. And when it comes to your shared creativity, the ideas you dream up are game-changing and original!

But even when you're in "play" mode, you'll eventually put a plan together behind it all. How else will you make these fanciful dreams a reality? As one of the zodiac's three earth signs (along with Taurus and Virgo), Capricorn is connected to the tangible, material plane. Even the body parts it rules are all about structure: the bones that shape us, the teeth that allow us to form words and chew food for strength and the skin that holds it all together.

Capricorn is in one of the zodiac's trailblazing cardinal signs, along with Aries, Cancer and Libra, the signs that begin every season. These are significant points on the zodiac wheel, much like the NSEW points on a compass. It's no surprise that you both often develop tight bonds with people you meet on the job or through a team project. Mixing business with pleasure may be the only way you'll have a social life together! Despite your relentless shared drive, when you slip into lounge mode with one another, you can relax with the best of 'em, becoming practically immobile! Work hard, play hard—together—is the name of the game!

Famous Capricorn Supercouples: Goldie Hawn & Kurt Russell, Justin & Hailey Bieber, Ryan Gosling & Eva Mendes, Elizabeth Taylor & Richard Burton, Brad Pitt & Jennifer Aniston, Elton John & David Furnish, Sarah Paulson & Holland Taylor, Demi Moore & Bruce Willis, Elizabeth Taylor & Richard Burton, Justin Timberlake & Britney Spears

SUPERCOUPLE SUN

AQUARIUS ✳ ♒

OR THE 11TH HOUSE

We feel most confident & united when we are:

- Communing with thought leaders and free spirits
- Having a transcendent moment on a shared vision quest
- Cracking people up (especially ourselves) with edgy jokes
- Being each other's best friend
- Playing sports or exploring for hours
- Participating in social change and activism
- Wiring up our home with the latest technology
- Co-hosting a party for 100 of our closest friends
- Festival-hopping and attending a community gathering
- Creating an idealistic social group from all walks of life

Supercouple Style: FRIENDLY FIRE

Release the unicorns! The Supercouple Aquarius Sun makes you a paradoxical pair. Together, you pull off the astounding feat of being hardcore individuals and an undeniable unit. Aquarius is the sign that rules the future, which may explain your cutting-edge and experimental approach to...everything. No matter how traditional you are in your individual lives, this connection brings out your rebelliousness. Shaking up the status quo is what you two live for, and you care little about judgments from the outside world.

Create your own Supercouple Chart at **SUPERCOUPLE.COM**

Avant-garde Aquarius is ruled by Uranus, the only planet in the solar system that spins on its side! Just like this quirky celestial body, relationships with Supercouple Sun in Aquarius will make you a pair who prefers to do things your own way, moving on a path that's anything but traditional. Even if you look like a classic couple, there's surely more going on behind the curtain. You have a refreshingly authentic shared style that inspires others to take more chances in their own lives.

Aquarius is one of the zodiac's three intellectual air signs, along with Gemini and Libra. This vibrantly social placement makes it essential that you form a shared community of friends ASAP. One of the best bonding agents for you two? Spending time among your people, telling jokes and introducing thought-provoking conversation topics. While you're not concerned with popularity contests, mutual friends truly do make your world go round. Of course "friend" is a broadly defined term that applies to people you partied with on New Year's Eve, shared a camp with at a festival or chat with every morning when you're picking up coffee.

Keep it casual? With the cool and logical Sun in Aquarius, intensely intimate interactions flood your circuits with too much passion. This sign also craves novelty, which can bring some struggles over the long-term. Even if you were clingy in the past, you may become a bit more avoidant in your attachment style here. Because of this, you may disengage from one another at times, even drifting outside the relationship for a fix. (A true risk, so don't underestimate the appeal of "new relationship energy!") A chief complaint? Giving platonic pals better treatment than you bestow upon each other. Learning to accept and express your emotions can help you two avoid the massive freakouts and anger flashes that come from pretending everything's cool when it isn't.

The symbol for Aquarius is the Water Bearer, which has been tied to the Greek legend of Ganymede, a good-looking young man who filled cups for the gods on Mount Olympus and was granted eternal youth. There's a teenage quality to relationships with Sun in Aquarius, which can show up as rebellion or the unwavering idealism that most cynical adults abandon.

While you two might be renegades, you're hardly slackers! Aquarius is one of the zodiac's four fixed signs, along with Taurus, Leo and Scorpio. Your shared role is to hold down the fort and make sure the work gets done between the planting and the harvest cycles. When it's time to roll up your sleeves, you're both as responsible and industrious as they come. With your shared intellectual savvy and people skills, you can manage projects well together. While as a couple you can be a bit unsentimental, you can be moved to tears—and action!—by the plight of animals, the environment or any suffering. You're also born team players, and when you're fired up about a mission together, no one is better at unifying the group than the two of you!

Blowing off steam with exercise together can help you relax into the sensations in your bodies that you may be wriggling away from. Since this sign rules the calves, you may enjoy leg sports together, like soccer or track and field. Plus, there's nothing like a long run or bike ride together to help you process the emotions that you inevitably cannot avoid. Meditative movement like yoga is especially powerful for getting out of a "Uranian side spin" and recentering your four feet on the ground. And hey, you two never mind catching a runner's high or having an out-of-body experience with a breathwork session.

Famous Aquarius Supercouples: Oprah Winfrey & Stedman Graham, Kourtney Kardashian & Travis Barker, Ellen DeGeneres & Portia DeRossi, Chip & Joanna Gaines, Megan Thee Stallion & Pardison Fontaine, Alec & Hilaria Baldwin, Bradley Cooper & Lady Gaga, Justin Timberlake & Jessica Biel

Create your own Supercouple Chart at **SUPERCOUPLE.COM**

SUPERCOUPLE SUN
PISCES ✳ ♓
OR THE 12TH HOUSE

We feel most confident & united when we are:

- Co-creating a fantasy world that's "just the two of us"
- Attending charity galas and fundraiser events
- Immersing ourselves in music—concerts, dancing, DJ sets, and speakers in every room
- Crying on each other's shoulders during cathartic conversations
- Getting holistic treatments from the same healer
- Long vacations at the beach
- Shopping (for shoes, crystals or vintage clothes)
- Setting up meditative spaces at home
- Sleeping in and staying in bed all weekend
- Talking about our dreams
- Scuba diving/sailing/other water sports

Supercouple Style: ESCAPE ARTISTS

Life is but a dream for the Supercouple Pisces Sun couple. This sign is akin to the elder years when the veil thins between reality and imagination. No matter your actual ages, you know how to escape into your own self-created bubble together, screening out anything unpleasant—until you want to deal, that is. As the 12th and final sign, Pisces is said to have experienced the energy of every other sign before it. As a couple, you two become profoundly empathic, with compassion that flows to the most neglected members of society. Whether you're fundraising for a shelter or offering pro bono legal services to immigrants, you are compelled to be there for those in need.

Pisces is symbolized by two fish swimming in opposite directions. Relationships with this blended Sun sign can be dualistic in nature. Enchanting and enigmatic, your connection may mystify you both! One moment you're elevating yourselves to a spiritual high, the next, you're plunging into sorrow and despair. You can be boundless in many moments, dissolving into each other's identities to the point of codependence. The next moment, you're toughening your scales, making it impossible for the other to penetrate your "cold fish" exterior.

As one of the zodiac's four mutable signs along with Gemini, Virgo and Sagittarius, Pisces is perpetually ebbing and flowing between states. The Supercouple Sun here creates a strong need for variety. Part of you both may always be trying to "swim away" or escape reality. The other part is so intuitive that you get swept into each other's fields, drowning in the ensuing feelings. Since Pisces rules the feet, you may love going dancing together. Certainly getting lost in a beat is an effective form of therapy!

Exploring life beyond the material plane can churn up equal levels of fear and fascination in this relationship. Ruled by hazy and elusive Neptune, this relationship may feel like an illusion on many days. Is it real...or just a mirage? As a result, you will need to reassure each other regularly of your devotion. As a couple, you may journey through realms of the subconscious via hypnosis, meditation and medicine ceremonies. Edgier types may explore legalized treatments like ketamine therapy or microdosing mushrooms to heal depression. Since setting boundaries can be difficult for you as a pair, these explorations come with a huge red flag around addictive substances like prescription pills and party drugs.

Pisces is one of the zodiac's three emotional water signs along with Cancer and Pisces. In this connection, you both play the roles of soulful, sensitive creatures who feel everything at an amplified intensity. As such, you might not always have the fortitude to be the rock for one another. You can lure each other into the depths, but if you're not prepared to deal with all the baggage, look out! You may paddle away, leaving your partner to drown in the emotion ocean.

When you're both underwater in your sorrows, best to fill up the tub for an Epsom salt bath—then find an adequate source of support outside the relationship, such as a therapist. Although you can feel helpless and overwhelmed at times, you're also much stronger than you think when you come together. The best way to experience your power in this relationship is to cultivate your incredible healing and artistic gifts together.

Because it's easy for people to make you two feel guilty, you should watch out for mutual friends who use you, or make you doubt yourselves. Surround yourselves with good-hearted empaths who have their acts together, and lean on one another. Finding a tranquil spiritual outlet, or spending time alone with each other, can ground you in your shared power. There's nothing like the sea to bring your relationship back to its Neptunian center.

Famous Pisces Supercouples: Brad Pitt & Angelina Jolie (Brangelina), George & Amal Clooney, Harry Styles & Olivia Wilde, Elvis & Priscilla Presley, Martin Luther King Jr. & Coretta Scott King

SUPERCOUPLE

Compatibility

WITH YOUR SUN SIGN

If our Supercouple Sun is in a fire sign:
(ARIES, LEO OR SAGITTARIUS)

And my personal Sun is in a fire sign
(ARIES, LEO OR SAGITTARIUS):

You'll feel at ease with the independent energy of this relationship, enjoying (and celebrating!) autonomy as part of your togetherness strategy. But make sure you aren't two ships passing in the night. Committing to plans doesn't have to kill spontaneity!

And my personal Sun is in an earth sign
(TAURUS, VIRGO OR CAPRICORN):

This relationship will challenge your structured nature—good luck scheduling and systematizing, even with a shared calendar. The silver lining? You'll learn to be more autonomous and live in "the now." You may have to be the rock in this relationship, so don't be afraid to bring your steadying energy to the mix.

And my personal Sun is in an air sign
(GEMINI, LIBRA, AQUARIUS):

Your time together will be fun and lively—and you may be more effusively expressive in this relationship than you are on your own. There is a tendency to be too spontaneous and leave things up to chance. Be sure to mange practical matters and talk about feelings before they become fiery and dramatic.

And my personal Sun is in a water sign
(CANCER, SCORPIO OR PISCES):
Because you crave alone time, you may find there is a lot of negotiation required to meet your needs. But you also like more security than this relationship may initially provide. This union will challenge you to be more forthright and self-advocating. No making sacrifices!

If our Supercouple Sun is in an earth sign:
(TAURUS, VIRGO, OR CAPRICORN)

And my personal Sun is in a fire sign
(ARIES, LEO OR SAGITTARIUS):

On your own, you prefer living in the moment, but this bedrock relationship demands stable routines and long-range plans. Your serious side comes out to play, which might even mute your effusive self-expression. If you tone it down too much, you could wind up rebelling. But don't let your restless side turn reckless. The stability this relationship provides can be the grounding force you need.

And my personal Sun is in an earth sign
(TAURUS, VIRGO OR CAPRICORN):

Sweet relief! You'll easily express your most authentic qualities in this relationship, which feels safe and natural. Your penchant for planning, building and creating legacies is met—and matched—in this union. In some ways, this relationship can be a little too predictable. Challenge yourself to be more playful, adventurous and emotionally expressive. Life won't fall apart if you take the occasional risk!

And your personal Sun is in an air sign
(GEMINI, LIBRA, AQUARIUS):

The responsibilities this relationship demands can weigh down your social spirit—and that can feel heavy at times. But if you don't flutter away at the first sign of boredom, you will vastly appreciate the stability this partnership brings. Once you create a shared friend group, your desire for a "chosen family" will come to life, anchoring you both in a beautiful way.

And my personal Sun is in a water sign
(CANCER, SCORPIO OR PISCES):

Ah, the safe harbor you've always desired! You'll love how dependable this relationship can be, which is anything but boring for your security-loving Sun sign. Just be careful not to get too insular as a couple. Nurture outside support systems so you don't weigh each other's spirits down with too much emotional processing.

If our Supercouple Sun is in an air sign:
(GEMINI, LIBRA, AQUARIUS)

And my personal Sun is in a fire sign
(ARIES, LEO OR SAGITTARIUS):

So much fun! Electrifying and expansive, this social relationship amplifies your playful nature. You may willingly sacrifice some of your signature independence for the sheer fun of bonding with all the great people you two attract. Together, you'll create a friend group, build a community and explore new intellectual vistas together. The catch? Intimacy can wither on the vine if you don't consciously devote one-on-one time to each other.

And my personal Sun is in an earth sign
(TAURUS, VIRGO OR CAPRICORN):

Ready for liftoff? This relationship can untether you from some of your stubborn old habits! Get ready to uncover new ways of thinking about life that are anything but traditional. Socially, this relationship will lure you into the wider world, where connections don't run quite so deep. This can be challenging, since you prefer to tend to your trusted crew of close friends and family.

And my personal Sun is in an air sign
(GEMINI, LIBRA, AQUARIUS):

Float away on that bliss bubble! This people-focused relationship is fun, social and a boon for your popularity. Get ready for game nights, group vacations and holidays with your crew. The struggle comes in around the practical realities of life together, like paying the bills and managing the household. Make a greater effort to set up routines and maybe (eventually) plant some roots so you don't float away from each other.

And my personal Sun is in a water sign
(CANCER, SCORPIO OR PISCES):

This relationship is simultaneously invigorating and unsettling. On the one hand, you'll love how it brings you out of your shell and into a world of people you might not otherwise meet. On the other hand, that's exactly what disturbs you about this bond. Don't sacrifice your need for alone time and intimacy, but do capitalize on the gift of this relationship, which is teaching you to lighten up.

If your Supercouple Sun is in a water sign:
(CANCER, SCORPIO OR PISCES)

And my personal Sun is in a fire sign
(ARIES, LEO OR SAGITTARIUS):

Send up the smoke signals! In the right balance, this relationship can be seriously steamy, channeling your passion in a focused and intimate bond. However, the emo vibes can also put out the flames if you don't create a healthy balance of autonomy and togetherness. The trick here is to co-create a special space for the two of you without getting flooded by the tidal wave of feelings this relationship can bring out. Boundaries are needed to ensure that you don't get flooded.

And my personal Sun is in an earth sign
(TAURUS, VIRGO OR CAPRICORN):

Surprise, surprise, your softer side is peeking out! This nurturing relationship is like a warm hug, softening your defenses and opening your heart. Your practical side will come in handy though, especially when feelings rise to critical levels of intensity or the two of you begin to get swept away by a romantic notion. Someone's gotta be the grounded one, and yep, that's you.

And my personal Sun is in an air sign
(GEMINI, LIBRA, AQUARIUS):

Wave goodbye to your logical side, because this relationship is all feelings, all the time. While at first it can feel unsettling to follow your heart before your head, once you learn to balance both input levels, you'll hit a steady stride. Your social side may feel a little suppressed in a relationship that's so focused on intimate one-on-one exchanges. Make sure to negotiate that, because you'll need some autonomy to continue feeding your long-standing friendships, which mean the world to you.

And my personal Sun is in a water sign
(CANCER, SCORPIO OR PISCES):

You'll easily flow into this relationship, which mirrors your caring, nurturing style of bonding. This ticks all the boxes for you: a safe space to be vulnerable, a comfortable feeling of home, and a desire for quiet closeness. Just don't get so insular that you fall into an "us against the world" mindset. Maintaining outside sources of support and interaction can keep you from putting too much pressure on this relationship to be your everything.

Create your own Supercouple Chart at **SUPERCOUPLE.COM**

SUPERCOUPLE

MOON

our emotional map

Use Your Supercouple Moon to Understand:

- The emotional temperament of your relationship
- How to find a common language during upsets
- Best ways to nurture each other
- The kind of home to create together
- How best to co-parent kids and pets
- The role parents and other family members should play in your lives
- How you respond and react emotionally when together
- What makes you feel secure and valued in this relationship
- Where you'll be most sensitive when together

WHAT'S THE EMOTIONAL NATURE OF YOUR RELATIONSHIP?

Ah, feelings—those messy, inconveniently-timed "vulnerability bombs" that detonate exactly when you wish they wouldn't. Even the most understanding, evolved partner will at some point get triggered or impatient with the emotional demands of the Moon, which has a habit of acting out like a naughty or exhausted child at nursery school.

In the birth chart, the Moon sign reveals your emotions, how you react, what makes you feel secure. We think the Moon sign (individual and Composite!) is one of the most important factors in compatibility, since it drives your core needs and how you need to be nurtured. If mama Moon's not happy, nobody's happy!

Feelings may not be facts, but they are a reality of relationships. And the Composite Moon can throw you an anchor when your individual boats hit stormy seas at high tide. When buttons get pushed, we tend to default to our lunar natures, and well, lunacy often follows.

For example, maybe your stinging Scorpio Moon and their pincer-like Cancer Moon go lower than low in a fight. Before you utterly savage each other's more sensitive points, you could lean into your Composite Virgo Moon, a grounded and discerning earth sign with problem-solving superpowers.

Heck, you might even decide to make "Composite Moon" your safeword, a phrase that helps you find the saving-grace pause between stimulus and response.

Healthy relationships provide a safe harbor for the people involved. The feeling of "coming home" to each other is a cornerstone of intimacy. On both a literal and metaphoric level, the Composite Moon is like the interior designer for your shared sanctuary.

How much privacy do you need as a pair—from each other or the outside world? Should you nab the highrise unit with 360° wraparound views or restore a Craftsman in the quaint commuter town outside the city? Separate bathrooms? Bedrooms? Homes?

And what about children? The Moon is classically associated with the mother figure, though in modern times, we look at it as the nurturing parental force. So it makes sense that the Composite Moon has a lot to say about your parenting style. Whether you're finding the best school district for your kids or crate-training your fur babies, you'll see your shared strengths and weaknesses show up. Lean in to the Composite Moon for a savvy co-parenting plan.

The Composite Moon can even reveal ways you nourish yourselves with food and how much meditative time you should build in to your relationship. Maybe you didn't ask for this "bonus MIL," but don't roll your eyes at luna's wisdom. Even if you embrace this cozy Composite placement in smaller doses, it's the stuff that keeps you both feeling safe and secure.

Supercouple MOON
THROUGH THE ZODIAC SIGNS

In the Sign of	Makes Us Emotionally	Strengths	Challenges
ARIES	Explosive	Passionate, exciting	Reactive, frustrating
TAURUS	Secure	Stable, loyal	Change averse, stubborn
GEMINI	Collaborative	Communicative, curious	Pettiness, avoidant
CANCER	Nurturing	Caring, tender	Taking things personally, codependence
LEO	Playful	Adoring, fun	Power struggles, drama
VIRGO	Analytical	Growing together, shared mission	Overly critical, controlling
LIBRA	Serene	Romantic, fair	Superficial, excessive
SCORPIO	Magnetic	Passion, trust	Jealousy, possessiveness
SAGITTARIUS	Adventurous	Honest, inspiring	Impatience, knee-jerk reactions
CAPRICORN	Responsible	Pragmatic, loyal	Repressed, rigid
AQUARIUS	Innovative	Calm, authentic	Detached, rebellious
PISCES	Soothing	Empathic, dreamy	Codependent, unstructured

FIND YOUR SUPERCOUPLE MOON AT
SUPERCOUPLE.COM

Create your own Supercouple Chart at **SUPERCOUPLE.COM**

SUPERCOUPLE MOON
ARIES ✳ ♈

OR THE 1ST HOUSE

To feel securely attached, we need:

- Undivided attention
- Adulation
- Compassion
- Physical affection
- Personal space
- Flexibility
- Excitement

Stay on your toes! The Supercouple Moon in Aries guarantees a relationship full of energy and excitement. With this courageous zodiac sign setting the mood, you are well equipped to fight any challenge that comes your way. Except, maybe, the ones that arise between you two. Feelings turn hot and passionate fast under this lunar influence. Explosive, too! You're a highly reactive pair whose connection should come with a heat advisory and maybe a warning label.

The reason for this? Impulsive Aries is ruled by Mars, the planet of aggression, which can make your connection temperamental and straight-up combative. With all the fiery feelings being served, you two get frustrated easily and blow up at the slightest provocation. Although temper tantrums pass quickly, even a brief rage spell can wreak havoc on your bond. If the bridge isn't permanently burned, the fallout could take years of recovery time.

The trick to elevating the love? Learn to be less reactive with one another. And set some ground rules for yourselves, like no calling names, throwing objects or raising your voices. (We aren't kidding here). The "proactive pause" between stimulus and response will do wonders for your communication. This will take practice; however, since you two are like a match and a powder keg. To sustain the peace, find healthy outlets for burning off intense emotions. Sports, regular sex and projects that challenge you (without an overly complex set of rules) are a must.

As the zodiac's baby, Aries demands a lot of attention. With this Moon sign, neither one of you will stand for being ignored. When one of you is upset, the other must learn to be responsive, even if sending a quick text to say, "I've got you," then setting up time to listen at length when you're free. By the same token, independence is essential to your emotional bond. If one of you feels trapped or chained down, look out! Any whiff of control can evoke intense arguments, knee-jerk reactions, and even running away to find "space."

These reactions can be especially problematic if you decide to have children together. More than ever, you will need to lean in to mature practices and temper the reactivity of your relationship. Otherwise, your kids may feel like they have to be YOUR parents—or you could witness them acting out frustrations in problematic ways like tantrums and bullying. No bueno!

THE MOON

Aries is the first sign of the zodiac, and this Supercouple Moon sign makes it easy for you two to initiate anything. Fittingly, this relationship stokes a competitive spirit, and you may find yourself using phrases like "crushing it" that were never in your lexicon before now.

One caveat: Starting a project is a lot easier than finishing it for this restless match. Regulate excitement with reality checks. (How long will this really take and how much will it actually cost?) Otherwise, your shared space could look like a warehouse full of half-done projects that you both lost interest in. While a pioneering spirit drives you to co-create something together that's never been done before, you two may need outside motivation in order to bring your big ideas to the finish line.

Here's a rule you two should follow to the letter: Always remember that you're on the same team. Rather than battle each other, buddy up. Winning as partners cements your bond in ways that few other activities can. So go ahead and drop your names in the hat. Whether it's a karaoke competition at the local dive bar or the grand prize on a survivalist reality show, the Aries Moon relationship gives you a co-star quality that is undeniably fierce.

Bottom line: If you want this relationship to be emotionally fulfilling, tear up the rule book! With this fervent Supercouple Moon, your connection must blaze its own trail. This won't be the easiest coupling, but it may very well be the most thrilling connection you'll have in your entire life!

SUPERCOUPLE MOON

TAURUS ✳ ♉

OR THE 2ND HOUSE

To feel securely attached, we need:

- Financial stability
- Loyalty
- Ease
- Comfort
- Familial connection
- Grounding
- Steady routines and rituals

Stability, loyalty, consistency: check! With the Supercouple Moon in Taurus, this relationship is here to provide security in every area of life. The desire-driven moon is "exalted" in Taurus, which is its most potent position in the zodiac. As such, your connection will be blessed with a dutiful and dependable vibe. While it might not be 24/7 fireworks, you know that you can count on one another, which is where the magic lies. You two aren't just "rocks" for each other. Together, you become pillars for your community. Shared friends become "our people" and you'll quickly be adopted into each other's family. What can you say? With this possessive Composite Moon, you like to claim your crew.

Create your own Supercouple Chart at **SUPERCOUPLE.COM**

Generally, this connection operates at two speeds: relaxed and contented like a couple of steers luxuriating in a verdant pasture or hyped-up and ready to charge. (Toro, toro!) This calming lunar energy provides a built-in energy conservation program that helps you to patiently assess whether something is worth an investment of time and resources. If the green light flashes, it's all systems go! But until then, slow and steady wins the race.

Since responsibility can be heavy in this bond, give yourselves ample quiet time to process every decision. People may accuse you two of being remote at times, but that's not the case. Giving so steadily can be exhausting! To bring your best to the world each day—and to each other—turn your shared space into a temple of serenity. A comfortable bedroom is particularly important for this Moon sign, which requires lots of snuggling, lounging and sensual touch as its love languages.

Relationships are investments for this match, and over time, yours will age like a fine wine. Repetitive routines may dull the sparks for some couples, but not you two! These are your romantic glue, like making each other the perfect cup of morning coffee and washing the dishes together after your nightly, home-cooked dinners. You don't just create memories; you turn them into traditions. In fact, the more "lather, rinse and repeat" things feel, the more bonded you become. As long as you each keep putting time and energy into one another, you'll experience increasing dividends in this relationship.

But there IS a catch: if you get too comfortable, your connection can flatline. Alas, the shared Taurus Moon can be stubbornly fixed. Even if you're the most experimental people on your own, together, you may grow set in your ways. Since you two appreciate the safe and familiar when united, you may resist change, digging in your heels when it's time to grow. Cleaving to outmoded ways can plunge you into an emotional rut, leading to hopelessness about your shared future. When one of you wants to evolve, it's important for the other to find ways of being supportive. Even if you eventually amble back to your old ways of doing things, you'll do so with a fresh perspective—and that's a win-win for everyone.

Same goes for children, if you have them. Raising a family comes naturally to this Supercouple Moon. But your offspring may not share every one of your values, which can challenge this bond. Do your best to instill a sense of kindness and decency in your kids, of course! But remember that allowing for individuation is a part of parenting too. Think of it as a duty to help your little ones find their unique path in this lifetime. That said, you're probably the parents who do holidays to the nines and print matching T-shirts for family vacations—and there's nothing wrong with that!

While your shared tastes may be modest in many categories, this relationship works up an appetite for luxury. There are certain possessions that must be top of the line. As a couple, you may grow into curators and collectors—and you'll need a shared budget to satisfy those urges! Your splurges will likely fall into the "practical luxury" realm, having a purpose and use for enjoyment. You might even be minimalists who simply enjoy a few high-quality items that suit your (highly specific) requirements to perfection.

Create your own Supercouple Chart at **SUPERCOUPLE.COM**

SUPERCOUPLE MOON
GEMINI ✳ ♊

OR THE 3RD HOUSE

To feel securely attached, we need:

- Open communication
- Synergy
- Compatible social styles
- Shared interests
- Attentiveness
- Playfulness
- Variety

Speak from the heart! Communication is the pathway to connection for couples with the Supercouple Moon in articulate Gemini. Words mean everything in this cerebral duo—and there's never a shortage of topics to discuss. Gemini is one of the three cool and breezy air signs (along with Libra and Aquarius), which lends a lightheartedness to your relationship. An agreeable one too! Since Gemini is the sign of the Twins, you're pulled to harmonize with each other, seeking consensus. You'll banter and squabble like siblings, but you have an easier time compromising than most.

Dialogue is a two-way street in this relationship. When one of you needs an ear, the other will actively listen. You'll spend hours dissecting dilemmas (and dramas!) until you distill a solution. These long, probing conversations are your favorite ways to bond. Just be careful that they don't devolve into gossip! When the two of you identify a shared enemy, you can resort to "mean girl" antics to punish them for their behaviors, like dragging them on social media or turning mutual acquaintances against them. Petty feuds with a common "villain" can overtake your relationship—which is NOT the distraction the Composite Gemini Moon needs.

You're much better off focusing on life-changing books, indie bands and other discoveries that you can share as a pair. At its best, this Supercouple Moon awakens a mutual curiosity about life. Since you enjoy learning together, sign up for classes, from wine tastings to couples' workshops. Weekend road trips will leave you two bubbling with excitement as you "discover" hidden gems. Private beaches, buzzy brunch spots, vintage shops with midcentury furniture and extensive vinyl sections: The secondary thrill comes in telling all your mutual friends about your finds and bringing them there to see for themselves. At the heart of it, you are a social pair. This Moon placement makes you two stellar community builders and the "crew glue" for your friend groups. Take the reins and expand your shared network, showing the world that there's strength and security in numbers.

Should you choose to have kids, you'll keep your little ones active with sports, music lessons and weekend outings. As they grow up, you'll be the "cool parents" who their teenage friends can confide in. (Hey, as a couple, you're like eternal teens yourselves.) Just remember that it's your job to set limits for your kids. Say no to their out-of-bounds requests. Show them that their actions have an impact—and consequences, in some cases. That's how you'll prepare your kids for adulting instead of turning them into entitled hedonists. The biggest challenge for you both? Modeling healthy behavior instead of raising them with an attitude of, "Do as I say, not as I do." Parenting can be a crash course in temperance for the two of you—at least when there are children in the room.

With this intellectual energy governing your Supercouple Moon, you may "think" your way to your feelings. Experiencing the fullness of your relationship's emotional range, however, can be challenging though. It's easier to rationalize ("She has attachment issues") and reason ("We were both raised by single dads") than go through the uncomfortable process of unpacking your feelings. But there's a cost to this avoidance! You may grow distant from each other, drift apart or never quite solidify your bond.

One emotional awareness technique that works well in this relationship? Write each other letters before having "the talk." Not only does this support the analytical nature of your connection, it gives you both a chance to edit prior to your delivery. Processing on the spot is never wise when confronting an issue between you. You'll struggle to be concise about your feelings in this relationship and may devolve into a stream of "verbal diarrhea" that leaves you both even more confused. Put it down on paper first and then extract your most salient points. For best results, arrive at the conversation ready to suggest a potential solution or three.

Another great technique for you two is "mirroring." Rather than responding to the other's words, first take a moment to repeat them back. Then confirm, "Did I understand you correctly?" With the twinning power of your emotional connection, you can easily pick up on the other's gestures and facial expressions, which is a proven signal of empathy and respect. The more you can reflect the other, the closer you'll feel—as long as you don't lose sight of your own perspective in the process.

While there's a BFF bond in even the most romantic Gemini Moon relationship, be careful not to crowd out each other's pre-existing support groups. Too much reliance on the other to be your "everything" can pull this pairing into the platonic zone fast. Find sounding boards outside your relationship, like close friends, mentors and therapists. You don't have to share every thought with each other, especially the unformulated ones!

Since curious Gemini likes to explore all the options, hours can be spent in a research rabbit hole as you hop from one idea to the next...and the next...and the next! It's this Supercouple Moon sign's prerogative to change your minds. Pressure to make any sort of choice will give you both anxiety—and that includes committing to each other or any "next steps." Our advice? Extend the decision-making process instead of rushing to choose. But don't wait SO long that outside circumstances make the choice for you.

SUPERCOUPLE MOON
CANCER ✷ ♋

OR THE 4TH HOUSE

To feel securely attached, we need:

- Emotional support
- Nurturing
- Safety
- Appreciation
- Acceptance
- Tenderness
- Sentimentality

So many feelings! The Supercouple Moon is right at home in Cancer, its "domicile" zodiac location. Sensitive, intuitive and family-oriented, this relationship is like a warm hug for your hearts. At last, you've found a safe harbor where you can drop your guard and open up about all the things you've never told another soul. This relationship is a judgment-free zone filled with compassion, nurturing and tender TLC—provided you can manage your moods.

Because of the intimate nature of your bond, you may prefer to slip off into your private bubble. And there's no place like your shared home for that! "Give me sanctuary!" is a mantra for this domestic duo. Together you'll create a comfortable (and comforting!)

environment. Surround yourselves with favorite books, craft supplies, music, pets and a well-stocked kitchen.

On your days off, you might retreat to your sanctuary or go into your shells. You'll make up for it later, when you emerge to shower everyone with your love. As a couple, your nurturing side comes out full force! Hosting dinner parties and family gatherings can fortify your connection, the perfect way to include your closest circle in your shared life.

That said, even the most hardcore extroverts may be surprised by how much LESS socializing they need when they slip under the soothing spell of the Composite Cancer Moon. While it's comforting to lean on each other, make sure to get out and circulate independently! This will refresh you both so you can bring your best back to your bond. Creating self-care rituals—and sticking to them—will keep your love tanks full and resentment at bay.

Even if you get shy during your initial approach, once you connect, it feels as if you've known each other for years. It's possible, in fact, that you've had past lives as relatives, which may be part of your uncanny familiarity. Parenting comes naturally to Cancer Moon couples. If you have pets or kids (or both), you'll create the perfect blend of safety and structures for your little ones to flourish. Get to know each other's family history—and if relationships are intact, their actual families. Or reinvent the paradigm with the "chosen family" of super close friends who you attract into your orbit.

Part of your connection may involve "re-parenting" yourselves. It's possible that you chose the other because they remind you of a beloved person who raised you. But you could just as easily be drawn together because you trigger each other's family-of-origin issues. Many couples with this Moon come together to do the work of healing intergenerational trauma. This will definitely come in handy if you wind up having kids. One of the big goals you'll share is giving your offspring the best life possible while also imbuing solid values in them. While there will be no shortage of hugs, there WILL be house rules that they'll have to follow. No spoiled brats allowed.

As your relationship grows, you become SO tapped in that you may absorb each other's moods like a sponge. Unchecked, that tendency can pull you both into an emotional undertow. A mantra for this Supercouple Moon sign? Don't take it personally! Within this connection you two find it hard to compartmentalize feelings or to shrug off anything that feels like an affront. But to avoid dragging one another down, you must learn to set boundaries and resist taking on each other's problems as your own. The best support you can provide your partner is getting a list of recommended therapists, healers or coaches to do the heavy lifting.

At the heart of it, you're a sentimental pair. As important as it is to feel emotionally and financially secure, the little things matter in this relationship! As time goes on, you'll amass a collection of objects to prove it: framed photos, vacation mementos, secret codewords and inside jokes. Oh, and the white picket fence too. Being known so intimately is a rare gift, and one that you'll bestow upon each other, thanks to your shared Cancer Moon.

SUPERCOUPLE MOON
LEO ✳ ♌

OR THE 5TH HOUSE

To feel securely attached, we need:

- Praise
- Adoration
- Fun
- Enthusiasm
- Pampering
- Validation
- Treats and gifts

Attention, attention! With the Supercouple Moon in showstopping Leo, you are quite an expressive couple. Even if, individually, you shirk the spotlight, as a pair you'll enjoy stealing it, turning heads the minute you walk in the room. Life becomes a costume party with this Supercouple Moon sign. If you're not rocking matching outfits, you may coordinate colors or dress in flashier, sexier ways to turn the other on. Or you'll dazzle one another with your flirtatious wit. This warm and lively connection is a highly entertaining one!

Encore, encore! When the velvet curtains go down on your two-person show, the behind-the-scenes production may be equally elaborate, especially during your courtship phase. After feeding each other dinner served by a private chef, rose-petals line a pathway to

Create your own Supercouple Chart at **SUPERCOUPLE.COM**

the bed, lit by over 100 pillar candles. (Or, uh, something to that effect!) What it boils down to is this: The Leo Moon turns you into full-on romantics. When you fall for each other, you go down hard! This relationship requires complete, absolute adoration in order to thrive. Would you do anything for love...even that? If the answer isn't a resounding yes, there will be trouble in paradise.

In this union, feelings are big, bold and impossible to ignore. What can you say? You're a passionate pair! While that can devolve into Broadway-level drama, your connection is equally compassionate. Over time, you may start mirroring each other's gestures, voices and movements in a dead-on impersonation. Bizarre as this may be, it also has the effect of making the other feel safe and seen.

Who's the boss? Regal Leo rules the ego, and this Supercouple Moon sign is bound to churn up a few power struggles. Within this relationship, you may both want to be in charge, and that can get tricky. Since you ignite the other's capacity to be noble, powerful leaders, here's a workaround: Carve out specific "realms of rulership" within your shared empire. This can be as mundane as "You do the dishes and I'll handle laundry" or as specific as choosing to have separate rooms in the house that you can decorate to your individual needs and tastes. Even when collaborating—which will be necessary if you become parents—this relationship fails when you ride on assumptions. Take time to share your visions then negotiate your way to common ground. While you won't be able to make many snap decisions, you're an unstoppable power couple when you're finally aligned.

The other glue for this relationship? Good old-fashioned fun. Activities that rev up a sense of childlike wonder will bring back the romance. Did you both love waterslides when you were little?

Tent camping? The circus? Whether or not you have kids, you'll love reviving pastimes and sharing them with each other. Since Leo is associated with fertility, this could very well be a union that thrives when there are little ones running around the house. (And what a perfect excuse to relive your own youth!) You'll make warm and nurturing parents who are both protective and encouraging. Regardless of the household headcount, keep the arts-and-crafts supplies handy! Creative activities are therapeutic in this relationship. Who knows? You might just hang your paintings in a shared gallery show, or start a band or a microbrewery. The sky is the limit for your royal union.

Create your own Supercouple Chart at **SUPERCOUPLE.COM**

SUPERCOUPLE MOON

VIRGO ✳ ♍

OR THE 6TH HOUSE

To feel securely attached, we need:

- Reassurance
- Acceptance
- Devotion
- Reciprocity
- Purity
- Acknowledgment
- Appreciation

Analyze this? Bring it on. No stone is left unturned by relationships with the Supercouple Moon in Virgo. Like a pair of professional critics, you two may be on a constant improvement quest. How can we make this better? What would feel nicer, safer and more secure? While perfectionism may be the Achilles heels for you two, there's no denying this relationship's role as an important growth agent in your shared life.

At its best, this connection stokes your curiosity about one another. You'll love learning how the other is wired. What are their preferences and dislikes? What causes them anxiety and what soothes their frazzled nerves? Pop open your hoods and get vulnerable. Over time, you'll become each other's greatest advisors. Since Virgo is the sign of service, being there for each other feels like a duty and an honor. This relationship thrives when you know each other intimately—from your attachment styles to your bodily functions, you're here for all of it.

As supremely helpful as such closeness may be, tread carefully through this terrain. Life partners who support each other through the ups and downs? That's a lovely goal. But life coaches who point out the other one's every misstep? Instant buzzkill. Sometimes you have to let your person learn things the hard way because it's the only way they'll grow. Rushing in with helpful hints or solutions can create unhealthy dependencies, even laziness. Or you may polarize with one of you playing the hero while the other is the victim. Once the high wears off, these roles get old really fast.

Individually, you may have very different tastes, and with the nitpicky Composite Virgo Moon at the helm, compromising will not come easily. If you're not acting out your control issues, you may get caught in a battle of "my way is better." Alas, there's no light at the end of that tunnel. If you want to persuade your partner, think of it as a game of show-and-tell. Model the behavior within your relationship and share the winning results. Even if you aren't met with instant adulation, trust that the other is studying you carefully. With enough compelling data, you will give each other's techniques a try.

Underneath the resistance to anything "different" may lie a swirling pool of shame and self-deprecation. Although you may cover it up with cynicism, this lunar duo gets you both emotional about "failure." In this relationship, you may both be anxious about making a so-called mistake. Lighten up on each other! It's great to keep a high bar raised, but try not to set impossible standards. When you encourage with positive affirmation and unconditional love, you're at your power couple best!

With the moon in this meticulous placement, cleanliness is next to godliness. There's zero patience for sloppy work or laziness within this connection. Integrity is everything to you both! Clean, serene environments put you two at ease. Clutter, on the other hand, gives you both anxiety. Tidying up is a great form of therapy for the Virgo Moon Supercouple. When you need to "stress clean" together, no one scrubs a tub with quite your combined ferocity. That said, your shared hobbies can border on obsessive as you amass more tools and supplies than you know what to do with. (Yes, even if they are shelved to Pinterest-level perfection.)

Virgo governs our well-being, so the connection between mind and body is powerful for you two! Self-care is directly correlated to your emotional health. Together, you can be diligent about exercising and eating clean in order to achieve optimal wellness. Thanks to this earthy energy, time in nature is deeply therapeutic. Cultivate a garden to grow fresh food and fill your home with plants.

Beyond the physical, be sure to pay attention to your thoughts. In this pairing, they can quickly manifest into moods. A mindfulness practice can keep you centered as a couple, but careful not to swing to the opposite extreme. Those healthy obsessions can make you neurotic. Remind yourselves regularly that moderation is key!

Keep this reality check in mind should you choose to become parents. The two of you will want to raise kids with integrity. Plans to get them sleep-scheduled, raised on vegan diets and reading by age three are noble. But at some point, you're going to have to release control or at least build in some flexibility. For best results, make it your shared mission to understand the tiny soul that chose the two of you as its parents and respect their nature as you nurture. Kids have as much to teach you as they do to learn from you.

SUPERCOUPLE MOON
LIBRA ✳ ♎

OR THE 7TH HOUSE

To feel securely attached, we need:

- Romantic gestures
- Compliments
- Peace
- Harmonious lifestyles
- Quality time
- Aesthetic stimulation
- Fairness

Peace, love and harmony! Emotional equilibrium is the ultimate goal for relationships with Supercouple Moon in Libra. Even if you're naturally fiery individuals, your relationship soothes the savage beast within. Like arriving at a serene oasis, you can finally relax, drop your guards and sink into the bliss of being with someone who simply wants to adore you. As chill as this nonstop spa date may be, your relationship is hardly boring! Libra is one of the zodiac's die-hard romantics, and this Supercouple Moon can make you quite the poetic (and decadent!) pair. Dress-up dates, stadium concerts, fresh flowers, slow and lingering dinners with wine pairings...you two can spin a lifelong fairy-tale.

Create your own Supercouple Chart at **SUPERCOUPLE.COM**

Bring on the beauty boosters! Since aesthetics are important in this lunar mashup, you'll work hard to keep yourselves fit and fashionable. Your approach to intimacy may involve a bit of modesty. Old-fashioned, yes, but it keeps the mystery. Who says couples have to share a bathroom—or even a bedroom? A healthy mix of togetherness and autonomy will keep the embers burning. With a little support from your respective glam squads, the fashion "reveals" in this relationship can be the stuff of red-carpet legends. Bottom line: You'll work hard to keep the honeymoon phase alive in this union. And nothing does that like regular dashes of novelty.

By the same token, you must guard against superficiality. Libra is one of the three air signs (along with Gemini and Aquarius). Emotionally, you two prefer to keep everything light and breezy. Too much levity can become "toxic positivity," turning you into resentful strangers who never skim past the surface. It may also leave you woefully unprepared for the inevitable challenges that life throws your way. For example, should one of you fall ill or be consumed by stressful responsibilities, the other may feel abandoned. For this reason, it's essential to cultivate sources of support outside of your partnership. Mutual friends can pull you back to shore or provide a reality anchor when you're in the throes of this relationship's romanticizing energy.

If you share space, keep inspiring visuals in your sight lines whenever possible. Decorate each room with care, choosing high-end textiles and art that evoke the mood you want to create. Walking through gorgeous scenery or a colorful outdoor market together can immediately pull you out of a funk. And yes, you two will have expensive tastes. This lavish moon sign can be excessive. Watch those retail therapy urges, but make a shared budget for indulgences.

At times, this connection feels SO calm and centered, that your serenity could be mistaken for indifference—wrong! With the sign of the scales setting your relationship's emotional gauge, you simply need to take your time. Every option must be carefully weighed and deliberated. Rushing into decisions brings up major anxiety within this relationship! Before you can move ahead together, you want to check out a situation from every possible angle.

Compromise is usually the goal for the Libra Moon Supercouple. With the diplomatic energy this provides, you'll have a knack for devising win-wins. While interpersonal harmony is your shared preference, there are a few things that tip the scales off balance. Social injustices will always fire you both up. You two hate to see people treated unfairly and instinctively stick up for people who aren't able to defend themselves. Animal rights can also be a huge conviction. When one of you gets moody, it can be hard for the other to deal. But hey, we all have bad days here and there. Give yourselves and each other room to be human and you can't go wrong!

SUPERCOUPLE MOON
SCORPIO ✳ ♏︎
OR THE 8TH HOUSE

To feel securely attached, we need:

- Trust
- Strong sexual chemistry
- Sacred connection
- Loyalty
- A safe space to be vulnerable
- Understanding
- Control

Intensity! Mystery! Seduction! Yes, please. Emotions are complex and, at times, downright enigmatic, for relationships with the Supercouple Moon in Scorpio. Strong sexual chemistry may have ignited your bond, but that's not all. Upon meeting, you had a knowing sense that you've met before, perhaps in another lifetime. With such an all-consuming love language, this relationship can be as demanding as it is exciting. You want—make that NEED—to know that the other is attracted to you and, preferably, thinks you're the hottest creature on Planet Earth. This erotic pull will be the healing salve when you find yourself on opposite corners of the ring.

But is there trust along with the lust? Loyalty is everything in the Composite Scorpio moon relationship. Building that rock-solid allegiance binds you together—and also gets you to open up. But here's the catch: the combined Scorpio Moon can make you both terrified of vulnerability! Hearing the other's trauma stories? You'd be there for it in a heartbeat, holding space for their revelations and healing process. Sharing your own deep, dark feelings is another story. It may take an excruciatingly long time before either of you "goes first" in the wound-revealing department.

Once the seal is broken, it becomes much easier to drop your guards. For best results, try going back and forth. "I'll tell you a secret, then you tell me one of yours." Honestly, seeing the other's scars will show you that you're not the only one who has (gasp!) been a perfectly imperfect human. If you sense that you'll be judged in any way, the vault remains locked. Betrayals are especially hard to forgive in this relationship. Guard each other's secrets like Fort Knox!

The Moon is in "fall" in Scorpio, which is said to be one of its most challenging placements in the zodiac. As such, the emotional current can be riptide strong, pulling you both into an obsessive undertow. But thanks to this deep-diving lunar placement, you don't mind going (way down) into the mysterious depths to "learn" each other. There's nothing light or superficial about this connection!

Scorpio is associated with transformation. Like the phoenix rising from the ashes, you may need to touch the fire of destruction together before you can elevate to the illuminated heights of awareness. Tough emotional lessons? You'll both weather plenty of them in this lifetime. It's part of your process together—and how you develop your superpowers as an evolved and empathic couple.

Because you're such a private pair, the Scorpio Moon relationship may feel isolating and heavy at times. As powerful as it feels to connect to each other, that can add a lot of pressure. But fostering outside support structures will take effort! The magnetic force field of your bond makes it far too easy to slip into a couple bubble. Build your shared community and remember: This can be fun! Join forces to host lavish dinners, organize group vacations to see your favorite band play live. Yes, you'll be "crew glue" for your people, but it goes both ways. When the seas get stormy for the two of you, having a shoulder to cry on (or a couch to crash on) can give your relationship the breathing room it needs.

Should you choose to become parents, you may revel in your children's magic some days and secretly resent them on others. Their presence interrupts the "just the two of us" energy of the Scorpio Supercouple Moon, and while you'd never admit it aloud, you may long for times B.C. (Before Children) for the sheer sexual freedom you felt when you weren't in parent mode. Training your kids to be independent and respect your "adult time" can be a great way to set boundaries once they're old enough to look after themselves. But this isn't a 24/7 thing. Watching the products of your spiritual bond grow up can be one of the most fulfilling things the two of you will experience. If you don't have actual kids, tending to a co-created project can generate a similar buzz for you both. Perhaps you'll start a band together or open up a B&B. The drive to "reproduce" in some way is impossible to avoid under the spell of the Scorpio Supercouple Moon!

SUPERCOUPLE MOON
SAGITTARIUS ✳ ↗

OR THE 9TH HOUSE

To feel securely attached, we need:

- Curiosity
- Honesty
- Supportive wisdom
- Willingness to explore the world
- Physical chemistry
- Independence
- Levity

Honesty is the only policy for relationships with a Supercouple Moon in Sagittarius. Whether the delivery is gentle or brutal depends on the moment. Obviously, kindness will always bring better results. But good luck with that! The excitable energy of your bond can give you both a case of "open mouth, insert foot." Before you remember to self-edit, you've already blurted a "helpful hint" that struck a nerve. Oops! Fortunately, there's nothing you two love more than a rousing round of real talk. (And you're suckers for a deep, philosophical conversation). No matter how intense the horn-locking gets, every mistake is a teachable moment meant to help you both evolve.

Tempers flare up quickly at times, particularly when one (or both) of you is impassioned about your point. A word to the wise: Set ground rules around how you express anger. No slinging personal insults, no interrupting the other before they've made their point and no raising voices or throwing things. (This is a legit thing to watch for here!)

Cooldown breaks will be necessary when discussions devolve into fiery debates.

Security in this relationship doesn't come from a white picket fence, but rather from a shared spirit of adventure. Where (and if!) you'll settle down is anyone's guess. With your Composite Moon in the sign of the worldly Archer, you may prefer the nomadic life, weaving through spells of 24/7 togetherness and long-distance. Independent Sagittarius is the sign of personal growth, and your relationship fosters that for each of you! But get ready for some lonely moments—and maybe even some jealous ones. At times, you may need to be apart, at least physically, to fulfill your destinies.

The peripatetic nature of the Sagittarius Supercouple Moon poses a challenge if you decide to have kids. You may opt to wait and become parents a little later in life, AFTER you've ticked enough boxes on your personal bucket lists. Commitment can be challenging for this ever-expanding relationship. With so much accelerated growth, it's anyone's guess where your trajectories will lead you in a year, much less a month.

Plus, Sagittarius energy is wild and free. If you haven't sown your wild oats, this exploratory connection can spin up major FOMO. One of the best ways to keep the fires burning? Travel together often! (Even for day trips or staycations if that's all you can swing.) Discovery and novelty produce dopamine—a sexy biochemical that your relationship thrives on, along with occasional rushes of adrenaline.

As a couple you'll attract a diverse friend circle! When it comes to creating a community, the Sagittarius Moon helps you both feel right at home among people of different backgrounds and religions—although you may all share some sort of spiritual connection or belief. Starting a business together can also be a powerful bonding agent as long as you share a similar work ethic. With this enterprising Supercouple Moon, you might even write a book or script together about your shared experiences!

SUPERCOUPLE MOON
CAPRICORN ✴ ♑
OR THE 10TH HOUSE

To feel securely attached, we need:

- Stability
- Wealth
- Integrity
- Patience
- Dedication
- Empathy
- Help with relaxing

Where is this all heading? With a Supercouple Moon in no-nonsense Capricorn, emotions are serious business. Even if, left to your own devices, you're the reigning oversharers of your Twitter feeds, you may feel a lot more reserved around each other. Capricorn is ruled by clock-watching Saturn (AKA Kronos), and this Supercouple Moon relationship understands that good things come to those who wait. Your relationship is no fly-by-night fantasy. It's an investment that must be handled first with caution and then, with care. The moon is in "detriment" in Capricorn, which is opposite its home sign of Cancer on the zodiac wheel. Because of this challenging placement, you may be hesitant to open up to each other. Your relationship may hover in the friend zone—or idle in neutral—for an extended period before you finally cross into intimate territory.

But here's the good news. You wouldn't be together if you didn't both sense a promising future here. True, you'll run through an extended checklist of requirements: financial stability, integrity, family values. If one of you isn't "ready" to adult, you may put things on hold and reconnect a decade later. Timing is everything in this relationship, and if it ain't divine, you'll both shy away. The Composite Capricorn Moon focuses on long-term success, period. Like a pair of goal-getters, you'll love setting benchmarks then working diligently to bring them to life. Hello, power duo!

Loyal and dutiful, you're both the rock for one another, as well as your shared friends and family. Parenting comes naturally for you, and if you're inspired to build a family, you might just create a legendary dynasty! You two will pull extra shifts to provide for your relatives, sacrificing sleep to emotionally support them through a crisis. But sometimes, you two can forget to tend to your own emotional needs. Don't ignore them! You'll just wind up resentful, angry or frustrated from putting obligations before your own heart's desires. Or you'll simply be too burned out to fill the love tanks in your own relationship. And that's not something you two should sacrifice!

Setting benchmarks together can be helpful in guiding your shared pathway. But there's also a tendency to be too rational in matters of the heart. If you sense yourself (or your partner) getting icy, red flag! Going cold is a defense mechanism for the Supercouple Capricorn Moon. Folding into a self-protective state instead of expressing yourselves authentically is a surefire intimacy killer.

A helpful tactic? Both of you can learn to name and claim your feelings instead of detaching when things get "intense." Within the energy of this relationship you both like to appear in control. Alas suppressing your feelings can be a self-fulfilling prophecy. If you don't speak up, those tempestuous emotions will erupt like a volcano...or in some cases, manifest as anxiety or depression.

With such an ambitious lunar placement, this union is wired for material world success—and you'll both work hard to achieve it. Your relationship imbues you both with the spirit of leadership. Some days, you two take pride in the struggle (or straight-up suffering). If you earned it the easy way, it doesn't count in your book. Perfectionism can be an Achilles heel for the Capricorn Moon duo, making it hard for both of you to enjoy the fruits of your labors, especially when you're in this energy together.

Like a good home, your shared projects may never really be "done." Celebrate the milestones together instead of waiting until you get to the finish line to raise a toast. This attitude of gratitude will help you manifest more of the abundance that your Supercouple Moon sign craves!

SUPERCOUPLE MOON
AQUARIUS ✳ ♒

OR THE 11TH HOUSE

> ### To feel securely attached, we need:
>
> - Friendship
> - Open-mindedness
> - Calm
> - Compatible social circles
> - Willingness to experiment
> - Help identifying and expressing emotions
> - Intelligent conversation

Hosting the Supercouple Moon in cerebral Aquarius can be a funny thing. It's not that your cool-as-cucumbers connection lacks sensitivity. You just see no reason to lose your $#!% to prove that you're passionate about each other! You may begin vibing from the friend zone, cracking each other up with satirical wit or admiring each other's sartorial choices. What's quickly evident: You appreciate what makes the other one unique. This bond has a rebellious flavor that makes you both feel like eternal teenagers.

Still, this outward-facing relationship vibrates at a high frequency, with a focus on humanity at large. While you may not weep at sappy movies, here's what DOES get you two choked up: human suffering, mistreatment of animals and the planet. You'll be the shared voice of reason that unite everyone for higher good. When you work together purposefully, you know exactly why your souls united on this plane.

Aquarius understands the concept of free love. Even if you're traditional individually, when together, you may suddenly become open-minded and willing to explore unconventional arrangements. Neither of you takes kindly to your partner restricting your personal freedom or trying to control your schedule. Life and liberty go hand in hand under this free-spirited Composite Moon.

But are you just rationalizing your emotions instead of feeling them? That's a strong risk in the Aquarius Moon relationship. Take a time-out before doing anything that may throw your connection into a tailspin. During moments of conflict, learn to consciously tune in to your hearts instead of going right to your intellects. This is especially salient when considering something "experimental" that could damage trust, even if it's consensual. Pushing boundaries can be fun but you need to set your limits—and choose your safe words!

Because Aquarius is community-driven, finding alone time can be challenging here. Your extended circles of friends, colleagues and teammates could cannibalize the time that could be used for "just the two of us" bonding. To keep your union strong, remember to establish some sort of emotional hierarchy, placing each other at—or at least near—the top. The pitfall for this Moon sign is that you can forget to do those little romantic things that make one another feel special. Ultimately, you both do want a mate who will also be your BFF and click with your close friends.

Should you have children, it's unlikely you'll raise them in a predictable way. They might even take a semester off for a family trip, getting educated in "the school of life." Or you'll imbue them with an early understanding of the power of diversity, inclusivity and equity, making sure they are exposed to all sorts of people in their youth.

Aquarius is an air sign, and this head-in-the-clouds Supercouple Moon can make you a quirky couple. At times, you WILL get lost in your own shared bubble. But that's the gift of your elevated matchup. As you model living by your own rules, you pave the way for progress. Ascend!

Create your own Supercouple Chart at **SUPERCOUPLE.COM**

SUPERCOUPLE MOON
PISCES ✳ ♓

OR THE 12TH HOUSE

To feel securely attached, we need:

- Empathy
- Spiritual chemistry
- Caring gestures
- Interdependence
- Clear boundaries
- Serenity & unhurried lifestyles

Dive into the depths! There's a bottomless well of empathy in relationships with the Supercouple Moon in soulful, sensitive Pisces. Yet, those feelings can be as enigmatic and ever-changing as the ocean itself. Emotions may ebb and flow by the minute, making it hard to put them into words. Sometimes, they aren't even your feelings.

This Pisces Moon can make you into psychic sponges, absorbing each other's moods and picking up the energy of everyone in the room. This intuitive trait can be a lot to deal with so prepare to slip off regularly to tune out the world and recharge.

This dreamy lunar placement lends a powerful element of fantasy to your connection. Some days, your relationship feels like a straight-up fairytale as you sweep each other into a magical bubble, where no one else exists but the two of you. Holding each other can be so soothing that it literally heals your frazzled nervous systems. You may lie in bed for hours, sharing daydreams, listening to music and tuning out the stress of the outside world. Pisces is the sign of escape and at its best, your bond can feel like a romantic retreat.

Just don't go MIA forever! With the boundlessness of the Pisces Moon, you can get swept out to sea by each other's emotional currents. Real-world responsibilities don't go away just because, together, you've realized that the only thing "real" is love. With the boundlessness of your bond, this couple is susceptible to codependence. You may regularly try to rescue each other—an effort that will leave you drowning. The trick to building a strong, supportive connection? Empower one another to "do for self." Pardon the Pisces pun, but it boils down to this: Teach each other to fish and you'll both thrive for days!

Relying solely on each other for security is unwise, however, since this relationship can make you both particularly sensitive. Instead, surround yourselves with people who are unconditionally loving AND practical. Living on a tight schedule can stir up anxiety in this "go with the flow" connection.

Bring on the life coaches! Think: Serene and organized experts who can help you create healthy, sustainable structures. The Pisces Moon relationship may need help thriving in the material world rather than just on the fantasy plane. Sometimes you need to remind each other to sleep and eat—and better yet, to cook and grocery shop—when you inevitably drift off to la-la land again.

Outside support will be particularly essential should you decide to become parents. With the boundless compassion this relationship brings, your children will feel doted on and loved. What might be more challenging, however, is setting limits with them, like regular bedtimes and finishing their homework before they play games on the iPad. The shared Pisces Moon is not given over to structure. But remember: It's the very thing that can help kids feel safe in the world, because they know what to expect.

Rushing to kiss the boo-boo and dry their tears is a natural instinct for protective Pisces Moon parents. However, little ones also need to learn from their mistakes. Joining a parents' support group can do wonders if you find yourselves struggling with the journey of raising kids. Beyond getting helpful tips, doses of encouragement remind you that you're not alone in this journey. You'll see when it's time to follow simple guidance and when

Create your own Supercouple Chart at **SUPERCOUPLE.COM**

there's room to improvise!

Protecting the disenfranchised is one thing that will charge up your fighting spirits. But you both must also be mindful of what you're taking in when you offer your help to wayward friends, family members and even strangers. With an empathic Pisces Moon, you can easily absorb other people's stormy moods, negative vibes or outright toxic energy.

Again, this is where the struggle to establish healthy boundaries can really show up for the Pisces Moon. Certain people simply can't be allowed in your lives, especially if they pull you into a toxic vortex with self-destructive addictions or behaviors. At the very least, you may choose not to have them in your home or around your kids. Step back from your feelings of guilt and shame, which are major Pisces themes, and do what will promote peace and health.

More than most, you both need to "shield your fields" from the emotions and energies you'll absorb as a duo. Learning to set healthy boundaries is essential to your shared sense of sanity and stability. Feel free to take that to the spiritual level with your mystic Moon! You could wear certain crystals or a protective talisman, burn palo santo and even explore the power of plant medicine. There are many ways that you'll open each other's psychic channels through your union.

Like the Fish that symbolize Pisces, let yourselves "swim away" from challenging situations when your circuits get overloaded. Learn to clear yourselves with salt baths, sage wands and quiet moments in your own spaces. Make it your mission to find a home together with a dreamy tub!

With your rich fantasy lives, a creative outlet can also be a huge bonding force for this relationship. You might channel intuitive feelings and deep emotions into art, music or dance. What you dream up together can be pure genius! Like a tsunami, you could rise up from "nowhere" and start a cultural wave that takes the world by storm. Your shared space may double as a studio where you both can let your imaginations soar. At the very least, make sure it's a peaceful sanctuary, only open to those who enter with good intentions and as their best selves!

SUPERCOUPLE

Compatibility

WITH YOUR MOON SIGN

If our Supercouple Moon is in a fire sign:
(ARIES, LEO OR SAGITTARIUS)

And my personal moon is in a fire sign
(ARIES, LEO OR SAGITTARIUS):

The good news is this relationship won't leave you feeling trapped or limited. Here your emotionally expressive style will be well-received. However, building security will take extra work. You may disrupt stability the minute it feels restrictive—or the responsibilities seem too heavy. The best way to stay grounded and united is through action: Work on a shared project or plan a trip. Any adventure will be a bonding agent.

And my personal moon is in an earth sign
(TAURUS, VIRGO OR CAPRICORN):

While you'll love how passionate your emotional exchanges can be, this connection rocks your sense of security to the core. You may feel like things are moving too fast without enough certainty for you to relax into. But don't abandon ship too quickly! Predictability and excitement CAN co-exist. Look for common ground. By cultivating your shared dreams and desires, you will grow emotionally. Simultaneously, lean in to other steady relationships for support, especially when the two of you aren't able to be together.

And my personal moon is in an air sign
(GEMINI, LIBRA, AQUARIUS):

Can we talk? Word is bond in this relationship! You may derive your greatest sense of security through communication and the exchange of ideas. Experimenting and exploring with a partner? Yes, please. Those desires find a happy home here—and those game-changing experiences will become your connective tissue. Just make sure you aren't always chasing the next sparkly thing. You don't have to map out a twenty-year plan, but SOME semblance of future security is important to lock down.

And my personal moon is in a water sign
(CANCER, SCORPIO OR PISCES):

You may never feel 100% secure in this relationship, which thrives on adventure and accelerated growth—both things that are contrary to your deep need for predictability. However, that's where the magic of this connection lies! Through your independent bond, you both become more self-sufficient, fortifying your internal security instead of seeking selfhood from outside validation. Hit the brakes if things start moving in a direction that feels scary or unsettling. Managing the strong emotional current is the biggest challenge of this match.

Create your own Supercouple Chart at **SUPERCOUPLE.COM**

If our Supercouple Moon is in an earth sign:
(TAURUS, VIRGO, OR CAPRICORN)

And my personal moon is in a fire sign
(ARIES, LEO OR SAGITTARIUS):

This relationship may feel SO secure that it sets off your independence alarm bells. Since your Supercouple Moon requires rock-solid material security, it may clash with your free-spirited, "whatever happens, happens" approach to life. Passionate spontaneity may be in short order here, which at first can feel like a bummer. But challenge yourself to sit through any "boring" and uncomfortable moments. The dependable structure of this relationship is a gift that allows you to explore a wider range of feelings within yourself.

And my personal moon is in an earth sign
(TAURUS, VIRGO OR CAPRICORN):

Kick up your feet and pour yourself a drink. This grounded, easygoing relationship feels like home to you. At last, you've found the serene stability required to relax into the rhythm of shared life. This bond is all about supporting and being supported! Just be careful not to become complacent or miss out on the thrills that come from taking emotional risks.

And my personal moon is in an air sign
(GEMINI, LIBRA, AQUARIUS):

You can be cool and detached about your feelings, so it's easy to hide out in the practical side of this Supercouple Moon. But if you do, you'll miss a key growth opportunity. So, go ahead... open up to the sensuality and stability this partnership can provide. Dive in deeper and get to know each other instead of scattering your attention among a wide group of strangers. Let this relationship teach you how to use your natural networking powers to create family bonds and long-lasting friendships.

And my personal moon is in a water sign
(CANCER, SCORPIO OR PISCES):

You'll love how grounded this relationship makes you feel! Finally, an opportunity to create the long-term security that you crave, but aren't always able to manifest on your own. There's a sensible quality to your emotional connection, however. Bringing your best to this bond may require some emotional restraint, but that's okay! Putting your melodramatic side in the timeout chair is not the worst thing.

If our Supercouple Moon is in an air sign:
(GEMINI, LIBRA, AQUARIUS)

And my personal moon is in a fire sign
(ARIES, LEO OR SAGITTARIUS):

It's never been easy for you to put your swirling hot-and-cold feelings into words—until now, that is. The elevated level of communication in this relationship provides an outlet you didn't realize you needed. (Just remember, your partner is not your therapist.) To keep the peace, cool down your hotheaded responses and utilize greater emotional restraint. Building a shared friend group is an excellent security measure. Not only will your community keep you honest, but it's a place you can return to when you find yourself on shaky ground.

And my personal moon is in an earth sign
(TAURUS, VIRGO OR CAPRICORN):

Get ready to compromise! All your dreams about home, family, finances and other benchmarks will be challenged by the novelty and experimentation this relationship stirs up. If you settled on a picture of the future without exploring a wide enough range of possibilities, this relationship will be sure to send you on a discovery mission. Don't bother clinging to the past. Seeing what else is out there could unveil a new definition of security that is anything but cookie-cutter.

And my personal moon is in an air sign
(GEMINI, LIBRA, AQUARIUS):

Does it make sense on paper? Logic reigns supreme in this relationship. You two may never be fully swept away in feelings—and that suits your cooler temperament just fine. Sharing ideas and inspiring each other to explore different perspectives are more important than stacking up material resources. And truth be told, that support WILL pay off, since the more you mirror one another's greatness, the brighter you'll shine in the world. Equally important is the social support you'll both receive by building a shared community. It takes a village!

And my personal moon is in a water sign
(CANCER, SCORPIO OR PISCES):

Your personal benchmarks for security, such as a home, family and warm fuzzy TLC are great, but they aren't the true glue in this bond. The magic here lies in being each other's best friends. The cooler emotional emotional temperature of this relationship may seem unromantic at first, but it may soon become a relief! Here, you can express your vulnerabilities without feeling overwhelmed, then shape your feelings into a plan of action. This partnership may calm some of your anxieties, which in turn allows you to be more functional in the world. From there, you can manifest the resources you need to live a stable life.

If our Supercouple Moon is in a water sign:
(CANCER, SCORPIO OR PISCES)

And my personal moon is in a fire sign
(ARIES, LEO OR SAGITTARIUS):

Can you shift from a "me first" mindset to a collective one? That's the key to finding security with this Supercouple Moon relationship. The trouble is, you're hard-wired to be independent. Thus, you may feel a little beyond your depth in this relationship, especially when you're called upon to make sacrifices for family or the greater good. Stick with it, and this union is sure to raise your EQ. (But first...tantrums.) This relationship brings a sweet reminder that you don't have to do it all alone. Utilize your natural creative abilities to generate resources, not just for yourself, but for both of you.

And my personal moon is in an earth sign
(TAURUS, VIRGO OR CAPRICORN):

This relationship adds heart and meaning to the practical productivity that is part of your security plan. Suddenly you're not just going through the motions of earning a paycheck and putting organic, non-GMO food on the table. You feel a sense of purpose, a desire to provide for something bigger than just yourself. The nurturing nature of this bond can also remind you to relax and kick your feet up. Now, who wants a shoulder rub?

And my personal moon is in an air sign
(GEMINI, LIBRA, AQUARIUS):

This relationship draws you into deeper waters that may feel unfamiliar and even a little intimidating at first. Come down from your lofty cloud. Words alone will not create security here. Tangible efforts, material rewards and abiding loyalty on the other hand? Non-negotiable must-haves! If you want this to last, you'll need to make good on your promises. That level of responsibility can be intimidating, but resist the urge to drift away when the going gets tough.

 And my personal moon is in a water sign
(CANCER, SCORPIO OR PISCES):

It's almost too easy to create a safe bubble here. Your natural desire for domestic bliss, safe emotional spaces and reassurance will be easily met in this bond. The only pitfall is that you can veer toward codependence and becoming overly reliant on each other for all your emotional needs. That level of enmeshment can become claustrophobic, too.

Create your own Supercouple Chart at **SUPERCOUPLE.COM**

SUPERCOUPLE

ASCENDANT (RISING SIGN)

Asc

how others see us

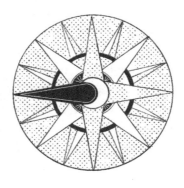

Asc

Use Your Supercouple Ascendant to Understand:

- How you "display" to others as a couple
- The ideal image you can present to the world
- Your relationship's main focus or orientation
- Ways to break the ice in early stages
- How to melt the ice in later stages
- How to be seen as a dynamic duo
- How others may initially view your relationship

WHAT IMAGE DO YOU PROJECT AS A COUPLE?

Ever wonder how others see you as a duo, especially when you step out in public? Your Supercouple Ascendant reveals the first impression you make together. Since the Rising sign governs appearances and a more consciously-crafted public image, it's the "us" that the two of you project into the world. But as they say, first impressions last longest!

Here's a case for the Supercouple Ascendant's power: On our reality show *Cosmic Love,* where we served as astrological matchmakers and guides, we paired a Leo (Chris) and a Capricorn (Maria). Their upbringings and cultures were as different as their Sun signs. He was a Connecticut-raised Italian mama's boy whose parents had been happily married for decades; she was a Dominican entrepreneur raised by a self-made single mom.

Asc

Maria and Chris had a Composite Ascendant in Taurus, the sign of values, sensuality and beauty. As soon as they discovered they were matched, they couldn't keep their hands off of each other. Hugging and touching progressed to some steamy scenes! In sync with their blended Taurus rising, they made a stylish couple, always groomed and dressed with impeccable attention to detail. When they weren't making out, most of their conversations centered around Taurus themes of family, traditions and core beliefs.

The Supercouple Ascendant shows how you'll break the ice when you're getting acquainted. Will you try to impress each other (Composite Libra or Leo Ascendant)? Or will you quickly shed the facade and keep it real (hello, Composite Aries Rising)? If you can get your hands on the other person's birth data without it being "too soon," this chart placement can help guide you through the awkward initial phases of your connection.

For established couples, the joint Ascendant gives you a shared orientation for your relationship. What are you striving for as a couple? Maybe you'll build a business with your Composite Capricorn Rising...or make a beautiful home courtesy of a Composite Cancer Rising (decorated to the nines for every holiday and a haven for friends and family).

Think of this chart placement as the direction your shared compass naturally points toward. It doesn't mean you have to follow that route, but you may find your way back to each other anytime you do.

Supercouple ASCENDANT
IN THE ZODIAC SIGNS

Asc

In the Sign of	The image we display is	Our main focus is	Sometimes we can be
ARIES	Fierce sexiness	Having a trailblazing mission	Overwhelming
TAURUS	Sweet affection	Being responsible	Set in our ways
GEMINI	Mischief waiting to happen	Intellectual connection	Two-faced
CANCER	Warm and nurturing	Being a safe, caring space	Oversensitive
LEO	Captivating glamour	Making life feel like a celebration	Competitive
VIRGO	Thoughtful and inquisitive	Looking like we've got it all together	Judgmental
LIBRA	Refined elegance	Dazzling the world with our beauty and grace	Superficial
SCORPIO	Sexy mystery	Exuding power and a touch of intimidation	Overpowering
SAGITTARIUS	Fun and adventurous	Being inspiring and thought-provoking	Too much
CAPRICORN	Polished pragmatists	Conquering the world and looking good doing it	Uptight
AQUARIUS	Quirky iconoclasts	Disrupting the norm, normalizing the weird	Eccentric
PISCES	Earth angels	Spreading compassion and high vibes	Flaky

FIND YOUR SUPERCOUPLE ASCENDANT
AT **SUPERCOUPLE.COM**

Create your own Supercouple Chart at **SUPERCOUPLE.COM**

SUPERCOUPLE ASCENDANT
ARIES ✳ ♈

> **People often notice our:**
>
> - Flamboyance
> - Take-charge energy and leadership
> - Fierce sexiness
> - Argumentative banter

With Aries as your Supercouple Ascendant, you two command a take-charge energy that's inspiring and motivating. No matter how shy you are as individuals, when you come together, you can turn into a pair of dynamic firecrackers.

Courageous and bold, Aries is a fire sign, ruled by warrior planet Mars. This can quicken your impulses and add some heat to your interactions. You can be a little bossy with each other, but that's okay! You're here to blaze trails together, and when you're on a mission, there's no time to mince words. In groups, you are seen as natural leaders and may set the bar for your entire community.

When you're out together, you can't help but make a statement— and oh, what fun this can be. Turn heads with wilder fashion choices, stepping out with outre styles that make people stop and take notice.

THE ASCENDANT (RISING)

Asc

You might even coordinate your outfits or rock the signature Aries hue of red. Hey, Aries is the first sign of the zodiac and with this Composite Ascendant, you two love to leave your mark.

Combative Mars is your "chart ruler," the planet that will be a beacon for your relationship. Track the movement of Mars through the zodiac to know the "mood" you two will embody on any given day. Mars changes signs every seven weeks, except when it turns retrograde every two years and hovers in a single sign (or between two signs) for seven whole months. During these backspins, your initiatives may stall, and the two of you are prone to locking horns more than most couples. You can find these dates by checking an ephemeris, which is a calendar of all the planetary transits, or by working with a professional astrologer.

With the red planet ruling the show, you can be a competitive and attention-seeking pair. You can overwhelm people if your shared passion doesn't have a proper outlet (or five). However, when you channel that impulse into physical and creative outlets, your combined zeal becomes a force to be reckoned with. With this fiery ascendant, you two need a lot of movement and action, whether through intense workouts, sexual marathons or even taking the stage as entertainers.

Create your own Supercouple Chart at **SUPERCOUPLE.COM**

SUPERCOUPLE ASCENDANT
TAURUS ✳ ♉

People often notice our:

- Sophistication
- Traditional ways
- Elegance
- Sweet affection

With sophisticated Taurus as your Supercouple Ascendant, you two are a class act. But you're also a tenacious twosome! You don't mince words, even if you set firm limits clear with style and grace. You can be determined and persistent when you want something—and you don't bother trying to hide those desires! Fortunately, you can be as tender as you are tough.

Taurus is ruled by aesthetic Venus, which makes the planet of love and beauty your Composite "chart ruler." Track the movement of Venus through the zodiac to know the vibe you two will exude on any given day. Venus changes signs approximately every four weeks, except when it turns retrograde every 584 days and hovers in a single sign (or between two signs) for four whole months. When Venus is retrograde, there's no escaping issues you two have swept under the rug—and more than most couples, your intimacy can be tested

Asc

by these periodic backspins. You can find these dates by checking an ephemeris, which is a calendar of all the planetary transits, or by working with a professional astrologer.

Your four eyes will develop a deep appreciation for art, beauty, design and gourmet everything. But this down-to-earth Ascendant keeps your feet on the ground. Although you may have expensive tastes, you're not snobs. As a couple you'd just as happily meet at a dive bar as you would a Michelin-starred trattoria. You don't always gravitate toward flashy stuff and might prefer refined items of lasting quality, procured at a sensible price. Did someone say "designer discount?"

Industrious Taurus works hard for its money. When duty calls, you'll both roll up your sleeves and get your hands dirty. As much as you two might love a 90-minute massage (with the seaweed wrap, salt scrub and oxygenating facial package thrown in), you savor a good day's labor. Being responsible gives you a shared sense of purpose. The family-oriented nature of this connection creates a natural desire to provide. But without ample funds in the bank, you both feel anxious and unmoored.

Although you're naturally focused on security in this relationship, together you can be overly stubborn and get stuck in a rut by refusing to try new things, opting rather to do things "the old-fashioned way." By the same token, your shared tenacity is what keeps history alive. You two may even dress as if you're from another era, or shape your lives around values of a treasured time.

SUPERCOUPLE ASCENDANT
GEMINI ✳ ♊

People often notice our:

- Social charms
- Friendliness
- Effusive and bubbly communication
- Expressive gestures

Can we talk? Having ultra-communicative Gemini as your Supercouple Ascendant blesses your relationship with unparalleled social skills. There's nothing you two enjoy more than being consumed in an engaging conversation—with each other or the ever-growing friend group you'll attract as a pair. You might lose track of time, but *c'est la vie*. A wink, a smile and a genuine apology is generally all it takes to get you both off the hook in this charmed alignment.

Gemini is a breezy air sign ruled by quick-witted and intellectual Mercury, which makes the messenger planet your Composite "chart ruler." Track the movement of Mercury through the zodiac to know the impression you two will make on any given day. Mercury changes signs approximately every three weeks, except when it turns retrograde 3-4 times a year and hovers in a single sign (or between two signs) for two and a half months. More than most couples, your

Asc

interactions and communication may be affected by Mercury's backspins. You can find these dates by checking an ephemeris, which is a calendar of all the planetary transits, or by working with a professional astrologer.

A convivial duo, you know how to get people talking. At gatherings, you'll be the people zipping around the room faster than the messenger planet itself! As a couple you might even get a rep for your short attention spans, or be accused of (glug) superficiality. This inquisitive Ascendant can drive you both to distraction. So many things pique your curiosity that it's hard to know where to focus. The upside of your dilettante nature is that it you could become knowledgeable experts on a variety of topics from books to music to movies. Soon enough, you'll be an in-demand pair for the bar trivia team or monthly Jeopardy night.

Watch out for a tendency to be manipulative. If you twist each other's arms, you may get jabbed with a sucker punch from left field. A propensity to gossip is the shadow side of Gemini Rising. Although your snarky commentary can be hilarious, it can also skew mean-spirited and divisive. You might leave people wondering if you're the next supervillains!

Since Gemini is the zodiac's twin, being by one another's side is crucial for this "BFFs with benefits" relationship. When one of you feels troubled, the other is there with savvy advice, witty commentary and playful ideas to pull them out of a rut. Warning: Make sure you don't develop an "us against the world" identity. Since this connection relies heavily on verbal processing, having a therapist or coach as a sounding board can keep you from taking out frustration on one another when the going gets tough.

Create your own Supercouple Chart at **SUPERCOUPLE.COM**

SUPERCOUPLE ASCENDANT
CANCER ✳ ♋

> **People often notice our:**
>
> - Nurturing and caring vibes
> - Stormy moods
> - Emotional tenderness
> - Love of comforts such as food

Who needs a hug? With nurturing Cancer as your Supercouple Ascendant, you'll be the connoisseurs of comfort, ready with a compassionate ear, a hot mug of tea and the kind of support most people could only expect from their family. When together, you may be more reserved than you are on your own. Cancer isn't necessarily quiet or shy, but this shared Rising Sign brings out a caretaking impulse in you both. Rather than focusing on how others perceive you, the two of you just want to make sure that everyone around you is doing okay. You might even feel like the de facto "parents" of your posse. Of course, the zodiac's Crab does have a pretty outer shell! And with this Ascendant, you two will exude a timeless grace. Stylistically, you may start spinning the classics as a duo, dressing in vintage or fashion inspired by a bygone era.

Cancer is a water sign, ruled by the shape-shifting moon, which makes la luna your Composite "chart ruler." Track the transits of the moon through the zodiac and you'll get a pretty good idea how to approach each other (and the outside world) on any given day. Oh, by the way? That vibe changes every 2.5 days, which is the length of

Asc

time that the moon spends in each zodiac sign before moving on to the next one. You can find these dates by checking an ephemeris, which is a calendar of all the planetary transits, or by working with a professional astrologer. As a couple, you have your own monthly cycle, and may be luckiest initiating plans with the new moon and harvesting results with the full moon. You'll have to stay fluid in this relationship!

Together you understand the ebb and flow of emotions more than most. In fact, yours are rarely far from the surface. With sensitivities heightened by your Cancer Rising, you become empaths who pick up on everyone's feelings. Some days, it may feel like you're carrying the weight of the world on your shoulders. But with this family-oriented Composite Ascendant, you are definitely the glue for your crew.

Because this relationship makes you both so touchy, it wouldn't hurt to develop greater emotional restraint. Reactivity can damage trust between you, especially if you blame or shame one another. With people outside your relationship, you may feel guarded, worried that they're taking advantage of your mutual generosity. Agree on boundaries, then set them clearly with friends and family. Then, you won't have to snap anyone with your claws because they didn't show proper appreciation for your boo!

All sorts of cultural activities appeal to you as a pair. Even if you were a beer and burgers type before, suddenly, you're picking up season tickets to the opera and cataloging the names of indie musicians and rappers. Quiet time at home is equally essential. When you're not engaged in another DIY project, you'll "parallel play" in comfortable silence.

Food is a major bonding agent, whether you're tucking into a home-cooked meal or ordering the tasting menu (with wine pairings) at a raved-about restaurant. Hosting intimate parties is how you show love, and it is a metaphor for the coziness you want others to feel on a heart and soul level. The act of stopping for a meal also allows you to ease into social situations without the anxiety that can accompany it. *Bon appetit!*

Create your own Supercouple Chart at **SUPERCOUPLE.COM**

SUPERCOUPLE ASCENDANT

LEO ✶ ♌

People often notice our:

- Expressive (and theatrical) interactions
- Glamorous fashion choices
- Scene-stealing presence
- Magnanimous ways

Look who just stepped into the room! With beaming, radiant Leo as your Supercouple Ascendant, you're a dynamic duo with major presence. Whether you're bouncing off the walls with excitement or brooding after a couple's spat, you two exude so much energy that everyone sits up to take notice. More than any other Composite Ascendant, you'll command attention—which is why it's important to be mindful of your surroundings. Leo is a fire sign, after all. You both don't merely change the temperature of your environment. When together, your flames fan out, licking everyone around with their heat. With Leo as your shared Rising Sign, you can warm hearts or scorch souls; the choice is yours.

Little Simba from *The Lion King* couldn't have sung it better with "I Just Can't Wait To Be King," a true musical ode to the power this Ascendant possesses. Yet there's a lot required to become a true power couple. Underestimating the level of responsibility involved can get you both in over your head. Ironically, although you two love to take charge, you can have a hard time with authority. If people fence you in or boss you around, they'd better prepare for your angry roars!

THE ASCENDANT (RISING)

Asc

Much like this sign's ruler, the all-powerful Sun, you two are a lot like the biggest and brightest star in the galaxy. Life revolves around you both! The Sun is the "chart ruler" of your Superchart, so track its movement through the zodiac for clues about where to find the most powerful opportunities at any given time. Every zodiac "season" is governed by the Sun (Leo season, Virgo season, etc.), and begins some time between the 18th and 23rd of every month. Use this calendar as your beacon. During the four weeks that the Sun is in a specific sign, your pairing will be lit up by that astrological energy—and if you focus there, you will crush it! You can find these dates by checking an ephemeris, which is a calendar of all the planetary transits, or by working with a professional astrologer.

The Supercouple Leo Ascendant gives you both a fierce competitive streak. When you come together, you know how to put on a show and deliver a winning performance! As a couple, you may attract famous friends or become a recognizable pair yourselves. Don't miss the opportunity to play this up. Life can be a nonstop costume party for this connection, so bring on the colorful couture and Paris Fashion Week "lewks." Play with your "lions' manes" and try eye-catching hair styles, wild colors and oversized hats. Matching outfits are not off the menu, especially if you create a den full of cubs. If there were ever a family destined to send out holiday cards in coordinated ugly sweaters, it's yours!

Because this relationship puts you in touch with your youthful spirits, you two can be great with children—once you've banked enough playful experiences yourselves. Your union may inspire you both to step into the role of parents—or to "birth" a creative brainchild together. Whatever the case, your efforts are sure to be showstopping. Lights, camera, action!

SUPERCOUPLE ASCENDANT

VIRGO ✳ ♍

People often notice our:

- Willingness to be helpful
- Curious and engaging conversations
- Elegant style
- Refreshing innocence and sweetness

Give the world service with a smile! With helpful Virgo as this relationship's Supercouple Ascendant, you're a dutiful, purposeful pair. Generosity is your shared compass—and you'll readily make a sacrifice in the name of greater good. Of course, your "pro tips" aren't always sugar-sweet. Virgo is the zodiac's critic, so when something's out of order, you two are the first to spot the flaw. Whether it's a misspelled word or a distasteful accessory that deserves a citation from the fashion police, nothing escapes your exacting eyes. To call you both neat freaks would be an understatement. But some couples with Virgo Rising may go in the opposite direction, collecting every treasure you find at an antique mall or on the sale rack until one day, friends threaten to give your names to the *Hoarders* camera crew. Eventually, there will be a wakeup call that snaps you into the systematic groove Virgo is famous for, and you'll live up to its regimented rep.

The detail-driven Virgo Rising blesses you two with a talent for any task that requires precision, from baking to editing to drawing up

Asc

architectural plans. However, you can easily fall prey to perfectionism, redoing tasks a thousand times before deeming them presentable. Easy does it! There's a tendency to come across as rigid or judgmental when you're together. We are all human beings trying to do our best. Remind yourselves of this regularly, whether you're turning that exacting lens on yourselves, each other or your neighbors.

Virgo is ruled by analytical, systematic Mercury, which makes this planet your Composite "chart ruler." Track the movement of Mercury through the zodiac to know where you two can lend your support and smarts on any given day. Mercury changes signs approximately every three weeks, except when it turns retrograde 3-4 times a year and hovers in a single sign (or between two signs) for two and a half months. More than many couples, you may find that your communication hits a snag during Mercury's backspins. You can find these dates by checking an ephemeris, which is a calendar of all the planetary transits, or by working with a professional astrologer.

Wellness is Virgo's domain—and this sign is associated with the digestive system. To say this Ascendant sharpens your gut instincts would not be wrong. For one thing, this chart facet can turn you both into clean-eating fitness nuts whose first question about your food is always to the tune of, "Is it organic and non-GMO?" Arguably, this IS a little obsessive. But regular workouts and eating a balanced diet together go a long way to combat the anxiety that a Virgo Supercouple Ascendant churns up. And when you're feeding your bodies pure fuel, your minds become sharper. This is a plus for everyone, since you're often tapped as the ethical barometers for mutual friends and family.

Your earth-conscious ethos doesn't stop at your plates. Organic cotton, sustainable brands and undyed fabrics—you'll cultivate a meticulous sensibility. You may adorn yourselves with spiritual talismans and fashion brands that are hand-sewn by women in a developing nation. Whenever there's a chance to share your high-minded values as a couple, you'll happily do so, inspiring others to elevate along with you!

SUPERCOUPLE ASCENDANT
LIBRA ✳ ♎

Asc

People often notice our:

- Calming presence
- Sense of fairness
- Adoring gazes
- Refined fashion sense

Hey, you beautiful people! With aesthetic Libra as your Supercouple Ascendant, you're an exquisitely elegant duo. Pack away the faded athleisure. This relationship has a polished dress code that's more upscale than "off duty." When together, you'll never meet a fine bottle of wine, soft-spun silk or luxury bedding set that you wouldn't try. From the curb appeal of your home to your choice in furniture and sartorial flair, you'll enjoy creating a feast for the eyes. People will compliment your presentation—and not-so-secretly want whatever you two are serving. To call you an enviable pair would be putting it mildly.

Libra is a free-flowing air sign, governed by radiant Venus, making the glow-up goddess your Composite "chart ruler." Track the movement of Venus through the zodiac for captivating clues on how to tickle your romantic fancy at any given time. Venus changes signs approximately every four weeks, except when it turns retrograde every 584 days and hovers in a single sign (or between two signs) for four whole months. When Venus is retrograde, there's no escaping issues you two have swept under the rug—and more than most

Asc

couples, your intimacy can be tested by these periodical backspins. You can find these dates by checking an ephemeris, which is a calendar of all the planetary transits, or by working with a professional astrologer.

Libra is symbolized by the Scales, so maintaining balance is a lifelong quest. It feels wonderful to delight people's senses with your luxurious tastes. But focus too heavily on external appearances and you two risk reading as superficial or vain. With the exquisite appetite this Ascendant incites, you both can overdo it on the shopping. That designer French sofa may scream "royale," but it could end up being a royal pain-in-the-a** to pay off! And nothing brings down the vibe of a Libra Supercouple Ascendant than a financial shortfall.

When life starts feeling flat, lean in together to the justice-focused side of Libra. Not only does this Ascendant make you a principled pair, but together, you're natural bridge-builders. Diplomatic Libra is a sign with a rare ability to bring together warring factions or open people's eyes to social inequities. Find a meaningful cause to get behind, even if "peace, love, and harmony" is your mutual M.O.

Libra is the partnership sign of the zodiac and this Ascendant definitely keeps you two joined at the hip. But you'll also enjoy socializing together with your ever-growing group of caring, cultured friends. Loneliness can be a real fear for you within this relationship, but one worth confronting head-on. Believe it or not, cultivating more independence can be incredibly liberating for you both. Maybe you set a night each week where you spend a few hours apart—or hey, even a few days. Before you know it, you'll be picking up a book, choreographing a dance or getting inspired to write a post after watching YouTubes of a legendary activist.

SUPERCOUPLE ASCENDANT
SCORPIO ✳ ♏

People often notice our:

- Mysterious allure
- Intense closeness
- Fierce loyalty
- Charged sexual chemistry

Piercing gaze or a faraway, mysterious look? With deep-water Scorpio as this relationship's Supercouple Ascendant, both will be familiar expressions for you two. With the famed "sex sign" governing your outward appearance as a pair, you both emit an energy as intense as a thousand burning suns. The attraction between you can be fiery one minute, cool and distant the next, but with this alchemical water sign guiding your relationship's outward expression, riding those waves is a part of the life-transforming experience of being together. Hey, at least your relationship won't be boring!

Probing Pluto is Scorpio's galactic guardian, and thus your Composite "chart ruler." Yes, this may explain all the magnetism you two exude—and why you may feel like twin detectives unlocking life's enigmas together. You can track the passages of Pluto through the zodiac for clues on where you both may be intently focused at any period of time. You can find these dates by checking an ephemeris, which is a calendar of all the planetary transits, or

Asc

by working with a professional astrologer. A slow-moving outer planet, Pluto hovers in a single zodiac sign for 12 to 30 years. Your relationship will go through extended cycles, where you're both deeply involved in a shared pursuit. Then, one day, Pluto moves to a new sign and you may completely transform your lives! These shifts may even seem radical, combustible or extreme, but that's just how a Scorpio Rising Supercouple rolls.

Having the lord of the underground directing your GPS is no small (or laughing) matter. As a pair, you can come across as relaxed and ultra-cool. But with your keen powers of observation, you two are ready to strike like a couple of king cobras should anyone cross you. The good news is, you both look hot as hell doing it!

No matter where you beam your attention, there's a power couple vibe going on in this relationship. When you two share a position of leadership, you're an unstoppable force! Whatever your life motto is, just tack on the phrase "or die trying" at the end. You'll go through hell and back to achieve your goals. Few can keep up with you, but that's not necessarily a good thing. The single-minded obsession with achievement a Composite Scorpio Rising brings out can make you workaholics, and your other relationships may suffer as a result.

Trust doesn't come easily where Scorpio is involved, and it may take a while before you warm up to each other. Then comes the "hazing" process of meeting each other's friends and families. Despite your otherworldly sexual chemistry, the early days can be a rough emotional period for you two! As much as you desire soulful bonding, you also want to make sure that your emotional investment will be returned. Be patient if you think the payoff of being together "forever after" is worth it. Once committed, you're a fiercely loyal pair, providing support in each other's darkest moments and champion one another's success.

Since Scorpio is a spiritual sign, it's helpful to have shared rituals with this Supercouple Ascendant, particularly ones that integrate shadow work. You're not afraid to get "woo," channeling messages from the departed or going on plant medicine journeys that help you touch other realms. Life is an endless mystery and following its clues together is your favorite treasure hunt!

Asc

SUPERCOUPLE ASCENDANT

SAGITTARIUS

Asc

People often notice our:

- Adventurous spirits
- Larger-than-life presence
- Booming laughter
- Vital energy

Quick...what's your opening line? Having wise and witty Sagittarius as your Supercouple Ascendant makes everything a laughing matter—and we mean in a "laughter is the best medicine" kind of way. Together, you see the absurdity of life and can dissect anything from a philosophical angle. Your relationship provides an enlightened lens on life that many people struggle to reach! Welcome to the nonstop salon of your Composite Sagittarius rising!

Candid Sagittarius is the zodiac's truth seeker and this shared Rising Sign does not mince words. There's no telling what will spill out when you two start talking, but it's bound to be memorable—and, uh, possibly controversial. If something's out of sync, you both are going to speak up, even if it clears the room! No matter how raunchy or recherche you get together, your intentions are generally pure. Fortunately, most people can sense that. You might accidentally

Asc

misfire your truth arrows at times, hitting below the belt. But as a couple you also have the power to shift people's mindsets!

Sagittarius is a fire sign ruled by bountiful Jupiter, which makes the larger-than-life planet your Composite "chart ruler." You can track the passages of Jupiter through the zodiac for clues on where to take a gamble together at any given time. As the first of the outer planets, Jupiter hovers in a single sign for 12-13 months before moving on to the next. Put yourselves on an annual schedule! This is an ideal cadence for you two—especially if you want to remain inspired without biting off more than you can reasonably chew. Just know that it will start on the day Jupiter changes signs, not necessarily on January 1. You can find these dates by checking an ephemeris, which is a calendar of all the planetary transits, or by working with a professional astrologer.

Jupiter's influence blesses your union with good fortune and a healthy appetite for all of life's pleasures. But there IS a catch! You two don't always realize when to stop indulging—and those hedonistic sprees can get expensive. When you're lit up about a goal, you'll pursue it like Centaurs galloping off on a hunt. Having something to chase keeps life interesting for you both. Just make sure you stop and integrate all the "wins" you achieve. It's not just about scoring the prize; it's also about learning how to incorporate these victories into your lives.

With worldly Jupiter as this relationship's beacon, this coupling inspires a global mindset. What else is out there? And who? Traveling together brings out the best of you both. But no matter your GPS coordinates, you two may become ambassadors, bridging together friends from diverse cultures and lifestyles. Because you're

Asc

always on the go, there's no need for fussy dress-up dates. The uniform for your relationship? Clothes that are a little bit "college quad" mixed with "backpacking bohemian" and accessorized with spiritual totems.

Life is a never-ending journey of growth and discovery for a Sagittarius Ascendant Supercouple. And you'll soon have the self-development workshops, spiritual ceremonies and teacher trainings to show for it. But watch out! When you're lit up about a new methodology, your evangelizing can get downright zealous.

In this connection, there's really no limit to your visionary reach, a superpower you two should wield with care. You're able to see so many options that you can wind up majorly overwhelmed. You may scale up too quickly or overshoot the mark, then suffer from a loss of freedom due to the outsized plans you co-create.

And here's the deal: Beyond any epic achievement, freedom is the ultimate need for this rising sign. There's nothing that frustrates you more as a couple than feeling restrained or fenced in. Record all your big ideas for posterity and put them on the bucket list. Then, remember that Rome wasn't built in a day!

Create your own Supercouple Chart at **SUPERCOUPLE.COM**

SUPERCOUPLE ASCENDANT

CAPRICORN ✴ ♑

People often notice our:

- Power couple presence
- Classic elegance
- Solid integrity
- Capable command of any room

Let's do lunch! Business is pleasure for relationships with ambitious Capricorn as the Supercouple Ascendant. An achievement-oriented pair, you'll discover lifelong opportunities to build and grow together—whether it's a family, an empire (or both) that you're out to create. Material security and success are a major focus of this union and you'll work tirelessly to achieve it. Capricorn is the provider sign of the zodiac. With this Ascendant, your combined efforts could leave a legacy to be enjoyed by the ones you love and the generations to follow.

Capricorn is a traditional earth sign, making you as a couple the rock for your families and friends. You're the dependable and loyal pair who brings everyone together for holidays and special occasions. Some may accuse you of being too caught up in status, but what can you say? You'll inspire each other to do, be and have the best—and no one can deny that you hustle for those victories. Your people know that you'll be there for them in a jam, but this can become a burden if you make too many sacrifices. Healthy boundaries keep you "protected and connected," as therapist and author Terrence Real advises, so find that middle ground between giving too much and cutting people off.

THE ASCENDANT (RISING)

Asc

Earth sign Capricorn is ruled by disciplined Saturn, which makes the planet of structure and authority your Composite "chart ruler." Though you might not be the most playful pair, you ARE the most productive. When you two commit to a mission, you are unstoppable. There's always a new challenge to conquer, but where to begin? Track the movements of Saturn to find the most fruitful focal point. A slower-moving outer planet, Saturn spends about three years in every zodiac sign before moving on to the next. That's a good chunk of time, which means there's no need to rush to your finish lines. Slow down and do things right the first time—that's the ringed planet's motto. You can track Saturn's dates by checking an ephemeris, which is a calendar of all the planetary transits, or by working with a professional astrologer.

With mature Saturn as your planetary PR director, together you may favor a polished look of black, white and gray. Luxury and heritage brands will find their way into your homes, closets and driveways. You two like to look good! However, Saturn's repressive energy can evoke an after-hours rebellion. When it's time to blow off steam, you may shed your business attire and head straight to the tattoo parlor for ink and piercings that you can conceal under your button-down shirts. In the bedroom, you might even have a penchant for fetishwear and a little BDSM. Hey, power plays don't just happen in the boardroom for Capricorn Rising Supercouples.

Legend has it that Capricorn is a sign that ages in reverse. While you'll definitely learn the art of adulting together, once you've handled all your duties, you'll have greater freedom to go play. Life doesn't have to be so heavy and serious! And once you two realize that, you'll start enjoying yoru life in ways that few couples can.

Another thing to grow out of? The compare-and-despair syndrome. Enjoy your status symbols but remember that the best things in life aren't actually things. Supporting each other emotionally can be far more fulfilling than rolling up in a Benz with a red ribbon tied around it. (Not that we're discouraging such gifting practices.) Dig into the soulful depths of your relationship, and you'll find a buried treasure that money can't buy.

Create your own Supercouple Chart at **SUPERCOUPLE.COM**

SUPERCOUPLE ASCENDANT

AQUARIUS ✦ ♒

People often notice our:

- Friendly attitudes
- Team spirit
- Quirky style
- Open-mindedness

Two tickets to outer space, please! With cosmonaut Aquarius as your Supercouple Ascendant, this relationship rockets you far beyond your familiar orbits. The spirit of innovation reigns supreme for you two, and like a pair of mad scientists, the world becomes your lab. It's time to experiment with anything that leaves you both with a sense of wide-eyed wonder. And yes, that covers an extremely broad range of possibilities. This relationship will pry you out of rigid thinking and inspire you to explore new avenues of... everything. What's the point of life if you don't experience as much as you possibly can before you die? In each other, you've found a daring playmate who will join you on the razor's edge!

Air sign Aquarius is ruled by Uranus, the only planet in the zodiac that spins on its side. This makes the quirky ice giant your Composite "chart ruler." No wonder you two do everything by your own set of instructions! Whether you're shocking the world with your sartorial choices or disrupting industries as a power couple, you're a highly original duo—and impossible to forget!

Asc

Since, Uranus is a slower-moving outer planet, it hovers in each zodiac sign for seven years before moving on to the next. Because of these longer cycles, you may find that certain areas of your lives are both exciting—and unstable—for the duration of each transit. You can find these dates by checking an ephemeris, which is a calendar of all the planetary transits, or by working with a professional astrologer. The seven-year itch is a real thing for the Aquarius Ascendant pair. Every time the side-spinning planet changes signs, you could shake things up in shocking ways. But hey, you're both here for novelty—and the next shared adrenaline rush awaits!

Hopefully you can embark on these journeys together. But this indie-spirited Ascendant gives your relationship a built-in insurance policy for times when you may need to live apart or even change the status of your relationship due to circumstances. Aquarius is the sign of friendship and as a couple you have a strong BFFs-with-benefits vibe. In this high-vibe relationship, you understand that life is long and people who are meant to be together always find each other again and again.

With this communal air sign as your Supercouple Ascendant, you become unrepentant social butterflies who love breezing around from group to group. When you're swept along in the "people current," you can work a room like no one's business. Watch a tendency to play it TOO cool, however. Rational Aquarius can intellectualize anything, but when it's time to feel the feelings, you may both get twitchy and uncomfortable. Don't hold each other at arms length or stonewall the other when a difficult subject arises. Conflicts need to be discussed or else intimacy dies.

THE ASCENDANT (RISING)

Wild and crazy as your relationship may be at times, you're not a superficial pair. With broad-minded Aquarius Rising, you'll entertain a kaleidoscope of perspectives—probably ones you never considered before meeting each other. Aquarius is the zodiac's humanitarian sign and this rising makes you two as a team naturally attuned to helping others in need. You may team up as activists, working together for a common cause.

Break out the crystals! We'll bet you have quite the collection.) The metaphysical realm is ruled by Aquarius, and you may enjoy dabbling in astrology, tarot and other esoterica. Meditating together is a great way to reconnect to the true essence of your connection, since Aquarius rules the higher mind.

No matter where you plant yourselves, you two are a popular pair. Your ever-expanding friend circle will groan at the seams, making it hard to choose a venue for your group hangouts. Warning: You may fail to pay attention to the people closest to you while you're busy interacting with the dazzling new people you both love meeting every day. Even if you're geared toward a non-traditional lifestyle, it's important to also prioritize family and partners—at least if you want them to stick around and have your back!

Asc

SUPERCOUPLE ASCENDANT

PISCES ✳ ♓

Asc

People often notice our:

- Serene auras
- Glamorous "Old Hollywood" style
- Go-with-the-flow adaptability
- Compassion

What's going on below the surface? With dreamy, esoteric Pisces as your Supercouple Ascendant, this coupling is a mystery unto itself. Like the current that carries the zodiac's Fish, feelings ebb and flow, along with your moods. You'll peer deep into each other's souls, intuiting whatever's happening below the surface. And with the compassion your bond ignites, others will feel touched and transformed by your shared presence. Sometimes you two crave extreme stimulation: lights, music, sensual touch! The next minute, you need to be far away from everything—including each other at times—in a safe, serene setting that helps you regain your chill.

Ooh la la! This imaginative Ascendant blesses your relationship with a rich sense of fantasy. When the lights go down, you're at your most playful together. Since nocturnal Pisces oversees the dream realm, you two could live out a literal fairy tale in the early days of bonding, sweeping each other off into a sweet escape that feels scripted by Disney Studios. Costumes may be involved—or fashion choices that are curated to heighten the mood of the moment. When you step out together, you two can be quite a glamorous pair!

Create your own Supercouple Chart at **SUPERCOUPLE.COM**

But look out! Just as easily, you can pull each other into the dark and stormy waters. Pisces is symbolized by two fish swimming in opposite directions. While there's nothing wrong with going "underground" here and there, you both would be wise to avoid anything nefarious: illicit substances, shady schemes or just the "perfectly nice" people who are involved in anything questionable. A pitfall of this relationship is that you two can give the wrong folks the benefit of the doubt and wind up in over your heads.

So here's the question: Where do the limits lie? Since Pisces is a water sign, this ascendant can give your relationship porous boundaries. It doesn't help that Neptune, the boundary dissolver, is the ruler of Pisces—and thus, your Composite "chart ruler." Neptune is one of the slow-moving outer planets, which hangs out in a single zodiac sign for 14 years. Track these cycles because as a pair, you may have prolonged phases of life that correspond to the watery planet's transits. Perhaps you'll be healing an issue for a decade and a half—or may be consumed by a shared cause for that period of time. You can find these dates by checking an ephemeris, which is a calendar of all the planetary transits, or by working with a professional astrologer.

Because this empathic Ascendant turns your relationship into a bigtime reflecting pool, it's easy to misread each other's signals. Without realizing it, you mirror your partner back to themselves, becoming psychic sponges or absorbing each other's personas like chameleons. You two deal with guilt a lot, and may be tempted to go AWOL because you feel "bad" about vocalizing boundaries. Push yourselves to speak up. Even if it tests your shared limits, under Supercouple Pisces Rising there is powerful healing potential.

When you're in a healthy flow together, you find one another to be incredibly soothing to be around. Pisces Rising can also evoke your talent for the arts, from creating otherworldly theater sets (perhaps in your own living room) to choreographing dance routines. Talk about living the dream! Just make sure you two line up ample support in your own lives too, so that you don't wind up drowning in your complex emotions.

Asc

Asc

SUPERCOUPLE
Compatibility
WITH YOUR
ASCENDANT SIGN

If our Supercouple Ascendant is in a Fire Sign: (ARIES, LEO OR SAGITTARIUS)

And my personal Ascendant is in a fire sign
(ARIES, LEO OR SAGITTARIUS):

The attraction is a no-brainer here. You'll feel an immediate spark that moves you to action, and you'll know just how to stoke the embers should they start to fade.

And my personal Ascendant is in an earth sign
(TAURUS, VIRGO OR CAPRICORN):

In your own life, you may present a little conservatively, but this relationship reveals your wild side. You'll open up readily here, but try not to push yourself out of your comfort zone too quickly.

And my personal Ascendant is in an air sign
(GEMINI, LIBRA, AQUARIUS):

Your calm, cool exterior evaporates under the heat of this relationship's smoldering chemistry. Forget about downplaying your feelings here. It's time for passion and tons of action!

And my personal Ascendant is in a water sign
(CANCER, SCORPIO OR PISCES):

There's no hiding your feelings in this exothermic relationship. But get ready to weather a few vulnerability hangovers, because you're bound to overshare.

Asc

If our Supercouple Ascendant is in an earth sign: (TAURUS, VIRGO, OR CAPRICORN)

And my personal Ascendant is in a fire sign (ARIES, LEO OR SAGITTARIUS):

While you'd never tone it down completely, this relationship elevates your snappy style to something a bit more sophisticated and refined.

And my personal Ascendant is in an earth sign (TAURUS, VIRGO OR CAPRICORN):

Eleganza! As a couple, you'll attract status and elite opportunities at twice the rate you would on your own.

And my personal Ascendant is in an air sign (GEMINI, LIBRA, AQUARIUS):

This relationship brings you out of your head and into your body. Less thinking, more touching, please!

And my personal Ascendant is in a water sign (CANCER, SCORPIO OR PISCES):

While this relationship may temper some of your wild feelings, it can teach you the art of restraint — a sexy quality, in the right measure!

If our Supercouple Ascendant is in an air sign: (GEMINI, LIBRA, AQUARIUS)

Asc

And my personal Ascendant is in a fire sign
(ARIES, LEO OR SAGITTARIUS):

Those wacky ideas and clever thoughts won't just stay in your head; you'll wear them on your sleeves. This creativity-stoking Composite Ascendant will inspire you to put them into action, fast.

And my personal Ascendant is in an earth sign
(TAURUS, VIRGO OR CAPRICORN):

Loosen up! Ready or not, this relationship reveals your lesser-seen playful side, and opens your mind to new types of people.

And my personal Ascendant is in an air sign
(GEMINI, LIBRA, AQUARIUS):

Unleash the social butterflies! If you thought you were popular before, get ready to be everyone's favorite power pair.

And my personal Ascendant is in a water sign
(CANCER, SCORPIO OR PISCES):

Feelings that you couldn't formulate into words suddenly become easy to articulate. Take a deep breath. This relationship helps you become more rational than reactive.

If our Supercouple Ascendant is in a water sign: (CANCER, SCORPIO OR PISCES)

And my personal Ascendant is in a fire sign (ARIES, LEO OR SAGITTARIUS):

You thought you were passionate before, but wait! This relationship helps you focus instead of scattering your energy far and wide.

And my personal Ascendant is in an earth sign (TAURUS, VIRGO OR CAPRICORN):

Your softer side peeks through under the emo influence of this pairing. You're less practical and more creative when together, which is playful and sweet.

And my personal Ascendant is in an air sign (GEMINI, LIBRA, AQUARIUS):

Forget about playing it cool. This relationship sweeps you into an emotional current and gets you out of your head and into your heart.

And my personal Ascendant is in a water sign (CANCER, SCORPIO OR PISCES):

You'll wear your hearts on your sleeves, modeling emotional intelligence and showing the world what a nurturing bond looks like.

SUPERCOUPLE

MERCURY

☿

our communication style

Use Your Supercouple Mercury to Understand:

- How to sync up your communication styles
- Where your social lives can easily overlap
- How you might trigger each other with your words
- How to use non-verbal signals and body language effectively
- The "words of affirmation" you'll need in this relationship ("You look hot!" or "Nice work!")
- Best ways to organize and systematize your shared space
- A common hosting style and how often to welcome guests

WHAT'S YOUR RELATIONSHIP'S LOVE LANGUAGE?

We've all heard that "good communication" is the key to a healthy relationship. But that old adage could use some serious unpacking.

What is good communication anyway? Should we just open our mouths and start spewing unprocessed thoughts? (Results will vary wildly.) Do we stare deep into each other's eyes and coo, "I hear you, babe" while seething with resentment inside? (Tried it, don't recommend.)

What if we could find a sweet spot, a place where our polarizing individual styles could take a time-out? A space where we could reach for something bigger than our own agendas, and both feel understood, satisfied.

Create your own Supercouple Chart at **SUPERCOUPLE.COM**

Enter Composite Mercury.

Composite Mercury is your relationship's central communications office. It reveals how you'll interact, socialize and compromise as a duo. And it can help you find a common "love language" when your own styles divide you.

For example, maybe one partner is soft-spoken (Mercury in Pisces) while the other tends to overtake conversations with strong opinions (Mercury in Taurus), even finishing their hesitant mate's sentences for them. Eventually, the quieter person could feel steamrolled and resentful. Communication breaks down, then the relationship.

Here's an opportunity to reach for the Composite Mercury: Let's say they have that blend in Aries, the sign of the fearless individual. This couple could consciously monitor conversations so that each partner has uninterrupted and equal time to talk. They might even set a timer for a while until they find their groove. The quieter person might become a lot more expressive and even confident in their own opinions from this tactic. And the talker could realize how valuable other people's contributions are when given proper airtime. They might even find relief in realizing they don't have to have all the answers or do other people's thinking for them!

While your individual communication styles divide you, Composite Mercury shows how to find common ground.

Supercouple MERCURY
IN THE ZODIAC SIGNS

In the Sign of	Makes Our Communication	Healthy Communication	Unhealthy Communication
ARIES	Bold	Direct, dynamic	Aggressive, combative
TAURUS	Pragmatic	Attentive, realistic	Stubborn, headstrong
GEMINI	Witty	Inquisitive, animated	Petty, bickering
CANCER	Emotional	Sensitive, intimate	Melodramatic, guarded
LEO	Enthusiastic	Loud, colorful	Bossy, competitive
VIRGO	Inquisitive	Witty, intellectual	Judgmental, critical
LIBRA	Diplomatic	Gracious, fair	Evasive, conflict-averse
SCORPIO	Charged	Engaging, penetrating	Secretive, vengeful
SAGITTARIUS	Vivacious	Hilarious, curious	Crass, exaggerating
CAPRICORN	Purposeful	Visionary, pragmatic	Melancholic, reserved
AQUARIUS	Idealistic	Entertaining, unconventional	Shocking, rule-breaking
PISCES	Dreamy	Poetic, compassionate	Vague, non-committal

FIND YOUR SUPERCOUPLE MERCURY AT
SUPERCOUPLE.COM

Create your own Supercouple Chart at **SUPERCOUPLE.COM**

SUPERCOUPLE MERCURY

ARIES ✳ ♈

OR THE 1ST HOUSE

Our communication style might best be described as:

- Bold
- Direct
- Fearless
- Aggressive
- In-your-face
- Clever

Blurt first, ask questions later? With Supercouple Mercury in Aries, your rapid-fire communication style can be hard to keep up with! An exhilarating energy courses through your conversations. You'll leave each other on the edges of your seats with the "incredible news" you have to share or the epic updates from your day. Some might say you two are prone to exaggeration, but it's not hyperbole as far as you're concerned. It's the passion you provoke within one another!

Stay on your toes in this relationship! Otherwise, you could get fast-talked right into something that you didn't realize you were agreeing to do. More importantly, check yourself! Even if you're the most cooperative angel in most interactions, this union comes with a built-in power struggle. Who is gonna be the Alpha in this round? Aries loves a challenge, and you two thrive on debating. But are you vying for domination? If you're interrupting each other mid sentence, being dismissive or insisting that your opinion is the right one (and the only one), well, we'd have to say yes.

Um, what's up with that? Aries is the warrior sign, bottom line. On a bad day, this Composite Mercury can make both of you straight-up combative. But there's a silver lining...at least for "the meek" who are here to inherit the earth. In this relationship, you'll have no choice BUT to speak up. And that makes it the best damn assertiveness training you'll ever get. The trouble comes in when you confuse assertiveness with aggression—a legit issue for couples with this shared Mercury sign.

As you shed any fears around speaking your mind—or learn to dial down your inner pitbull—this relationship can prepare you to be powerful leaders in the world. When you're in the zone, you two can own the room, strutting in like a charismatic power couple and inspiring people into action. (Just don't go and form a cult, okay?)

Should you enter any competitions together, look out, world! Aries begins the zodiac, and your mental Mercury makes you serious contenders. Together, you like to be first—and best—as often as possible. Sometimes, it sounds like you're bragging or being egotistical, but you just love pulling off the impossible and proving the haters wrong! To channel your fiery Supercouple Mercury productively, turn shared projects and goals into challenges. This will stoke your competitive energy and keep you both interested. When teaming up, reserve the right to do part of a project "my way" and brag on the other's behalf. Work in short sprints with a clear win when you complete a task—Aries energy has a brief attention span!

Socially, you enjoy trends and exploring the new, but you can lose interest just as quickly. Careful about spending a fortune on your latest hobby, or your basement may become a graveyard for gaming equipment, sports gear and DIY kits that you never actually use more than once.

SUPERCOUPLE MERCURY

TAURUS ✳ ♉

OR THE 2ND HOUSE

Our communication style might best be described as:

- Straightforward
- Attentive
- Pragmatic
- Realistic

Does it make sense on paper? With Supercouple Mercury in Taurus, your relationship thrives on practical magic. Together, you are master manifesters in the material realm. The secret sauce of this placement: You play by the rules and follow due process. Sounds easy enough, right? Guess again. This is not something most couples have the willpower to muscle through. Mercury is the planet of systems and mindsets, and in Taurus it ushers you along the tried-and-true track to success. Get ready to discover the surprising joy (and profitability) of KISS: Keep It Simple, Sweetheart.

But don't worry, you're hardly "basic" as a pair. Once you've figured out the strategy for covering your bases, your minds wander into far more luxurious terrain. Taurus is ruled by sensual Venus, and your wide-ranging conversations can easily span from the monthly financial spreadsheet to your bedroom sheets—particularly where to find the highest thread count set in the softest natural fiber.

Composite Mercury in Taurus loves any trivia, as long as the category is "The Best of X." From Spanish wines to contemporary jazz to Cannes-winning documentaries, your shared social life is a decadent discovery mission that centers around beauty, art and earthly pleasures.

Warning: Mercury in Taurus adds a stubborn streak to the mix. Even if you're the most open-minded individuals in your personal lives, when united, you dig your heels in, resisting change or getting stuck in the rut of a routine. Taurus is the sign that rules ethics and values, and when yours diverge from each other, the battle to be "right" can turn you both into raging Bulls. Try to remember that no two people will see eye-to-eye on everything. But if core values are completely misaligned, it can be a dealbreaker for you both.

Sorting it out might best happen in bed...or anywhere comfortable and relaxing where you can untangle the web of disagreement without feeling pressured or rushed. Tactile Taurus encourages you to communicate through touch and affection. Science has proven that hugs lasting 30 seconds release the bonding hormone oxytocin and can lower blood pressure and the stress hormone norepinephrine. That's the kind of "conversation" your Supercouple Mercury thrives on. The more you touch, the easier it is to talk!

As a couple, you like to be productive, and may always have a project in the works. With Mercury in this fiscally savvy zone, start with a budget before sourcing materials. Then, systematically work through a to-do list and make incremental achievements. You two process information best with clear, step-by-step instructions and through concrete evidence from the physical, material world. A solid upfront understanding of the desired outcome gives you an incentive to act. You might even make a binder with step-by-step instructions for essential household tasks, important contact information and logins. Having all that data in one place will make your efficient Supercouple Mercury swoon.

SUPERCOUPLE MERCURY
GEMINI ✶ ♊
OR THE 3RD HOUSE

Our communication style might best be described as:

- Inquisitive
- Animated
- Gossipy
- Distractible
- Playful

How fast is your "processing speed?" You might up it a few extra GHz in THIS dynamic duo. Supercouple Mercury is right at home in the sign of chatty, "always on" Gemini. If you're not texting each other all day long, you'll come armed with juicy nuggets of gossip, trivia and cultural commentary every time you meet. "We stayed up all night talking and never stopped from there," you may tell friends when recounting the story of how you met.

With this eternally curious Mercury, you'll want to know the "why" about everything—for no reason in particular. You make effortless small talk with each other and can carry the conversation in group settings. Mutual friends will come to count on you both to be their cultural activities planners and "idea people." You spark that intellectual curiosity in one another and may search things no one thought to type into a Google window...until now.

Since Gemini energy will stoke your desire to learn, you two may devour books, articles, podcasts, and more! Sign up for seminars and watch your relationship grow. You may become regulars on the workshop and retreat circuit, at least for a period of time. Hey, whatever gives both of you something stimulating to talk about is a true bonus.

Are you tired yet? Or are you just plain wired? With dualistic Gemini governing your communication style as a couple, you could volley between extremes. There aren't enough hours in the day for you to tell each other every story in your vault, and invariably, you'll reach a point of mental exhaustion. When one of you needs space, the other had better learn to hit pause, or else! Your fluid back-and-forth could turn into nasty bickering—and you'll both hit below the belt when annoyed.

Socially, you can "twin" each other easily. You're the enviable couple who shows up at every party together and never seems to get jealous when the other works the room. You're probably the co-hosts of many events yourself. In garrulous Gemini, your Supercouple Mercury draws you both out of your shells. Still, too much together time can definitely dial down the romance factor and make your bond feel platonic. Developing separate interests can keep the sparks alive, even if it goes against what feels like your natural impulse. Having at least one other sounding board outside of your relationship will ensure that you won't be pacing the floor while you wait for the other to be available to help you talk things through. And yet, this truth is self-evident in the Composite Mercury in Gemini partnership: Through dialogue, you can figure anything and everything out.

Create your own Supercouple Chart at **SUPERCOUPLE.COM**

SUPERCOUPLE MERCURY
CANCER ✳ ♋

OR THE 4TH HOUSE

Our communication style might best be described as:

- Emotional
- Sensitive
- Intimate
- Nurturing
- Moody

"How do you FEEL about that?" This question is central to a relationship with Supercouple Mercury in highly sensitive Cancer. The planet of mental processes becomes supremely heart-centered when it lands in this emo water sign. While this Mercury placement helps you both put feelings into words, you don't necessarily need to speak in order to communicate. A tender, "I got u" gaze, a wraparound hug or nod of approval: gestures like these may become the preferred language for you two. Cancer is the "mother sign," and with this Mercury, you're wired to nurture each other.

Bring on the mirror neurons: Because you're such a tapped-in pair, you may preemptively react to the other's oncoming feelings. Quickly, you'll start to catalog each other's subtle expressions—the twinkle of mischief that indicates things are about to go off the rails, or the terse smile that belies a brewing storm. Despite your loving intentions, this caretaking impulse can shut down your authentic communication.

Don't rush to put a Band-Aid on every "boo boo" or grab for the Kleenex box to stop a deluge of tears. Instead, let the feelings flow! Widen the range of emotions you "allow" yourselves to discuss, then keep on processing them together. Not only will you raise your collective EQ, you'll enjoy a level of intimacy you never dreamed possible in a relationship.

Just like the Crab tucks away in its shell, your Supercouple Mercury in Cancer can make you guarded and self-protective in the early days of your bond. Even if you sense the potential depth of your connection, you may skim the surface, waiting for each other to open up before you share any personal intel. To overcome this, make a point of being a "safe space" for each other. And no matter how long you've been together, watch the assumptions. True, you may be more psychic than most couples, but don't expect the other to "just know" what you need. When you DO open up and articulate your needs, it's a win-win. Your brand of vulnerability is not only magnetic, but it gives your partner permission to open up and do the same.

Socially, you'll enjoy finding little ways that your hobbies and tastes overlap. You both may enjoy entertaining in your shared home, whether you're hosting an intimate dinner party for a few close friends or opening up every sleeper sofa for holiday guests. In family-minded Cancer, getting to know each other's relatives is a must—and they may become preferred company for you two, especially if you share extracurricular interests or wind up having kids. Warning: You can be a moody duo! Keeping upbeat people around can offset your arguments—not to mention reducing stress-eating or the risk of sinking into melancholy spells together.

The arts are another great outlet. Give yourselves something to look forward to with season tickets to the symphony or a music festival that you return to annually. Rituals like these can keep you bound together, even when one of you feels clingy and the other needs space.

SUPERCOUPLE MERCURY

LEO ⁕ ♌

OR THE 5TH HOUSE

Our communication style might best be described as:

- Colorful
- Enthusiastic
- Competitive
- Loud
- Bossy

A flair for the dramatic? That's putting it mildly. With Supercouple Mercury in theatrical Leo, your exchanges bubble over with passion, angst or whatever mood the curtain lifts on that day. It's all part of having the zodiac's most flamboyant sign governing your communication style. In this colorful union, you'll bring out the storytellers in each other. No detail will be spared—get ready to scroll through a barrage of descriptive texts!

How many ways can you say, "I love you?" Leo is one of the zodiac's die-hard romantics. There's lots of hugging, gift-giving and spoiling that goes on with this Composite Mercury. Those gestures provide the proof that words alone can't. Spare no expense. If you're sending flowers, opt for the oversized bouquet. When you're treating for dinner, think "Michelin-rated." And don't even think about showing up with costume jewelry on a birthday or Christmas.

☿

In the early stages, you won't be able to take your eyes off each other—much less your minds. Your connection is all-consuming! Dress up dates will give you a chance to show off your sartorial flair—or perhaps, develop it for the first time. Shopping together can become a favorite activity, even if you're just trying things on and stepping out for an admiring twirl. There's no one else you'd rather text first, whether you have epic news to share or simply want to review the highlights of the day. Praise is the fuel that keeps this fiery Supercouple Mercury sign burning bright, so be generous with those words of affirmation! They are the primary love language in your bond.

But don't confuse them with insincere flattery. True, delivering constructive feedback can be a delicate matter for you two, but when it means sparing the other a costly misstep, don't hold back! You'll get over a harsh critique but being left to free-fall without a net? Unforgivable. The reason for this? Leo is zodiac royalty and for you both, looking good in public is a must. You like to represent like polished pros or glamorous celebutantes—not misguided fools. (Perish the thought!) So if that means shutting down a terrible idea that the other is excited about from time to time, suck it up. You'll thank each other later.

Socially, you're particularly playful, which can make you the resident party-throwers of your circle. Entertaining is a great way for you both to bond, provided you don't allow plans to get stressfully over the top. Sunday barbecues can be casual potlucks without a theme or dress code, okay? Like lions, you two need your pride of loyal friends to champion, protect and shower with generosity. When you believe in someone—especially each other—there are no fiercer advocates out there!

Create your own Supercouple Chart at **SUPERCOUPLE.COM**

SUPERCOUPLE MERCURY

VIRGO ✦ ♍

OR THE 6TH HOUSE

Our communication style might best be described as:

- Witty
- Intellectual
- Analytical
- Inquisitive
- Judgmental
- Critical

So many questions, so little time! With Supercouple Mercury in analytical Virgo, you're a detail-driven duo. Witty banter is fine, but forget about small talk! Your conversations are more like data-mining sessions, journalistic interviews and competitive trivia nights. But that's okay! It's rare to find another human who is so curious about what makes you tick. While you may feel like a specimen under a microscope some days, this inquisitive energy is mutual. Welcome to the lab of your shared Mercury in Virgo.

And what a lucky laboratory it is! Mercury is not only at home in Virgo, one of the two signs it rules, but it's also "exalted" here, which is said to be THE most potent placement for the buzzy planet in the entire zodiac. If you were lazy about learning before, get ready for a switch! This relationship will sharpen your mental skills—and make you more spiritually mindful to boot.

Virgo is the sign of systems AND service. Not only do you enjoy organizing your lives in practical ways, but you'll love sharing "pro tips" with each other. DIY projects are a great way to bond, especially things like making a live indoor plant wall or growing your own food. Set up a creation station with all your materials, tools, and books. Who knows? You might wind up starting a YouTube channel or even showcasing your skills on HGTV.

Supercouple Mercury in Virgo thrives when life is orderly. Sync up your schedules on a shared calendar, get your devices on an affordable family plan and create a household budget. Since Virgo rules health, you'll be eating clean and working out together regularly. But please, be willing to deviate every now and again. There's a risk of you two becoming SO practical that you forget to have fun.

Speaking of which, your social style may center around the great outdoors. Virgo is an earth sign, so you may have a shared group of ski buddies or camping friends, or maybe you'll both join a cycling club or CrossFit gym. Life is a constant improvement mission for you both! Having a "stretch goal" keeps you inspired and motivated. Mutual friends count on you two to share all the helpful hints that you learn along the way.

One thing to watch out for? Virgo is the sign of the critic, and this Mercury can turn your relationship into a hot mess of nitpicking, perfectionism and bickering over what's "appropriate." As a rule, do NOT dole out unsolicited advice—especially when it comes to inconsequential things like your partner's off-duty clothing choices or where they part their hair. It will be SO tempting to play life coach in this union, and for a while, it might feel flattering. But soon enough, a parent-child dynamic will creep—or you may polarize into "overfunctioner" and "underfunctioner." Draw a bright line between "helping" and "enabling," and don't play the damsel in distress when you know you've got a situation handled. Ultimately, you'll want to meet each other's needs, but not if head games are involved!

SUPERCOUPLE MERCURY

LIBRA ✳ ♎

OR THE 7TH HOUSE

Our communication style might best be described as:

- Diplomatic
- Gracious
- Charming
- Classically romantic
- Peaceful and easygoing

Peace, love and harmony? Yes, please. With Supercouple Mercury in Libra, your communication style is naturally collaborative. You're all about finding the common ground and turning struggles into win-wins. Libra is the zodiac's diplomat, and this gracious Mercury placement makes for easy discussions about any (pleasant) subject under the sun: Fashion, the art world, even politics (Libra rules justice)…you'll keep each other up on whatever's current.

The spirit of partnership arises naturally in your cooperative interactions. But is it always best to seek a middle ground? While diplomatic Libra wants to keep the peace, this can come with a price. If you suppress the conflicts that naturally (and invariably!) arise, you'll never TRULY know one another. To create real intimacy, make "understanding" the goal rather than "harmony." A little dissonance doesn't mean doom—not by a long shot. Let the scales swing off balance from time to time instead of rushing to get back on a level playing field. You'll open each other's minds in the process.

Move over, Rumi. Composite Libra Mercury is poetic and romantic. There won't be a shortage of sweetness flowing between you. Surprise one another with little love notes tucked in bags, drop off gifts "just for the heck of it" and never forget to call (not text!) to say goodnight. This relationship thrives on a steady diet of affectionate gestures. Don't forget the grand ones, too! This Mercury loves luxurious expressions of love. Start saving up for that resort vacation or the significant piece of jewelry you want to gift each other.

When it comes to socializing, you're a glamorous pair and your shared calendar won't have much white space! While you both may love to throw an elegant party, you're just as happy to be the guests—or to join your roster of generous friends on their boats and at their vacation homes. And you'll look good doing it! With aesthetically oriented Libra as your joint Mercury, you may enjoy a rep as the most stylish pair in town. Match your tennis whites or après-ski knitwear, then show up with a well-chosen bottle of wine and your charming smiles. This Supercouple Mercury definitely ups your dazzle factors!

As much as you two drift off on flights of fancy, you're also sensible sounding boards for each other. Since you process information best together through dialogue, you may stay up until the wee hours talking until you hit on the answer to whatever problem you're tackling. It's rare to find a connection with this much range, but like all things Libra—it's a perfect balance!

©2022 Astrostyle. All rights reserved.

194   Create your own Supercouple Chart at **SUPERCOUPLE.COM**

SUPERCOUPLE MERCURY
SCORPIO ✴ ♏

OR THE 8TH HOUSE

Our communication style might best be described as:

- Observant
- Engaging
- Empathic
- Secretive
- Erotically or energetically charged

How spicy do you like it? Supercouple Mercury in sexy Scorpio charges every conversation with intensity and innuendos. Can you read between the lines? What exactly did you MEAN by that? In this relationship, neither of you will be satisfied with surface explanations. In fact, you might become a pair of ace detectives after a short time together. But that's where the thrill of it all lies! This Composite Mercury provokes a fascination with figuring things out, and you could spend a lifetime unpacking the inner workings of each other's psyches. Just when you think you've cracked The Case of the Soulmate Cypher, you'll discover something new about one another. Juicy!

Trouble comes when you start dissecting each other's motives rather than communicating directly. As the cliche goes, the word "assume" will "make an ass out of u and me." That's a rock-solid truth for Mercury in Scorpio relationships. This placement can spin up all sorts of paranoia if you let yourselves spiral into guesswork without actually talking! Not that your intuitions are always astray. In this transcendent connection, you may legitimately share a psychic bond, picking up on the other's unspoken signals, even getting vibes when you're miles apart. But still...check in and get confirmation before you let emotions wrest hold of your brains. The Scorpio horseman of jealousy can take your relationship down.

Your bond is a close one—too close for OTHER people's comfort at times. But ignore their raised eyebrows and feel no compulsion to share the inner workings of your dynamic duo. Instead, create a "fortress of solitude" where the two of you can commune. A private home is a must if you cohabitate, and if kids are in the picture, put a lock on your bedroom door.

At times, you two may feel like you're "too much" or "too deep" for the rest of the world, but that doesn't mean you should isolate in your couple bubble. Your shared inner circle will be an intimate one! True friends serve as an unbiased safe space that can hold the emotional ups and downs of your relationship in confidence. Some secrets may never escape your joint vault!

Still, it's important to find your own trusted sounding boards. Both of you can pay a price for holding things in, sinking into self-effacement or depression or numbing out when around each other. With this Mercury placement, you two may do well with your own individual therapists, spiritual advisors, or impartial counsel that you can "confess" to without worrying about your admissions impacting your relationship. Feelings are definitely NOT facts for the Supercouple Mercury in Scorpio pair, but they are certainly fiery.

SUPERCOUPLE MERCURY
SAGITTARIUS ✦ ↗

OR THE 9TH HOUSE

Our communication style might best be described as:

- Flamboyant
- Hilarious
- Cocky
- Exaggerated
- Open-minded
- Hopelessly optimistic

What's the big idea? That depends on the day, but one thing's for sure: with Supercouple Mercury in Sagittarius, you will inspire each other to expand, explore and expound upon every discovery. The zodiac's Archer aims its arrows high! Hitting the mark isn't guaranteed, but that's okay. In this wise and idealistic connection, half the fun lies in pursuing whatever target you have in your crosshairs. From entrepreneurial ventures to adventure travel, everything's on the table in this bond.

No more pencils, no more books? Guess again. There's both an old soul quality and a refreshingly youthful curiosity to Sagittarius, and inside this relationship, you're bound to feel both. Even if you swore off school, get ready to enroll in the "university of life." Sagittarius is the eternal student, and this Composite Mercury sign will turn you two into hardcore seekers. Before you know it, you're collecting passport stamps as you climb high peaks, attend global conferences on climate change activism, greet your inner children in self-development seminars and stretch your bodies and minds at yoga retreats on every continent.

Get ready to diversify your social lives. Sagittarius is the zodiac sign of cross-cultural connections, and with the horizon-broadening curiosity you'll share, your mutual crew could turn into a "rainbow coalition." As the co-ambassadors of your social circle, you'll love bringing people together from varied backgrounds, even folks who have difficulty bridging differences and breaking the ice.

Now for the challenging part: How to keep it real without tearing each other to shreds. Supercouple Mercury in no-filters Sagittarius can make you SO honest with each other that it becomes a fault. On the one hand, you'll appreciate having a partner who doesn't B.S. you. The candor in your relationship is refreshingly authentic. But when you bring the truth hammer down with blunt force, you can crush each other's self-esteem. There's also a tendency with this Mercury to speak without thinking and blurt tactless comments in total innocence. To avoid "foot in mouth" syndrome, slow down and be present! And check yourself before you exaggerate. Hyperbole is an issue for Mercury in Sagittarius.

The saving grace for you two? Humor! Laughter is truly medicine for Mercury in Sagittarius couples. When one of you goes too far—which will be often—you can cool things down by cracking a joke. (Ideally at your own expense...not another jab at your partner, please!) Arguments may get so fiery that you need to go to your corners from time to time. Thankfully, absence makes the heart grow fonder in this relationship.

SUPERCOUPLE MERCURY
CAPRICORN ✴ ♑
OR THE 10TH HOUSE

> ## Our communication style might best be described as:
>
> - Pragmatic
> - Mission-oriented
> - Visionary
> - Melancholic
> - Reserved

Let's get to the point here, shall we? With Supercouple Mercury in Capricorn, you two communicate in a businesslike way. It's not that you can't lighten up and have fun, but first you'll both need to know: What's the plan here? Or maybe, what's our five- or ten-year plan? With this goal-oriented Mercury placement, you are naturally strategic together. When you put your heads together, you process information in a linear, structured manner, considering a larger system. How does this fit into the big-picture agenda? Power couple vibes are plentiful: You're a dynamic duo and you thrive when you have a purpose.

No matter how free-flowing you are individually, this Composite Mercury brings out a dutiful and responsible side to you both. Capricorn is the "provider" sign, which may explain why you two become interested in supporting the people in your lives with wisdom and any resources you have to share. Your individual family relationships may improve as a result of the thoughtfulness cultivated within your relationship. And if you raise kids together, you'll structure their lives with educational activities, making sure they are surrounded by positive influences—and influencers. If the people in your direct lineage can't hang, you'll create a chosen family of loyal friends who you can rely on and vice versa.

But go easy on each other, please. You two may become harsh and officious when you feel that other isn't cooperating. At times, you might even be imperious or dismissive to each other. Try to remember that you're both only human—and sometimes you need a break from the 1,001 projects you're both trying to crush. The perfectionism of a shared Mercury in Capricorn can be weaponized if you turn it on each other.

Capricorn loves all things time-tested, and this Supercouple Mercury may inspire mutual interest in history and worldwide traditions, especially learning about the powerful leaders who have ruled over time. Mentorship is a theme in this connection. When together, you'll enjoy guiding younger people—you have an eye for that "diamond in the rough." Learning from older, wiser and more experienced people is also part of your shared success strategy.

While both of you may be more work than play, you know how to cut loose together. This Mercury sign incites a dry sense of wit that can crack you both up in the tensest of moments. When you combine these Mercurial planning powers and put them toward a party or vacation, it can be absolutely legendary. Make it a non-negotiable to treat yourselves to some earthly pleasures as a payoff for your hard work! Have a "bucket list" investment—put a portion of your profits or paychecks toward it, whether it's a dream trip, owning a home or creating a college fund for the kids.

SUPERCOUPLE MERCURY
AQUARIUS ✳ ♒
OR THE 11TH HOUSE

Our communication style might best be described as:

- Entertaining
- Unconventional
- Shocking
- Rule-breaking
- Open to everything

Just as water seeks its own level, the Supercouple Mercury in Aquarius relationship elicits a sense that you're coming together with a kindred soul. In this friendly, idealistic sign, you'll share a high-minded union that thrives on intellectual exchanges and a mutual desire to change the world. Even if you were complacent about things like politics or the environment in the past, once you meet each other, you feel driven to be part of something greater than "just" yourselves. So externally focused is this relationship, in fact, that you may have to consciously flip the lens back to each other's feelings. Don't get us wrong: It's amazing that you two can work so well side by side. But you should also get curious about each other's inner workings. There's a lot going on in there too! And if you don't pay attention to it, someone else probably will...

Heads up: Emotions are tricky terrain for cool, rational Aquarius. With Composite Mercury here, it's likely that you both will need an assist to articulate what's happening in the feeling realm...with feeling, that is. You two can intellectualize to your heart's discontent, but that's not advised. True intimacy happens when you can talk about what's bothering you without adding a disclaimer like, "It's not really a big deal but..." or "I already know this is my anxious attachment style at play, so..." What if you could cry when you were sad or stop smiling when you were angry? This may be a new challenge you face in the Mercury in Aquarius relationship—even if you were a big emoter before meeting one another.

Aquarius is a liberated sign and you'll both rail against the idea of "couple-think." In this intellectually curious pairing, you get turned on by differentiating from each other. But watch a tendency to be contrarian just to keep things "interesting." You're not rolling over if you agree with each other from time to time! And sometimes, it's best to just acquiesce, like in the case of whether to use aged cheddar or smoky gouda for burger night. (Yes, you two might waste time debating things THIS trivial.)

With humanitarian Aquarius helming your social interests, you may be drawn to activist work. This cutting-edge Mercury sign may lead both of you to any sort of workshop that falls into the "self-actualization" realm from a survivalist weekend to tantric yoga. Experimental theater camps and offbeat festivals may also become your shared jam—and the places where you meet the delightfully eccentric thought leaders who will soon join your shared crew. Or maybe you're the sporty types, and live for your summer regattas and winter ski lodge weekends.

One thing is for sure: You'll become each other's best friends. No matter how long your time as a couple lasts, this Supercouple Mercury sign provides the objectivity needed to discuss anything. From open relationships to a "conscious uncoupling" (should you go your separate ways), you'd rather be in one another's lives in some capacity, no matter the labels. Ironically, this foundation is a firm one for keeping you together through the years.

Create your own Supercouple Chart at SUPERCOUPLE.COM

SUPERCOUPLE MERCURY

PISCES ✳ ♓

OR THE 12TH HOUSE

Our communication style might best be described as:

- Poetic
- Compassionate
- Esoteric
- Elusive
- Fantasy-weaving
- Noncommittal

Cast a spell! With Supercouple Mercury in dreamy Pisces, your communication style is nothing short of "pure enchantment." Long after the honeymoon phase passes for most couples, you still have the power to draw each other into a web of desire. Poetic words? You both will serve up heavenly haikus and sexy stanzas, but the unspoken signals are fire too! Flashing gazes, enigmatic moves, and even the occasional disappearing act will bait the hook and keep the other on your line. That ebb and flow is what keeps this connection so intriguing, even if it CAN be emotionally disruptive at times.

Two tickets to Fantasy Island? Pisces is the sign of escapism, and with this Composite Mercury, it won't take long before you're luring each other off on an enchanted voyage. The scene for your fairy tales could be absolutely anywhere, from a five-star luxury hotel to your own bathtub. Pisces rules the dream realm, so sleeping, cuddling and meditating in one another's arms can be as exciting as a night on the town for you two. Just remember to check in with your people now and again. It's easy to get lost in each other's quantum fields, but alas, linear time keeps on ticking.

Creatively, this Supercouple Mercury gives you a deep well to draw from. If you're not actually making art, you'll surely appreciate it together. Film fairs, music festivals, gallery openings: with the interests Mercury in Pisces piques, the two of you could soon be the hottest couple on the scene. Mutual friends will enjoy a nonstop roster of cultural activities, with you both as their guides.

Since this Supercouple Mercury can be abstract, you might struggle to verbally articulate your ideas to each other. On the upside, your "show and tell" sessions can be incredibly sexy! But trouble comes in when you ride on assumptions. With this psychic Mercury sign at play, you two come close to reading each other's minds, but you're still not 100% accurate with your "intuitive hits."

Check in with one another often, and make clear agreements around everything from what time you're meeting for dinner to whether or not you're actually exclusive. We kid, sort of, but Pisces can be a slippery Fish. Spending TOO much time together can leave you feeling trapped in a net—and that's when you need to swim away. To combat that, give each other plenty of space and privacy.

You have boundless compassion for each other, which can be a beautiful support network. But careful! This can slide into codependent territory if you take on the other's problems as your own. Without realizing it, you can become psychic sponges, absorbing one another's emotions and energy. Make sure to maintain give-and-take friendships—outside of your relationship— so you don't lean TOO heavily on your partner. With enough room to splash around, the current will naturally pull you back to one another's shores.

☿

SUPERCOUPLE
Compatibility
WITH YOUR
MERCURY SIGN

Create your own Supercouple Chart at **SUPERCOUPLE.COM**

If our Supercouple Mercury is in a fire Sign: (ARIES, LEO OR SAGITTARIUS)

And my personal Mercury is in a fire sign
(ARIES, LEO OR SAGITTARIUS):

The rapid-fire excitable communication style of this relationship dovetails perfectly with your natural way of expressing yourself. You'll enjoy lively debates, surprise announcements and passionate exchanges. Be sure to bring the heat down to a simmer from time to time. You may feel like you always have to be "on," but comfortable silence is also a part of intimacy.

And my personal Mercury is in an earth sign
(TAURUS, VIRGO OR CAPRICORN):

Pick up the pace! Conversations are invigorating here, but may move faster than you're used to. At times, you may feel like decisions are being made before you've had time to properly mull them over. In this expansive relationship, you must stop stubbornly clinging to what you already "know." You can grow immensely by opening your mind. That said, tap the brakes when things accelerate in a way that upsets your equilibrium.

And my personal Mercury is in an air sign
(GEMINI, LIBRA, AQUARIUS):

Your logical mind will love parsing all the new data that this novelty-oriented relationship brings. For you two, no subject is off-limits. However, you won't be so eager to adopt any radical notions until you've checked out enough case studies. The true gift of this relationship, however, is that it teaches you to speak from the heart, not just your head. Get ready to feel a stronger sense of passion!

And my personal Mercury is in a water sign
(CANCER, SCORPIO OR PISCES):

This relationship feels refreshingly optimistic, teaching you to explore the bright side of life. Through conversation, you'll expand your capacity for being with "scary" emotions like hope and excitement that can leave you feeling vulnerable. Your innate ability to troubleshoot can save the two of you from leaping without looking. This is your chance to adopt the principle of "and" instead of "either/or." For example, the glass can be half-empty and half-full, so view and discuss the full range of possibilities together as a pair.

If our Supercouple Mercury is in an earth sign: (TAURUS, VIRGO, OR CAPRICORN)

And my personal Mercury is in a fire sign
(ARIES, LEO OR SAGITTARIUS):

Can you repeat that please? Your rapid-fire communication style won't fly in this relationship, which demands that you talk things through, think things through and really make sensible decisions. While it's great that you can bring all these novel concepts to the mix, you won't be able to hit go on them simply because they excite you. A buzzkill? Perhaps, but you'll waste so much less time and energy thanks to the maturing influence of this Composite Mercury.

And my personal Mercury is in an earth sign
(TAURUS, VIRGO OR CAPRICORN):

Sweet relief! In this relationship, your planning powers and pragmatic communication style thrive. Conversations morph into savvy strategy sessions, which then turn into successful and profitable projects. Your natural interest in building material security will be well-appreciated here. Cultural activities dates will be epic, but also expensive. Make an entertainment budget, fast!

And my personal Mercury is in an air sign
(GEMINI, LIBRA, AQUARIUS):

Your logical mind and experimental social style may feel like a plus and a minus here. On the one hand, your genius ideas won't get lost in the ether. But those blueprints you draw up also bring more responsibility than perhaps you like to lock yourself into. Your flirtatious style may disrupt this relationship's demands for fidelity, so get ready to tone it down and focus that wandering eye on your partner.

And my personal Mercury is in a water sign
(CANCER, SCORPIO OR PISCES):

Your sweet-talking ways may not have the same heart-melting impact in this relationship as you'd prefer, but here's something that's just as delicious: The serious conversational style of your

Supercouple Mercury provides a deep sense of security—and you'll love that! If you wish for greater vulnerability, don't hold back. Take the helm and guide your talks into the intimate waters you crave.

If our Supercouple Mercury is in an air sign: (GEMINI, LIBRA, AQUARIUS)

And my personal Mercury is in a fire sign (ARIES, LEO OR SAGITTARIUS):

Communication will be lively, excitable, and charged with novel ideas—just the way you like it! However, turning the visions into reality can get expensive or turn into a long list of pipe dreams. Careful not to race off on a lark just because you're both so pumped about a plan!

And my personal Mercury is in an earth sign (TAURUS, VIRGO OR CAPRICORN):

Communication can be challenging here because you like to speak in certainties, while this relationship enjoys abstract ideas and "maybes." Expand your capacity for exploring the unknown, which is a gift of this relationship. You'll tap into dimensions of thought that you never knew were possible.

And my personal Mercury is in an air sign (GEMINI, LIBRA, AQUARIUS):

The lively conversational style of this relationship is right up your alley when you're bantering, word playing and teasing each other in fun. But it can also devolve into unhealthy debates, nonstop arguing and extreme levels of FOMO as you battle for social dominance. Having a shared friend group is a plus for offsetting argumentative tendencies.

And my personal Mercury is in a water sign
(CANCER, SCORPIO OR PISCES):

This relationship stirs up deep feelings, yet in this intellectual Mercury Supercouple, it's challenging to communicate your emotions effectively. Frustration can devolve into angry battles, gaslighting and manipulation. On the plus side, you may learn to lighten up and look at the facts, and not just your feelings. Train yourself in coping skills for difficult interactions.

If our Supercouple Mercury is in a water sign: (CANCER, SCORPIO OR PISCES)

And my personal Mercury is in a fire sign
(ARIES, LEO OR SAGITTARIUS):

Holy smokes! This relationship provides the receptive audience for your passionate communication style—provided you don't blast it with high heat 24/7. This watery Mercury opens up a safe space for vocalizing your emotions and talking about how all those creative ideas will feel for you. However, make sure you don't dominate conversations. The gift of this union is how it helps expand your listening skills.

And my personal Mercury is in an earth sign
(TAURUS, VIRGO OR CAPRICORN):

When was the last time you labeled your emotions—or even stopped to hear what they had to say? This empathic relationship might shake up your equilibrium, forcing you to think everything through on more dimensions than simply the pragmatic ones. Conversations about the future can be powerful and creative, especially when exploring what will bring you personal happiness and fulfillment.

And my personal Mercury is in an air sign
(GEMINI, LIBRA, AQUARIUS):

Awkward! Your cool communication style may read as standoffish in this relationship, and even deter its profound potential for intimacy. But herein lies the opportunity for growth. Unpack your resistance to being vulnerable and sharing from the heart, because the greater your capacity for this, the closer the two of you will become. The question is, who is going to show their scars first? It might have to be you. Dare!

And my personal Mercury is in a water sign
(CANCER, SCORPIO OR PISCES):

No words required! In this intuitive mashup, you may feel as if you can read each other's minds. The unspoken intimacy can make it easy for the two of you to connect, but there's also a greater proclivity for secrecy here, especially when it comes to any topic that could make the other person emotional or stir up shame. Working with a mediator, therapist or coach may be necessary to draw out deeper truths. The art of active listening and mirroring can do wonders to help you both feel understood.

SUPERCOUPLE

VENUS

♀

> our romance & desire

♀

Use Your Supercouple Venus to Understand:

- What will turn you on (and off) as a couple
- How to make peace when you're at odds
- Keys to affection and keeping the romance alive
- The right "love language" for your relationship
- The colors, scents and ambience to evoke passion when together
- How to decorate and furnish your shared home
- The best gifts to give each other
- Ideal ways to celebrate special occasions and holidays

ROMANCE, COURTSHIP AND ATTRACTION: HOW CAN YOU KEEP THE FLIRTATIOUS FIRES BURNING?

Endless honeymoon, anyone? It's a lofty goal, but if any planet's gonna rise to the challenge, it's Venus. The galactic guardian of beauty, harmony and romantic connection, Venus is "in love with love" and serves it up morning, noon and night. Surrender to the goddess of goodwill and her sensual superpowers when you want to stay in sync.

In your blended chart, Venus shows how you'll spoil and seduce each other, what your flirting style will be and whether you love some hands-on PDA or prefer to express your affections behind closed doors.

When you're fighting and you need an instant peacemaker, you can also turn to your Supercouple Venus. Her location in your chart is the map back to harmony and mutual appreciation. Date planning and gift selection are both Venus specialties. (Why yes, you should splurge on that high-end designer watch for your Composite Venus in Capricorn anniversary.) Not sure where to meet your love interest or celebrate a relationship milestone? Let Venus play event planner.

Venus is also the planet that reveals what you'll find valuable—specifically what you'll spend money on, often based on the object's overwhelming beauty! Like the Ascendant, your Supercouple Venus has a hand in styling your image as a pair. Will you match your couture outfits or are you the laid-back, athleisure-loving pair who always looks like you're on the way back from your high-end gym?

Once you move into your shared home, this tasteful and gracious planet shows you how to decorate and entertain together. Will you be the consummate co-hosts of every lavish dinner party (Venus in Leo, anyone?) or social directors of your Burning Man camp (paging Venus in Aquarius)? Will you source an original Eames chair or make an overstuffed, L-shaped sofa the centerpiece of your living room?

Of course, couples don't always value the same things. Here's where Supercouple Venus can be a life-saving mediator. Maybe one of you has Venus in Taurus and a passion for utilitarian black leather furniture and ridiculously impractical sports cars. The other of you has Venus in Scorpio with a passion for endless variations of black clothing and environmentally-friendly electric vehicles.

Your Composite Venus likely falls in Leo, helping you understand the other's need for their version of luxury. Dressing up and riding in the (sustainable) sports cars? Hey, sounds like a killer date. Yet, more than most couples, you'll need to create a budget for indulgences—perhaps with the support of a third party—so you can enjoy them responsibly.

The same holds true for your tastes in the bedroom. If one of you is a generous giver and the other a pillow prince(ss), the lopsided dynamics will eventually get old. Supercouple Venus can reveal an entirely new formula for pleasure that casts you in entirely new roles!

Dog-ear this chapter as the ultimate olive branch, because if you're like any two humans attempting to merge your lives, you're gonna need to refer to this one a lot. Good news: Supercouple Venus has your shared love language locked into Google Translate. *Oui! Si! Da!*

Supercouple VENUS
IN THE ZODIAC SIGNS

In the Sign of	Makes Our Romantic Style	In Sync, We're...	Out of Sync, We're...
ARIES	Passionate	Spontaneous	Combative
TAURUS	Decadent	Sensual	Judgmental
GEMINI	Magnetic	Flirty	Distant
CANCER	Nurturing	Nurturing	Smothering
LEO	Luxurious	Passionate	Exhausting
VIRGO	Supportive	Helpful	Withdrawn
LIBRA	Dignified	Elegant	Scattered
SCORPIO	Magnetic	Soulmates	Mortal Enemies
SAGITTARIUS	Freedom	Uninhibited	Wishy-Washy
CAPRICORN	Patience	Majestic	Dominating
AQUARIUS	Experimental	Liberated	Aloof
PISCES	Seductive	Otherworldly	Isolated

♀

FIND YOUR SUPERCOUPLE VENUS AT
SUPERCOUPLE.COM

SUPERCOUPLE VENUS
ARIES ✳ ♈
OR THE 1ST HOUSE

We get turned on by:

- Captivating the room as the hottest couple
- Walking around naked
- Competing with each other
- Winning together as a team
- Being the first couple to do (fill in the blank)

With Supercouple Venus in assertive Aries, you are fiery and passionate lovers. In each other, you have found an all-encompassing attraction, but not necessarily an easy one. Was it love at first sight...or were you mortal enemies before you saw the light? With the warrior sign of Aries governing your romantic profile, the line between love and hate can virtually disappear some days.

One thing's for sure, there's nothing neutral in a Composite Venus in Aries relationship. The spark of emotion is immediate, provoking an intense reaction from you both. You're the couple that may argue constantly, forgetting to use your "inside voices" when other people are around. Is this the healthiest dynamic? Some would say no. But learning how to transmute fiery feelings into fierce devotion is undeniably hot.

Venus is "in detriment" in Aries, which is a challenging position because Aries sits opposite Libra, the zodiac sign that Venus rules. Fittingly, there's a lot of pushing and pulling that goes on in this relationship.

Create your own Supercouple Chart at **SUPERCOUPLE.COM**

VENUS

Good luck tapping into the harmonious, loving feelings that Venus usually provokes! At times you can be so diametrically opposed in your views that you wonder how you got together in the first place.

But then...makeup sex. Or the wild nookie in the back of the car because you just couldn't wait to get home to tear each other's clothes off. The attraction is downright animalistic, especially if you haven't seen each other for a while. Patience is not a virtue of Venus in brash, impulsive Aries. It's likely that things got physical on your very first date, followed by a need to know, "Are we doing this or not?"

In bed—or wherever you set the scene for your sexytime—you may add a performative element. Aries can be a showoff, begging for mirrors on the ceiling or a multi-angle camera setup to build a private video collection of your greatest moments. Build rock-solid trust before the "lights, camera, action!" With the hotheaded vibes that crackle through a Venus in Aries relationship, the last thing you need is to hand the other a cloud storage drive worth of revenge porn. (Do. Not. Go. There.)

Aries is fundamentally independent, which means this liberated (and sometimes fickle) Venus placement might make it hard for you two to settle into monogamy. Attraction may fire up, then disappear, then fire up again. Jealousy can become a troubling issue in this connection. While your book of love may be filled with steamy and half-finished chapters, at least it won't be boring! Try not to write each other off SO quickly during heated moments that you don't give your relationship a fair shake.

Venus is also the planet of beauty, and your Supercouple placement has a thing to say about your shared style. In Aries, think: edgy and nouveau. Fill your home with showpieces that have a one-of-a-kind flair. Even if it all feels a little over the top to some people, you two won't mind turning one room into a full-on tiki bar or game room. The color red is especially evocative for Venus in Aries. If one room looks like a bordello or a glam rocker's L.A. apartment with crimson walls, black couches and music blaring from the speakers, well, you know exactly why!

SUPERCOUPLE VENUS

TAURUS ✳ ♉

OR THE 2ND HOUSE

We get turned on by:

- Sensual and tactile play objects (feathers, soft leather)
- Luxury bedding
- Full body massages
- Sexy, ambient music
- Breakfast in bed
- Consensual rough sex

Who wants to cuddle...or how about a nice, stimulating massage? With Supercouple Venus in sensual Taurus, touch (and lots of it) is always on the menu. The planet of love, beauty and seduction is literally right at home in decadent Taurus, one of the two zodiac signs that it rules. No matter how reserved you are individually, this relationship brings out a hopeless romantic in each of you. To say your union has Cupid's blessing would be an understatement!

Let Coltrane pipe softly through your speakers while the vintage Pinot breathes alongside haute stemware on your counter. For a Composite Venus in Taurus couple, paying attention to life's finer things is foreplay in and of itself. Were you a beer and burgers type before? You'd better upgrade that to a share plate of Kobe beef sliders paired with a craft-brewed IPA. Or maybe a dry-aged porterhouse and reserve bottle of Pinot. Venus in Taurus has officially upgraded you.

That said, Taurus is highly sensual but equally sensible. You're also a practical pair who learns what to splurge on, and also what to pick up at IKEA and hack it with knobs or paint. Taurus is an earth sign, so plants may fill every corner—a great way to keep things lush if you're balling on a budget! Your appetite for luxury is certain to grow, however. Get ready to develop gourmet-level kitchen skills and fill your shared home with elegant décor and a collection of tasteful art that costs a pretty penny.

With your shared Venus in Taurus, being relaxed is the key to being receptive to love. Do you both work stressful jobs? Don't bring that energy home if you want this relationship to last. It might be wise for you two to stop by the gym together (and use the sauna!) on your way back from work, so you can burn off the stress of the day. It's a transition ritual that will help you both sleep better at night—and trust us, a good night's rest (and languorous mornings on the weekend) will keep the "raging Bull" aspect of your relationship at bay.

Here's hoping you aren't addicted to the Type A lifestyle. Venus in Taurus will virtually force you two to slow down and luxuriate! And that goes for your courtship rituals, too. While attraction may be hot and immediate, there's also a sense that this chemistry lesson is not to be rushed. You may have lingered over candlelit dinners, walked hand-in-hand under the stars and basically enjoyed every second of the dynamic build-up before your first kiss. If you didn't have a signature fragrance before, welcome to a new era where looking like a million bucks and smelling even richer is essential foreplay. When it's finally time to do the deed, a lavish boudoir is the ideal place for the scene to unfold. Add to the list a plush, organic mattress, silky sheets, a down comforter and piles of pillows—all aphrodisiacs for this comfort-loving Supercouple Venus sign.

As a pair, you may love to entertain, which can be a wonderful way for your shared creativity to unfold. From lavish dinner parties to family gatherings, you create a comfortable and beautiful home that guests never want to leave. Don't be surprised if your leather sofas wind up doubling as beds after talking and dancing into the night during one of your unforgettable shindigs.

SUPERCOUPLE VENUS
GEMINI ✴ ♊

OR THE 3RD HOUSE

We get turned on by:

- Flirty texts
- Talking dirty
- Making out at concerts and on the dance floor
- Wearing each other's clothes
- Deep metaphysical conversations
- Manual stimulation

They say talk is cheap, but for relationships with Supercouple Venus in Gemini, that's hardly the case. Your love zone centers around frequent communication! Right from the jump, it's witty banter and emoji-laced texts and, of course, the hottest damn pillow talk you've ever experienced. So you weren't the verbally expressive type before? Ha! Suddenly you're articulating every desire. "Touch me there...wait, a little bit lower. Firmer. Faster." Who ARE you even?

And that's just the beginning. Wordplay is foreplay in this Composite Venus configuration. It's also an essential part of the act itself, your lingering "aftercare" and every moment when you're not in each other's company. Gemini is the sign of the Twins, after all. Lucky you! Your shared Venus delivers a best friend and lover rolled into one. You'll keep each other spellbound with juicy gossip, fascinating stories and even a few head games.

Be warned though! With dualistic Gemini orchestrating your symphony of seduction, attraction can swell one moment and decrescendo the next. Along with the extreme magnetic pull between you come polarizing moments where you literally repel one another. This can be managed once you realize the

Create your own Supercouple Chart at **SUPERCOUPLE.COM**

trigger...and here it is. The swing toward repulsion generally comes when you've overdosed on the doppelgänger "just the two of us" vibes. Yes, it's great to find so much common ground and have a partner who can hang out with your BFFs and spend every second with you and never get boring. But without ample autonomy, you'll start to feel more like siblings than sexed-up adventurers. Venus in Gemini relationships come with a warning label: Don't get too close for comfort!

Pick-up artists have a technique they call "negging," where you teasingly insult the person you're attracted to. While moves like these can be manipulative, you might use them with a light touch. Differentiating from each other keeps the attraction dynamic in this relationship, so as you get closer, make space to pursue independent interests.

More than most other couples, you two must interrupt lazy habits that can dull the sexual tension. Socializing as a couple is also essential. Co-host game nights and organize trips with your mutual crew. Mix it up too! Everyone who tags along doesn't HAVE to be a couple. The point is that you're sharing a fun and memorable time—something the two of you can talk about for days.

Gemini rules the hands and arms, which is a definite plus in the seduction department. Whether you're furiously typing love texts or enjoying some, er, manual stimulation, you'll touch each other in ways you probably never experienced before. This Venus makes the two of you quite curious and experimental—both in a physical and intellectual way. Your bond is sapiosexual and getting in the mood often begins with arousing conversations.

As a couple, you are intrigued by life's offerings and want to explore them all. As a result, it can be hard to settle on a style for your shared home... beyond "eclectic," that is. You may switch up your living space season by season to reflect your current moods, so think in terms of collections. The summer might be time to bust out the inflatable hot pink couch; winter, your Moroccan wedding pillow collection on an oversized shag rug. Eclectic prints, vintage signs and vision boards may crowd your walls—fascinating conversation pieces for all the glittery intellectuals in your shared friend circle to discuss...that is, if you're home long enough to entertain them!

SUPERCOUPLE VENUS
CANCER ✴ ♋
OR THE 4TH HOUSE

We get turned on by:

- Lingerie
- Cuddling
- Dinner dates at sexy restaurants
- Being introduced to each other's families
- Chest rubs and nipple stimulation
- Sex on the beach
- Oral sex

Whoever said "secure" is the opposite of "sexy" never met a couple with Supercouple Venus in Cancer. The recipe for seduction in this relationship? One part caretaker, two parts coquette. Nurturing each other in and out of the bedroom is all part of the same dance. You'll pack lunches with little love notes slipped in, rush to support the other through a family crisis, and offer a full-body massage after the other's had a rough day at work. You feel safe in each other's lives, and thus in each other's arms. And suddenly, that means more than any hot-air balloon ride at sunset or a weekend in Paris. Not that you two won't enjoy such romantic delights! But in this relationship, they're the cherry on the sundae of the sweet, sacred life you create.

Want to get each other hot and bothered? Set up the pillow fort! Cozy spaces get you both feel comfortable and relaxed, which puts you in the mood for lovin'. Since Cancer is the zodiac's foodie, early

Create your own Supercouple Chart at **SUPERCOUPLE.COM**

dates may revolve around luxurious dinners. Soon enough, you may try out those recipes at home, taking a road trip to a seafood market then cooking a vat of mussels in white wine. In between bites? Clear the kitchen counter for a sexy "secondi" course, as you both get hotter than the steaming pots on the stove. Hey, it doesn't hurt to have a Composite Venus that's also orally fixated. The main course on the menu? Each other!

But hold the PDA: Venus in Cancer is deeply private and your intimacy is a two-person affair. While you two may be modest in the streets, you're definitely tigers in the sheets. Cancer is a water sign and once the passion starts flowing, it's a rushing river that cannot be contained. While lovemaking usually begins in a tender way—perhaps after drying some tears or sharing a sentimental moment—it's hardly boring! You'll definitely want to take care of the other's urges, playing out fantasies and assiduously studying the most pleasurable points on each other's bodies. The "hot mama" energy of your shared Venus can give way to some consensual power dynamics, spankings and light BDSM. ("Who's been a naughty baby?")

Cancer rules the chest area, and this can be an erogenous zone for your Venus. You may tease one another with an open button or low neckline that shows off your chiseled pecs or décolletage. Fill your lingerie drawers with sexy little numbers and trot them out for an erotic fashion show. The crab comes in a shell, after all, so costumes are part of the erotic package.

Nesting can be pure paradise, since Cancer is the sign that rules home. This Supercouple Venus sign is family-oriented and kids may figure into your long-range plans—at least fur babies will. And hey, since you both have SO much love to give, getting a pet can be a great outlet for some of your warm-fuzzy TLC. Whether you're setting up your starter apartment or building a family home, you're at your most creative together when behind closed doors. Your abode will be a cozy and well-appointed palace with overstuffed sofas and sentimental objects like souvenirs, family albums and framed photos. The heart of your home? The kitchen of course!

SUPERCOUPLE VENUS

LEO ☀ ♌

OR THE 5TH HOUSE

We get turned on by:

- Dressing up for each other
- Sex in luxury hotels
- Champagne in bed
- Taking sexy photos
- Hair-pulling and other "rough" play
- PDA
- Play parties
- Public sex (with occasional guest stars)

Dim the house lights! Romance is performance art for relationships with Supercouple Venus in theatrical Leo. This fiery, flamboyant placement imbues your relationship with megadoses of passion—and plenty of drama, too. If you're not working the room like a pair of red carpet stars, you're dreaming up your next high-key playdate or hosting the most legendary party your friends have ever attended without having to pay cover. This hedonistic relationship thrives on a mix of adrenaline, raucous laughter and childlike wonder.

PDA? Yes, please, and plenty of it. You can be wildcats in the streets AND in the sheets, scratching, nipping and pulling each other's manes. Your bedroom may look like a high-end bordello, complete with all the accoutrements needed to put on a show or even make a few home videos. Decorate it like a set with all the lushness, sound effects and lighting that you need to set many moods. Leo rules the heart and upper back so try focusing on these areas when seducing each other. A tight squeeze, bodies pressed together? You'll feel the electricity. You might even sit face to face with your hands on each other's hearts, sharing the current of energy that pulses between you.

When it comes to how you live your daily life, you're a creative couple! Your home will be luxurious and decadent—ideally with a giant walk-in closet, a full-on party room and a mattress big enough to host an orgy. You're fine going "off-script," writing your own rules of engagement. Do you both need your own lions' dens? While sharing comes naturally in this generous coupling, forcing a compromise can dull the sparks. You may opt for separate bedrooms or home offices so you can each spread out and decorate to your unique specifications.

In this fiery relationship, some of your most heart-opening moments may be ad libbed when you throw caution to the wind. But who's going to be the adult in the room? Composite Venus in Leo can bring some true spoiled brat moments. If there's one thing you two cannot abide by, it's being ignored. And when you're not getting the attention you want, look out! You may give yourselves way too much license to act out, whether throwing a tantrum or storming off for a revenge date...with someone else.

To combat this, make sure to worship and adore each other regularly. A roaming eye or an ambivalent heart? Instant dealbreakers. (And maybe the cause of an epic blowout that wakes up the neighborhood.) Even if you've never been a "vocal appreciator" before, start speaking up and letting each other know how gorgeous and special they are. Praise them for their sexiness and tell them how good they made you feel. Say thank you regularly for "the little things" and give lavish gifts that are thoughtfully chosen very, very often.

With all the narrative arcs this page-turner of a relationship brings, you could sell your story to a Hollywood studio. And while the cliffhangers might make you rich, they probably won't bring you happiness. This Supercouple Venus sign will quickly reveal where the two of you need to grow up—fast! And it might require separate therapists to deal with the inner child who comes storming out when you both unite. Once you nail the balance, oh, baby, it's on! You'll become the reigning royals of your own realm, where everyone comes to be spoiled. From kids to fur babies to your ever-growing circle of friends, life together can be rich and sweet.

SUPERCOUPLE VENUS
VIRGO ✳ ♍

OR THE 6TH HOUSE

We get turned on by:

- Sex in nature
- Soft white bedding
- Naked skin
- Tantric massage
- Exploring each other's bodies while talking about it

Can you fall in love with your life coach? We kid...sort of. Wise, analytical Virgo is the sign of service—and this Supercouple Venus makes you a pair of helpful heartthrobs. Your relationship might begin with one of you supporting the other through a rough time, like a breakup or custody battle. Or you could literally meet as client and service provider: "personal trainer and fitness-lover" or "bartender and Thursday-night karaoke regular." The common factor? You two cannot stop talking. Quickly, you realize that the other has something useful to offer, something that will improve your life significantly. There's a sense that you could really be there for one another—that is hot!

It's particularly sexy when the dutiful generosity spills over into the bedroom. You'll please the other with full-body massages, hours of oral sex, lap dances...whatever thrills them, you'll want to discover. And if it's one of your "offerings," you'll serve it up with a smile. In

Create your own Supercouple Chart at **SUPERCOUPLE.COM**

this relationship, it might be easier to give than receive. But since you'll both want to deliver the goods, take turns being the pleaser and the pleased. Aftercare will be particularly illuminating. When you're lying in post-coital bliss, talk through whatever feelings arose. What would you love more of...and what would you prefer to do differently the next time? Practice makes perfect, as Virgo knows. Plus, your shared intellectual curiosity is an aphrodisiac. Go ahead and analyze away!

Getting out of the friend zone might take a while. Virgo IS the zodiac's sign of the virgin, after all, and this Venus can make you adorably shy around one another. Venus is "in detriment" in Virgo, a challenging position because it's the opposite sign of Pisces—Venus' most exalted and powerful home. Relax! This doesn't mean you're romantically doomed. But expressing affection might not always be easy. Virgo is the zodiac's perfectionist, which can make you second-guess yourselves, particularly in the early stages. To push past your fears of making a "mistake," lean into Virgo's communicative powers. Asking lots of questions—in and out of bed—will get you all the information you need to earn that shiny gold star.

With modest Virgo ruling your Supercouple Venus, a clean and comfortable indoor environment is ideal for basically every shared activity. It's easier for the two of you to relax and get in a sexy headspace when you're in a tidy room with a chilled Pinot or mocktail. Since Virgo is an earth sign, getting it on in the great outdoors could also be your jam. Well, as long as there's a freshly-laundered (organic cotton) sheet to lay down on the ground.

While you may be uncomfortable being fussed over, it's part of the dance in this relationship. You're here to help the other become their best self—it's part of your bonding ritual! Know when to back off though. You don't have to be the chicken soup to each other's souls 24/7. That can create an awkward (and deeply unsexy) parental vibe that dulls the sparks. When that starts happening, get up and move your bodies! Hold hands while you walk under the stars and talk your dreams of making the world a better place.

Expensive gifts aren't required, but thoughtfully chosen ones are everything! Order a favorite book in a leather-bound hardcover or a consciously sourced, handmade treasure that donates half the proceeds to an important charity. Anything that's both useful and artfully crafted will win instant points, so listen up and you'll know just what's needed by the other.

Venus is the astro-aesthete and when it comes to decorating, you two go for a Zen-like palette of whites, browns and earthy neutrals, offset by loads of plants. Keep your home orderly and accessorize with natural objects like crystals and plants. Bookshelves are a must! Reading side-by-side in bed in the hush of comfortable silence might be your idea of foreplay. Or maybe you'll fall asleep at a set hour then rise for a blood-pumping round of morning sex. How sweet it is!

Create your own Supercouple Chart at **SUPERCOUPLE.COM**

SUPERCOUPLE VENUS
LIBRA ✴ ♎

OR THE 7TH HOUSE

We get turned on by:

- Spa dates as foreplay
- Love letters
- Expensive gifts
- Sexy playlists
- Dressing up together (then peeling it all off in a sexy striptease)
- Piles of pillows
- Grabbing each other's butts
- A back massage with warm scented oil

Hopeless romantics? That's putting it mildly. With Supercouple Venus landing in her home sign of Libra, you've come together to co-author a lifelong fairy tale. The planet of love and beauty reigns supreme here, blessing your relationship with megadoses of charm. Every season of your union is cause for celebration, from the sweep-you-off-your-feet courtship phase to your first couples' vacation to planning the wedding and ultimately, locating the perfect warm-weather retirement community for your sunset years.

But don't go pre-ordering the matching rocking chairs yet! Complacency has no place in the Venus in Libra relationship. You'll do everything in your power to prevent the "old married couple" vibe from kicking in prematurely: Showering each other with lavish gifts, working out with a trainer, strutting around in sexy lingerie, and booking luxury vacations. The element of surprise is always at play with the two of you! Socially, you're a power pair who may entertain frequently. The #blessed energy of your union is likely to attract abundance your way—and you'll share the goods graciously with your golden circle of friends.

This thoughtful Venus hates to be rushed. Even if you felt some twinge of love at first sight, committing to one another may have taken a while. True, the chemistry was bubbling like a freshly uncorked bottle of Veuve, but you knew this connection was to be sipped, not swilled! When clothes invariably DO come off, it's bound to be an elaborate processional. Rather then ripping bodices, you'll slowly peel off each item in a sensual *paso doble*. Tender gazes and gentle caresses crescendo slowly (but surely!) into uptempo pleasure-fests that you'd happily to enjoy for hours in your ridiculously high thread-count sheets.

This is not a "hit it and quit" it relationship by any stretch, although it wouldn't kill you two to have a quickie every now and again. Libra rules the derriere, which can make this area a hotspot of your "bootylicious" bond. Squeeze it, spank it, grab it hard in a moment of ecstasy. And be sure to get up off it when it's time to be at each other's beck and call. Spoiling one another is delicious as long as you keep the scorecard even. Yes, we said that. Libra is represented by the scales, and for this Supercouple Venus, keeping the romance alive is a lifelong balancing act. How much togetherness do you require...and when do you need to pull yourselves free from the couple bubble? Expect to adjust this formula often, along with the give and take.

Separate bathrooms, even bedrooms—that level of mystery may be the key to always feeling like you're in the honeymoon phase. But make sure that intimacy doesn't suffer in the process! (Hello, everyone poops!) You two can get so hung up on aesthetics—a speciality of Venus in Libra—that you remain somewhat superficial or formal with each other, even after years of being partners. At some point, one of you may get sick, depressed or struck by grief—all things that make a morning blowout and primping session seem far less important. If you can't love one another in sweatpants and bedhead, well, maybe you don't deserve each other in red carpet glam.

Not that anyone can stop you two from strutting around like Fashion Week royalty. Your shared sensibilities scream "Paris couture house," with a timeless sophistication and elegant sparkle. Nothing cheap or tacky belongs in a relationship with your combined Venus in Libra. It's all about harmonizing the elements and zhushing every ensemble and room of your home into the perfect balance. Keeping the visuals "museum quality" is part of the seduction for the both of you.

With peacekeeping Venus in fair-minded Libra, as a pair you easily sense when your partnership is out of sync and you'll quickly adjust. The only pitfall? You can be SO focused on creating unity that you sweep important issues under the rug. Cooperating, compromising and co-creating? No problem! In this relationship, you'd rather avoid the unpleasantness of a conflict at all costs. But this can actually be detrimental to intimacy. Learning to "diplomatically disagree" and even differentiate from one another is what will truly keep the peace for years to come.

SUPERCOUPLE VENUS

SCORPIO ✳ ♏

OR THE 8TH HOUSE

We get turned on by:

- Wearing sexy clothes
- Dancing or "performing" for each other in bed
- Just enough distance to feel a tiny bit jealous
- Other people being attracted to us
- Cat and mouse games
- Having our bodies worshipped
- Feeling irresistible
- Almost getting caught
- Nighttime sex (indoors or out)

Mystery, intensity and unspoken attraction! With Supercouple Venus in secretive Scorpio, the buildup is as exciting as the act itself—hell, maybe more so! This attraction is magnetic in every way. When you're "on" there is no greater high than being in the dynamic field of one another's molecularly charged presence. But when things go south, you can rebuff each other with an equally repellant force. Heed the warning label: This complex relationship should not be entered into lightly. Not that you'd listen to that advice...

Create your own Supercouple Chart at **SUPERCOUPLE.COM**

There's nothing casual about your communion, not even during the getting-to-know-you phase. Whether you're exclusive or not is irrelevant. Chances are, you won't be able to stop thinking about each other after your first encounter. You may live rent-free in each other's heads for weeks, months, even years, before you muster up the courage to admit that you're hooked, much less go "all in." Cat and mouse games are *de rigeur* in most Venus in Scorpio bonds. You'll just have to play them strategically and be patient while you wait to catch or be caught.

One of the reasons this union is so complicated? Venus is in "detriment" in Scorpio, which is a challenging position because it falls opposite to Taurus, the sign that Venus rules. This connection has an "all or nothing" spirit when it comes to commitment. The stakes are definitely high, but erotically, the risks are well worth it. Scorpio is the zodiac's famed "sex sign," and in this Venus connection, love is a mind-blowing, soulful trip to ecstasy.

Erotic encounters are legendary—especially in a darkened bar, hot tub or any body of water. Tantric rituals, BDSM and other consensual power games can turn your bedroom play into a form of therapy. At its best, this relationship can heal some deep scars, helping you emerge from the erotic fires like a pair of phoenixes rising from the ashes. You can get lost together in a transcendent space during sex! In the early part of your connection, it's difficult to concentrate on much else in your daily life besides the mental replays of your mind-blowing encounters.

Now for the REAL question: Can you pass one another's hardcore loyalty tests? When either of you feels hurt or rejected within this relationship, you may come across as withholding and even downright cold—and losing that love connection can devastate you more than most. There's a possessive nature to this Venus, and jealousy can take you two on a swift descent to Hades! Feelings are tender in this relationship and because you hold such power over your partner's emotions, you can put your guards up around each other. The vengeful nature of this zodiac's sign could rear up to sting, poison and destroy. Hell hath no fury like a Venus in Scorpio scorned, so if you're not ready to give your all to this bond, keep it firmly in the friend zone.

Fortunately, once your deep connection is solidified, you'll give the relationship your all. Sharing is more than just "caring" here since Scorpio is the sign of joint ventures and merging resources. This Supercouple Venus yields a magical melding of bank accounts and living spaces that increases security, and likely wealth, for both of you.

It's just a matter of getting there! You'd each happily plunge into the depths of intimacy and find out the other's most tightly locked secrets. And yes, you'll create a safe space! The trouble is, you may both resist feeling vulnerable or exposed. So who's gonna be the first to open up? Since trust does not come easily with this Venus placement, it's important for you to create a safe, non-judgmental space together for you two to bare your souls. That's when the magic happens.

When it comes to sartorial flair, as a pair you have the most discerning of eyes. In this connection, style and design may be big themes! Shopping is like a treasure hunt for you both, whether sourcing hand-woven pillows or the perfect festival wear. Though you're pros at choosing color palettes, *noir* may be your signature hue, from lingerie to tuxes to ebony paint and more!

Create your own Supercouple Chart at **SUPERCOUPLE.COM**

SUPERCOUPLE VENUS
SAGITTARIUS ✦ ♐

OR THE 9TH HOUSE

We get turned on by:

- Adventurous vacations (a change of scenery!)
- Grinding on the dance floor
- Couples' retreats
- Sex in cars
- Getting naked in public
- Play parties
- Wild sex
- Hair pulling
- Grabbing each other's hips

Love without limits? Yes, please. With Supercouple Venus in broad-spectrum Sagittarius, nothing gets you two hotter than feeling wild and untethered, like a pair of stallions galloping across the open plains. Or maybe the desert...or the tundra. With worldly Sagittarius directing your love jones, it won't be long before you two are exploring new terrain together. Getting frisky on every continent? That's #lovegoals for Venus in Sagittarius. When attraction starts to flatline, pack your bags and go! A change of scenery gets your motors revving.

Together, you'll expand your global sensibilities—and your cultural sensitivity. Diversity and equity are a couple of Sagittarius' favorite words, and your inclusive Venus sign will give you a broader lens on the human experience. It's highly possible that your relationship is a cross-cultural one, but regardless, together you attract friends from all walks of life. The parties you throw will be awakening moments for your entire crew—and no one is soon to forget.

Since Sagittarius rules education, part of your exploration as a couple may involve taking workshops together. Whether a tantric retreat in Maui or a wine-pairing class at the local vineyard, you'll love geeking out and experimenting with whatever you learn. Laughter is another crucial key to your connection! If you didn't have killer senses of humor before, you'll sharpen your wit in this relationship. Just note: Some of those inside jokes may be a little off-color, so keep them between the two of you, like a private language you share.

What both of you cannot tolerate, however, is feeling restricted or possessed. A relationship of two whole individuals is your shared ideal, not losing your identities in some claustrophobic couple bubble. Sagittarius is fundamentally expansive—and you're here to foster each other's purposeful growth! This Supercouple Venus will inspire you both to do, have and be MORE. At times, these pursuits may send you to different cities, even corners of the globe. Fortunately, a long-distance arrangement won't be a dealbreaker, provided you stay in touch regularly. And of course, to travel! Your boo's visiting professorship in Buenos Aires is just another excuse to collect the passport stamps that make your bond so luscious.

Some Venus in Sagittarius relationships might be polyamorous arrangements, or open under agreed-upon circumstances. For example, maybe you give each other a pass to kiss other people (as long as it doesn't go further!) or have a vacation fling if you're traveling separately. Or you may at some point open up to other full-on relationships, depending on how progressive you are.

The built-in truthfulness of this candid Venus makes it impossible for the two of you to pretend that you're not red-blooded humans. To only be attracted to one person for the rest of your lives? That's a Mission: Impossible. So even if your idea of fidelity means "flirting is acceptable as long as the other isn't present," you'll need to keep it real with one another. Either way, freedom is a core value of this high-vibe relationship. That might simply mean giving each other space to explore independent hobbies and intellectual curiosities. The best part is, you two get to make the rules.

Shake that thing! Sagittarius rules the hips and thighs, which may be an erogenous zone for the both of you. Dancing lessons—or just lots of nights getting down to DJ sets—should definitely be on your date night list. You might even perform a private dance number for each other. (Move over Magic Mike!)

Venus lends us our fashion sensibilities and your shared tastes could run from the bizarre to the "bazaar." Treasures you scoop up along your travels together will become favorite pieces in your home, from hand-embroidered pillowcases to largescale wood carvings. Your eclectically decorated nest may look a bit like a shamanic tent or a hookah lounge! A couch is optional: In fact, you two may prefer piles of embroidered pillows for your seating, the perfect perch to check out all your woven tapestries, religious artifacts and cleverly placed vintage suitcases!

SUPERCOUPLE VENUS
CAPRICORN ✳ ♑
OR THE 10TH HOUSE

♀

> ## We get turned on by:
>
> - Being seen as a power couple
> - Planning the future together (Capricorn foreplay!)
> - Outdoor sex
> - Locking the office door and getting it on
> - High-end vacations
> - Consensual BDSM (leather, whips, restraints)

Ready to play the long game in love? Here's hoping. With Supercouple Venus in Capricorn, your relationship wants to go the distance—or bust! This practical, persistent earth sign knows that good things come to those who wait. You'll see each other as an investment that's meant to be nurtured, cultivated and treasured. But first, do your values align? Do you have common future goals? Don't get it twisted. In this relationship, you're not just enjoying each other's delicious company, you're building something legendary together! And that's what keeps it hot in this power-couple configuration.

Let's be honest, it's rare to find someone with whom you can fortify such a stable and fruitful life together. For this reason, you may be willing to wait it out while the other wraps up some "interfering circumstances." One or both of you may be in other relationships when you meet—yikes! Or perhaps you're living long distance and will be for the foreseeable future. Patience is not just a virtue in the Venus in Capricorn relationship; it's a requirement.

But here's the beautiful part, and the very glue that holds your bond together: You allow each other to be full-range humans. Venus in Capricorn brings a hardcore realism to the relationship. You both understand that no one can be "perfect" 24/7. And while this relationship DOES thrive on social status and looking good together in public, behind closed doors, you offer each other a huge dose of grace. Part of the trial period involves revealing every dimension, from your tucked-away erotic personas to your stormy shadow sides. You want to know what you're getting into...and you want to know it all.

Once you've passed each other's rigorous entry tests, you're all in, shopping for housewares at Crate and Barrel, making Pinterest boards of iconic engagement rings, scouting out hillside mansions for your wedding ceremony and figuring out which grandparent you'll name the first kid after. Family isn't just valued, it's prized in this union. Venus in Capricorn strengthens the "provider" instinct for you both.

That desire to provide extends to the bedroom, too. A natural generosity flows between you. In this relationship, you want to know what turns the other on. Because Capricorn is interested in power, you might even try using restraints or playing with BDSM. The trick is getting past some of the shyness this reserved Composite Venus can spin up. Being the receiver isn't as easy as lying back like a pillow prince(ss) and letting your partner "do" you. When you stop to take in their touch, you also have to be with whatever thoughts and feelings come up in your psyche. Those could include perfectionistic standards you're applying to your body or any shame around your sexuality.

♀

For the Venus in Capricorn Supercouple, sex is like a hero's journey that will plummet you down into the shadows to learn about yourselves AND each other at the same time. The best part about this? Exploring each other's bodies isn't just for the honeymoon phase for this Venus. Capricorn rules time and you'll enjoy learning one another's turn-ons through every age and stage.

With this career-driven Venus directing your love jones, you may become both bedmates and business partners. What could be more satisfying than being able to sit back with your S.O. and witness all that you've built together? Since this earthy energy connects to your shared creative impulses, you get inspired in nature together. Bring the outdoors in, decorating with lush houseplants, crystals, stone floors and reclaimed wood furniture.

Venus in legacy-builder Capricorn also favors classic "grandfather" décor: large clocks, leather sofas, wood cabinetry...even taxidermy. Hunter green, navy and brown are go-to hues within this coupling, and you might need to add fresh flowers or white linens to keep rooms bright. Well-appointed home offices are vital since in this productive pairing, you'll spend lots of time at your desks!

SUPERCOUPLE VENUS

AQUARIUS ✳ ♒

OR THE 11TH HOUSE

We get turned on by:

- High-minded erotica (VR and AR included)
- Intellectual chemistry
- Being BFFs and building a shared friend group
- Sex toys
- Experimenting with edgy fantasies (possibly involving others besides the two of us)

Rip up the rule book! With Supercouple Venus in iconoclastic Aquarius, you're doing "relationship" by your own design. Even if you ARE the traditional types by nature, you'll reinvent your rituals with a fresh and modern twist. Restrictions dissolve in this high-vibe union—including the ones that family and society have foisted upon you in the past. Pleasing them? So not a priority anymore. Now that you've met one another, you are ready to discover your unique purpose as a pair. And surprise! It may be edgy, avant-garde and kink-positive.

Not that this is anyone's business! But we feel compelled to remind you of that. Since Aquarius is the sign of community, you'll get so excited about the discoveries you make together that you shout them across every social media platform. (Heck, you might even start teaching workshops.) Generous, but when it comes to the seamier stuff, don't rush to make any PSAs. First, allow yourself to integrate the progress privately and with supportive confidantes only. When (and if!) you go public with a lifestyle change, you should be able to confidently respond to any questions—and critiques—that come your way. Plus, not everyone deserves a seat at your future duo burlesque cabaret or a slideshow from your Burning Man engagement party. But the friends who make it into your joint inner circle are sure to be some of the most liberated futurists on the planet!

Are you two a little more vanilla than that? That's totally cool. Venus in Aquarius has all sorts of range, including the intellectual type. In this sapiosexual union, you'll get turned on by each other's minds. Get ready for fascinating conversations that draw your thinking WAY outside the box. You'll grow as people in the world—and that's hot! But be aware that as the sign of friendship, Aquarius CAN pull your relationship in a platonic direction. Jealousy is a pretty foreign concept for Venus in Aquarius, in fact. Alas, that levelheaded approach might dull the sparks at times. Be careful not to minimize one another's feelings. Learning about neuroscience and its effect on human emotions can give you each a template for empathy.

To get back into your bodies when things get too "heady," tap into the air sign quality of this zodiac sign. Tantric breath work can give you access to your lower chakras, filling your bodies with the sexy life-force energy that starts your motors. Plus this spiritually aware Supercouple Venus enjoys anything with a high-minded twist. A copy of the *Kama Sutra* should be the first book on your nightstands!

No matter what, experimental Aquarius can make for some fun times in bed. As the zodiac sign that rules electricity, have fun trying out erotic toys and gadgets, even a rotating cast of partners and "extras." Marriage might not be your shared ideal with this ultramodern Venus placement. Under this liberated influence you two may chafe at the idea of anyone "owning" you. That said, neither of you minds exclusivity! This emotionally cool sign finds it a relief to plant into a relationship instead of playing all those aggravating head games of the courtship phase. The non-negotiable for each of you within this connection? Your mate must be a strong individual with a lush life, both inside and outside of the relationship.

Stylistically, Venus in Aquarius allows you to express an eccentric flair and anti-fashion sensibility. Your shared home may be more curated than cozy, a pastiche of midcentury modern and industrial pieces in glass and steel. Art will be provocative and large-scale, the conversation-starters that will have people settle down for a salon-style discussion. With humanitarian Aquarius guiding the design process, textiles may be sourced from ethical brands that support the artisans in developing nations. If you don't go full-vegan and non-GMO together, Meatless Mondays are sure to become a tradition.

SUPERCOUPLE VENUS

PISCES ✳ ♓

OR THE 12TH HOUSE

We get turned on by:

- Complex and creative experiences
- Tons of affection and healing touch
- Sharing transcendent metaphysical experiences (in bed)
- Sweep-you-off-your feet romantic gestures
- Aquatic aphrodisiacs (candlelight baths, skinny-dipping, walks on the beach)
- Kink and fetish play
- Foot massages
- Rescuing each other from disaster
- Shoring up each other's emotions
- Melancholy moments in each other's arms

Sweet, seductive rhapsody! With Supercouple Venus flowing in fantasy-fueled Pisces, your relationship is pure poetry, pulling you away from the stress of everyday life and into a bliss bubble for two. Reality? Not so much. This bond brings romance with all the trappings: oversized bouquets of fresh-cut flowers, gourmet picnics at a scenic overlook, decadent dinners by candlelight and of course, kissing endlessly under the stars. But your connection goes far deeper than the surface. Spiritual, esoteric Pisces lends a "meant to be" energy to your union. Yes, it's as if you've known each other for lifetimes—and indeed you probably have.

The best opening gambit for this Venus sounds like this, "Hey, I've got two tickets to a show this weekend." Pisces is one of the zodiac's die-hard music lovers, so get ready for a sonic seduction of live bands and playlists for every occasion. It won't be long before you two build up a vinyl collection, pick a theme song and set up speakers in every room of your shared home. Visual and performance art is also Pisces terrain. Favorite date nights may involve gallery-hopping or going to the ballet. Immersive experiences are just as fun as spectator sports! Schedule your disco naps: This nocturnal Venus placement could turn you both into the stars of the salsa club or the luminaries of your all-night plant medicine circle.

With this watery energy directing your loving feelings, you could feel your friskiest together at the beach or in a tub. Since Pisces rules the feet, this Supercouple Venus could give you quite the fetish. As you artfully weave empathy with an intuitive understanding of what turns each other on, you'll be quite the high-vibe lovers. One soulfully sexy gaze between the both of you might be all it takes for clothes to go a-flinging. Venus is "exalted" in Pisces, meaning this is its most potent placement in the zodiac. Lucky you!

But since Pisces is symbolized by two Fish swimming in opposite directions, attractions may run hot and cold. One minute you're worshiping at one another's altar, the next you're gasping for air... and even pulling a "slippery fish" disappearing act! Commitment issues may sneak up on you both, appearing in the form of a triangulating "emotional affair." Easy does it! In a bond as spiritual as yours, it can feel like a breach of trust if one of you starts pouring your helpful, compassionate energy into someone else's tanks. The problem is, the more you demand attention, the faster the other will swim away (or hide under a coral reef). In this relationship, you must learn to give each other an ample amount of space. Be affectionate, but never smothering. "Fluid" is a keyword for Venus in Pisces pairs to remember.

By the same token, do your part to NOT trigger one another's abandonment issues by going MIA. Even if your body is in the room, if you're checked out mentally, it can be deeply wounding. Such a balancing act! To make matters more complex? A Supercouple Venus in boundless Pisces is also susceptible to codependence. Getting swept up in each other is a beautiful thing, but if you start enabling destructive behaviors—especially ones that pull you each too far from your "real world" responsibilities, bring in a grounded third party to snap you back into action...fast! More than most pairs, you'd benefit from working with a couples' therapist or coach—even doing buddy workouts with a personal trainer who can remind you to pay attention to your bodies instead of floating off on a pink cloud.

Since Venus governs your aesthetic sensibilities, your home should be a soothing oasis that might feel a bit like a seaside resort. Decorate with a serene palette of soft neutrals and aquatic hues like sea foam green, coral and lilac. A fountain or aquarium could be the showpiece of your home—or perhaps you'll put in a pool. Make sure décor plans involve a quiet room for meditation and lots of creative "studio" spaces throughout. And if you can actually get a water view? Score!

Create your own Supercouple Chart at **SUPERCOUPLE.COM**

SUPERCOUPLE

Compatibility

WITH YOUR VENUS SIGN

♀

If our Supercouple Venus is in a fire Sign:
(ARIES, LEO OR SAGITTARIUS)

And my personal Venus is in a fire sign
(ARIES, LEO OR SAGITTARIUS):

Love at first sight? Before you can hit the brakes on the runaway train, this relationship is off to the races. You may have an immediate sense of knowing that you've met someone special—and a burning attraction that makes you want to pursue! In this connection, you may also feel like you're applying pressure to your partner, and indeed it would be wise to temper yourself. Make sure you're not just chasing a fantasy. Slowing down won't be easy; however, and if you both jump in, just know that when the new relationship energy fades, there's no avoiding the practical realities of forming a fast and furious bond.

And my personal Venus is in an earth sign
(TAURUS, VIRGO OR CAPRICORN):

Throw another log on that fire! While the passionate courtship style of this relationship may move at a faster pace than you're instinctively comfortable with, you'll find yourself wanting more, and even neglecting some of your earthly responsibilities to get swept away in the fairy tale. In some ways, this can bring an important transformation. Perhaps you're avoiding love by keeping yourself busy. But make sure you're not ignoring your values or shucking key responsibilities around work, money and family. If you do, there could be some pretty significant consequences when the honeymoon phase ends.

Create your own Supercouple Chart at **SUPERCOUPLE.COM**

And my personal Venus is in an air sign
(GEMINI, LIBRA, AQUARIUS):

Why yes, it is getting hot in here—perhaps more so than you think you can handle. While part of you loves how your heartbeat accelerates when the two of you are together, you'll definitely need to take cooldown breaks. You may be the rational one in this union, which can be a saving grace when passion gets too hot to handle. Not only will this relationship beckon forth your creative side, but it makes you far more playful and adventurous than you would be on your own.

And my personal Venus is in a water sign
(CANCER, SCORPIO OR PISCES):

Too much too soon? You may feel overpowered by the intensity of this connection, which could be off to Fantasy Island before you've had time to check your emotional temperature. While you'll share incredible life-changing experiences, you may miss out on the processing time between each experience—and that can stir up insecurity, even panic. It's up to you to set the pace here! The challenge for you is internal: Face the fear of being rejected if you say "no" to an offer, and set some boundaries before you get swept up in resentment.

If our Supercouple Venus is in an earth sign:
(TAURUS, VIRGO, OR CAPRICORN)

And my personal Venus is in a fire sign
(ARIES, LEO OR SAGITTARIUS):

Get ready to play the long game! This relationship can hold your interest for more than a fleeting few, since it innately brings out the part of you that wants to build and create something lasting. While the seduction style may be slower than you're used to, it's also steadier, like the fuel instead of the tinder. Take it upon yourself to spice things up with sexy adventure when you feel like you've fallen into a rut.

And my personal Venus is in an earth sign

(TAURUS, VIRGO OR CAPRICORN):

Break out the massage oil and the organic cotton sheets. There's an earthy sensuality in this combination, which appreciates natural beauty, vibrant health and supporting each other's self-care. (Talk about a sexy glow-up!) The pitfall is that your romantic style can get a little too routine and even boring at times. To keep the spark alive, get out of your familiar environment and do something that produces dopamine, like having a novel experience, adventure sports and travel.

And my personal Venus is in an air sign
(GEMINI, LIBRA, AQUARIUS):

You'll feel more embodied in this relationship than you might on your own. How scintillating! This relationship heightens your senses and tunes you in to life's richer pleasures. For a change, you may prefer skin-to-skin contact, no toys and props required. Since you woo through a meeting of the minds, you will have to adapt for this affectionate Venus. Make sure there's as much touch and TLC as there is talk.

And my personal Venus is in a water sign

(CANCER, SCORPIO OR PISCES):

Break out the corsets, fans and Tudor heels! This relationship

Create your own Supercouple Chart at **SUPERCOUPLE.COM**

is old-fashioned romance at its finest. Go ahead and enjoy the prolonged feeling of desire burning in your belly. Before you act upon it, take the time you need to process all the feelings that flutter up to the surface. You might even play into traditional gender roles or enjoy some frisky power dynamics. Best of all, no one but the two of you will ever know the naughty details of this bond.

If our Supercouple Venus is in an air sign:
(GEMINI, LIBRA, AQUARIUS)

♀

And my personal Venus is in a fire sign
(ARIES, LEO OR SAGITTARIUS):

Kink with a wink? Your playful seduction style meets the experimental energy of the Supercouple Air Venus—and oh, the places you will go! Before much time passes, you may have a drawer full of toys, a trunk full of costumes and a memoir's worth of naughty stories to write about when you're 80. Commitment, on the other hand, may be challenging here. This relationship may have the capacity to hold unconventional structures such as non-monogomy, polyamory or living in different locations. Just make sure every agreement is discussed and clarified.

And my personal Venus is in an earth sign
(TAURUS, VIRGO OR CAPRICORN):

Your prim and proper ways get a shakeup in this relationship, which demands open-mindedness and experimentation. Holding fast to your traditional values could short-circuit the pleasure, creativity and high-minded connection this union has to offer. Although you may need to pace yourself and choose a safe word, see what happens if you ease in to some of the kinkier opportunities available here.

And my personal Venus is in an air sign

(GEMINI, LIBRA, AQUARIUS):

At last, an opportunity to break out the liquid latex, fur-lined handcuffs and bondage-wear. This connection gets freaky fast, since no subject is off-limits and the propensity to say "Why not?" is amplified. But don't skip the aftercare or suppress emotions as they come up after swinging out of your comfort zone. Make room for processing time as part of your exploration.

And my personal Venus is in a water sign

(CANCER, SCORPIO OR PISCES):

In some ways, this relationship can feel lacking of the passion and emotional depth that is innately your M.O. However, there's a levity here that can be a relief. Through this relationship, you'll realize that seduction can be playful, humorous and fun as long as you have enough emotional reassurance (which incidentally, you may have to ask for). You'll delight in the frisky, freaky bedroom play. Role playing can also help bridge the gap: nurse-patient, detective-spy—oo la la!

If our Supercouple Venus is in a water sign:
(CANCER, SCORPIO OR PISCES)

And my personal Venus is in a fire sign
(ARIES, LEO OR SAGITTARIUS):

Turn down the heat! Coming on like a house on fire is NOT actually hot in this relationship. The real seduction happens in the deeper emotional bonding. You may have to hold back a little with your forward seduction style in the name of creating trust. Once a safe space is established, feel free to take charge. But always take time to connect emotionally before you shift into sexual mode.

And my personal Venus is in an earth sign
(TAURUS, VIRGO OR CAPRICORN):

Your tender, tactile seduction style will work like a charm, as long as you're both feeling emotionally connected. Touch is a powerful love language, one that can break you both out of verbal gridlocks and misunderstandings. However, you may be challenged to broaden your emotional range here in order to meet this relationship's desire for intimacy as a key component of the erotic equation.

And my personal Venus is in an air sign
(GEMINI, LIBRA, AQUARIUS):

Your experimental approach to seduction can be both exciting and destabilizing in this relationship. You may realize that your desire to talk about everything and anything fuels anxiety and insecurity, which in turn can feel suppressive. The trick is to frame these "wouldn't it be hot if?" conversations with reassuring statements like, "This is something I want to do with you."

And my personal Venus is in a water sign
(CANCER, SCORPIO OR PISCES):

TLC, tender gazes, tears and all—you'll feel safe letting it all hang out, and that is such a turn-on. Creatively, this is a dreamy match. You'll make art, music, drawing and creating beautiful spaces together part of your courtship dance. There's a risk of becoming SO emotionally enmeshed; however, that it dulls the sexual spark. Don't let your pillow talk turn into therapy sessions too often. A night or two away from each other every month can also bring an important reboot.

SUPERCOUPLE

MARS

our drive & sex life

Use Your Supercouple Mars to Understand:

- How to keep things sizzling in the bedroom
- The erotic hot spots to explore as a couple
- What triggers anger and frustration for the two of you
- How to negotiate different drives, especially physical ones (from exercise to sex)
- Where you'll be impatient or overreact when together
- Strategies to break past your comfort zone
- Ways to motivate yourselves into action
- What ambitious plans you'll have the energy to co-create (scaling mountains, renovating an 100-year-old cottage)

HOW DO YOU KEEP THE SEXY FIRES BURNING…WITHOUT BURNING DOWN THE RELATIONSHIP?

Human beings are animals, and our best intentions to be civilized can betray us when our primal levers get pulled. Lust, greed, wrath, envy, pride—most, if not all, of the Seven Deadly Sins could be filed under "Mars made me do it." Yet, Mars also supplies us with drive, motivation, and life force energy. It helps us keep our edges sharp and our sex drives humming. (Tali likes to call Mars the "planetary pelvic thrust.")

In your combined chart, Mars shows how your primal reactions will fire off. When your ancient brain tells you to fight, flee or fornicate, that blended Mars sign will step in as first responder. And you'll feel its influence from the bedroom to the battleground (which might be one and the same).

Mars the warrior doesn't back down from a challenge or a conflict. This physical and fearless planet leaps into the fray without looking. If you want to know where your buttons will get pushed—or where you'll both do something stupid and regrettable—the scarlet planet will occupy the hot seat and will be ego-driven enough to defend those wrongs instead of simply apologizing.

In traditional astrology, Mars is one of the "malefic" (harmful) planets, along with Saturn. While the ancients may have been more deterministic than we are, there's no denying that this planet has a shadow side. Your Composite Mars shows where you'll be impatient and possibly hurtful to each other. It reveals what you'll fight about and which issues could be hot-button topics. Red flags are served, courtesy of the red planet.

Here's what we love about Mars: The right dose of its yang energy can make a couple feeling hot and sexy, motivated to fight for the relationship. It keeps the edges sharp, the attraction sizzling. From a purely primal POV, Mars gets the procreation population multiplying, helping our wayward species carry on.

Like spice in a recipe, your Supercouple Mars should be considered an accent flavoring, not the whole dish. If it's a purely sexual thing, disregard this advice and lean into the lust until it's too hot to handle! But if you're in it for the long haul, think of Mars like the shiny red sports car in the garage–it's fun to take it out for a drive, but it can be fast and hard to control unless you really know how to operate it.

Supercouple MARS
IN THE ZODIAC SIGNS

In the Sign of	Makes Our Sexual Style	In Sync, We're...	Out of Sync, We're...
ARIES	Fiery	Passionate, exciting, assertive	Combative
TAURUS	Sensual	Tender, sensual, thoughtful	Stubborn
GEMINI	Stimulating	Flirtatious, provocative, handsy	Argumentative
CANCER	Intimate	Heartfelt, sentimental, nurturing	Guarded
LEO	Uninhibited	Bold, lavish, exciting, playful	Dominating
VIRGO	Attentive	Measured, tactile, eager to please	Anxious
LIBRA	Luxuriant	Pampering, affectionate	Resentful
SCORPIO	Soulful	All-consuming, enchanting, intimate	Ruthless
SAGITTARIUS	Limitless	Passionate, adventurous, daring	Competitive
CAPRICORN	Calculated	Tactile, sophisticated, deliberate	Businesslike
AQUARIUS	Unscripted	Unexpected, Quirky, Experimental	Commitment-phobic
PISCES	Healing	Transcendent, generous, fantasy-fueled	Self-sacrificing

♂

FIND YOUR SUPERCOUPLE MARS AT
SUPERCOUPLE.COM

Create your own Supercouple Chart at **SUPERCOUPLE.COM**

SUPERCOUPLE MARS
ARIES ✴ ♈

OR THE 1ST HOUSE

Our attraction is:

- Immediate
- Hot
- Passionate
- Physical
- Exciting
- Assertive
- Bold

On the scale of spiciness, there may not be enough chili peppers on the menu to rate the heat factor of a Supercouple Mars in Aries relationship. You probably felt an immediate click, that rush of energy from the other's presence. Suddenly, you were standing up straighter, twirling hair around your finger, and puffing up a little to make sure you were noticed. That's how explosively exciting this Composite Mars can be!

Since instinctual Mars is the natural ruler of Aries, there's a raw, sexual energy that ripples between you. No need to put this lust into words! Once the attraction is acknowledged, you'll be ripping each other's clothes off in a frenzy before you have a chance to formulate a poetic stanza about the other's irresistible body. While this "see it, want it, grab for it" ferocity may work in the beginning, as time goes on, you'll need to be careful you don't come on TOO strong and cross one another's boundaries. No two people are ever "in the mood" on exactly the same schedule, especially when life's responsibilities enter the realm of your ongoing relationship.

Since Aries rules the head, your noggins may be erogenous zones in this shared Mars connection. To get the sexy vibes flowing during a dry spell, start with a scalp massage, touch your partner's face seductively or draw them in to a mentally stimulating conversation. When the spirit of excitement has entered the room, you'll naturally gravitate to each other. From there, your animal natures will take over every damn time.

Heads turn when you two enter the room, although you might not actually notice. Generally, you're too engrossed in each other. Whether you're swapping exciting updates or shamelessly battling about whose opinion is right, you often forget to use your "inside voices." Warrior Mars is the ruling planet of fierce, take-no-prisoners Aries, which can be a double-edged sword. On the one hand, this Mars imbues you both with a straight-shooting confidence that you may not have access to before meeting each other. This relationship is absolutely an ego booster! However, the combative vibes can accelerate from zero to "bridge-burning drama" in record time.

To rescue this relationship from ruin, you'll both need to develop cool-down techniques, especially in moments when one of you seems to be picking a fight. (TBH, this will happen regularly, so be on guard for that sabotaging behavior!) Learn to call a timeout, pass a talking stick (one person shares at a time!) and schedule "appointments" to discuss triggering topics instead of dropping them on each other out of the blue. You might channel that anger into a passion project or an activist cause worth fighting for together—after you've both hit the gym hard!

SUPERCOUPLE MARS
TAURUS ✴ ♉
OR THE 2ND HOUSE

Our attraction is:

- Tender
- Slow-jamming
- Multi-sensory
- Thoughtfully planned
- Traditional

Sensuality is the "drug" in a Supercouple Mars in Taurus relationship. With the lusty planet in this tactile sign, good luck keeping your hands off each other. If you're not stroking palms, rubbing each other's legs or enjoying other skin-on-skin contact, you're probably delighting yourselves with rich edible delicacies, eye-popping visuals, dreamy aromas and anything else that falls squarely in the "earthly pleasures" category.

What can you say? For the two of you, attraction doesn't necessarily begin in the erotic realm. Stimulating your erogenous, body-based senses, on the other hand, gets things cooking—fast! Feed each other chocolate-dipped strawberries (in or out of bed) and the next thing you know, buttons start to come undone. Hopefully, you two will lean into this energy and bring this multi-sensory experience to the bedroom. Seduction is truly an art form in the Composite

Mars in Taurus connection! Scented candles, sexytime playlists, even feasts served in bed are totally on the menu here. Spa treatments too! Luxuriate with massage oils or a perfumed bubble bath, or splurge on side-by-side bodywork treatments. Since Taurus rules the throat, kissing one another's necks artfully could make you putty in each other's hands.

But it's not all hedonism all the time. Taurus is as sensible as it is sensual, and this Mars sign makes you industrious, practical and tenacious when you come together. As your relationship progresses, you'll work tirelessly to obtain financial security—mostly because of your shared desire to be comfortable, but also because, as a couple, you love enjoying the finer things in life together. When you've saved up enough to indulge, you two will spare no expense! Fortunately, your relationship inspires a diligent work ethic and the patience needed to keep the coffers full.

Having speed-demon Mars in the sign of the slow and steady Bull can be a bit of a paradox. Should you hit the gas or pump the brakes? It can be extremely agitating when one of wants to coast in autopilot while the other wants to burn rubber on the Autobahn! Extreme stubbornness is a pitfall of this Supercouple Mars placement: When disagreements arise, you may both dig in your heels and refuse to budge. Or you may get so settled in "workability" to the point of getting stuck in a rut. It might take a wise family member or a couple's therapist to pull you out of that hole and set you off on a more productive path.

What upsets you two most, however, is when your material needs aren't being met. But with a Supercouple Mars in Taurus, you also realize that laying a solid foundation takes time. While you're building your shared dream, you may need to hold down nine-to-five jobs that keep food on the table. Just be careful not to swing to the opposite extreme. Being overly cautious can limit your wealth-building goals, so it may be wise to develop a greater risk appetite together.

Create your own Supercouple Chart at **SUPERCOUPLE.COM**

SUPERCOUPLE MARS
GEMINI ✳ ♊
OR THE 3RD HOUSE

Our attraction is:

- Flirtatious
- Communicative
- Provocative
- Teasing
- Spontaneous
- Activity-based

With Supercouple Mars in Gemini, the way to the heart (and the bed!) is through the mind. With the passion planet mixing it up in the zodiac's wittiest sign, it won't take much more than clever banter to get you two hot and bothered. Intellectually stimulating dialogue? That's almost as good as sex...and if you throw in a heated debate, you're verging on orgasmic terrain. With warrior Mars in this expressive sign, daring to challenge one another will be a major turn-on, and fiercely so, even if your values seem diametrically opposed!

But to keep the fires burning for the long haul, there must also be plenty of common ground. With Mars in the sign of the Twins, it's worth putting in the effort to find those areas where you are on the same page. Then, turn them into a shared obsession that you can pursue as a pair. Do you both have a thing for Marvel movies? Next up: themed Halloween costumes and a yearly trip to ComicCon. Both love to cook? Start a roving supper club with mutual friends and save up for a food tour of your favorite Italian region. Become the couple that plays together...and slays together!

Along with communication, dextrous Gemini rules the hands and arms. With lusty Mars in this analytical placement, you'll love touching each other and talking about each caress. "How does this feel?" and "Faster or slower?" There's no need to leave anything to guesswork in this union. Roaming fingertips can be your favorite playtime activity together—and besides sending one another into paroxysms of pleasure, this relationship may inspire you both to start making things by hand. (And yes, sewing sexy fetishwear absolutely counts!)

The two of you may text each other all throughout the day: Mars in Gemini relationships have a lot to say! In this pairing, you've found your "other half," someone who you are eager to share every detail with. Caveat: Mars in Gemini can make you both argumentative and sometimes prone to flying off the handle about minor grievances. Usually, this is a result of not vocalizing your needs or clarifying your feelings. It can help to regularly scribble some of those thoughts in a journal—or to engage in talk therapy that can allow you to make sense of those jumbled up thoughts moving between you both at lightning speed.

At the end of the day, your "best friends with benefits" chemistry is the glue that keeps you together. But even in Gemini, lusty Mars needs sparks to fly—so don't get complacent about creating them. Even if you CAN be around each other 24/7 without getting bored, set some limits, or your sex life may suffer. You don't want to get SO used to each other that you fall into lazy habits. In this relationship, make an effort to nurture friendships with the people who were in your life before you met. Supercouple Mars in Gemini is naturally curious, and there's nothing hotter than a little bit of mystery!

SUPERCOUPLE MARS
CANCER ✳ ♋

OR THE 4TH HOUSE

Our attraction is:

- Heartfelt
- Sentimental
- Attentive
- Caretaking
- Intimate
- Affectionate
- Moody

Lower the blinds, turn up the slow jams. Home is where the HEAT is for relationships with Supercouple Mars in private, domestic Cancer. This relationship is at its sultriest behind closed doors. In the early stages of your connection, you'll count down the minutes until you can race back to your private enclave and have your way with each other. With the right playlists and sensual bedding, these bodice-ripping sessions can go on for hours.

As a couple, you two rule in the kitchen, the bedroom and every room in between—whether you're artfully preparing a gourmet feast or whipping off layers of clothing, and then "power cuddling" after marathon lovemaking. No apologies for wanting to be tightly held! Cancer is the zodiac's most nurturing (even maternal) sign, and this Composite Mars placement can churn up the very human urge to be cradled like a baby. It's kind of like being in a sensual crab shell. Even if, independently, you aren't super affectionate, you may suddenly morph into the clingiest "little spoon" in town. The feeling of safety can be a huge turn-on in the Mars in Cancer relationship. And, hey, it doesn't hurt that physical touch releases the feel-good, bonding hormone oxytocin. As you grow to trust each other with your tender emotions, you can't get close enough!

During courtship, it's likely that you wooed each other with home-cooked meals and nostalgic tales of your childhoods. Once you finally feel safe enough to drop your guards and get physical—which can take a little while for this guarded Mars—sex should always have an element of tenderness. Gaze into each other's eyes and use words of affirmation, even if you're pulling their hair or administering a sexy little spank.

Nesting and building a family is often a primary goal for Mars in Cancer—if not with kids, then with pets. As a pair, you are fiercely protective of your loved ones. No one crosses your crew without feeling some serious retribution. If your biological families didn't provide a safe haven, you may spend your adult lives remixing the past by creating a "chosen family" and being the ultimate caretakers for those you love.

Warning: With aggro Mars in this emo water sign, moods can run hot and cold when you're together. Mars is "in fall" in Cancer, meaning this is one of the more challenging zodiac signs for the red planet to be housed in. It makes sense: Mars is fierce and flamboyant while Cancer is nurturing and private. With such a paradox afoot, you may serve each other a prickly outer shell when you're feeling your most sensitive. Learn to drop your defenses and ask for what you need—without throwing an accusatory jab or coming from a place of suspicion and doubt. Passive-aggressiveness can cut both of you deeply in this relationship, so avoid it at all costs!

Another thing to look out for? Triggering each other's family issues. What attracts you to each other may indeed be wrapped up in some intergenerational healing. Perhaps you remind the other of a beloved parent—or fill in the gaps where a negligent caretaker was remiss. Tread lightly with this dynamic, should it arise. Not only can it steal the sexiness from your bond, but it can lead you down a path of projection and codependence that will take hours of therapy to untangle.

SUPERCOUPLE MARS
LEO ✳ ♌
OR THE 5TH HOUSE

Our attraction is:

- Palpable
- Theatrical
- Uninhibited
- Bold
- Playful
- Lavish
- Exciting

With Supercouple Mars in theatrical Leo, the world isn't just your oyster, it's your shared stage! This expressive placement makes you a flamboyant and magnanimous pair who steal the show when you step into any room. Whether you're grabbing first prize in a costume competition or bringing down the house with your karaoke duet of *Islands In The Stream,* you'll bring out the daredevils in one another. With the childlike wonder this Mars stirs up, life becomes seriously FUN again! As a couple, you can be counted on to pump up the passion in any social situation.

When together, you rarely hit the "off" button. And why should you when there are so many entertaining avenues to explore on the goddess' green Earth? Pleasure and playtime are what this hedonistic Composite Mars sign lives for. From lavish vacations to spontaneous road trips (with detours for hand-dipped ice cream and live DJ sets you discovered while flicking through Instagram) you're like a pair of kids when together. Just make sure you consider things like budgets and timelines. It's easy to get carried away by the magic of the moment, but that gets expensive! And there are only so many morning meetings you can reschedule due to "a wild night out" before eyebrows are raised and reprimands roll in.

Leo rules the heart and upper back, which are two erotic zones for this Mars connection to explore. When you need to get in the mood, take turns giving each other massages with warming oils—and don't be surprised if you only make it partway through the "treatment" before flipping over for deep, sensual kisses. Sit, cross-legged, with your hands on each other's hearts while you lock into a deep gaze. While some people may be too giggly to pull off such an intimate exercise, you two could ride the electromagnetic waves of bliss right into each other's souls.

The zodiac's Lion thrives on praise so with Mars in Leo, words of affirmation are a love language to use liberally. But watch out! It's one thing to desire validation, but when you become hooked on each other's approval, resentment can follow. As a couple, make sure you share the stage—and the power! The same people who love what leaders you both are may see you as dominating if you take charge too often. You're at your best when you're working together for a noble purpose instead of the shiny gold star. (Not that you can't have both.)

The Mars in Leo relationship values rituals, especially ones that can be done in public. Those early date nights had better give you both bragging rights when you're debriefing around the brunch table. There's no room for being cheap or unromantic in this pairing. Get ready to send and receive all the works: red roses delivered to the office, serenades outside your bedroom window, and dress-up dates that peg you as the power couple about town.

SUPERCOUPLE MARS

VIRGO ✦ ♍

OR THE 6TH HOUSE

Our attraction is:

- Attentive
- Ritualistic
- Measured
- Fussy
- Tactile
- Service-oriented and pleasing

♂

Details, details! With Supercouple Mars in fastidious Virgo, the "little things" are everything. This placement brings out the curator and critic in you both. Finer points that you glossed over in the past may become glaringly evident in this connection, which drives you both to be your absolute, personal best. Bottom line: Everything can and should be improved as far as you two are concerned! But you're not trying to be fussy or difficult. Mars in Virgo makes this relationship service-oriented by nature. Together, you'll work to make your corner of the world a safe and ethical place where every member of the community has a voice.

Rising to this elevated status can be a double-edged sword. On the one hand, this relationship will wipe away any willingness to "settle" for less than what you can achieve. But it can also bring out a sense of elitism and entitlement—yes, even when you're trying to do the right thing. The woke perspective you two eschew may indeed be "correct," but watch your delivery! As a pair, you can come across as judgmental and holier-than-thou if you aren't careful. Even if people resist listening at first, they inevitably admit that you two were right. Just try not to hammer them with the "I told you so's" when they do, or hold them to unrealistic expectations!

With athletic Mars in wellness-fixated Virgo, taking great care of your bodies may become an obsession. Get that buddy pass for the gym or yoga studio—and share a punchcard at the cold-pressed, organic juice bar while you're at it. Should this go-getter Mars lead you in an enterprising direction, you might even find your fortune together in the wellness world, guiding people to improve their lives on every level. Warning: An obsession with going "clean and green" can go overboard, turning you into a controlling pair. Learn to loosen up and enjoy a "cheat day" here and there...with food and drink, that is!

Analyze this! You will study each other's habits like scientists in a lab, thanks to Mars in investigative Virgo. If you catch your partner quietly observing you, don't make it weird! In a short period of time, you both know exactly what the other wants, desires and needs, and you'll do everything in your power to please one another.

With Supercouple Mars in anxious Virgo, you two may require a clearly defined relationship status—perhaps before you even unzip a single item of clothing. And let's be real: Having the sign of the Virgin lord over your lustiness can be, well, contradictory. You both may need a relaxation ritual like meditation or non-sexual touch before you can move into the erotic space together. Clean sheets, pleasant scents and a freshly-showered and well-groomed partner are also musts for getting in the mood. And also privacy—cameras off, please.

The only exception? Virgo is an earth sign, so the great outdoors can be a true aphrodisiac. Pack a blanket in your backpack before you head off on a hike. You two may get so charged up that you have to slip off the trail for a spontaneous forest romp!

Create your own Supercouple Chart at **SUPERCOUPLE.COM**

SUPERCOUPLE MARS

LIBRA ✦ ♎

OR THE 7TH HOUSE

Our attraction is:

- Luxurious
- Glamorous
- Leisurely
- Sweetly romantic
- Easygoing
- Affectionate
- Showy

♂

Why can't the honeymoon phase last forever? For couples with Supercouple Mars in Libra, a lifelong fairy tale is the goal. And why not? With this ultra-romantic sign governing your lust profile, it only makes sense that wining and dining is the precursor to mind-blowing sex. Foreplay happens long before you make it to the bedroom. And it often begins with oversized bouquets, five-star dinners, and two tickets to an incredible show, ideally in the VIP section. The boudoir experience isn't hot unless it's *haute*. So make a budget! You'll be spending a pretty penny on luxe scented candles, fine lingerie and silver serving trays for your breakfasts in bed.

Facts: Spoiling each other may become a competitive sport in this relationship. But if the scorecard gets uneven, look out! Libra is symbolized by the Scales. With feisty Mars here, keep the give and take as balanced as possible. If you've been a "pillow princess" or a "quickie king" in past relationships, you'd better step up your game pronto! Lie back and enjoy the pleasure when it's your turn to receive, but don't even think about slipping into a nap until you've both had your O. Another option? Take turns being the pleaser and the pleased of each "session," so that you can each lose yourselves in the sensual frequency. Just make sure to swap roles frequently so you're both getting your fill. (Is there a tracking app for that?)

Since Libra rules the, er, lower back, you two enjoy a different kind of booty call. Squeeze it, grab it, spank it, peg it—wherever the comfort level lies for you two, this Supercouple Mars will make you both "ass obsessed." Now, where is that feather tickler riding crop?

Want to keep it hot for the long haul? Aesthetics are a big deal for couples with Mars in beauty-loving Libra. At its best, this relationship inspires you both to get (and stay) in shape, dress in flattering clothing and decorate every square inch of your shared home as if it was a designer showroom. Your life together may be adorned with enough decadent accoutrements to make the love goddess Venus (Libra's ruling star) a tad envious. At worst, however, your bond can skew superficial with too much emphasis on how you look together and not enough on how you actually feel about each other. If you don't want to be each other's "starter spouse," you two will need to develop realistic standards around things like aging, weight gain and the normal evolutions we all go through in life.

But here's the real paradox you'll need to navigate. Mars is the planet of combat while Libra is the sign of harmony. With the red planet in this placement, this may be a relationship of "peaceful warriors." But it can also be challenging to synthesize those two forces: Astrologers say that Mars is in "detriment" in Libra because this zodiac sign is actually opposite on the horoscope wheel from Aries, the sign that Mars rules. Unhappiness may hide behind a false cheer, but you can only say, "I'm fine!" so many times before the sparks begin to dull. Rather than suppressing natural disagreements that arise between couples, you two should consciously cultivate tools for resolving conflicts. We suggest Nonviolent Communication, developed by compassionate Libra Marshall Rosenberg, one of the most validating methodologies for co-understanding that we know!

Find healthy outlets to release any pent-up rage, too. But since anything that isn't beautiful can make your skin crawl, try singing! Belting out a power ballad at karaoke or in your car might be the best outlet—and a calming breathwork exercise, to boot. Dancing together can also be a great release. Libra is an air sign, so do what you can to keep the current moving, and your bond will never grow stale.

SUPERCOUPLE MARS

SCORPIO ✶ ♏

OR THE 8TH HOUSE

Our attraction is:

- Mysterious
- Enchanting
- Sacred
- Intimate
- Soulful
- Purposeful
- Erotically intense

Too much intensity? There's no such thing for relationships with Supercouple Mars in Scorpio. As a couple, you dial up the passion to Level: Extreme. Why chuckle wryly when you can laugh so hard that you feel like you took five consecutive abs classes? And what's the point of a surface connection when, together, you plumb the depths of the universe and uncover life's full-bodied pleasures?

Until you met each other, you may not have realized such a range was possible! Here you've found someone you can be truly vulnerable with. You can drop your guard safely and confess secrets you thought you'd take to the grave. So potent is the Composite Mars in Scorpio attraction that you might forget that the rest of the world exists—at least in the early stages of your relationship. We can't blame you! But as incredible as it feels to be stripped of your ego defenses, then witnessed, adored and ravaged for your soul's essence, you'll need to come up for air...eventually.

If you don't, look out! There's a thin line between love and hate for Scorpio. The same gaze that vaulted you up on a high-priestess' pedestal can rake you over the most critical coals. Translation? Take breaks regularly, even if you have to tear away from each other.

There truly is such a thing as "too close for comfort" with Mars in Scorpio. Without realizing it, you may begin to engulf the other, growing possessive, even controlling. And that's where the trouble begins. Should one of you feel stung by rejection, interactions can turn cruel fast. Mars in Scorpio is not famous for emotional restraint, whether in the throes of joyful lust or the fury of scorn. But in both moments, the heat can break temperature records, and by extension, "break" the relationship. Pro tip: Master the pause between trigger and response. You may need to get as far away from each other as you can when you feel irritation building. "Taking space" will be the saving grace for you two.

A blessing of the Mars in Scorpio Supercouple? Once you've cooled down a bit, you're a pair who can actually work things out in the "arena," as Scorpio Brené Brown calls it. And for you two, the arena might be a king-sized bed. Intensifier Mars is actually happy in the passionate sign of Scorpio; in fact before astronomers knew that Pluto (Scorpio's ruling star) existed, Mars was considered the ruling planet of Scorpio, along with Aries. Sex is the lifeblood of your relationship. But with Mars in this deeply private sign, you two may only turn on your full-tilt eroticism behind closed doors. That said, you're certainly not anti-PDA! To seduce each other, you may dress in sexy clothes that fit your bodies well and show off your creative flair. You'll be an appreciative audience for one another!

Asterisk: Mars in Scorpio relationships have periodic phases of celibacy—particularly when the two of you are pouring your energy into a shared mission like moving house, raising an infant or tackling a business venture together.

When it comes to your shared drive, you draw from a deep well and regenerate more quickly than many. Most people can't keep up with your productivity together—and when the two of you put a goal in your crosshairs, you'll work tirelessly to pursue it. Be careful not to get ruthless and single-minded in your quest. That's often when the sexual fire goes out. A lack of physical interactivity is a solid warning light. Have you become a little too obsessed about achieving a goal? Hire a babysitter, loosen up your timelines, or go on a long weekend vacation. Fun can be easily forgotten in this relationship, but it's as vital a "vitamin" as anything else!

If and when it's ever time to call it quits, brace yourself for a drawn-out process. Goodbyes are especially hard for you two. Supercouple Mars in play-for-keeps Scorpio can make you possessive AND obsessive about each other. Even if you've followed every step of the "Conscious Uncoupling" protocol, parting may still feel like you're ripping out a piece of your soul. One thing's for sure, this transformational relationship will have a lifelong impact on you!

SUPERCOUPLE MARS

SAGITTARIUS ✳ ♐

OR THE 9TH HOUSE

Our attraction is:

- Forward
- Obvious
- In-the-moment
- Passionate
- Flamboyant
- Adventure-based
- Daring

Wise, wild and free! That's the trinity that a courage-boosting Supercouple Mars in Sagittarius is sure to deliver. No matter how singular your focus was before you met, this relationship is sure to expand your horizons. Bye-bye, comfort zone. You've met the person with whom you can explore every corner of this rich and beautiful planet. From its geographic wonders to its ancient philosophies, you'll want to soak it all up before your time here is done. How exhilarating!

Limits? What are those! The ceiling can't hold the Composite Mars in Sagittarius relationship, which needs lots of movement and physical activity. Globetrotting Sagittarius rules travel, and you two are happiest while on the road together, whether you're meandering along a cobblestone street in Rome or slipping off to a Tanzanian wildlife preserve. Athletic challenges—especially in the great outdoors—are a great way to bond. Think: hiking, mountain climbing, bike riding and camping. Mars is competitive and you two may be fierce on the court AND in the stands cheering on your favorite team!

Speaking of limits, Sagittarius isn't exactly a fan of being reined in sexually. With Mars here, you may be a couple who prefers non-monogamy or needs to create a few "allowances" around flirting with other people (within agreed-upon bounds). You can't help but arouse each other's lust for life, which may be so powerful that it spills out beyond the confines of your relationship. Better to be open about your desires than to sneak around—especially since Sagittarius is the sign of candor and honesty. Even if you both feel like the one-person type when you're together, you'll each need lots of autonomy within the relationship to develop your personal hobbies, and connect to all the fascinating humans on planet Earth.

All the same, fidelity is as essential for you two wanderers as it is for any other couple. Finding a non-sexual outlet for all that lusty energy can keep your commitment strong. Whether you work it out at ecstatic dance or volunteer to build houses in impoverished nations is up to you. Having a high-minded focus is always helpful for this Supercouple Mars since Sagittarius is an idealistic sign that wants to make the world a beautiful place for everyone.

When you two get into an optimistic flow, no one can hold you down! With warrior Mars in expansive Sagittarius, you're a pair of "no limits soldiers" who will go to battle for the people and principles you both hold dear. But easy does it with the gambling! This capricious cosmic energy can make you a pair of daredevils who take unnecessary

Create your own Supercouple Chart at **SUPERCOUPLE.COM**

risks with your finances AND your personal safety. Living for the moment—or even for some lofty goal—could complicate your future together if you don't take practical considerations into account. But your bounceback rate is also higher than most—lucky for both of you!

Each of you appreciates being with someone who is a little bit of a challenge—strong-willed and able to stand up to you. So no people-pleasing, unless you want to kill the magic. With this fiery Mars, you're better off staying in a conflict until it's resolved than backing down to keep the peace. Having a solid spiritual connection to your partner is also a must. The aphrodisiac in this relationship: contemplating the meaning of life together while cuddling under the stars.

Because of your shared boundless craving for thrilling experiences, you might get a rush from making out together in semi-public places and "almost" getting caught—or literally being observed in the act. Sagittarius rules the hips and thighs, and these areas can be total erogenous zones—and quite possibly the reason why you two may have met on the dance floor!

SUPERCOUPLE MARS
CAPRICORN ✴ ♑
OR THE 10TH HOUSE

Our attraction is:

- Lusty
- Persistent
- Sophisticated
- Undercover freaky
- Challenge-loving
- Has stamina and endurance
- Calculated

Can't stop, won't stop! That's the motto of Composite Mars in Capricorn. Having the warrior planet in this driven, ambitious zodiac sign blesses you with VIP power couple status. Success is in your shared destiny! And if you stick together for the long haul, you'll leave a legacy behind you. But no matter how brief your time together is, look out, world! When you set your sights on a worthy goal as a couple, you will work tirelessly to achieve it, your tanks filled with rocket fuel.

Mars is said to be "exalted" in Capricorn, its luckiest placement in the zodiac. Like a double-dose of high-achiever energy, this Composite Mars boosts Capricorn's inherent qualities: persistence, leadership, industriousness and wealth-accruing skills. Capricorn is symbolized by the mythical Sea Goat and having Composite Mars here gifts you with a special brand of magic as a pair. Together, you are as creative as you are productive, drawing inspiration from a deep well, then finessing it to the heights of success.

Warning: your relationship can get SO mission-driven that the
romantic, pleasurable aspects take a backseat. Learn to enjoy
the moment instead of always fixating on that future "someday"
where you'll feel as if you've "arrived." But will that someday ever
come? With Composite Mars in Capricorn, you two are prone to
eternally raising the bar. Plus, life comes with no guarantees. Make a
practice of going on weekly dates, taking regular vacations and even
setting "zero work allowed" hours to just focus on unwinding and
connecting through playful activities. Capricorn energy thrives with
structure—and that goes for extracurriculars too. To ensure that the
two of you engage in delicious bonding activities, schedule it! Join a
pickle ball league, natural wines club or take a three-month seminar
together. Anything that brings in a new subject matter besides work,
work, work!

Sexually, this relationship can be a force of nature. When you
channel your drive toward erotic pleasures, it's on, baby! The
legendary lovemaking can last all night—and this Composite Mars
can give you insatiable appetites for each other. Choose your safe
word! In bed, you may enjoy role-playing different power dynamics
together, even switching from "top" to "sub" depending on the day.
Light bondage or full-on BDSM could add to the fun—and it can
be a relief to cede control in the bedroom after taking charge in the
office all day. Capricorn rules the skin, bones and teeth. Sensual
touch and massages can be turn-ons in this relationship—and so can
those gentle (or not so-gentle) bites!

But you can also go long spells without sex! In the book *Think And
Grow Rich*, author Napoleon Hill wrote of "the transmutation of sex
energy," postulating that the same energy used for sex is required
to fuel the creative genius—and that periods of abstinence are
advisable for those wishing to develop their magnum opus. You both
may understand this concept when you're in the energy of your
connection, indulging in the pleasure principle "by season" instead
of at will.

©2022 Astrostyle. All rights reserved.

THE ASTROTWINS   283

SUPERCOUPLE MARS
AQUARIUS

OR THE 11TH HOUSE

Our attraction is:

- Refreshingly unexpected
- Mind-melding (sapiosexual)
- Quirky
- Experimental (including rechargeable devices)
- Unscripted (even random)
- Casual

Ready to break the mold? The "weird" is wonderful in relationships with Supercouple Mars in Aquarius. No matter how buttoned-up you've been in the past, when you come together, restrictions loosen. Aquarius is the great experimenter of the zodiac and your relationship is the hottest "lab" in town. Get ready to meet an alter ego (or three!) and have the most memorable erotic exploration of your life. Inside this passionate petrie dish, it's safe to go from vanilla to kinky and play every role in between. Building up a toy drawer and a costume chest can bring playful fun and wacky humor to the bedroom: an awesome bonding agent in this relationship! The calves and ankles are erogenous zones for this Mars sign, and you two may be crazy about each other's legs.

Create your own Supercouple Chart at **SUPERCOUPLE.COM**

Idealistic, futuristic Aquarius is the sign of social progress. With warrior Mars here, you'll fuel each other's passion for making the world a better place. Along with vibrating toys and latex fetishwear, a bullhorn and picket sign may be accessories the two of you can't live without. When you join forces, you become gifted organizers with the motivational powers of pep-squad co-captains. And once people get a taste of that electrifying enthusiasm—Aquarius is the sign that governs electricity, in fact—they'll engage in any mission, whether caravanning to a music festival or heading to a capital city for a protest.

When it comes to commitment, Composite Mars in Aquarius may skew your relationship in an open-minded direction. The desire for "universal love" might be stronger than the need for monogamy, which makes it challenging to "settle down." The truth? Conventional moires of relationships may feel confining to you both. This Supercouple Mars energy allows you two to fully adore more than one person at a time—provided you maintain a tight and trustworthy bond with each other. For this reason, you may opt for an open relationship or polyamory.

Of course there are other influences in the astrological chart that affect love, like your Supercouple Moon and Venus signs, so you two may indeed prefer the one-on-one. All the same, this relationship will not survive if the rules get too rigid. Make some clear agreements and stay in communication before, during and after you "play" outside your partnership. Maybe you won't get jealous if one of you dives into the occasional cuddle puddle or kisses someone on the dance floor. A level of casualness is a hallmark of Mars in Aquarius, and you'll be each other's BFFs even if your days as lovers are numbered. With the rich social life this Mars creates, you may regularly invite your squad to tag along on your supposed date nights.

Just make sure you aren't using these edgy explorations to avoid closeness! Cool-as-a-cucumber Aquarius isn't so comfortable with the "scary" terrain of conflicting emotions. Intimacy and vulnerability may be skills you have to work toward developing together, even using a "model" of sorts, like the "10 Guideposts for Wholehearted Living" laid out in Brené Brown's *Daring Greatly*. Ease into emotional subject matter bit by bit, but don't avoid it! It can help to take an academic approach, if you must. This intellectual Mars will love pontification about the way the brain does love. Check out the work of anthropologist Helen Fisher, who has researched the science behind attraction. This is the sexiest pillow talk you two can nerd out on while you're lounging in post-coital bliss.

SUPERCOUPLE MARS
PISCES ✳ ♓
OR THE 12TH HOUSE

Our attraction is:

- All-encompassing
- Fantasy-weaving
- Transcendent
- Addicting
- Ephemeral
- Nurturing
- Sexually healing

So. Many. Feelings. With Supercouple Mars in the compassionate sign of Pisces, you are quintessential romantics—and this relationship is your one-way ticket to cloud nine. At last! You've found the soul-nourishing connection that elevates you to your highest selves. Plus, it feels like a straight-up fairy tale. During the dating phase, there's no shortage of prolonged eye gazing and worshipping each other's bodies. Dreamy, watery Pisces is the sign of escape and you're bound to go where neither of you has before.

Who wants to play footsies? Pisces is the last sign of the zodiac and rules the feet. The Composite Mars in Pisces may give you two a full-on foot fetish (not to mention a shoe fetish) for each other. Maybe you'll enjoy some pedi-pleasures as foreplay. Pisces is the sign of fantasy, and this Mars supplies rich imagination in the bedroom. Costumes, role-playing, blindfolds and handcuffs—that's just the beginning!

You may plunge "below the surface" to get your erotic fix. The taboo can be a turn-on for a couple with Mars in Pisces, but careful not to get sucked into anything unsavory or addictive. Boundaries are hard to maintain in this relationship. While you may think it's "no big deal" to experiment in ways that you haven't before, tread lightly. It's a slippery slope when the zodiac's Fish gets involved. Don't underestimate the emotional impact something like, say, having a threesome or making a sex tape, will have on you.

Mars is the planet of pursuit, and in ultra-romantic Pisces you can be SO focused on winning over (and pleasing!) each other that other areas of your life begin to suffer. It's a wonderful thing to be swept away, but watch out! Mars in Pisces comes with a lifeguard's warning. Drift too far away from the shore of reality and you risk drowning. In this relationship, you will need to work harder to keep healthy structures in place. It's too easy to lose track of time, staying up all night binging rom-coms or having champagne-fueled (and utterly mind-blowing) sex. But showing up late for work, slipping on responsibilities and forgetting to pay the bills? This is the spiral that a Mars in Pisces Supercouple can tumble down when you let go a little too much.

Because Pisces is the sign of healing, you may come together during a particularly hard time in your lives. One or both of you may have suffered a loss or trauma; maybe you were struggling with depression or loneliness. At first, your relationship is like a magic salve, taking your mind off a persistent pain that you couldn't shake...until now. Alas, that emotional bypass is a temporary shortcut. It takes time to metabolize grief, trauma, anger or any "shadow" emotion, and there's no accelerating the process.

A wiser use for your shared Mars in Pisces? Empower each other to do your individual healing. Once you learn to detach, set boundaries and to "shield your field," you'll enjoy a new level of serenity in this relationship. Plus, you can always cheer the other on from the front row of the bleachers! Remember, you're supposed to be partners, not the object of the other's rescue mission. Plus, absence makes the heart grow fonder with Supercouple Mars in "ebb and flow" Pisces. Be sure to both create ample solitary time for meditative activities like journaling, gardening, swimming (a Pisces pleasure) and listening to soothing music. And of course, come together to do the relationship's work, providing generous listening and the best hugs you've ever had in your life.

♂

SUPERCOUPLE
Compatibility
WITH YOUR
MARS SIGN

Create your own Supercouple Chart at **SUPERCOUPLE.COM**

If our Supercouple Mars is in a fire sign:
(ARIES, LEO OR SAGITTARIUS)

And my personal Mars is in a fire sign
(ARIES, LEO OR SAGITTARIUS):

There's no such thing as "extra" here! Quite the contrary—your lust for life is amplified in this adrenaline-pumping relationship. Things can get too hot to handle sometimes, and your spirited debates can turn into a battle of wills pretty quickly if you don't temper your my-way-or-the-highway attitude.

And my personal Mars is in an earth sign
(TAURUS, VIRGO OR CAPRICORN):

If you can't stand the heat, should you get out of the kitchen? You might wonder that often, since this relationship is sure to get you more fired up than you're accustomed to being on your own. As exciting as it is, you may feel like plans and physicality are moving too fast. But you may also be the one who is always hitting the brakes or trying to cool things down.

And my personal Mars is in an air sign
(GEMINI, LIBRA, AQUARIUS):

Whee! This relationship can be nonstop fun and adventure, setting some of your wild ideas into motion. Your daring side comes out to play, especially when you're socializing or traveling together. Just don't lose sight of safety measures in the heat of the moment.

And my personal Mars is in a water sign
(CANCER, SCORPIO OR PISCES):

In many ways, you'll feel out of your element here, as if the relationship moves at a very different pace than you prefer. Normally you would take your time to feel things out, but here, you drop your guard and expose personal intel faster than usual. You may have to nurse a few vulnerability hangovers before you find your footing. But if you establish trust here, you'll love how intimate this bond can become.

If our Supercouple Mars is in an earth sign:
(TAURUS, VIRGO, OR CAPRICORN)

And my personal Mars is in a fire sign
(ARIES, LEO OR SAGITTARIUS):

This relationship is like a stable hearth that you warm with your caring, expressive energy. You may feel more grounded emotionally than you're used to, which can provoke some rebellion if you feel TOO secure. You might even pick fights to keep things "interesting," so check yourself! Building something together can be your saving grace, whether it's a family or a business.

And my personal Mars is in an earth sign
(TAURUS, VIRGO OR CAPRICORN):

What can't the two of you accomplish together? This relationship revs up your natural inclination to provide lasting stability and material comfort. Careful that you don't get too formulaic or rigid—or else the sparks can fizzle!

And my personal Mars is in an air sign
(GEMINI, LIBRA, AQUARIUS):

Your free-flowing work style can feel restricted in this partnership, which demands certain outcomes—a direct opposition to your experimental "let's see what happens" style. The gift, however, is that by learning to be more structured, this relationship helps bring your half-completed ideas to the finish line.

And my personal Mars is in a water sign
(CANCER, SCORPIO OR PISCES):

This relationship can serve as a stable container for your dreamy ideas, which may become profitable quickly if this is a business relationship, or materialize into something tangible like creating a home or growing a family. At times, however, you may feel like your emotions are dulled by the practical vibe of this shared Mars. Careful not to start drama just to keep things "exciting."

If our Supercouple Mars is in an air sign:
(GEMINI, LIBRA, AQUARIUS)

And my personal Mars is in a fire sign
(ARIES, LEO OR SAGITTARIUS):

This relationship will either fan the flames of desire and excitement or put them out before they've built into a passionate pyre. Here you learn to think a little more before you act, which can be a good thing, at least for your wallet, schedule and reputation. The excitement may be more conversational than physical. Don't be afraid to bring more daring, tactile energy into the mix if you find it lacking.

And my personal Mars is in an earth sign
(TAURUS, VIRGO OR CAPRICORN):

All talk and no action? In some ways it may take longer for you to achieve liftoff in this relationship, because it may feel unmooring or destabilizing to race off in pursuit of lofty goals. Indeed, you may have to be the planner here, or the one who makes sure all these exciting dreams and ideas actually become something tangible. Bring your earthy sensuality into the mix when things get too heady.

And my personal Mars is in an air sign
(GEMINI, LIBRA, AQUARIUS):

Up, up and away! This relationship is a booster pack for your already enthusiastic, visionary nature. As a partnership it will be playful and experimental in a way that you love. Just make sure the two of you come down from the clouds sometimes, so that it doesn't turn into an all-talk, no-action situation.

And my personal Mars is in a water sign
(CANCER, SCORPIO OR PISCES):

Finding connection points is the key to unlocking the passion here. Without common interests or a shared mission, you may always feel like you're "too emotional" or grasping for validation. In some ways this relationship can teach you emotional restraint and temper your tendency to retreat quickly and hide out. The more you verbalize your needs, the more fulfilling this relationship becomes.

If our Supercouple Mars is in a water sign:
(CANCER, SCORPIO OR PISCES)

And my personal Mars is in a fire sign
(ARIES, LEO OR SAGITTARIUS):

Where there's smoke, there's fire, right? Not necessarily! This relationship can throw cold water on your enthusiasm, but it's actually teaching you a different way of expressing your passions. While you might normally charge in, throw spaghetti at the wall, and see what sticks, this union shows that your actions have an emotional impact, something you might not have considered so seriously before.

And my personal Mars is in an earth sign
(TAURUS, VIRGO OR CAPRICORN):

This relationship brings the flow back into your life—and the chemistry here is palpable. Suddenly you feel safe opening up, sharing your feelings and being a little less practical than you normally would be. This is a great place to nurture your dreams and do everything with a lot more feeling than you would on your own.

And my personal Mars is in an air sign

(GEMINI, LIBRA, AQUARIUS):

In moments, this connection can feel like a downer. You're all about experimentation, exploration and novel ideas, but the passion principle here centers around creating security and doing things the safe way. Do your research and collect the data! Then, this relationship becomes a wishing well that you can dip your bucket into and draw up prosperity and abundance—along with gallons of emotional support!

And my personal Mars is in a water sign
(CANCER, SCORPIO OR PISCES):

What a sweet sentimental symphony! This relationship was orchestrated to bring out your passionate, romantic nature and expand your feelings into the vastness of the ocean. You'll feel secure unleashing your creativity, sharing your feelings and letting yourself get messy and vulnerable. It's great that you're not so guarded and defensive. Just try not to let your sense of humor get washed away!

SUPERCOUPLE

JUPITER

our luck & opportunity

4

> Use Your Supercouple Jupiter to Understand:
>
> - Where you're lucky as a duo
> - Growth opportunities you can tap into
> - What inspires you when you're together
> - Best places and ways to travel
> - Where you'll feel optimistic as a duo
> - The risks or gambles you'll take
> - When to take a leap of faith with each other
> - How to combine your visionary powers

WHERE WILL YOU GROW AND BE LUCKY TOGETHER?

Every relationship needs a vision, something to believe in. An adventurous, "look what we did!" outlook that keeps you inspired and fist-bumping like the badass co-conspirators you are.

When you want to get high on your own supply of #CoupleGoals, you'll get plenty of support from Composite Jupiter. The joyful and abundant planet rewards you for taking risks. It serves up megadoses of good fortune and reminds you why you came together in the first place.

It also shows you where you might be headed next! As the global nomad of the skies, Jupiter is the planet that pushes you out of your comfort zones and off to explore new vistas. Use it to dream up a list of places you'll travel to together. Sidenote: Due to Jupiter's penchant for blithe optimism, lean into Composite Mercury and Saturn when it comes to actually planning those trips.

Your Supercouple Jupiter will give you a lofty vision to strive for. It's the planetary pop-up reminder that there's something way bigger than

Create your own Supercouple Chart at **SUPERCOUPLE.COM**

all of "this." (Why ARE you squabbling over petty B.S. like pulling lint out of the dryer box anyway?) With Composite Jupiter, you don't even have to know what that "thing" is. You just have to be willing to believe in a greater intelligence...to open up, take a leap of faith, stretch out of your familiar comfort zones.

You know those times when you're really pissed off at each other, brooding and punishing them with icy silence? Then, suddenly something makes you both laugh, and you can't hold that mean mug together to save your life. That's kind of how Composite Jupiter works. It tells you to lighten the f*** up, cut the drama and go do something worthy of your genius.

In other words, Jupiter reminds you to keep the faith.
And sometimes, that's the only thing that two people have to hang on to. Sure, "making it last" means sticking to your commitment through the plateaus and trials. But that's not Jupiter's domain. Composite Jupiter injects your relationship with a current of excitement and possibility. It paints the picture of an exhilarating future you could step into together.

One note of caution: Jupiter is a gambler. Not every risk pays off, especially if it isn't mitigated by a strategic and sensible backup plan. Your Composite Jupiter can also make you foolhardy and reckless as a couple. It's where you indulge or have "too much of a good thing."

A duo with Jupiter in Libra could have a closet full of couture and a pocket full of sawdust. Jupiter in Sagittarius might have great ideas for starting an independent business or a retreat center or a school...but have you mapped out a long-term plan to scale and sustain the place?

Other planets in the Superchart can help with those details. Just bear in mind: Composite Jupiter is the entrepreneur in your relationship, the Pied Piper who rides into town with flamboyant and enchanting ideas. Follow along, but call in the practical reinforcements before you get totally swept away!

Supercouple JUPITER
IN THE ZODIAC SIGNS

In the Sign of	We grow together through	But may be too
ARIES	Adventures and challenges	Impulsive
TAURUS	Working steadily, shared values	Risk-averse
GEMINI	Intellectual curiosity, building a social circle	Indecisive
CANCER	Expressing empathy, building a home and family	Protective
LEO	Being creative and magnanimous, celebrating life	Lavish
VIRGO	Intellectual pursuits, learning skills, being in nature	Meticulous
LIBRA	Active listening, supporting a cause, compromise	Even-keeled
SCORPIO	Trust, intimacy, vulnerability, erotic exploration, transformational wisdom	Intense
SAGITTARIUS	Travel, entrepreneurship, learning, expanding our comfort zones	Restless
CAPRICORN	Pursuing an inspirational goal, building an indie venture	Obedient
AQUARIUS	Exploring cutting-edge ideas and communities	Out-there
PISCES	Spiritual connection, creativity, learning esoteric wisdom	Unstructured

4

FIND YOUR SUPERCOUPLE JUPITER AT
SUPERCOUPLE.COM

Create your own Supercouple Chart at **SUPERCOUPLE.COM**

SUPERCOUPLE JUPITER
ARIES ✳ ♈
OR THE 1ST HOUSE

> ## Together, we expand by:
>
> - Competing/pushing ourselves to the edge
> - Diving into projects that challenge us to grow
> - Taking off on independent journeys
> - Leading the pack and learning to work cooperatively
> - Fearlessly blazing trails and setting trends
> - Asserting ourselves without being combative

♃

Hello, trailblazers! With self-starter Aries as your Supercouple Jupiter, you two jump in the ring and take initiative—no permission or consensus required. When you join forces, life becomes a game of Choose Your Own Adventure. And there's sure to be an adrenaline rush as you dive into each cutting-edge escapade. From starting businesses to scaling mountain peaks, you two love anything "extreme." Daredevil Aries loves pushing past the edge, even if it leaves your loved ones both terrified and in awe.

As the first sign of the zodiac, Aries loves to lead, and you're such an inspiring duo that others will readily follow. But here's the catch: Independence and freedom are qualities the zodiac's Ram hold dear, and this Composite Jupiter will keep you both focused on "life, liberty and the pursuit of happiness." You two may be more comfortable as inspiring role models than CEOs who are responsible for a giant org chart.

No matter if you're an army of two or commanding legions of troops, it's wise for you two to build a "cabinet" of advisers. The excitable and impulsive energy of Jupiter in Aries can cause you to leap before you look. Not only will you chase after the latest, greatest thing, but you wind up with your hands in far too many pots. Either that, or you'll both become so distracted that your visionary ideas take forever to make it to the finish line. Money managers can help you as a couple offset the impulsive spending and gambling instincts this Jupiter Supercouple placement bestows.

With your active minds, there's an ageless quality to this connection. No matter your generation, you two stay abreast of trends in fashion, business, lifestyle and spirituality. Heck, you might even set them! When you both believe in something, you're the most zealous proselytes. But just as quickly, you may move on to your next obsession, at times earning a reputation for being a fickle couple.

Rather than looking for the ultimate truth, accept that you're a pair of dabblers who may always be drawn to the panoply of new, exciting developments. Once you find something that holds your attention, honing your expertise will be a lifelong quest for the two of you. Step up to the podium or record a TED talk together! With this larger-than-life Jupiter placement, you may grow to become charismatic speakers who hold audiences rapt with your shared conviction.

♃

Create your own Supercouple Chart at **SUPERCOUPLE.COM**

SUPERCOUPLE JUPITER

TAURUS ✳ ♉

OR THE 2ND HOUSE

Together, we expand by:

- Trying out new routines
- Working steadily towards a shared goal
- Embracing (gentle) change
- Creating a life with people who share our values (while also learning to engage with those who have different values)
- Working with the earth and natural resources

♃

An endless appetite for luxury? Boundless desire for romance? Whatever Supercouple Jupiter touches, it expands. And in sensual, decadent Taurus, that includes your desire to enjoy the finer things in life. Tap into this planet's globetrotting powers and it might just lead you from the Champs-Élysées to Madison Avenue to Shanghai's Huaihai Road—and all the tiny collectors' markets in between. The shared possessions you two curate are the artifacts of your love story—so why not show off the good taste you've cultivated?

When it's time to travel together, your ideal place would have gorgeous scenery and five-star accommodations. A mountain lodge with in-room spa services, a boho-chic Airbnb near a surf town? Yes, please—and bonus if there is a known food scene in the area! Even if you're "roughing it," you may retire to an RV with a comfortable mattress. Sleeping is important in this relationship. (Picture two bulls lounging in the pasture.) With this earthy Composite Jupiter placement, explore ecotourism—journeys that allow you to visit natural destinations without disturbing or damaging the environment.

Ironically, Jupiter in Taurus gives you both a low risk appetite. Yes, you two may burn through cash while refining your shared style. But once you become clear about your desires, you are savvy investors who can spot a killer deal! At the end of the day, Taurus is a pragmatic earth sign, and this Supercouple Jupiter wants "practical magic." Together, you may opt for steady paychecks over the wild fluctuations that an entrepreneurial lifestyle brings. You two won't be the biggest gamblers by any stretch of the imagination. Sure, you'll take SOME chances, but only after all your basic needs are covered. With your killer tastes, it wouldn't hurt to put some of your discretionary funds into NFTs or chic fixer-uppers you can rent as vacation properties. You both need to be anchored on solid ground before you feel safe flying as a couple.

Philosophical Jupiter is the planet that rules our faith and with ethical Taurus here, you may be a rather traditional pair. Earthy spirituality or conventional religion may figure into your shared belief system. A comfortable, beautiful home and healthy family relationships are the key to your expansion together. If you two decide to co-parent, your brood may grow fast, perhaps including adopted and birth children. Raising them with solid values will bring you a sense of deep fulfillment.

SUPERCOUPLE JUPITER
GEMINI ✳ ♊

OR THE 3RD HOUSE

> ### Together, we expand by:
>
> - Building a supportive social circle (so we don't put all the pressure on each other to be "twin flames")
> - Following our intellectual curiosity,
> - Participating in local initiatives and traveling to see how other cultures live
> - Discovering the power (and adventure) of commitment

♃

So many options, so little time! With Supercouple Jupiter in ever-curious Gemini, you two could develop a raging case of FOMO. Even if you weren't a seeker *per se* before meeting, together, you'll develop a deep curiosity about the wider world. With this intellectual Jupiter sign, you may soon be devouring books and articles about every subject under the sun from ancient philosophy to postmodern art.

Candid Jupiter pulls no punches in Gemini. Get ready for a game of 20 Questions. (Or make that 20,000 Questions.) There's no subject you two aren't brave enough to explore: financial crashes, flesh-eating bacteria, paranormal activity. You two are the ideal trivia night teammates! But your communication style as a couple can give friends mental whiplash. Learn to pause and take a breath, giving others a window to enter the dialogue. And allow people to fully make their point before you two start formulating questions. With practice, both of you can master the art of active listening.

One reason for all this inquisitive energy? Jupiter is the educator and Gemini has an insatiable appetite for data. Endlessly hungry for knowledge, you may backpack across every continent or spend years as nomads. With this etymologically obsessed Jupiter, words are your shared passion. While traveling, you two might do a stint as language teachers—a great way to form an authentic connection with the locals. With the natural charm you exude as a duo, it won't be long before you're invited to the insider spots, where few (if any) foreign tourists are ever allowed!

As fun as it all sounds, Jupiter is in "detriment" in Gemini, a challenged position. Translation? Gemini is opposite on the zodiac wheel from Sagittarius, the sign Jupiter naturally governs. As a result, you two may hesitate when it's time to leap. Opportunities may pass you by as you endlessly deliberate, compare and despair.

Money that you could have invested may sit stagnant in a basic savings account—or simply be burned away on impulsive retail therapy binges. You could even wind up with a clutter issue. And with worldly Jupiter in the mix, traveling together can trigger the urge to splurge. If you're not mindful, shelves may become cluttered with souvenirs and five versions of the same dip-dyed caftan. Develop a healthy risk tolerance for long-term investments. Create metrics that help you assess any calculated risks. That way, you can enjoy life's greatest adventures while also giving yourselves a safety net...and a cushion!

SUPERCOUPLE JUPITER
CANCER ✴ ♋

OR THE 4TH HOUSE

Together, we expand by:

- Creating a stable home base while pushing ourselves outside of our comfort zone
- Articulating our needs (instead of bottling them up inside)
- Honoring our feelings without confusing them for facts
- Surrounding ourselves with loyal and loving people

Hosting Supercouple Jupiter, the planet of global adventures, in home-loving Cancer might sound like a total paradox. But guess what? The red-spotted titan is "exalted" in this sign, which makes this the most fortuitous placement in the zodiac! Cancer rules the home, and when you two build your nest, it's more than just a cute 2BR with fireplace. It's a warm and thriving epicenter where guests come to exchange ideas, share their feelings and gather around the heart. Some days, it might feel like you two have a revolving door at the front of your house!

In Cancer, Jupiter's expansive powers may bless you two with a huge family. If not, you'll create a "world family" by developing deep friendships with people all over the globe. But where do your boundaries lie with your people? In nurturing Cancer, this Composite Jupiter placement may cast you two as the glue holding everyone together. While you have plenty of kitchen-table wisdom to dispense, too much caretaking drains the *joie de vivre* in your relationship. So rather than be everyone's "adopted parents," empower your inner circle (and your own growing kids, if you have them) to "do for self." With freedom-loving Jupiter here, the last thing you both want is to have people heap THEIR responsibilities onto your four shoulders.

Home on the road! When you're traveling together, you'll quickly nest in your space. While you may never admit it aloud, getting away from familiar people can be liberating for you two, freeing you from the dutiful roles you play with friends and family. While this potent Jupiter can make you a pair of Alphas, it can be a relief to kick back and follow someone else's itineraries too. Yoga retreats, guided tours, all-inclusive anything can be downright restorative. Even while "roughing it," you two need an element of glamping. With watery Cancer here, proximity to a beach (or pool) is a must. Your accommodations should be comfortable and curated. Bonus if they have a kitchen that allows you to prepare a few of your favorite meals. And a killer food scene within walking distance is a definite benefit.

Though you'll trek many miles together in this lifetime, your most profound journeys are the ones that foster emotional evolution. Empathy is a hallmark of the Jupiter in Cancer connection. Through your relationship, you'll gain fluency in the universal language of feelings, while mastering the wisdom of your hearts. And who knows? Since Jupiter is the planet that rules publishing and education, you may team up to write a book (or teach a workshop) dispensing advice on interpersonal relationships.

Jupiter is the planet of entrepreneurship: If your kitchen table doubles as a workspace, we wouldn't be surprised! With Supercouple Jupiter in cozy Cancer, you two may be lucky as real estate investors, building a portfolio of properties all over the world. Is there a food truck in your future? A retreat center or mobile medical station? Feeling and healing on wheels might be your favorite way to move through the world together.

SUPERCOUPLE JUPITER
LEO ✳ ♌

OR THE 5TH HOUSE

Together, we expand by:

- Being a power couple while also learning how to be of humble service to others
- Supporting each other's creative passions (and making art or music together)
- Following our hearts and pursuing what we both feel passionately about
- Sharing our "toys" and wealth with each other and our loved ones

---

4

Twirl! When Supercouple Jupiter lands in spotlight-stealing Leo, all the world is your stage. This magnanimous placement gives your relationship a larger-than-life presence. You two can't help but light up every room you walk into! After making your entrance, you'll dive right into the action, sparking conversations, moving people from the bar to the dance floor and flirting with shameless abandon. As a couple you would sooner start a buzz than fade into the background—fashion police citations, be damned! But when a stormy spell strikes, you can just as readily bring down the whole room. Moods are big, colorful and impactful in the Jupiter in Leo relationship.

Some might accuse you both of being prone to exaggeration; even stirring up drama. And they're not altogether wrong. Jupiter is the planetary truth teller, but it can also be a legendary smack talker. Nevertheless, your colorful stories will always draw an audience. You might even start a social media feed together or pitch a reality show.

Warning: Theatrical Leo's version of "speaking the truth," could stir up intense feelings in other people, from rivalry to rage. Careful not to egg each other on when one of you is feeling emboldened for a fight! It's great to have each other's backs, but Jupiter in Leo can supersize both of your egos. Know the difference between courageous action and foolish risk.

Life is a party for couples with Jupiter in this playful sign! Your eternally youthful spirits will rise up when you're together. As a couple, you may love to dwell in the heart of the action—and the parties you plan together will be epic. But learn your limits! Overindulging can deplete your resources, leaving you both with empty bank accounts, closets full of too-small clothes and friends on the verge of storming your apartment to host an intervention. Of course, these very slip-ups may become the source of your shared spiritual evolution. As you bound back from rock bottom (or wherever you land), you two may become mouthpieces for your recovery programs. Before you know it, all of your mutual friends have signed up for the "life-changing seminar" that got you back on a pious path.

But here's one area of life where no one will EVER put you two on a budget: Love, sweet, love. With Jupiter in romance-junkie Leo, you'll go to the outer limits to woo each other. Jupiter rules travel and you may rack up frequent-flier miles together with Cupid as your copilot. If you marry, the wedding may be an extravagant affair filled with theatrical and luxurious effects. Since Leo rules fertility, abundant Jupiter could bless you with a large family. If kids aren't in your plans, a flourishing creative life may be for at least one of you. Starting a band or working on large-scale art pieces or building your dream "castle" together can be a potent way to bond.

SUPERCOUPLE JUPITER

VIRGO ✳ ♍

OR THE 6TH HOUSE

Together, we expand by:

- Participating in charitable activities and community service
- Being active and outdoorsy
- Fueling our bodies with clean food and a green lifestyle
- Learning time-tested wisdom to help make our lives more organized and fulfilling
- Learning to unconditionally accept one another (instead of constantly trying to fix or improve each other)
- Calming our minds through breathwork and meditation

4

Hello, wise ones. When Supercouple Jupiter lands in savvy Virgo, your twin powers of practical magic and intellect are unleashed! Don't be surprised if this turns you into the community sages...or maybe the traveling ones! Wherever the compass directs you both, there's bound to be a high-vibe mission to achieve. Virgo is the sign of service, and together, you'll walk a purpose-driven path.

This magnanimous Jupiter placement could lead you both to "voluntourism," combining your vacations with humanitarian missions. Eco travel is also appealing for you two. Learn how to sojourn without doing damage to the environment of your destination—then, pass along your teachings to the rest of the world. Since Jupiter rules education, the two of you may lead retreats or do stints as instructors or tour guides. Who knows? One day you may team up to open a wellness center in a gorgeous destination.

Bringing dreams to fruition probably won't happen from pure luck for both of you, alas. Jupiter isn't at its most venturesome in risk-averse Virgo; in fact, the planet is "in detriment" here, landing opposite on the zodiac wheel from its home base of Pisces. As a result, you two may go through a series of stops and starts before you find your cruising altitude.

As a couple, you are constantly on a "make better" mission, and have lots of field notes to share with others. But of all the Jupiter placements, having yours in Virgo makes you both prone to perfectionism.

If you're not stuck in analysis paralysis, your play-it-safe M.O. may impede progress. The two of you can only research so much before it's time to make a move. Embrace the process and be willing to learn from your mistakes. Like scientists, the data you glean from your "failed experiments" could open up new paths of exploration!

Wellness is Virgo's domain and Jupiter is the god of the feast. Growing your own food can be a spiritual experience, connecting you both to the abundance of Spirit. You'll make excellent accountability buddies for one another, whether you're going on a vegan cleanse or taking a 21-day challenge at your fitness studio. It's all about learning!

Channel the kinetic Jupiter energy into outdoor activities like mountain biking, horseback riding, rock climbing, whatever! The precision of Virgo can mean that technical movement, such as choreographed dancing, is a great way for you two to burn off stress AND improve non-verbal communication. Traveling together with a fitness component is also fun: yoga retreats, a week at a ski lodge. Wherever you go together, the itinerary will be impeccably planned.

SUPERCOUPLE JUPITER

LIBRA ✴ ♎

OR THE 7TH HOUSE

Together, we expand by:

- Learning to balance the give-and-take in our relationship
- Participating in social justice efforts together
- Learning to navigate conflict instead of avoiding it
- Enjoying the finer things in life without overindulging
- Following our hearts and our heads
- Living according to our principles
- Reading sage wisdom and ancient philosophy

4

Two is more than a magic number for those with Supercouple Jupiter in Libra. It's your access to mutual expansion in every way! Romantic idealism flows freely in this connection. If you're going to be in it for life, why settle for anything less than a soulmate? With global Jupiter here, you might have met each other while traveling, at a retreat or a love workshop. What matters most for longevity, however, is that your philosophies about life align. It's not just about where you're from...but also about where you're going.

"Let's make a deal!" could be a favorite opening gambit for you two. There's going to be a lot of negotiation in this relationship, which might even have an "opposites attract" quality. Represented by the Scales, you may always feel as if you're weighing options. Sometimes, it's best for you to go off on separate pursuits, especially if a compromise feels like a sacrifice. Learn to be okay with autonomy—it's part of being in a healthy relationship! And heed the FOMO alert. It's great to explore the bounty of prospects, but if you don't make a decision, you both may wind up spinning your wheels and missing out on opportunities.

As a dynamic duo, you love joining forces. But with liberated Jupiter at the helm, you won't tolerate being possessed or restricted in any way. If you're taking this journey together, it's going to be one that you both go on by choice! Get ready to write some of the most exciting chapters you've ever co-authored, complete with mind-expanding studies, no-holds-barred conversations and treks to every corner of the world!

Make a shared budget—and stick to it. With indulgent Jupiter in luxury-loving Libra, you can't get enough of those five-star experiences. But #resortlife CAN get expensive, especially with the planetary god of the feast whetting your appetites. Still, there's nothing you two may love more than opening up a reserve bottle of wine and slowly sipping under a starlit sky.

Libra is also the sign that rules justice. This compassionate Composite Jupiter placement will make you both quite aware of social inequities, and you'll want to devote some time to work that helps people who are less fortunate. As you two evolve in your spirituality together, your shared path may involve helping others find balance, perhaps as yoga teachers, counselors or life coaches. With the planet of publishing here, there may be a draw toward writing, podcasting, or YouTubing as relationship experts. With harmonizing Libra working the dials, your voices could uplift the masses.

Create your own Supercouple Chart at SUPERCOUPLE.COM

SUPERCOUPLE JUPITER
SCORPIO ✳ ♏︎

OR THE 8TH HOUSE

Together, we expand by:

- Practicing being vulnerable and open together (instead of secretive and suspicious)
- Surrounding ourselves with people we trust and creating an intimate community of mutual friends
- Treating our bodies like temples (in and out of bed)
- Slowly and steadily allowing our relationship to grow more intimate
- Investing wisely for long-term financial security
- Exploring our sexual chemistry in a sacred manner

♃

Simply irresistible or too close for comfort? The bewitching powers of Supercouple Jupiter in Scorpio create quite a magnetic bond. But this won't be an easy one. Independent Jupiter is the planet of limitless expansion, living its truth loud and proud. Cloak-and-dagger Scorpio needs to have control and operates more powerfully behind the scenes. So how to unite the disparate energies in your relationship?

First and foremost, accept that the two of you may always run hot and cold. You may draw each other into your passionate quests only to wind up feeling stifled by a power struggle. But after a periodic separation, you will long for the other's dynamic energy and sage input. And back together you go.

Another thing to remember? Amplifier Jupiter will turn up the volume on some of Scorpio's, er, dramatic tendencies. The "life or death" intensity that you ascribe to situations may very well be overblown. Once you accept that Jupiter in Scorpio can lead to overreaction, you can support one another with deescalation. A little box breathing—four sets of inhales and exhales, each held for four seconds—can bring you both back to your senses. From there, you can get back to making magic!

And we do mean magic. When the two of you are in the zone, there's no challenge too mighty for you to transform. Financially, this is a lucky placement for abundant Jupiter! Scorpio rules shared resources and long-term investments. Not only is this relationship a money magnet, but you manage money well together. Throughout your time together, this relationship can build a strong, diversified portfolio that includes profits from your own ventures.

You two may grapple with trust issues but once you get past the vulnerability hurdles, there's no secret that you won't share with each other, including your fantasies. Scorpio is the famous sex sign, and this Jupiter brings a "seeker" vibe to the party. Exploring in the privacy of your bedroom is hot, but it may not stop there. Expansive Jupiter loves to learn and travel which might lead to things like OM-ing circles, sex-positive retreats and play parties.

Are kids on the agenda for you two? With the planet of abundance in the sign of reproduction, you could be quite the fecund duo. You may have plans to raise a large brood, possibly adopting a few of your family additions. Even if you opt out of childbearing, both of you will be fertile in other ways, whether you're starting businesses, making art or finding new ways to creatively collaborate. Bottom line: Sharing this esoteric Jupiter makes life a nonstop vision quest—and in Scorpio, you're bound to set new depth records in your explorations!

Create your own Supercouple Chart at **SUPERCOUPLE.COM**

SUPERCOUPLE JUPITER
SAGITTARIUS ✴ ♐

OR THE 9TH HOUSE

Together, we expand by:

- Traveling to new corners of the world together
- Studying principles of world religions and philosophies
- Enjoying the banquet of life without overindulging
- Expressing our opinions freely after we have thoroughly researched the facts
- Taking bold but calculated risks
- Pursuing our desires while also learning to be patient about getting results

---

Double down! With Supercouple Jupiter in its home sign (domicile) of Sagittarius, your relationship has Lady Luck on its side. No matter how many times you test her limits with your daredevil antics, you manage to land on your four well-shod feet! With limitless Sagittarius running the show, love knows no bounds for you as a couple. Many relationships with this Jupiter placement bring together partners from two vastly different backgrounds. Or you may literally meet while traveling. Regardless, you'll love exploring the world as a pair!

A naturally nomadic duo, you may disappear for long stretches, leaving mutual friends wondering of your whereabouts. Often these are purposeful journeys like consulting gigs, visiting residencies, or teaching abroad. But sometimes, they're purely for adventure! You two may go backpacking into the wild, living amongst the locals in a tiny surf village. Note: This can happen at any stage of your relationship, from the halcyon to the sunset years.

One thing that CAN become problematic for couples with Jupiter in Sagittarius is a resistance to putting down roots. It's hard to build a community or connect to family when you're always on the move. For every exotic passport stamp, there's a missed 30th birthday or a best friend's wedding that happened while you were building a school for a rural population. At some point, it can be healing for you two to drop anchor and create your base camp. Near an international airport, ideally—and of course, the people you both love dearly.

Thanks to this visionary Supercouple Jupiter, there's no shortage of lofty ideas flowing between you. Sagittarius is the zodiac's gambler. Together, you'll take some serious leaps, pouring all your resources into a shared passion! To avoid tumbling into debt, learn the difference between a calculated risk and a foolish one. Some "exciting opportunities" are far more laborious than they are pleasurable. And in this relationship, nothing is more painful than clipped wings.

Both Jupiter and Sagittarius rule publishing and media—and you two have a lot to say! There's a lot of creative potential for you both. Maybe you'll team up to create a podcast or YouTube channel or to co-host an open mic night. But be warned: Mouthy Jupiter is unleashed and unfiltered in its native sign of Sagittarius. Indeed both of you are a regular comedic duo, leaving each other in stitches with your inside jokes. But will other people find your brand of humor funny? That's questionable. Keep the off-color (and downright offensive) commentary off social media and out of the public sphere or you could get yourselves canceled.

Since Jupiter rules higher education, this Composite placement will keep you on a permanent quest for knowledge. Taking classes together is an excellent way to bond. If the ivory tower isn't your thing, you could be "retreat junkies" on a quest for self-development. As you two gain mastery in a field, you may earn your living by leading workshops as a pair in remote destinations. Put that one on your bucket list and see what happens!

4

SUPERCOUPLE JUPITER
CAPRICORN ✳ ♑
OR THE 10TH HOUSE

Together, we expand by:

- Creating wealth and security to support the ones we love
- Training with master teachers and coaches
- Setting challenging goals and steadily building until we achieve them
- Learning to communicate our feelings instead of acting like you've got it all handled
- Committing for the long-term

♃

To the top...and beyond! When no-limits Jupiter breaks through the sound barrier in ambitious Capricorn, this Supercouple placement turns you into a supersonic Supercouple. Your relationship is as much "business" as it is "pleasure." When you come together, you're like a cosmic C-Suite! And with this competitive Composite Jupiter, you two are in it to win it. No one has to raise the bar for you as a couple. You'll keep elevating it higher with the next challenging mission that you decide to crush together.

But when is enough enough? Thrill seeking Jupiter is in "fall" in cautious Capricorn, a sign that's considered its most challenging position in the zodiac. This can mute the otherwise jovial, risk-taking qualities of Jupiter—or create a self-defeating, "never say die!" stubbornness.

Create your own Supercouple Chart at **SUPERCOUPLE.COM**

Adaptability? Not a strong suit for couples with Jupiter in Capricorn. But sometimes you NEED to change gears or just throw in the towel.

Here's something you'd both benefit from remembering: Mistakes and "failure" are part of the roadmap to success. Rather than trying to achieve perfection, build more experimentation into your relationship. It's like that Thomas Edison quote you've probably seen on a refrigerator magnet before, "I have not failed. I've just found 10,000 ways that won't work." Cliche as it may be, this could be a mantra to adopt, especially when you're trying to accomplish something truly meaningful. Let yourselves "fail faster," and you'll see your success rate soar.

Family-oriented Capricorn is the provider sign and with Jupiter placed here, the two of you may be the rocks for relatives across multiple generations. Noble though this may be, saddling yourselves with too much responsibility can be a drag on your relationship. Perfectly capable grownups may act like helpless children when in your company. But if you don't want to wind up as "foster parents" for adult children, you both will need to learn the art of setting firm boundaries. Repeat after us: "No, you cannot stay on my couch for a month."

When it IS time to relax, this earthy Supercouple Jupiter placement sends you into the great outdoors. Settle back together at a mountain lodge or boho-chic beach cabaña. Just try not to log on to their wi-fi 24/7 or you'll get sucked into work and miss out on all the romantic opportunities that arise when you FINALLY unplug and give yourselves that blessed 24 hours to truly relax.

Not that you two MIND combining business and pleasure. The digital nomad life was made for couples with Jupiter in Capricorn. With your many obligations, it may be hard to pick up (pack up) and go as much as you'd like. Traveling for work can create a happy compromise. Build a solid support structure at your base—and check in frequently—so no one feels abandoned by your wanderlust.

SUPERCOUPLE JUPITER
AQUARIUS ✳ ♒♒

OR THE 11TH HOUSE

Together, we expand by:

- Creating a community of eclectic thought leaders (IRL and on social media)
- Trying out cutting-edge methodologies
- Allowing ourselves the freedom to break and rewrite the rules
- Getting involved with social justice and activist causes
- Getting a daily RDA of laughter
- Centering ourselves with yoga or another physical practice

♃

Set your spirits free! With Supercouple Jupiter in avant-garde Aquarius, you two would happily soar into the stratosphere together and never come down—if it weren't for this little thing called gravity. Rules? What are those? Most don't apply to the two of you, as far as you're concerned. As a couple, you enjoy flouting convention and leaving jaws on the ground with your cheeky brand of shock value. Systems were meant to be revolutionized, right?

With Jupiter in mad-scientist Aquarius, you two think so far outside the box that you're not even sure if it's a box anymore. But how much should you share with the rest of the world? Some of the concepts both of you dream up may be too far afield for the average bear. Not that this should silence you. But do you really want to spend time defending and explaining to people who will probably NEVER get it?

Create your own Supercouple Chart at **SUPERCOUPLE.COM**

Your precious energy would be better devoted to finding (or forming!) a soul squad of seekers who think more like you both. You can't ever have too many mutual friends. Aquarius is the sign of community and with Jupiter here, you might start a fast-growing movement. When it's time to get away, you don't often slip off for a "just the two of us" voyage. Group travel, festivals, voluntourism and humanitarian missions: your nomadic spirits come to life when you're around other people.

One caveat: Don't get stuck in an echo chamber or rush to cancel people who don't readily adopt your woke ethos. This idealistic Jupiter believes in equity but can become intolerant and zealous. It's a good idea for you two to interact with folks outside your friend group, especially if they come from a different economic class or cultural background. Their ideas may be "unusual," but their perspectives could also be valid and worth incorporating into your own future thought processes.

Technology and science fall under the futuristic realm of Aquarius. With this enterprising Jupiter placement, you both could make your fortune in digital entrepreneurship, tech investing or any sort of inventing. Your shared charisma comes through on camera too: Hello, YouTube instructors, TikTok influencers and mad scientist superstars! Together you might create media that shines a light on social change, or develop a business committed to green energy, sustainable sourcing, and cooperative ownership.

Spiritually, this rational Jupiter position prefers interpretive systems over codes of ethic. Astrology, which is ruled by Aquarius, has tangible concepts that give you two access to the divine. Numerology, tarot, even quantum physics can be a form of "religion" with this Jupiter placement, especially if you both connect them to ancient philosophies and more open-ended wisdom traditions. (No hellfire and brimstones please!) Since Aquarius rules the higher mind, together you may connect to source energy through meditation and mindfulness practices. Finding that space between stimulus and response is where the magic lies!

4

SUPERCOUPLE JUPITER

PISCES ✳ ♓

OR THE 12TH HOUSE

Together, we expand by:

- Escaping into creative passions like music or poetry
- Traveling to sacred sites and going on spiritual retreats
- Learning how to express buried feelings (perhaps with the help of a couple's therapist)
- Taking time to be with our thoughts through meditation and journaling
- Learning to set healthy boundaries in love (and avoiding codependence)

♃

Bring on the mystical mojo! As the secondary ruler of Pisces (along with Neptune), philosophical Jupiter is right at home in this ethereal zodiac sign. Does someone out there need support? When your shared empathy is evoked, there's hardly a more compassionate couple. In a healthy setting, this boundlessness is your greatest gift. You two may feel as if you can intuit people's needs before they even vocalize them, then provide the comforting solution that makes everyone feel warm, fuzzy and spiritually uplifted inside.

But take heed: Hosting no-limits Jupiter in this watery sign can turn you both into psychic sponges. When together, you may feel like a pair of tuning forks picking up every vibration in the room. Develop

Create your own Supercouple Chart at **SUPERCOUPLE.COM**

techniques for "shielding your fields," like wearing protective crystals and literally developing your "outro" to slip away from energy vampires who may be attracted to the bright energy you two exude.

In the energy of this relationship, you ARE more attuned. (Welcome to the woo!) And that includes with each other. You must be careful not to absorb one another's emotions too. You hate to see your partner upset, but give them space to have a healing cry or a week of moping. Feeling your feelings IS part of the healing process. Use crystals, salt baths, and sage to clear yourselves after particularly intense exchanges. Because emotions get big under your Jupiter's expansive influence, you'll need to find healthy outlets for metabolizing them—and not just in each other's arms. Vent regularly to your journals, close friends and therapists.

The truth is, you'll always tend a bit toward hedonism when you're in the energy of this connection. With its untethered creativity, Jupiter in Pisces will bring music, art and dance into your lives. Basically anything flowing and non-linear is right up your alley. Optimistic Jupiter buoys your faith and Pisces is the most hopeless romantic of them all. You'd both do anything for love—yes, even that. The problem? Spoiling each other can get expensive and even unhealthy. Since Pisces is prone to addiction, it's more important than ever that you two avoid using food, alcohol or drugs to escape reality together.

Boundaries may not be your relationship's strongest suit with Supercouple Jupiter here. But learning when and how to set them can keep your batteries charged, ensuring that you'll have enough energy left over for your partner. Even then, you must be careful not to slip into a codependent groove. Give one another a safe space to say "no" to requests without feeling guilt-tripped or punished. This will curb the victim mindset that can flare up for Jupiter in Pisces Supercouples. Blaming and shaming? No fun! Cheering on each other's soul growth? Now we're talking.

SUPERCOUPLE
Compatibility
WITH YOUR JUPITER SIGN

4

Create your own Supercouple Chart at **SUPERCOUPLE.COM**

If our Supercouple Jupiter is in a fire Sign:
(ARIES, LEO OR SAGITTARIUS)

And my personal Jupiter is in a fire sign
(ARIES, LEO OR SAGITTARIUS):

Your leap-first, look-second M.O. will be thoroughly appreciated, but who's got the safety net? This is a risk-forward relationship that can propel you to the heights of abundance or further the possibility of you betting the farm and losing it. Work with this energy in small careful doses, because it's best used for planning vacations, tackling big projects and exploring the world together—and make sure you read the safety precautions first.

And my personal Jupiter is in an earth sign
(TAURUS, VIRGO OR CAPRICORN):

Easy does it! This relationship could burn down all the things you've worked so hard to build. You may even feel shy or "uncool" about how cautious you are in your personal life, but if you try to prove something by racing ahead, you could make some costly mistakes and give yourself a whole lot of anxiety.

And my personal Jupiter is in an air sign
(GEMINI, LIBRA, AQUARIUS):

Safety third? This relationship is sure to bring out the daredevil in you, making you less mindful and rational than you would be on your own. Even if you are aware of all the steps and precautionary measures, you can jump into things faster than perhaps you should. Remember to check your speedometer regularly.

 And my personal Jupiter is in a water sign
(CANCER, SCORPIO OR PISCES):

Feel it loud and proud! When it comes to sharing what's in your heart or following an exciting relationship, you're more ready than ever to throw caution to the wind here. But you're also at greater risk for getting burned, especially if you haven't had the honest conversations that are necessary to give you a realistic picture of what you're getting yourself into.

If our Supercouple Jupiter is in an earth sign:
(TAURUS, VIRGO, OR CAPRICORN)

4

 And my personal Jupiter is in a fire sign
(ARIES, LEO OR SAGITTARIUS):

Hold your horses! You may be ready to leap out of the starting gate, but this relationship is fundamentally more risk-averse than you are on your own. While this may be frustrating to suppress your gambling instincts, it's an important lesson in adulting. Create some metrics for stop-or-go so that you don't have to kill off every dream, but be able to move forward at a pace that serves your relationship.

And my personal Jupiter is in an earth sign
(TAURUS, VIRGO OR CAPRICORN):

Manifestation heaven! Your natural productivity is doubled here since this connection supports your ability to turn big ideas into profitable ventures or life-changing explorations. This relationship could literally make you rich—or at the very least, satisfied and secure.

And my personal Jupiter is in an air sign
(GEMINI, LIBRA, AQUARIUS):

Your enterprising ideas could become literal enterprises in this relationship, which is grounded in material success. You're the one who keeps things fresh, edgy and groundbreaking, rather than predictable and boring. Just don't reject every traditional notion.

And my personal Jupiter is in a water sign
(CANCER, SCORPIO OR PISCES):

This relationship will appeal to your risk appetite! It's cautious enough to allow time for you to process every potential gamble—before any plans get into motion. You'll have lots of room to use your intuition, but be sure to back up your knowing feelings with empirical data.

4

If our Supercouple Jupiter is in an air sign:
(GEMINI, LIBRA, AQUARIUS)

 And my personal Jupiter is in a fire sign
(ARIES, LEO OR SAGITTARIUS):

Your big ideas benefit from the balance of rational thinking here. Rather than rushing ahead without a plan, this relationship teaches you to put more thought and research into your vision. Your outspoken nature could be challenged, and you'll need to use more diplomacy. Same for your my-way-or-the-highway mentality. Tone it down, and you could become a supreme negotiator.

 And my personal Jupiter is in an earth sign
(TAURUS, VIRGO OR CAPRICORN):

This relationship quickens your pace and helps you get into motion faster. While you may feel like things are growing and expanding faster than you're used to, the rational cool of the Composite Air Jupiter provides enough reassurance for you to expand your risk profile.

 And my personal Jupiter is in an air sign
(GEMINI, LIBRA, AQUARIUS):

Your visionary nature is right at home in this relationship! Together, you'll love to explore big ideas and new thought. You'll be able to test out unconventional approaches to everything from your living arrangement to the dynamics of the relationship itself. Be careful not to get too heady here! And think about how you'll feel after you take these leaps.

And my personal Jupiter is in a water sign
(CANCER, SCORPIO OR PISCES):

While you're accustomed to taking emotional and creative risks, this Supercouple Jupiter is more about exploring interpersonal dynamics, systems of thought and communication styles. Get ready to be more honest and vulnerable in your expression than you may have bargained for. Learning to verbalize and communicate your feelings is a gift of this relationship.

If our Supercouple Jupiter is in a water sign:
(CANCER, SCORPIO OR PISCES)

And my personal Jupiter is in a fire sign
(ARIES, LEO OR SAGITTARIUS):

You won't be able to hit the gas and check the GPS later. You'll need to know where you're heading before you leap off the high starting block—otherwise, you'll rock this relationship's stability to the core.

And my personal Jupiter is in an earth sign
(TAURUS, VIRGO OR CAPRICORN):

Your sensible nature flows easily in this pond. You might even realize that you're being a little too practical in your decision-making. This relationship expands your appetite for pleasure, beauty and doing things because they feel good, even if they don't make sense on paper.

4

And my personal Jupiter is in an air sign
(GEMINI, LIBRA, AQUARIUS):

You're out of your depth here because you won't be able to simply race after an exciting idea. If you want this relationship to work, you're going to have to live with major FOMO. Take a chance on situations that bring a promise of lasting security, not just another adventurous tale.

And my personal Jupiter is in a water sign
(CANCER, SCORPIO OR PISCES):

Dive in deep. This relationship can feel like a scuba mission to the bottom of the ocean, and there are few dark places the two of you won't explore together. While you'll expand your emotional intelligence, you could also drown in the emotion ocean if you don't come up for air.

♃

Create your own Supercouple Chart at **SUPERCOUPLE.COM**

SUPERCOUPLE

SATURN

our goals & boundaries

♄

Use Your Supercouple Saturn to Understand:

- Boundaries and how to set the right ones together
- The challenges you'll face as a couple
- Structures needed to keep your relationship strong
- How to co-manage the responsibilities of day-to-day life
- Your long-term goals as a couple
- Where your relationship could use some "adulting"
- Traditions: How you'll approach them as a couple
- Where you may have to sacrifice and learn tough lessons together

---

WHAT ARE THE BOUNDARIES IN YOUR RELATIONSHIP? HOW CAN YOU BUILD A LONG-TERM LIFE TOGETHER?

Can this relationship go the distance? Enter astrology's Inspector Gadget: Supercouple Saturn. When it's time to have the "so, where is this thing going..." talk, the planetary taskmaster steps up to be the adult in the room.

It's no mistake that Saturn has a ring on it—because this planet reveals how you'll deal with long-term commitments like marriage. Will a lifelong partnership be as fulfilling and magical as the honeymoon phase?

Create your own Supercouple Chart at **SUPERCOUPLE.COM**

Maybe you've hit the dreaded seven-month mark and the novelty is fading. You've stopped dressing up for dates and starting peeing with the bathroom door open. Someone's eye wandered, or you caught them texting an ex. One of you had an illness or a death in the family. The exhaustion of parenthood turned you into sleep-deprived zombies. How did something so enchanted turn into...this?

Challenges happen in relationships. And when you need a slow-burning source of resilience, Saturn comes through, helping you find the magic in the mundane aspects of your commitment.

At a certain point, every relationship needs a structure to keep it humming along. Real talks. Hard talks. Hat-in-hand honesty about how you see your life unfolding in the next few years—and whether or not it makes sense to walk that path together. There might be tough decisions or compromises, especially in these times when we all have robust individual lives that don't always have space for someone else's equally full existence.

Without solid goals and clear commitments, there's literally no foundation for a long-term love. Some couples are smart enough to talk about this before acting on their attraction, but most of us sail to the bedroom (and possibly the altar) on the fumes of body chemistry and "new relationship energy."

Fortunately, Saturn likes to simplify. In your Superchart, Saturn identifies the bottom line, pinpointing shared priorities and defining dealbreakers. From there, it's up to the two of you: Can you both give your word to that shared agenda? Is a lasting life partnership worth what you may have to sacrifice in order to build this bond?

Composite Saturn outlines the vows you'll take, the sacrifices you'll make, the short-term payoff you'll give up in the name of a greater shared goal. In your blended chart, it shows how you'll face those tough choices as a couple, where you might have to delay gratification or work arduously for a reward.

Saturn rules obstacles, barriers and boundaries. It tests our will and makes us sing for our supper, pay our dues, prove we want it through grit and resilience. If you have Composite Saturn in Scorpio, the sign of sex and intimacy, it might take you a minute to find your bedroom groove. Or, your busy schedules could make it tough for you to carve out time to actually get it on. Composite Saturn will show exactly where you need to establish clear agreements with each other and stick to them like your life depended on it.

The silver lining? Once you earn Saturn's bounty, it's yours to keep. So even if it feels like you're spinning your wheels in the mud, you're actually making tire tracks that will one day become a familiar path home to each other. Turns out the key to long-term happiness might demand a hero's journey and a few dark nights of the Composite Saturn soul as you mature and learn emotional self-regulation and discipline.

Sound like a buzzkill? It will feel like one too for a minute. The ringed planet rules longevity, wisdom and bonds that stand the test of time. (Saturn is also known as Chronos, which is the root of the word chronology.) Those anchors you establish and the memories you create? Those become the container that keeps your relationship safely cocooned.

There's no growth—and as time goes on, no freedom—without leaning into your Composite Saturn. So feed each other those vegetables, then head over to another planet for dessert.

Create your own Supercouple Chart at **SUPERCOUPLE.COM**

Supercouple SATURN
IN THE ZODIAC SIGNS

In the Sign of	We mature through	But may be too cautious about
ARIES	Taming our selfish impulses	Putting yourselves out there
TAURUS	Following good habits and healthy routines	Spending money
GEMINI	Sharpening our intellects and communication skills	Saying what you mean
CANCER	Building emotional resilience, creating home and family	Opening up to others
LEO	Overcoming a need for attention and validation	Letting your playful side out
VIRGO	Sticking to healthy routines, mastering a skill, helping others, sharing quality time	Making mistakes
LIBRA	Learning the art of compromise and adult relationship skills	Committing
SCORPIO	Powerful alliances that build wealth, investing, property ownership, intimacy skills	Letting your guard down
SAGITTARIUS	Experiencing new cultures, countries and philosophies, personal growth work, being honest and transparent	Taking a risk
CAPRICORN	Accomplishing long-term goals, building a legacy, modeling your highest values	Breaking the rules
AQUARIUS	Championing a cause, building something with new technology and ideas, a leadership role in community	Joining a group
PISCES	Developing artistic or spiritual gifts, cultivating compassion and helping those in need	Sharing your emotions

ħ

FIND YOUR SUPERCOUPLE SATURN AT **SUPERCOUPLE.COM**

SUPERCOUPLE SATURN

ARIES ✴ ♈

OR THE 1ST HOUSE

To feel stable together, we need:

- Attention and positive feedback
- Consistency
- Calm
- Support with sticking to day-to-day structures and routines

---

Should you hit the accelerator or slam on the brakes? Expect plenty of stops and starts in a relationship with Supercouple Saturn in Aries. Structured Saturn is cautious, deliberate and slow. Aries is impulsive and "go, go, go!" Saturn plays by society's rules. Aries is the zodiac's renegade. Clearly, it's going to take a minute to find your ideal speed—not to mention the right label for your relationship!

There's an age-old saying that "fools rush in," and it's a lesson that this Saturn serves you two on auto-repeat. When you're both lit up by an idea, you instinctually dive in headfirst, kickstart a project or ignite a new trend. But just when things start getting off the ground, Saturn's self-sabotaging effects creep in! You two may feel overwhelmed by the scope of your mission, which could lead you to question its legitimacy. Oy! Or you get frustrated by the drudgery of mundane tasks. It's a hot fire-sign mess.

Create your own Supercouple Chart at **SUPERCOUPLE.COM**

Go easy on yourselves. Saturn is in "detriment" in Aries, its least favorite spot in the zodiac. There's a fundamental mismatch between this ultra-cautious planet and the daredevil zodiac sign. But here's some good news! You two can build in support to get past tough-nut Saturn's hurdles. The most effective technique? Form a pep squad of solid friends who aren't afraid to deliver straight talk when you two start spiraling. Sometimes an unwavering, "You've got this!" can get you both back in the ring. And sometimes, you need a wise soul to call, "Game Over" before you two do any more damage.

With headstrong Aries at Saturn's helm, power struggles can and will arise. There are so many strong ideas about what's "right" that you may constantly be battling each other for domination. Needless to say, a "my way or the highway" attitude can sink the ship. More than most couples, you'd benefit from learning basic conflict negotiation skills. Life doesn't always have to be an uphill battle!

Lessons in "right timing" won't come overnight. It can take a while to outgrow the impulsivness, self-sabotaging stubborn DIY-ing and hair-trigger frustration that Saturn in Aries incites when you two are building together. Remember that Saturn is all about process, process, process! Rather than flying into "doing" because you have a dream, stop and develop a plan. If you're not ready for the pro leagues, you can build your confidence by training with the masters. Learning together can actually be a brilliant way for couples with Saturn in Aries to bond. Best of all? You'll save yourselves and everyone who loves you both a whole lot of anxiety!

SUPERCOUPLE SATURN
TAURUS ✳ ♉

OR THE 2ND HOUSE

To feel stable together, we need:

- Regular affection
- Financial stability
- Motivating validation
- Family loyalty
- A relaxing environment...but not so comfortable that we become stagnant

---

Sweet stability! Routine-driven Saturn feels right at home in pragmatic Taurus! You two aren't just each other's biggest cheerleaders, you're sexy accountability buddies. When there's a goal to be accomplished, you'll roll up your sleeves and work steadily to achieve it. Friends may marvel at how much you two accomplish as a duo. What can you say? The practical magic of Supercouple Saturn in Taurus casts a disciplined spell that delivers!

You're also quite the dependable pair. Thanks to your unwavering reliability, you're the rocks for your extended community of family and friends. Taurus is the sign of values and you two may uphold a gold standard of integrity. But this CAN become problematic if you grow dogmatic or wind up making too many sacrifices to help others. One of the core lessons for your shared Saturn is learning to value yourselves!

The best way for you to remain balanced and thriving? Ground yourselves in simple, healthy routines and repeat them on a regular schedule. Sleep for eight hours on weeknights, fuel your bodies with plant-based and high-protein food. Exercise at least three times a week with free weights and cardio moves. It sounds easy enough, right? Yet with the demands of modern life, you two may have to work at "doing less" instead of pushing for more.

With "never say die" Saturn in stubborn Taurus, you could swing to the opposite extreme and become TOO rigid. There's a reason celebrity trainers are fond of cheat days. We all need to cut loose every now and again—something you two can easily lose sight of when you're caught up on your quests. A little flexibility goes a long way with this Supercouple Saturn placement!

Fortunately, when it's time to treat yourselves, you WILL go all out. Even rigid Saturn can't completely suppress Taurus' decadent tastes. Once your relationship becomes official, open up a joint bank account earmarked for your "entertainment budget." When it's time for that long weekend in Belize or to pop the cork on a reserve bubbly, you'll have the funds chilling on ice. This Supercouple Saturn understands the art of delayed gratification!

As a rule, you two may prefer simple luxury over anything ostentatious. With the refined tastes this status-conscious Saturn brings, you may eventually become collectors of fine art, vintage cars, natural wines... Such pristine specificity can be a double-edged sword. If you lose the down-to-earth qualities of Taurus, you can veer into elitism. (Not a good look!)Because of the grounded wisdom Saturn in Taurus brings, you two may live an economically privileged life. Good on you! It's fine to share about your journey, especially if you came from humble beginnings. But know your crowd. Bragging about your expensive purchases to less-fortunate friends and family will alienate them, fast.

Another trap to avoid? Becoming set in your ways. Too much sameness also leads to stagnation, so try to break out of your shared bubble from time to time. This won't be easy since Saturn in Taurus loves comfort and familiarity. It may take a village—plus a couple's therapist, life coach and celebrity trainer—to pull you out of a well-worn groove once you've settled in together. Don't resist the call to growth! With legacy-builder Saturn in this rooted earth sign, your shared life is meant to yield a bumper crop of abundance.

SUPERCOUPLE SATURN
GEMINI ✴ ♊

OR THE 3RD HOUSE

To feel stable together, we need:

- Shared social interests
- To be listened to/have our ideas and opinions respected
- Frequent communication (ideally multiple times a day)
- Being best friends with each other

Say what? Every word counts for couples with Supercouple Saturn in Gemini, the zodiac's most communicative sign. Mic drops? No shortage of those between you two. Really getting to know each other? That can be a slower process, thanks to Saturn's suppressive influence. Behind the hilarity and intellectual musings, what ARE you two actually talking about? One of you had better get real already. Otherwise, you'll never get to experience the richly rewarding bond this blended Saturn has to offer.

Gemini is the zodiac sign of the Twins. Have you met your missing puzzle piece? Your twin flame? Yes, sort of. With weighty Saturn here, you two can sense the relationship's gravitas immediately. And THAT can stir up worries about losing yourselves in the couple bubble if you get together. Here's the good news: You're not here to "complete" each other. Rather, you'll mirror one another's greatness. And that means you simply have to celebrate what makes each of you so awesome. (Think: fraternal twins.)

With Composite Saturn in Gemini, this begins by exploring all the common ground between you. What do you both love doing? When you find those crossovers, you cooperate skillfully—and often profitably!Since Gemini is the BFF sign, your relationship may blossom out of a deep and abiding friendship. There's a natural desire to see the other succeed and, naturally, to score some victories as a tag team. Fortunately, neither goal is out of reach. Savvy Saturn in this placement makes you excellent co-strategists who navigate life's chess board with keen awareness.

As a couple, your novel ideas may be SO groundbreaking that they turn into something bigger than late-night discussions over pizza and wine. Gemini is the messenger sign and enterprising Saturn could lead you to a platform where you broadcast your visions. Start the Spotify podcast, the TikTok feed; co-author a book. When you put your heads together, brilliance emerges and quickly takes form.

As your relationship progresses, you may hit some stumbling blocks around individualization. The urge to "twin" is so strong that it can feel like a betrayal to break off on an independent mission—or to contradict the other's opinions. But here's the deal: Differentiation isn't merely healthy for couples, it's what creates a dynamic spark. With Supercouple Saturn in Gemini, you can deal with this in a structured way. For example, on Thursdays you spend time with your separate friend groups. On Tuesdays, one of you takes a dance class while the other goes indoor rock-climbing.

Equally important? Respecting each other's right to privacy. While you may be each other's #1 confidantes, the pressure to share EVERYTHING can churn up resentment. Therapy can be particularly helpful for couples with Saturn in Gemini—and we mean with your own separate counselors. Processing every thought together is NOT a good move for you two, especially when you're in the heat of frustration. Your tongues can be sharp and critical. Although you'll regret being "mean" to each other, the damage can be hard to undo. Learn to take cooldown breaks. They will be the saving grace of your relationship!

SUPERCOUPLE SATURN

CANCER ✳ ♋

OR THE 4TH HOUSE

To feel stable together, we need:

- Emotional security
- Safety to express our feelings
- Family bonding time
- A peaceful and nurturing home

Comfort, safety and security: That's the ultimate trinity for relationships with Supercouple Saturn rooted in Cancer. And you take this very seriously! Saturn in Cancer doesn't merely heighten your nesting instincts. It calls you to create a serene home, to heal intergenerational trauma and perhaps even build a family of your own. Nothing light and fluffy here!

The catch? Opening up and getting personal won't happen overnight. The Crab's emotionality doesn't flow easily through Saturn's buttoned-up reserve. Saturn isn't super stoked to be in Cancer; in fact, astrology calls this position in "detriment" because Cancer sits opposite the ringed planet's home base of Capricorn on the zodiac wheel. But once the trust develops between you, there's no emotion too profound to share! As feelings become rock solid, you'll readily lean on each other.

Having a private space is a must! Your shelter is your "crab shell" and you need it to be a place where you both feel safe dropping your guards. Without that, you feel vulnerable and exposed, making it difficult to bring your best to the relationship. If you weren't naturally gifted with the

♄

decorating gene, you two can (and should) develop it. Studious Saturn can help you master all the hacks for making a basic room feel like a sacred oasis that's stamped with YOUR personal touches.

Nurturing Cancer is associated with the archetypal mother, making you a caring pair. But having your Supercouple Saturn in this sign can anchor you with heavy family responsibilities. Set boundaries fast! Otherwise your home can turn into a revolving door for relatives who are down on their luck. Guests who overstay their welcome will stress you out and cause you to bicker. Then, everyone suffers. You'd never leave loved ones out in the cold, of course. Find ways to support them that don't turn into a "home invasion."

Children can be another sticking point for the two of you. This karmic Saturn can churn up a strong desire AND a deep resistance to becoming parents. If your own youths were troubled, you may fear repeating patterns, or worry that you're not up to the task of being role models. Surprise: Raising kids (and pets) could be your greatest joy together! Saturn's restraint reins in just enough of Cancer's caretaking instincts to make you two both loving and firm. You'll be adored and respected—every parent's dream! In fact, part of your dharma work within this connection may be healing ancestral trauma and shifting your lineage's tide in a healthy, new direction.

A little real talk about your ultimate home: your bodies. No matter how many security blankets you swaddle yourselves in, you can't escape the fact that you are made up of flesh and blood. Emotional eating can be a shared vice in this relationship, leaving you both with extra pounds, inflammation and other undesirable conditions. Getting yourselves on a structured eating and exercise plan is #SaturnGoals for you two.

Frivolous spending is another "comfort" you two would be wise to give up. More than most duos, Saturn in Cancer Supercouples need savings in the bank and an ever-growing nest egg in order to REALLY relax. If you two tap into Saturn's enterprising powers, you might even team up for a successful home-based business. Anything in the hospitality or real estate industry may be your shared jam, like opening a restaurant, flipping houses into a vacation-rental empire, building coworking spaces. With a solid vision, you could set yourselves up for a secure future that gets Saturn's seal of approval.

SUPERCOUPLE SATURN

LEO ✳ ♌

OR THE 5TH HOUSE

To feel stable together, we need:

- Encouragement to express our voices and talents
- Words of affirmation
- Support with managing finances
- Daily doses of romance

Glamour, fame and fairy-tale romance: Sounds good, right? But wait...when will this magic moment happen? How much will the experience cost? Oh, and what's the dress code? Womp womp. With restrained Saturn rolling up the red carpet in Leo, you're not exactly floating off to a castle in the clouds. For couples with this Saturn placement, the pursuit of pleasure comes with a hefty side of anxiety and hesitation. This normally romantic zodiac sign struggles to "surrender to the moment" under Saturn's rigid control. If ever there were a couple who needed a date night calendar, it's you two!

Leo is a zodiac sign that hates to be ignored, so it's not like you'll be flying under the radar. But with your Supercouple Saturn here, you want to be seen in the best possible light. Modesty may be overrated, but together you're allergic to anything that carries a whiff of narcissism. You two may downplay your contributions as "no big deal." Hell, even a humblebrag can be extra. You'd rather walk into the room like a magnanimous duo who earned everyone's respect through your hard work and humility. (Even if you DID get a little help on that down payment from your folks...shhhh.)

ħ

Life hacks and shortcuts are not your preference, by and large. Whether you're raising a family or building a business that supports the entire community, you prefer to take the long route together, experiencing every step of the journey. Along that winding road, you two gain a Saturnian mastery of the process. How else can you grow as wise, compassionate leaders if you don't get your hands dirty? That in-the-trenches experience is a badge of pride for you both. It makes you relatable. And then you can sidestep the power dynamics that you find excruciatingly uncomfortable.

Lest you think we're accusing you of asceticism, here's an important footnote: Saturn in Leo Supercouples DO love their earthly pleasures and luxury brands. But your tastes are more classy than flashy. You'll roll up in matching black Mercedes, outfit your kitchen with Carrara marble countertops, send your cubs to an elite private school. But you probably aren't vocally trumpeting your privilege around town.

Behind the scenes, you two may struggle with excess. Saturn in Leo can serve tough lessons about overindulging. Word to the wise: Cut up the plastic! And go easy on the loans. Just because you CAN get that home equity line of credit doesn't mean you should— at least not without heeding cautious Saturn's warnings about overspending.

Your shared struggles with authority can be epic. No one had better think they're the boss of you two! When outside forces attempt to constrain you, it's not a pretty sight. So you were supposed to get a permit before building that addition onto your house? The Airbnb you rented has quiet hours? Grrrroar!

Create your own Supercouple Chart at **SUPERCOUPLE.COM**

Epic power struggles can arise within your relationship, too, especially if one of you feels like they are always compromising their desires. One workaround? Carve out independent realms to reign over within your shared kingdom. Knowing that you have full authority over the home decor while your partner handles vacation planning, for example, can give you both a sense of agency. But times will come when you need to compromise, which is not Leo's strongest suit. Lean into Saturn's penchant for adulting. Giving an inch doesn't mean the other one has the right to take a mile!

ħ

SUPERCOUPLE SATURN
VIRGO ✳ ♍

OR THE 6TH HOUSE

To feel stable together, we need:

- Quality time together
- Shared values and a high level of integrity
- Daily communication
- Healthy routines
- Constructive feedback

Let's keep it simple, shall we? With Supercouple Saturn in orderly Virgo, life together works best when you two have clearly defined rules, roles and operating systems. Are we exclusive or allowed to see other people? Who is going to manage the household finances? What side of the bed do you sleep on? Yes, these little things matter! Virgo is the zodiac's most discerning critic and it knows a Pima from an Upland cotton. Throw in Saturn, the planet of status, and suddenly, your four eyes are wide open. Have you become fussier since the two of you got together? Get used to it. Saturn in Virgo is here to elevate everything in your lives to the purest standards. This is where the "virgin" symbolism comes in. And you'll soon have the undyed, organic, ethically sourced wares to prove it.

Create your own Supercouple Chart at **SUPERCOUPLE.COM**

While your lifestyle may bring some eye rolls from less awakened friends, you're not trying to be a pair of prima donnas. Quality matters to Virgo, the zodiac's integrity hound, and it's not just about snobbish standards. In this conscientious earth sign, serious Saturn wakes you up to the impact you're having on the planet—and yourselves. Wellness is a a big deal to Saturn in Virgo Supercouples. You want to live long lives together, after all. The sooner you start eating clean and working out together, the better. And guess what? You two actually ENJOY setting up systems that make your worlds run like a well-oiled machine. Get yourselves on that fitness app and start sharing your daily macros, stat!

Financially, the two of you can become savvy savers and investors. While you won't have the hugest risk appetites, you're okay with delaying gratification. Your nest egg grows steadily as you squirrel away a percentage of every paycheck into compounding-interest accounts. Knowing that you'll have breathing room in your elder years is more of a luxury to the two of you than blowing everything on a one-time splurge.

Perfectionism is the obvious Achilles' heel for Saturn in Virgo duos. When it's time to cut loose and say, enjoy a slice of birthday cake or stay up five hours past your usual bedtimes, it may occur as a massive disruption to the field. Anxiety can be rife in your relationship and you may spin each other out into worry spirals at the first sign of a "mistake." Remind yourselves often that chaos is a naturally occurring phenomenon. This will be especially essential if you have kids!

Speaking of which...who don't you two try to parent? Virgo is the sign of service. And in this relationship, you may shift naturally into the roles of "the responsible ones," doling out advice and rushing in for the save when people fail to heed your words of warning. While charity indeed begins in the home, it doesn't stop there for Saturn in Virgo Supercouples. It can be deeply satisfying for you both to get involved in community service work. Whether you're fundraising for a youth after-school program at a block party or managing the holiday food drive, you make quite the power team.

The dutiful nature your Saturn in Virgo spins up CAN feel heavy at times. Caring for elderly parents, helping out friends who have hit hard times—there will always be a place where help is needed. The question to ask is this: where do your limits lie? It's one thing to support your loved ones when you have the resources to do so. But when you put the needs of your relationship last, your connection suffers. Be sure to include YOURSELVES in the list of people who need your giving touch.

ħ

SUPERCOUPLE SATURN
LIBRA ✦ ♎

OR THE 7TH HOUSE

To feel stable together, we need:

- Loving gestures
- Strong physical attraction
- Compliments on each other's beauty and style
- A clearly stated commitment (ideally leading to marriage)

How sweet—and supportive—it is! Libra is the sign of committed partnerships, and when Supercouple Saturn lands in this zodiac sign, it acts like a stability beam for your relationship. Once you two find each other, it's game on! You quickly become a "we," with a natural drive to think, act and move through life as a conscious couple. And with beauty-lover Libra at the wheel, you look damn good doing it. You two are an enviable pair!

Saturn is an industrious planet, and it helps people build long-term security. Through harmonious Libra, this can be a fun and decadent process that doesn't need to be rushed. As the saying goes, "A good house is never done." And you two will apply this broadly to your life together, upgrading and elevating one step at a time.

Sourcing missions can be fun in architectural salvage shops or luxury showrooms, after all. There's no shortage of creativity for Saturn in Libra couples. You two understand that the power of aesthetics has little to do with the price tag. (Not that you won't splurge often with this decadent placement!)

Working together comes naturally to you two, both at home and in business. As the sign of the Scales, Libra blesses you with a natural ability to compromise. Together, you'll weigh options and pick up where the other leaves off. There's a reason you're such a force when together! Saturn is "exalted" in Libra, the planet's most powerful spot in the zodiac. And thanks to that, you two won't be hit with the usual challenges that the taskmaster planet brings. (Sweet relief!) But you WILL have access to the diplomacy and negotiation skills of Libra—and combined with Saturn's wisdom, you can use these to good measure for creating long-term security in your life.

Saturn in Libra makes you natural networkers. It really IS all about who you know—and you two are a naturally popular pair. Settle down in a city with award-winning restaurants and a notable arts scene. You'll love being around stylish folks who take great care of their appearances. We're not calling you superficial; you're just an aesthetically oriented pair.

That said, Libra is also the sign of justice, so you two will feel a duty to help underprivileged members of society. With the party-planning skills this Supercouple Saturn gives you, how about raising funds at a charity gala? (Your good friend who runs the local museum would surely open up the space...and maybe your sommelier bud would donate some wine...) The contact database you two build over time is bound to be impressive. But beyond that, you'll call these people your genuine friends. As a generous couple,

ħ

you are natural relationship-builders. Your community will be one of goodwill, fairness and equal give and take.

Some of Libra's romantic proclivities can be stifled by this Supercouple Saturn. You two can get so caught up in making life beautiful for everyone around you that you forget to turn those beams on each other. Or you may "save it all up" for a special occasion, like a birthday or wedding anniversary. And while those shared celebrations are sure to be epic (and highly Instagrammable), it's important to make regular gestures so your love tanks don't get depleted. Set up a shared calendar and commit to a weekly date night that's only about the two of you. Create "device free" hours in your home where you put down the phones and tablets and concentrate on each other. You'll be amazed by what activities you, er, get your hands into when they aren't busy scrolling.

SUPERCOUPLE SATURN
SCORPIO ✳ ♏

OR THE 8TH HOUSE

To feel stable together, we need:

- Respect for each other's privacy and personal space
- A soul-deep connection
- Strong sexual attraction
- Financial responsibility
- Unwavering loyalty
- Attentiveness to each other's specific needs and tastes

Who's the sexiest tag team in town? With Supercouple Saturn in bewitching Scorpio, you two are a force of nature—and a pair to be reckoned with, thank you very much. Scorpio is the sign of power and Saturn is all about achievement and status. Your twin ambition is hard to match. People may simply step out of the way when you two come barreling through.

But is that a good thing? Pump the brakes! More than most couples, you'll need to be aware of how much energy you exude when together. Domination should NOT be the goal, and it probably isn't. The trouble is, you two can easily overpower others when you show up as a united front. Push it too hard and you'll get a reputation as villains. Ouch! Despite the legends about Scorpionic evil, this

ħ

Create your own Supercouple Chart at **SUPERCOUPLE.COM**

sign can be used to do great good. The trick is to focus on what you're creating, then tap into this empathic water sign to make sure everyone involved in (or affected by) the mission feels safe, cared for and secure.

The truth is, Saturn in Scorpio can help you both develop deep levels of empathy. This is the sign that rules death, spirituality and rebirth. Being such an alchemical couple, you may become "space holders" for your community, supporting others through their most critical life passages. When you love people—including each other— you do so fiercely. That unwavering loyalty can revive people's spirits—and even bring them back from a "dead" existence, such as hopelessness or depression. And you two will do it without a single false platitude!

Scorpio is said to evolve through three incarnations: scorpion, serpent and eagle. Your relationship may go through a similar phased approach. Early on, you're like the threatened Scorpion, ready to unleash its deadly sting if the other dares hurt you. When you realize it's safe, the enchanting serpent rises and you'll charm each other with every seductive tool you have in the arsenal in an effort to prove that you're "The One." Finally, having chosen the other as your mate for life, you soar together like visionary eagles, viewing the world from your perch.

But that doesn't mean you can rest on your laurels up there in your treetop nest. As a couple, you can be triggered by outside forces that send you spiraling back into Scorpion mode. Trying to take on too many responsibilities all at once? Spending money you don't have to keep up with the Joneses? Becoming competitive with others in your community? All very bad ideas for you two. Not only can these things spin up a shared vengefulness, they can spin you both out into unhealthy addictions. In this relationship of extremes, you can be each others champions OR enablers. It's a slippery slope when you start opening up bottles of bourbon to cope with anxiety or get obsessed with status markers that are not in your budget, like sending your kids to an elite private school because "everyone else is doing it."

For you two, creating a solid sense of inner security will be your joint key to freedom. Some astrologers believe that the phoenix is the fourth phase of Scorpio. Cycles of death and destruction are often what lead to rebirth. Transformation is a huge theme for Saturn in Scorpio—and yes, this placement intensifies the "lessons" of your souls' journey together. A shared spiritual path is often the entry point to this elevated existence for you two. With disciplined Composite Saturn in mystical Scorpio, you're open to all kinds of guides from plant medicine shamans to meditation gurus. Sharing that enlightening journey may be the best investment you two make in your relationship!

SUPERCOUPLE SATURN
SAGITTARIUS ✳ ♐

OR THE 9TH HOUSE

To feel stable together, we need:

- Total honesty
- Space to explore our independent interests
- A warm and welcoming home
- A willingness to grow together—to explore the world and learn

---

With Supercouple Saturn in global Sagittarius, the world is your oyster. But there IS a catch: You two will have to shuck a lot of mollusks before you find your pearl. This slow-and-steady planet tempers a lot of Sagittarius' fiery zeal, but it also brings a profound enthusiasm for the learning process itself. Teachable moments? Let's go! You two will turn them into growth experiences, and these will become part of your ultimate fortune as a pair.

Higher education is governed by Sagittarius, and with Saturn here, you become eternal students of life. But academia isn't the only place to thrive. One of your best "education centers" as a couple is the school of life. Sagittarius is the zodiac's traveler, and Saturn here challenges you both to broaden your horizons. Couples' retreats are the ultimate getaways for you two. A chance to absorb knowledge while exploring a brand-new region? Nirvana for you two!

But here's the rub: restrictive Saturn can also throw hurdles in your path, making it harder for you to slip off on these getaways. Your sojourns must be carefully planned with lots of advance preparation. Embrace the journey TO the journey, whether you're building up stamina for a backpacking trip with regular hill climbs near home or getting your diving certification in a local pool before heading to a coral reef. One of you may sign up for grad school in another country or get a gig as a visiting professor. Work may send you on a build overseas. Adventures like these, while exciting, can feel like disruptions, throwing off your stability. Moments like these are when Saturn's systematic planning powers will really be necessary!

If you hope to drop anchor, be patient. Karmic Saturn can slow the clock, which can make it hard for you two to settle down and find a home. But that's not necessarily a bad thing. You could do a long stint as digital nomads, working remotely with views of the rain forest or ancient temples. Stick around long enough and you two might even become adopted into a culture that's different from your native ones. If you haven't traveled extensively before meeting, each other's Saturn in Sagittarius could nudge you both to live abroad. And if not? You two may team up to work with people all over the globe, rising early for Zoom meetings with colleagues who are already eating dinner in their time zones.

Many cross-cultural couples may have Saturn in Sagittarius. With the challenger planet here, you may really have to adopt the "love will conquer all" mantra. Hurdles may come at you left, right and center, from disapproving family to figuring out how to raise the kids. Putting up boundaries will be a necessary, but at times painful, experience. However, your relationship is nobody's business but your own.

Enterprising Saturn gets especially entrepreneurial in Sagittarius! Opening a business together may be one of the toughest AND most rewarding things you'll do together. This Supercouple Saturn gives you two the grit, determination and hustle that you need to succeed—plus it tempers this fire sign's gambling instincts. The secret to your success? Move ahead thoughtfully, and keep "scope creep" in check as you expand. The point is to build a sustainable empire, even if it isn't an overnight hit.

SUPERCOUPLE SATURN
CAPRICORN ✳ ♑

OR THE 10TH HOUSE

To feel stable together, we need:

- A long-term commitment
- Shared financial values and work ethics, a strong sense of family
- To be appreciated (and needed) for what we are each providing

---

Step aside, the power couple has arrived! When Supercouple Saturn struts through its native sign of Capricorn, it blesses your relationship with extra prestige. When you two join forces, it feels like you can achieve anything—and you keep the bar raised high. It won't be long until the VIP invites start rolling in.

You're here to bring out the best in each other at every phase of the game. You'd make excellent business partners, thanks to the double-strength diligence of both masterful Saturn and tenacious Capricorn. When you find a shared passion, you'll throw yourselves into it! And quickly, it will be monetizable. If one of you is in grad school or the other doing corporate life, that's fine too. You'll easily design a lifestyle that supports both of your ambitions. Either way,

Create your own Supercouple Chart at **SUPERCOUPLE.COM**

you two will be happiest when you're whirring away together toward your loftiest goals.

While you're not clout chasers, you DO have a healthy respect for status. As a couple, you enjoy being around accomplished people who have earned their "merit badges" through grit and determination. Membership has it privileges for Saturn in Capricorn, so join groups that speak to your common interests. Miracles happen when you're rubbing shoulders with the VIPs. Maybe it's an arts society or a business ignition group for people looking to break into the seven-figure income bracket. Structures like these support your growth—and can introduce you each to mentors that are a vital part of your shared success story.

While your hustle together is unstoppable, it flashes a few yellow lights. In your zeal to prove yourselves to the world, you can easily become workaholics, missing out on crucial milestones with the ones you love. Check your priorities: If you're more worried about asking your boss for a deadline extension than you are about missing your mom's 60th birthday party, it's time to recalibrate.

Nurturing strong family bonds is particularly important for Saturn in Capricorn Supercouples. (So yeah, definitely don't miss that birthday party.) Capricorn is the legacy-builder, the provider, the zodiac sign most likely to have a family crest. With responsible Saturn here, you two may become the pillars for your respective clans, organizing intergenerational activities that keep traditions alive. If you decide to have children, you won't necessarily be in a rush. But slowpoke Saturn doesn't calibrate his watch to the biological clock, so you might need to set a few "reminder alarms" if you don't want to miss your prime fertility window. There's more to life than "work, work, work" and if anything can top the joy of achievement for you two, it's building a family, as you define it!

SUPERCOUPLE SATURN
AQUARIUS ✳ ♒

OR THE 11TH HOUSE

To feel stable together, we need:

- A non-judgmental atmosphere
- Conscious lifestyle choices (socially, environmentally, etc.)
- A shared community
- Being each other's best friends
- Regular date nights and outings
- Acceptance of each other's "eccentricities"

Can you change the world for the better? With Supercouple Saturn in idealistic Aquarius, you two are certainly going to try—cynics be damned! You are the pair that cares. And thanks to integrity-hound Saturn in this conscientious placement, you want to live by values you can both be proud of, like sustainability and inclusivity.

You can also be quite the rebels, although your renegade moves are generally for a good cause. Aquarius is the sign of social justice and this Saturn puts a supportive structure behind your activism. Whether you're attending (or organizing!) a protest or setting up a charitable fundraiser campaign on social media, you two know how to rally the community into action. As a dynamic duo, social impact is the name of your game.

Whatever plan is at stake, you have a knack for hyping up team spirit and getting everyone engaged in the mission. And it's not just lip service!

Create your own Supercouple Chart at **SUPERCOUPLE.COM**

Together, you know how to draw out people's highest potential and turn it into kinetic energy. Others feel important around you two—a talent that makes you a power pair when it comes to leading any group effort.

Here's where the paradox comes in: For Saturn in Aquarius Supercouples, freedom is the ultimate form of success. Living life by your own design? Yes, please. While you'll happily participate in groups, you rebel against any collective that expects people to conform to a uniform standard. Your ideal community celebrates diversity and trusts people to follow their own moral compasses—and of course whatever guidelines you agree on in a democratic vote.

On the subject of liberation, what about work? Despite briefly considering "Breatharian" theory that says sunlight and air are proper sustenance, you two still need to put food on the table. The good news is that Saturn in tech-savvy Aquarius is wired to thrive in the digital age. You two may team up successfully on an innovative venture, like launching a time-saving app or building an online peer-to-peer platform that helps people share goods and services. Not feeling quite so entrepreneurial? You could polish your skills as designers or developers and live that independent contractor life, perhaps as digital nomads for part of the year.

Who wants to pull some tarot cards? There's no escaping the "woo" for you two, even with pragmatic Saturn pulling your attention back to the material plane. Channel your metaphysical interests in a Saturnian way—as TOOLS for self-awareness and personal development that you can bring back into your relationship. There's not much you two will do in life "just for the heck of it." No, your souls are far too evolved for that. Life is a brief and wonderful opportunity to help humanity gain greater consciousness—and you're both here for it!

ħ

SUPERCOUPLE SATURN

PISCES ✳ ♓

OR THE 12TH HOUSE

To feel stable together, we need:

- Uninterrupted dreamtime
- Fantasy dates and personalized romantic gestures
- Confidence-boosting support
- Appreciation for the "little things" that each of us do
- Healing touch
- A safe space for our highly sensitive emotions

Hey, you lucid dreamers! When pragmatic Supercouple Saturn lands in fantasy-spinning Pisces, the effect is definitely weird. Your relationship won't unspool according to traditional security measures or standard operating procedures. And that's the beauty of it. You're together because your souls have found one another (again). Even if it takes a while to nail the correct structure to house this big romance, that's okay. The steady stream of creative juices flowing between you keeps your love tanks full. And with that premium fuel, there's no telling what amazing things you'll build together in this imaginative relationship!

Discovering your shared magic may lead you to remote corners of the world. Since Pisces is the sign of escapism and solitude, you

Create your own Supercouple Chart at **SUPERCOUPLE.COM**

may be at your best being together in semi-isolation. With Pisces' seafaring energy, a remote island can be your dream destination for a couple's getaway. Since Saturn loves to push people to their edge, there could even be a survivalist challenge involved in some of your journeys. We're not saying you'll be contestants on *Naked And Afraid* or go off-grid to be healed by a sacred medicine practitioner. But it's not out of reach either...

We're not going to lie: Saturn in Pisces, the sign of sacrifice, can be heavy some days. Together, you may feel like Atlas, carrying the weight of the world on your shoulders. This trait is noble when put toward a world-changing purpose. But it's easy to get swept into "rescue missions" for random people who probably need to be handling their own affairs. Money can be particularly slippery, especially if you fail to utilize Saturn's systematic powers to create a budget. It's easy for you two to rack up debt, loaning funds that are never returned then leaving yourselves bereft of rent money.

To preserve your combined energy—and ensure that you have enough space (and cash!) left over for one another—school yourself on Saturn's boundary lessons. Get clear on where your limits lie. Practice saying "no" gracefully without feeling guilty or justifying your reasoning. This doesn't make you bad people, okay!

There's no sidestepping the shadow work in this relationship! We all come into this world with karma and you two will move through plenty of powerful soul lessons together. In esoteric, enlightening Pisces, stoic Saturn guides you both deeper into your "hero's journeys." At moments, you will definitely trigger each other, mirroring hidden pain. But if you can see this process as the gift of your relationship, you'll grow together. Not through codependence, which is a Pisces pitfall. Instead, encourage each other to do your individual healing work and be supportive through the ups and downs. This is certain to bring you closer as a couple!

SUPERCOUPLE

Compatibility

WITH YOUR
SATURN SIGN

ħ

If our Supercouple Saturn is in a fire sign:
(ARIES, LEO OR SAGITTARIUS)

And my personal Saturn is in a fire sign
(ARIES, LEO OR SAGITTARIUS):

This relationship supports your natural desire to build something big and game-changing. At times, however, you may feel creatively blocked or thwarted by the practicalities of your day-to-day life. Manage your anger and impatience so you don't destroy things before they're erected.

And my personal Saturn is in an earth sign
(TAURUS, VIRGO OR CAPRICORN):

This relationship will inspire you to build things faster and bigger than you normally would on your own. However, that can also arouse anxiety. Create a system of checks and balances for assessing whether or not you should leap ahead or move at your innately cautious speed.

And my personal Saturn is in an air sign
(GEMINI, LIBRA, AQUARIUS):

Cranes in the sky! This relationship can elevate your plans and inspire you to move full steam ahead. You're more creative than you would be on your own, but don't forget to apply your logical powers to the blueprints.

And my personal Saturn is in a water sign
(CANCER, SCORPIO OR PISCES):

Passion in action! Because this relationship amplifies your feelings, you'll need to create emotional structures and boundaries. Otherwise, you can get flooded or make unwise decisions just to keep the peace. The challenge here is to continue listening to your own feelings as a compass while also staying open to novel ways of doing things.

If our Supercouple Saturn is in an earth sign:
(TAURUS, VIRGO, OR CAPRICORN)

And my personal Saturn is in a fire sign
(ARIES, LEO OR SAGITTARIUS):

Pump the brakes! This relationship will make you healthier, wealthier and wiser, but you won't get there at your usual acceleration. Prepare to learn the fine art of budgets, timelines and project management.

And my personal Saturn is in an earth sign
(TAURUS, VIRGO OR CAPRICORN):

Sweet stability! This relationship feels blessedly centering and moves at the grounded, measured pace you prefer. There's great promise for material wealth and success here.

And my personal Saturn is in an air sign
(GEMINI, LIBRA, AQUARIUS):

Getting past the ground floor can be challenging here, but on the upside, you may experience more stability in a relationship than you ever have before. Find a way to communicate your vision by using empirical data, numbers, statistics and studies so that you can inspire growth rather than fear.

And my personal Saturn is in a water sign
(CANCER, SCORPIO OR PISCES):

Just as the ocean finds its shore, this relationship can be a very safe harbor for you. However, some mood management may be necessary so you don't flood the relationship with emotional intensity when what's needed is calm, centered thinking.

If our Composite Saturn is in an air sign:
(GEMINI, LIBRA, AQUARIUS)

And my personal Saturn is in a fire sign
(ARIES, LEO OR SAGITTARIUS):

Fasten your seatbelt, because grandiose visions could take off at warp speed in this relationship. Big ideas that no one's tried or done before will feel possible (and could be profitable). Just make sure not to cut corners.

And my personal Saturn is in an earth sign
(TAURUS, VIRGO OR CAPRICORN):

It's time to move! Your plodding pace accelerates in this relationship, which may not feel 100% practical, but can finally create some of the results that you've been ruminating on. Read the safety instructions, but don't let yourself stall the action out of fear of change.

 And my personal Saturn is in an air sign
(GEMINI, LIBRA, AQUARIUS):

Little ideas evolve into mind-blowing concepts in this relationship, which is characterized by a powerful ability to communicate. Get ready to write your TED talk or publish a study. Whatever you're fascinated with could become an even more serious pursuit in this relationship.

 And my personal Saturn is in a water sign
(CANCER, SCORPIO OR PISCES):

Your emotional intelligence may not be immediately understood here, but don't back down from your inner knowing. The gift of empathy is what you bring to this relationship. Once the two of you find the words to describe your feelings, you could build a powerful support structure for each other.

Create your own Supercouple Chart at **SUPERCOUPLE.COM**

If our Supercouple Saturn is in a water sign:
(CANCER, SCORPIO OR PISCES)

And my personal Saturn is in a fire sign
(ARIES, LEO OR SAGITTARIUS):

This relationship will require more emotional maturity than perhaps you're accustomed to. You may have less time for your self development study, shifting into the relational field, where your growth comes from learning about interactivity rather than solo pursuits. This relationship will force you to be your most emotionally mature self, which may mean learning better skills for cooperation and navigating shared activities, such as working with a team or building a family.

And my personal Saturn is in an earth sign
(TAURUS, VIRGO OR CAPRICORN):

Your sensible nature may feel cold and detached in this relationship, which requires a greater emotional intelligence than you may have developed in the past. In many ways, the fluid energy of this shared Saturn can feel destabilizing for you, since decisions may be made based on feelings rather than facts. At times you may need to pull back into your sensible personal earth Saturn to bring the relationship back into a grounded equilibrium.

And my personal Saturn is in an air sign
(GEMINI, LIBRA, AQUARIUS):

Differing ideas of what constitutes stability could make it hard to feel like you're on an even keel sometimes. Your reliance on empirical data won't hold up in this relationship that is heavily weighted toward emotional intelligence. Learning how to incorporate and make space for feelings and not just logic will surprisingly anchor this connection.

And my personal Saturn is in a water sign
(CANCER, SCORPIO OR PISCES):

Let the adulting commence! This relationship has a high EQ and will bring out your own facility with the world of feelings. At times, however, emotions may be given too much weight and should not be the only metric for making big important decisions.

ħ

SUPERCOUPLE

URANUS

how we feel young & free

Use Your Supercouple Uranus to Understand:

- Where you need freedom and autonomy in your relationship
- Best ways to get experimental (and a little freaky)
- The rebellious streak in your relationship
- Shared activism and social causes to get involved in together
- How much you break away from tradition and family patterns
- How to bring novelty and freshness into the mix
- Where you two should be innovative and open to new ideas

WHERE WILL YOU BE REBELLIOUS AND EXPERIMENTAL?

Traditions are lovely, but there comes a time when every duo needs to break the mold and escape expectations. Enter Supercouple Uranus: galactic freedom fighter, rebel and radical disruptor. The celestial shock jock marches in without an appointment, spray paint in hand, ready to tag the world with its signature stamp.

But is the "relationship graffiti" of your blended Uranus creating art or an eyesore? There's a fine line to walk where this planet is concerned. Uranus, like uranium, must be handled with care and measured in small enough doses to avoid a nuclear explosion. If you want to blow up the stability of your partnership, Uranus will certainly provide you with a chemistry lab for that. But we don't recommend you handle this planet's powers with a devil-may-care, "safety third" mentality.

What you two will find, in fact, is that "just a touch" of Uranian genius and originality goes far. Because really, what the side-spinning planet craves most is freedom. If Mars is the adrenaline junkie of your chart, Uranus is the dopamine supply. When you hit a plateau, turn to either of these planets to bust up the monotony.

Do something you've never done before and let Supercouple Uranus guide you there. Fun fact: Novelty can actually reboot attraction for couples, bringing back the butterflies and early-stage excitement. If your Composite Uranus is in sexy Scorpio, you might unlock this electrifying ripple through the kind of erotic experimentation that is as emotionally intimate as it is physical. In equality-minded Libra, Composite Uranus encourages couples to mix up those old-fashioned gender tropes. (Stay-at-home dad? Why yes. Got a problem with that?)

Experiment. Innovate. Ideate. Think outside the box. Dare to define love in terms that work for the two of you, no matter what your friends, family or society thinks. Uranus gives zero f***s about the neighbors' opinions. So uhhh, why do you?

Can you change the world together? And how? As the humanitarian planet, Supercouple Uranus also awakens a shared sense of activism. This idealistic juice can be like a high-voltage charge for couples who need to be snapped out of a "lather, rinse, repeat" rhythm. Much like Jupiter, Uranus reminds you that there's something bigger than both of you out there—and Uranus holds an important key to discovering what that is.

Supercouple URANUS
IN THE ZODIAC SIGNS

In the Sign of	We find freedom through	And rebel against
ARIES	Non-conformity, original ideas, breaking barriers	Feeling controlled or told what to do
TAURUS	Being resourceful and financially free	Restrictive budgets, cheapness
GEMINI	Articulating our opinions, learning and exploring novel ideas	Authority and rules, closed minds
CANCER	Creating a sense of home wherever we go	Feeling smothered or "infantilized"
LEO	Creativity, celebration and iconic style	Compulsive spending, feeling bored or ignored
VIRGO	Sharing our impeccable taste and discerning advice, mastering a craft or subject	Anxiety-inducing situations, micromanaging, information overload
LIBRA	Reinventing the rules of relationships, fighting for justice	Commitment-phobia, conflict avoidance
SCORPIO	Transformation of mind, body and soul; all-consuming sex	Sharing power, trusting people, being vulnerable
SAGITTARIUS	Adventure, novelty, taking risks, exploring metaphysical ideas, travel	Small-town mentalities, ignorance, echo chambers, fear-based thinking
CAPRICORN	Being methodical, building a legacy around shared values	Other people's authority, outmoded systems and institutions
AQUARIUS	Inventing new paradigms and starting radical movements	Conformity, groupthink, a "law and order" mindset
PISCES	Escaping reality, exploring fantasy, arts and spirituality	Not having enough privacy, too many rules, rigid schedules and deadlines

FIND YOUR SUPERCOUPLE URANUS AT **SUPERCOUPLE.COM**

Create your own Supercouple Chart at **SUPERCOUPLE.COM**

SUPERCOUPLE URANUS
ARIES ✳ ♈

OR THE 1ST HOUSE

We rebel against:

- Feeling controlled
- Conforming to conventional rules
- Giving up our individual interests or self-expression to please each other

---

Rules? What are those? This relationship is a two-person rebellion here to disrupt the status quo. Originality is the calling card for Supercouple Uranus in trailblazing Aries. And it shows, from the clothes you wear on your date nights (or just your joint errand runs) to the unconventional lifestyle you may embrace. It's not that you're trying to leave jaws on the ground, but with shock jock Uranus here, you don't mind pushing the envelope, especially if it makes people question the status quo.

In many ways, this is an eternal teenage romance, searching for the next hit of excitement and a deliciously sneaky thrill. No matter your ages, this relationship never totally outgrows the impulse to rail against authority or question societal norms. Sometimes you'll turn that on each other, going rogue on the relationship or accusing the other of being controlling. While it's necessary for you both to have agency here, there's a stronger-than-usual tendency to project your authority issues onto one another. Try not to let this union devolve into a power struggle!

With the game-changing perspective that emerges when you're feeling lit up by your connection, the two of you could spearhead a movement! Maybe you'll unveil a business model that shifts an entire industry in the most deliciously disruptive way. With Uranus in Aries, you don't mind courting controversy if it supports your ideals.

The spotlight loves both of you! For the most part, you're happy to bask in it, and you'll just as readily use this attention-stealing power to share visionary art as you will to take down an infuriating political candidate. With digitally savvy Uranus in this position, you two could become "Internet famous" or use social media as a tool for spreading a shared message.

Warning: Anger can be destructive in this relationship! Because Uranus is combative and Aries is the warrior sign, you'll need to watch your tempers—with each other and any "offending party" that crosses your path. In the heat of the moment, bridges can burn with family, service providers, dear friends. Tap into Uranus' high-minded practices like breathwork and meditation to get your reactive impulses under your own command.

Impatience is another Achilles' heel of Supercouple Uranus in Aries. In your haste to create results, you could steamroll one another— or anyone who dares to stand in your path. Make sure the radical ideas that you're drawn to aren't so far from center that you wind up in a constant struggle. As much as we hate to burst your bubble, sometimes, you have to abide by agreements and boundaries.

SUPERCOUPLE URANUS

TAURUS ✴ ♉

OR THE 2ND HOUSE

We rebel against:

- Stultifying routines
- Backing down from our ethical beliefs
- Anything so comfortable it becomes a snoozefest

Bring on the practical magic! Nothing is wasted or frivolous in relationships with Supercouple Uranus in resourceful Taurus. With this innovative placement, you'll utilize material assets in genius ways, making sure there is enough to go around for yourselves and all the people you love.

Uranus is in "fall" in Taurus, meaning it's in a weakened position in this zodiac sign. These energies are fundamentally diametric: Chaotic Uranus is rebellious and disruptive while Taurus loves structure, order and routine. Uranus is the futurizer while Taurus cleaves to tradition. But once you both learn how to blend these forces, you'll tap into a true superpower.

©2022 Astrostyle. All rights reserved.

In money-minded Taurus, your tech-savvy Uranus could bring financial security through cutting-edge means. Clean energy developers? Crypto gazillionaires? It could happen. That said, destabilizing Uranus can bring some ups and downs to your bank account. As a couple, you'll have lean years where you both have to hustle and periods where you enjoy the fruits of your labor. There's no resting on your laurels with Uranus in this industrious sign.

Taurus is an earth sign and with humanitarian Uranus landing in here in your Superchart, you two can't bear to waste or pollute. This could lead you toward environmental activism...and unfortunately, some packrat tendencies. Outmoded objects (even the expensive ones) need to be released at some point; otherwise, you get stuck in a time warp. Embracing minimalism won't be easy. This tactile Supercouple Uranus makes it hard for you to eschew all luxury. But who says you need to buy everything new? Treasure hunting for salvaged, reclaimed and repurposed objects is a fun and eco-friendly bonding experience for you both.

SUPERCOUPLE URANUS
GEMINI ✳ ♊

OR THE 3RD HOUSE

We rebel against:

- The predictability of long-term relationships
- Social constraints
- Communicating in ways that don't feel "spontaneous"

Speak your piece! With Supercouple Uranus in articulate Gemini, there's no off switch for you two. This relationship bubbles over with clever banter and rich conversations about how to change the world. Neither of you will shy away from an intellectual debate when you have a point to make. No subject is off-limits here, even if it rocks the romantic boat!

With all the new ideas flowing between you both, your connection feels a lot like a think tank. Record them! The keyboard is mightier than the sword for couples with Uranus in communicative Gemini. You may use your words to shift the cultural dialogue in a meaningful way—within your local community or across social media. Humor and intellect are not-so-secret weapons in your shared arsenal. You might even team up to record a podcast or write a book.

You love working together on projects, but for how long? For this distractible Uranus duo, attention spans may vary. With so many avenues to explore, you tend to switch directions before your work together has reached anything close to its full potential. Discipline is not the strongest muscle in this relationship, but it's something you can build.

Gemini is the sign of the Twins and with radical Uranus here, this relationship is a magnet for all sorts of interesting folks, from artists to activists to the scholarly elite. If you're ever home long enough to throw a dinner party, it will surely be legendary!

Socializing together can be a mixed bag, however. When aligned, you two can work a room like champion agents, locking down deals and gathering supporters for any cause. But when your enjoyment levels aren't synchronized, look out! The unhappy one may feel betrayed if the other doesn't leave the party with them. And the head games can go nuclear with ghosting, undercutting and fights that turn into embarrassing public scenes! You'll have to temper those immature urges on a regular basis if you don't want to blow up this bond.

Snap judgments can be another shortsighted pitfall. Look past superficial "evidence" and research your options thoroughly before making any final decisions. When you two dive down a rabbit hole, you're sure to emerge with fascinating data!

SUPERCOUPLE URANUS

CANCER ✳ ♋

OR THE 4TH HOUSE

We rebel against:

- Smothering attention and affection
- Conventional ideas of home and family
- The culture of oversharing

Stability? What's that? With Supercouple Uranus buzzing in domestic Cancer, "home" can be a moving target. Just when everything settles into a predictable groove, bam! This spontaneous planet takes the wheel. You two have got your bags packed and your flights booked and you're off on a new adventure.

Long periods of nomadic life can be fun for both of you to share, especially if you're traveling in connection with a humanitarian cause—or hey, being seasonal surf and ski instructors. (How about both?) With nurturing Cancer at the wheel, you care deeply for your fellow Earthlings. You'll also be right at home around water in all forms, from vast oceans to mountains of powdered snow.

You make home wherever you are together—it's a true superpower of Composite Uranus in Cancer! But even the most free-spirited souls need to touch down eventually. With the planet of disruption in rooted Cancer, you may feel perpetually ungrounded as a pair. Until, that is, you find (or create!) a solid base camp together. And that's when your shared creativity REALLY kicks in. With Uranus' innovative influence, a sanctuary is yours to design. Whether it's an Airstream trailer, an Earthship or a pod-sized apartment on the 42nd floor of a metropolitan high-rise, you'll put a fresh spin on nesting.

Family is another area where you both will color outside the lines. If you aren't close to the people who share your DNA, you'll form a "chosen family" with hand-selected friends. Or you may be "adopted" by the locals in every place you settle down in. Even if you're only there for a few months, you two will be welcomed back with open arms. Interestingly, the Baby Boom occurred while Uranus was in Cancer from 1948 to 1956. After a time of depression and war, it was almost an act of liberating rebellion to settle down and create a family again!

But does anyone REALLY know the two of you? As warm and fuzzy as Cancer energy can be, it's deeply private. Behind the scenes, you both are bound to have a lot going on. High-minded Uranus can lead you to all sorts of cutting edge methodologies for relationship building, but unless you're willing to come out of your joint shell, it will be hard to access these resources. The key to your evolution? Find trusted guides who can help you navigate the issues that ultimately arise for every couple. Then, slowly work your way into more public healing settings like seminars and retreats. Knowing that you're not alone with these feelings will be a bigger relief than you two realize!

Create your own Supercouple Chart at **SUPERCOUPLE.COM**

SUPERCOUPLE URANUS
LEO ✳ ♌

OR THE 5TH HOUSE

We rebel against:

- Toning ourselves down
- Predictable romantic gestures
- Restrictive budgets

Is this real life...or the makings of a reality show? Some days it might be hard to tell. Passion is the ruling force for Supercouple Uranus in Leo, and it runs through your relationship like an electric current. Together, you love to thrill and be thrilled, entertain and be entertained—and your wild streaks can be legendary. With this relationship's unbridled creativity and disruptive fashion sensibilities, you could become an iconic duo, thriving in the limelight as uncompromising "artistes" or the faces of a movement.

Romance reigns supreme for Uranus in Leo pairs, and you two will find all kinds of interesting ways to woo one another. You're the pair who will surprise each other with sunrise breakfast in a hot-air balloon or front-row seats at a sold-out arena show. If it comes with bragging rights, you'll know you hit the mark!

This relationship is refreshingly liberated, and as you become more secure in your bond, you both may prefer an unconventional arrangement, such as living in separate spaces or non-monogamy. Even in a traditional coupling, you'll work hard to keep the connection fresh—often by keeping yourselves feeling fit and beautiful.

Because Leo is associated with luxury, you two may develop a weakness for the finer things in life. Thanks to Uranus' high-minded influence, however, you'll justifying the expense by opting for "ethically sourced" and "organically farmed" goods. Money burns a hole in your pockets until together you master the compulsive urge to splurge that this Uranus placement evokes. Uranus transited through Leo from 1955 to 1962, a time of increasing affluence and a growing middle class in the U.S. The Civil Rights Movement was also in full swing as freedom-fighter Uranus called forth noble leadership to allow all U.S. citizens equal access and rights.

Learning how to use all this potency effectively can take a minute though! While you'll both love all the attention your relationship brings, you may lose sight of the line between "fame" and "notoriety." One possible reason? Uranus is in "detriment" in this zodiac sign, a challenging position since Leo is the sign opposite the planet's home base of Aquarius.

Since Uranus rules radical thought, your relationship may go through a period of notoriety, especially if you two rail against entrenched systems before gathering proper data and support. When both of you align behind a cause, the whole world knows it. But appearances can be deceiving. Don't get swept along by a charismatic guru! Remaining independent in your thinking will be the saving grace for you as a couple.

SUPERCOUPLE URANUS

VIRGO ✳ ♍

OR THE 6TH HOUSE

We rebel against:

- Structures that are static with no room for growth
- Being told to act (or look!) your age
- Anyone telling you, "that's impossible"

If "organized chaos" is a legitimate thing, the Supercouple Uranus in Virgo relationship is here to prove it. When the planet of disruption lands in the sign of structure, it produces madness with a method. What matters is that you two understand the system you design, right? In this relationship you get to rewrite the rules and amend them whenever you both please. Clear benchmarks and agreements are what make your union thrive.

But this is hardly restrictive! Think about it this way: Once you understand the rules, you have the freedom to play with them. You're not breaking the law; you're evolving it. This is something every great artistic master understood. Before blocking figures in his Cubist phase, Pablo Picasso perfected realism. That's a solid metaphor for the journey you two are on together in this lifetime. Interestingly Uranus transited through Virgo from 1961 to 1968. During this time, the industrious Baby Boomers passed the torch to the highly adaptable Gen X-ers.

Perfectionism is the Achilles heel of your partnership. And when it wrests control, your frustrations can turn destructive. If you're not beating yourselves up for a "failure," you could turn that critical lens on each other—and that's never pretty. Learn to embrace the process of growing and learning instead of getting fixated on results. The "lab" of experimentation in your relationship is a mighty brilliant place.

Anxious Virgo energy can get a little neurotic (okay, a lot). With mentally alert Uranus here, both of you worry incessantly when anything feels out of order. Like a couple of canaries in the coal mine, when you spin each other up, you start chirping warnings of what portends. Although you're rarely wrong, that panicked approach can be counterproductive—especially if it spirals into fearmongering. Careful with that! Fortunately, you're brilliant at designing solutions when you come together. Allow Virgo's levelheaded, analytic thinking to dovetail with Uranus' scientific and engineering sensibilities. Can you present both the problem and the fixes simultaneously? That's the way to get people's attention!

Is it clean and green? Having Uranus in earth sign Virgo can turn you both into health nuts. Discovering the connection between mind and body can be a fascinating exploration. You two may find your way to naturopathic practitioners, plant-based remedies and medicinal herbs. You'll voraciously consume the latest research on age-defying, life-extending nutrition and try every trending program. Get yourselves on a fitness app and share recipes, workout stats, macros and more. In each other, you may have found your ultimate workout buddy!

Create your own Supercouple Chart at **SUPERCOUPLE.COM**

SUPERCOUPLE URANUS
LIBRA ✳ ♎

OR THE 7TH HOUSE

We rebel against:

- Cookie-cutter relationship structures
- Being like other couples
- Sacrificing individuality to be half of a "we"

Can relationships be "conventionally unconventional"? As far as couples with Supercouple Uranus in Libra are concerned, absolutely, 1000 times yes! Having the planet of disruption in the zodiac sign that rules committed partnerships can be a bit of a head trip. On the one hand, you gravitate toward the traditional trappings: exchanging vows, celebrating anniversaries, uniting your resources. But how you "do" your everyday life together is another story altogether—a story, in fact, that you'll insist on co-authoring from scratch. It will be a modern love fairy tale, and yes, you'll have the framed photos to prove it!

Couples with Uranus in Libra want "a love like no other." Literally. Originality ranks high on the list of Uranus' must-haves. Can you skydive into your wedding reception? Raise a family as homesteaders? Crowdfund a food truck business? It's not that you're looking for romantic street cred—at least, not that you'd ever admit. But hey, if you happen to raise the cultural bar on what actually makes a relationship awesome—and in the process, reignite people's belief in the power of love—your souls will be deeply satisfied.

But there's a secret hurdle to overcome: the not-so-obvious fears of commitment that pop up in this connection. Liberated Uranus is not exactly at home in couple-y Libra. No matter how long you two stay together, you are hoping that THIS time around, you've found your twin flame. Every moment you share will either prove or disprove the hypothesis, a disquieting quality of this bond. Libra is the sign of the Scales, forever weighing and seeking balance. The slightest "disruption to the field" can throw one of you into a doubt spiral—your partner's new cologne, their nervous laugh, an ugly pair of shoes. Beauty-loving Libra can bring an insane level of pickiness to the mix. Reality check1: It's not really the cloud of Dior or the dirtied-up Vans. Nope, it's your defense mechanisms pushing them away because (sigh) you're afraid of being "stuck" with the wrong person for life.

If you want longevity, start with this simple rule: Give up the idea that people can (or even SHOULD) exist in perfect harmony. Conflict negotiation will probably be a weak muscle in the early days of your union. But it's an essential tool for Uranus in Libra Supercouples to have in the arsenal. Without proper systems for talking through disagreements, you'll polarize in one of two directions: people-pleasing and making sacrifices, or raging on each other for being "selfish" and "uncooperative." Clearly there are many shades of grey in between there. The journey of your relationship involves discovering those.

Interestingly enough, divorce rates skyrocketed when Uranus was in Libra from 1968 to 1975. But you two can sidestep that fate by entering your relationship with eyes wide open. Rather than seeing marriage as an ideal state of existence, what if you viewed your union as an ever-evolving journey—and a commitment to support one another's growth? The real balance to achieve here is this: How to tend to your individual fields AND your relational field in a way that gives both equal airtime.

SUPERCOUPLE URANUS

SCORPIO ✳ ♏

OR THE 8TH HOUSE

We rebel against:

- Old-fashioned rules around "propriety"
- Playing it safe with investments
- Vanilla sex

Hello, you sexy rebels! With Supercouple Uranus in seductive, transformational Scorpio, this is a power pairing at its finest. There's not just a spark here; there's a current of pulsating energy that flows between both of you. Every planet has a favorite sign to land in, and for side-spinning Uranus, it's Scorpio. Here, Uranus is "exalted," meaning its powers are most potent. But Uranus in Scorpio is cosmically odd, and here's why: Uranus is a free-spirited, unabashedly eccentric planet—but Scorpio is the zodiac's most secretive and controlling sign. As these forces unite, they allow you to shock (Uranus) and awe (Scorpio).

When you dial it up, you can seduce anyone with your dynamic duo charms. But you're not here for superficial encounters. Scorpio bonds deeply, so when you two invest in your shared community, you'll give people all that you've got. You'll build lifelong friendships with people—unless they betray your trust—providing rock-solid emotional support for loved ones through all the highs and lows. Uranus in Scorpio helps you make a difference in ways that might be invisible to the public but are deeply felt in your private, most intimate connections. If your innermost circle feels like a secret society, well, we wouldn't be surprised!

We'd be remiss if we didn't mention that Scorpio is the sign that rules sex and reproduction. With liberated Uranus here, you are definitely a sex-positive pair. But herein lies another dichotomy. Uranus is progressive while Scorpio is possessive. Experimentation will be super hot for you two, as long as you've built equal amounts of "trust" and "lust." When you're in the game together, explorations can lead you down all kinds of tunnels: tantra, group sex, OM-ing, and, since Uranus rules technology, testing out all kinds of state-of-the-art toys... even AI and VR experiences. Power struggles are a real thing, but with consent, playing with power dynamics can also be incredibly hot for you two.

Since Scorpio rules long-term investments, this Supercouple Uranus can lead both of you to high-risk—but potentially high-yield—investments. You two may team up for all sorts of ventures from collecting NFTs to building commercial real estate in developing areas. Don't expect the journey to wealth to be a straight line with chaotic Uranus in the mix. Before you make your fortune, this relationship could test the vow of staying together "for richer and for poorer!"

Speaking of long-term investments, let's talk about kids. Scorpio is the sign of reproduction so there's little doubt that this topic of conversation WILL be raised. However, Uranus is a rule-breaker. If you co-parent, there may be something unconventional about the way you decide to raise your little ones. Interesting fact: the rate of single parenting rose exponentially while Uranus was in Scorpio from 1974 to 1981, one if its sharpest growth rates in the U.S. to date. You may blend families from prior relationships, home-school kids while you take years abroad or even get support from the "village" of grandparents, cousins and other relatives. Anyone who is part of your shared world has made it through enough loyalty tests to earn your trust—even with your most precious "commodities," your children.

SUPERCOUPLE URANUS
SAGITTARIUS ✳ ♐

OR THE 9TH HOUSE

We rebel against:

- Being stuck in one place for too long
- The idea that anything is "impossible"
- Keeping things simple

Global nomads or kitchen-table entrepreneurs? Life is an eternal adventure for couples with Supercouple Uranus in Sagittarius. No matter your GPS coordinates, you will always find something to explore together. Do other people think it's impossible, overwhelming or just "too much"? Perfect. Where do you two sign up?

Novelty is the fuel that pilots your twin engines. Sagittarius is the zodiac's gambler and thrill-seeker—and side-spinning Uranus loves anything cutting-edge. While your adventures may give friends and family anxiety, you two always seem to land on your feet. And there's no continent, philosophy or subject too "out there" for you to dive into as a couple.

But how much success can both of you handle? This naturally lucky placement pours Miracle-Gro on whatever you two touch. Bigger isn't always better—especially if it impinges on the freedom that's equally essential to Composite Uranus in Sagittarius. If you aren't willing to tame the growth, you both may need to hire a full-on team to manage all the front-burnered plans you have cooking. Luckily, your fortune can be good for the economy, and your entire community stands to benefit. That's a win-win progressive Uranus can get behind.

Another risk to assess? Expansion plans can take you in so many directions that you feel utterly unrooted. It's nice that Uranus in globetrotting Sagittarius turns you into citizens of the world. At some point, however, you may want to drop anchor and set up permanent residence in your favorite hub city. Pro tip: Make sure there's an international airport within driving distance, a thriving cultural scene and a diverse population to mingle with.

Limits and boundaries are not a favorite of Uranus in Sagittarius couples, but you may want to set a few ground rules when it comes to how you speak to one another. This "honest to a fault" placement can add heft to your truth hammers, but you lose sight of the pain you're inflicting on each other (or the people who are trying to help you two) by being so blunt. Humor is a saving grace for both of you, especially if you can poke fun at yourselves. But irreverence is not enough to reverse the damage of any offensive comments you let fly. Check yourselves when you're posting on social media too. In this coupling, you could get yourselves canceled! Millennials born between 1981 and 1988 arrived while Uranus was in Sagittarius. Fittingly, this group has carried the language torch to be more inclusive, from self-selected pronouns to woke discussions about race.

Sagittarius is the zodiac's media maven, and when you two are steeped in the high-vibe expression of this Supercouple Uranus, you may team up to publish some important work. Since Uranus governs technology, you could find your inspirational outlet as bloggers, YouTubers, e-commerce merchants or influencers. With the educational spirit of your connection, you may develop a series of online courses or start your own school. There's no limit to what you'll try with this free-range Uranus sign. Just try not to do it all at the same time!

Create your own Supercouple Chart at **SUPERCOUPLE.COM**

SUPERCOUPLE URANUS

CAPRICORN ✳ ♑

OR THE 10TH HOUSE

We rebel against:

- Selling out to be successful
- Working in a rigid office environment
- Unethical companies and practices

Talk about an odd combination! Side-spinning Uranus is the planetary renegade, here to shake up the system. Methodical Capricorn works within conventional frameworks, navigating these structures like a VIP. So how do you balance these dueling desires? With Supercouple Uranus in Capricorn, you two can blaze an unconventional trail to the top of your game.

Here's a question you might ask yourselves: How can we succeed as a power couple without selling out? That's a lofty goal indeed—and perhaps unachievable during periods where you're both still paying your dues. Go easy on each other, please. One (or both) of you may need to comply with corporate restrictions in order to learn the industry you're destined to crush. Keep your endgame in sight, and cheer each other on to your ultimate victory, which is living life on your own terms. Motivating one another is a must if you want to achieve the high-vibe potential of this pairing.

One of the most important conversations you can have is around shared values. Figure out two to three tenets that shape your path; for example, "do no harm" or "live sustainably." Then make those your operating principles. This can be an incredibly helpful decision-making shortcut during moments of uncertainty. You might even draft a mission statement or a charter for your relationship. With company-man Capricorn as your Supercouple Uranus, it's not a bad idea to treat your union like an enterprise unto itself.

The good news is you don't have to abide by stuffy CEO rules. Maybe you take a cut in your salaries for ethical reasons or because you want to live a flexible lifestyle. Digital nomads who bookend coffeeshop workdays with sunrise surfing and sunset yoga on the beach? Not a bad way to live if you can swing it! Millennials and Gen Z-ers born between 1988 and 1996 have Uranus in Capricorn in their natal charts, so reinventing business as we know it has been a theme for this group, which you may be a part of.

No matter where you hunker down, with innovative Uranus in Capricorn, you two are here to remix traditions. You may move to suburbia to raise a family in a well-rated school district, but that doesn't mean you have to be just like the neighbors. Maybe you'll install a chicken coop in the backyard and a VR game room in the basement. Your kids might even call you by your first names or take part in shaping holiday traditions. Sure, you might color inside the lines, but you'll use all 64 Crayons in the pack!

SUPERCOUPLE URANUS

AQUARIUS ✳ ♒

OR THE 11TH HOUSE

We rebel against:

- Conforming to societal expectations
- Putting labels on anything, even our relationship
- Privilege and exclusivity

Belly up to the genius bar and make it a double shot! Supercouple Uranus thrives in its home sign of Aquarius, where it feels free to express its eccentric and inventive qualities. When together, you two won't just think outside the box—you'll abolish the notion of a box altogether! (Fractals and sacred geometry are more your speed, TBH.) It's not that you're trying to be different. Aquarius is the sign that rules the future, and when you're together, you are like a pair of mad scientists. Your relationship is an excellent lab for experimentation, which you'll take into all sorts of realms, from sexual exploration to gender identity roles to biohacking nutrition. Since you'll be so supportive of the other's discovery missions, you'll naturally grow through this bond.

Corralling behind a cause is a major bonding agent for couples with Uranus in Aquarius. Gen Zers were born with the side-spinning planet in this zodiac sign, a generation that inherited massive global debt, systemic racism, a climate crisis…to name a few issues. Saving the Earth from doom is embroidered into the "survival brain" of this group (which you may be a part of). The future WILL be different, like it or not, and your plans as a couple are sure to include some discretionary measures for all the foreboding warnings in the news.

Popularity: rising! Whether you're geeky gamers, performance artists or rebels with a cause, you'll thrive as a couple when you assemble a squad of mutual friends. And it's sure to be a motley crew since Uranus in Aquarius is all about inclusivity. With the keen sense of justice this democratic placement inspires, you want everyone to feel equal. You don't have to conform to the same lifestyle (perish the thought!). But privilege has no place in your chosen family.

Like it or not, you two may have the "It Factor" of a couple of pop stars. Once both of you embrace this as a gift, you can use your twin superpowers to spread a message of love and kindness. Social media and the Internet are Aquarius' playgrounds, whether you start an online business or amplify a powerful cause with your artfully hashtagged posts.

But use some discretion! Not every school of thought is wise to explore, particularly ones wrapped up in conspiracy theories. Sure, you may have many late night discussions about alien life and insidious government control. But space cadet Uranus in Aquarius doesn't always know when it's flown out of safe orbit. More than many couples, you two are susceptible to getting swept along by fringe groups masquerading as activism. Remain independent but open, and you'll hit the right mark.

Create your own Supercouple Chart at **SUPERCOUPLE.COM**

SUPERCOUPLE URANUS
PISCES ✳ ♓

OR THE 12TH HOUSE

We rebel against:

- Being tied down by the relationship
- Making too many sacrifices for love
- Hiving up privacy and personal space
- Making a commitment
- Being expected to share all of our secrets and fantasies

Ready, set, elevate! Or should we say, levitate? With Supercouple Uranus in ethereal Pisces, it's hard to keep your feet on the ground—or even remember that there's such a thing as gravity. Pisces is the sign of escape and your relationship may feel like a blessed escape from reality at times. But because Uranus is the planet of activism and Pisces brings deep compassion, there's no way you two WON'T be affected by the suffering going on in the world. As a couple, you will ride some tall waves, in one minute getting swept up in the current of blissful romance, and in the next, crashing down from the weight of your empathy.

Later-born Gen Z-ers (from 2003-2011) and early Generation Alpha have Uranus in Pisces in their birth charts. They have never known a world without the Internet and mobile devices. Virtual reality is part of their consciousness—a form of escape unto itself. Similarly, your relationship may feel unbound by material world constraints. Being in the same room (or even meeting each other IRL) may not be a requirement for your relationship to thrive. The connection for you two spans across the invisible realm, whether it involves wi-fi or astral projection!

Uranus in Pisces makes you a spiritual Supercouple who enjoys exploring the metaphysical realm. Your idea of a dream vacation might involve the beach, but you could travel there for a plant medicine ceremony or a sound healing circle. And while you're thinking about it, be sure to book a few days of activism, pulling plastic out of the ocean and protecting the hatching turtles. This Uranus sign makes you highly aware of the environmental impact of tourism.

As deeply tuned-in as you are to others, you two may struggle to articulate feelings ABOUT your relationship. Emotions are so fluid for the Uranus in Pisces couple that it's hard to pinpoint a single word to describe them. So don't bother trying! Instead, accept that you'll ebb and flow between a range of emotions, just like the two fish swimming in opposite directions that represent this zodiac sign. You love one another...but you may worry that you'll hurt the other's feelings if you pull away. Having your own private spaces to retreat to can be a lifesaver, but that's not enough. Make a rule: no guilt-tripping each other for needing time alone!

Still, you may have to pull each other out of isolation every so often. You're ultra-sensitive to partner dynamics, but you don't want to get lost obsessing in your head while you wait for that text to come in. You two may benefit from deeper forms of therapy, such as hypnosis and EMDR, that can help you release generational trauma and recondition your entire outlook on what it means to love.

SUPERCOUPLE

Compatibility

WITH YOUR URANUS SIGN

If our Supercouple Uranus is in a fire sign:
(ARIES, LEO OR SAGITTARIUS)

And my personal Uranus is in a fire sign
(ARIES, LEO OR SAGITTARIUS):

You like to be seen as different, flamboyant, and special. This relationship is a great stage for all of your wild notions, fanciful wardrobe pieces and renegade moves. This Composite Uranus can rev up your immature side, especially the part of you that says, "You don't own me!" Careful not to rail against anything couple-y or collaborative—or you may miss some of the best parts of this bond.

And my personal Uranus is in an earth sign
(TAURUS, VIRGO OR CAPRICORN):

You'd rather make new rules than break old ones, but in this relationship, you could find yourself being more rebellious than is your normal nature. There is a tendency to be more hot-headed and impulsive than is your normal speed, which can stir up anxiety. Don't lose sight of your personal values. Instead, take calculated risks.

And my personal Uranus is in an air sign
(GEMINI, LIBRA, AQUARIUS):

Your revolutionary nature gets a megaphone and soapbox, which can expand involvement in activism. You may go further out on a limb here than you would on your own, so make sure you're also centered in logic and not just the fire and fury of the moment.

URANUS

And my personal Uranus is in a water sign
(CANCER, SCORPIO OR PISCES):

Put an extra battery in the smoke detector, because this
relationship can set off false alarms. You're generally more
cautious, but suddenly you find yourself taking wilder risks
than you would on your own, especially when it comes to your
creativity, self-expression and the face you show to the world.
This may provoke an identity crisis as you meet a wilder side of
yourself. Don't rush to tame it, but do be mindful of your impact
on others.

If our Supercouple Uranus is in an earth sign:
(TAURUS, VIRGO, OR CAPRICORN)

And my personal Uranus is in a fire sign
(ARIES, LEO OR SAGITTARIUS):

Your daredevil manner may need to be tempered in this
relationship, which is more about discovering innovative ways to
build material security than sharing wild adventures. Make sure to
rock the boat sometimes so you don't get bored.

And my personal Uranus is in an earth sign
(TAURUS, VIRGO OR CAPRICORN):

Real estate moguls, crypto collectors, Silicon Valley power
couple? Your savvy wealth strategies could open up some financial
freedom, allowing you to play more and enjoy luxury as a pair. You
should also learn to give each other a killer massage.

And my personal Uranus is in an air sign
(GEMINI, LIBRA, AQUARIUS):

Your experimental style could hit a few roadblocks here. If you get out of your head and into your body, you'll find plenty of pleasurable ways to play together. Less talk, more touch, please! (Toys allowed.)

And my personal Uranus is in a water sign
(CANCER, SCORPIO OR PISCES):

Emotional experimentation may not fly quite so much in this relationship that demands focus and fidelity. In order to relax and bring more fun to the mix, you may need to prove that you're a trustworthy and loyal companion.

If our Composite Uranus is in an air sign:
(GEMINI, LIBRA, AQUARIUS)

And my personal Uranus is in a fire sign
(ARIES, LEO OR SAGITTARIUS):

Naughty, naughty! Your impish and experimental ideas will catch on like wildfire in this relationship, but who's going to be the adult in the room? Think through the impact and consequences before you rush off on every wild lark. Prepare to have the best belly laughs of your life.

And my personal Uranus is in an earth sign
(TAURUS, VIRGO OR CAPRICORN):

This relationship puts words to concepts, helping you articulate your five-point plan for social justice or dreams of creating anything in community. Your desire to give back to the world will be amplified, and you may get involved in activism together.

And my personal Uranus is in an air sign
(GEMINI, LIBRA, AQUARIUS):

Talk about a Vulcan mind meld! When it comes to shaking things up, you're not just in-sync. You'll play off each other's "Wouldn't it be crazy if?" notions. Just don't ignore the laws of the material plane while you're ascending to intergalactic heights.

And my personal Uranus is in a water sign
(CANCER, SCORPIO OR PISCES):

Your desire for emotional variety might be taxing in this relationship, but that doesn't mean you won't find it exciting. However, the joy comes from conversations, adventure dates and big ideas, rather than the vault of feelings.

If our Supercouple Uranus is in a water sign:
(CANCER, SCORPIO OR PISCES)

And my personal Uranus is in a fire sign
(ARIES, LEO OR SAGITTARIUS):

There's no shortage of passion here, and this relationship will amplify its intensity. Unexpected feelings could arise that you may not be prepared for, however. Choose a safe word and make time for aftercare.

And my personal Uranus is in an earth sign
(TAURUS, VIRGO OR CAPRICORN):

Your unconventional ideas about money and security could find a home here—literally. This relationship helps you set up a lifestyle by your design that may not be white picket fence, but feels safe and snug for you.

And my personal Uranus is in an air sign
(GEMINI, LIBRA, AQUARIUS):

What impact do you make? This relationship forces you to reckon with the results of your words and actions. The bad news? You may realize that you've been hurting people's feelings. The good news? You'll learn to be impeccable with your word.

And my personal Uranus is in a water sign
(CANCER, SCORPIO OR PISCES)

Nothing more than feelings? You'll move through so many emotional spaces in this relationship that it might make your head spin. If you remain fluid and open-hearted, sailing through these sensitive seas can help you find mastery in love.

SUPERCOUPLE

NEPTUNE

our secrets & fantasies

ψ

Use Your Supercouple Neptune to Understand:

- Where your relationship needs to be more flexible and fluid
- Where your relationship needs boundaries, too.
- Where you'll be idealistic together
- Shared fantasies to explore (or simply talk about for a high)
- Where you might be gullible and overly trusting as a duo
- How, when and where to get more vulnerable with each other
- The secrets to deeper sensuality
- Where you may go into denial as a pair
- Areas of addiction that should be avoided
- How to release control and surrender in the relationship
- How to give and receive with an open heart

FANTASY, ESCAPISM AND DENIAL IN YOUR RELATIONSHIP

Lovesick. Infatuated. Swept off your feet. That's Neptune-speak for "romance," which is the drug this planet traffics in. You want reality? Head due west to Saturn. Fantasy agent Neptune wants no part of that sobering buzzkill, thanks.

Love's most addictive properties are brewed in ethereal Neptune's cosmic kitchen. And a small taste can hook even the strongest among us. Even when we "know better," we can still tumble headfirst into Neptune's net, seduced by its siren song. Under its intoxicating spell, we become pure magic, suddenly possessing irresistible attractiveness and sensual superpowers.

In your Supercouple chart, Neptune reveals where you're most vulnerable and willing to surrender control. And hey, that's not a bad thing! If we don't let down our walls and allow others to contribute to us, intimacy can never flourish. Neptune is the "power bottom" of the solar system. Its strength lies in helping us find the willingness to trust and fall into the unknown. It allows us to be more fluid with our boundaries, gives us the courage to receive, to melt into oneness with another soul. In exchange, we get to commune with the divine.

But the planet of illusion and sacrifice must be enjoyed responsibly. In large doses, Neptune can lead couples down a destructive rabbit hole of addictions, enabling and codependency. Boundlessness is Neptune's gift to your relationship. But without healthy boundaries to match, the slope is more than just a little bit slippery.

With fervent faith, Neptune believes. In unicorns. Soulmates. Happily ever after. This blissed-out state can bring your relationship to the holiest heights or leave you stranded in the gutter, wondering how you could have been so foolish, so gullible, so trusting. You may need a recovery program as you experience the side effects of withdrawal.

There are ways to microdose Neptune for a healthier plan(e)t-based high. Notice when you start to loosen the reins a little too much, losing track of what's fact and what's fantasy. As the planet of illusion, Neptune can't help but project hopes (and sometimes fears) onto the relationship. The trouble is when we hoist someone onto a pedestal so high they can only fall from grace. And oh, is that abyss bottomless too: Neptune also shows where we feel like victims in a relationship.

Lean into Composite Saturn, Neptune's nearby neighbor, for a reality check when things get too porous. Find your fierceness with Composite Mars, your independence with Composite Uranus.

Still, what would that dappled honeymoon phase be without the rose-colored vistas, the longing, the escape from the monotony of daily human existence? Supercouple Neptune is the high we'll chase, an inevitable hazard in the contact sport of love.

Supercouple NEPTUNE
IN OUR ZODIAC SIGN

In the Sign of	We find healing through	But struggle to
ARIES	Self-actualization	Express anger
TAURUS	Leisure and pleasure	Budget wisely
GEMINI	Connection with kindred spirits	Individuate
CANCER	Comfort and domesticity	Open up and feel safe
LEO	Pageantry and passion	Know our limits
VIRGO	Serenity and health	Trust our own decisions, overcome imposter syndrome
LIBRA	Companionship and compromise	Say "no" and ask for what we need
SCORPIO	Chemistry	Find healthy expressions of power
SAGITTARIUS	Travel and adventure	Calculate risks accurately
CAPRICORN	Responsibility and long-term goals	Create healthy boundaries, loosen up
AQUARIUS	Building community	Separate from the pack
PISCES	Compassion, art and spirituality	Stay connected to reality

Ψ

FIND YOUR SUPERCOUPLE NEPTUNE AT
SUPERCOUPLE.COM

Create your own Supercouple Chart at **SUPERCOUPLE.COM**

SUPERCOUPLE NEPTUNE
ARIES ✶ ♈

OR THE 1ST HOUSE

Our idea of a fantasy may involve:

- Exploring our individual identities with each other's support
- Taking on an "us against the world" challenge

Hello, shape shifters. With Supercouple Neptune in Aries, you make an enchanting and enigmatic pair. You may inspire each other to change your looks frequently, enjoying the art of being chameleons. This theatrical Neptune placement can make every day feel like a costume party—and you two probably have the outfits to prove it. This relationship has an element of performance art to it that's enjoyable to experience...AND watch.

At times, you may choose to keep a low profile, playing the role of selfless supporters within this partnership. You can be powerfully attentive for one another, reflecting each other's highest selves. All the same, it can be hard to get a clear read on your partner's intentions. With boundless Neptune here, you may shape shift regularly to win the other over. This can be a blessing and a curse. The two of you can "become" what the other one wants, even intuiting their needs before they realize what they want for

©2022 Astrostyle. All rights reserved.

413

themselves! But too much adapting can leave you feeling lost, hooked on validation or stuck in a cycle of people pleasing. Until you gain awareness of this tendency, feelings of self-doubt or victimization could divide you.

A Neptune in Aries relationship is bound to have the occasional identity crisis, but that's something to explore. One of your core lessons as a couple is to "know thyself." Breaking free from Neptune's hall of mirrors may require assertiveness training. As both of you grow comfortable speaking up and taking charge, you can emerge together feeling like two beautiful, whole individuals who complement one another instead of "completing" each other.

Neptune is passive and Aries is aggressive, creating a paradox for you two. Getting in touch with anger—an Aries touchstone—can be a sticking point. Learn to recognize it and express it before it festers. Otherwise, it can turn inward and manifest as self-abuse or deep resentment.

With your Supercouple Neptune in this warrior sign, this relationship is imbued with a fighting spirit, but you two may find it easier to stick up for each other than for yourselves. Remind yourselves often that you are BOTH worth it, then find the most peaceful, loving way to navigate conflict.

Create your own Supercouple Chart at **SUPERCOUPLE.COM**

SUPERCOUPLE NEPTUNE
TAURUS ✳ ♉

OR THE 2ND HOUSE

Our idea of a fantasy may involve:

- Enjoying a leisurely and romantic life
- Spending on luxury

When flowy, dreamy Supercouple Neptune lands in the practical, structured sign of Taurus, things get weird. This cosmic "conflict of interest" can make it hard for you two to anchor in any sort of daily schedule. But there IS a workaround: Turn your routines into rituals. Sure, you may have to wake up an hour (or three) earlier so you can do cardio and connect over coffee before heading in to work. But at least you'll be in the zone! With the glamorous planet in this beauty-loving position, you may fight for the mirror. Escape to separate bathrooms for your grooming and primping rituals. That's how it was back in the day, and old-fashioned Taurus understands that.

At the end of the day? Bond through Neptune's spiritual practices before drifting off to sleep. Nightly meditations or yoga can help you relax into quietude. Who knows? You might wake up to discover that you've been in each other's dreams!

NEPTUNE

Taurus is associated with the throat (and throat chakra). With Neptune here, this relationship's healing gift may lie in helping you find your voices or learn to speak up for yourselves. You might even unite to heal other people through podcasting, chanting or raising the roof at a karaoke bar.

But get a good financial manager! With your joint Neptune in this decadent sign, money slips through your fingers. Whether you're splurging on impulse couture, buying everyone's dinner or lending cash (again) to every relative in need, generosity can't be reined in for you both. But it CAN be redirected. Have funds auto-transferred into a household savings and individual retirement accounts. Earmark your favorite charity for monthly donations.

Ultimately, a shared life of comfort and peace is a must for this relationship's survival! With earthy Taurus ruling this meditative placement, nature dates help you regroup and fall back in love again. If you don't have a garden, surround yourself with house plants— just make sure to set reminder alerts for watering time!

ψ

Create your own Supercouple Chart at **SUPERCOUPLE.COM**

SUPERCOUPLE NEPTUNE
GEMINI ✳ ♊

OR THE 3RD HOUSE

Our idea of a fantasy may involve:

- Staying up talking until dawn
- Being the most popular Supercouple of our friend group

Compassionate communication and genuine connection! With Supercouple Neptune in Gemini, it's almost too easy for you to merge your lives. Your identities too! With the boundary-blurring planet here, you'll be "twinning" before you know it: matching haircuts, matching outfits, you name it. There's so much common ground to explore that you quickly become inseparable.

But that level of closeness comes with a warning label. It's wonderful to find someone with whom you have so much comfort and ease. But codependency is a Neptune pitfall. With your Supercouple placement in Gemini, you can wind up taking on the other's problems as your own. That's when your once-playful connection becomes mired in complicated dynamics. Don't let outside relationships with friends, family and supportive people (like therapists and coaches) lapse!

The good news is social planning can be a delightful creative outlet for your relationship. You're both always dreaming up fun things to do—so why not bring your loved ones along for the fun? Just make sure to set up calendar reminders! With foggy Neptune, it's easy for you two to double-book, forget plans, or worse, get guilt-tripped into inviting people along who exhaust you. (Beware those energy vampires!)

Unchecked, this Supercouple Neptune position can spin up insecurity, especially if you listen to gossip instead of communicating directly. This can zap hours of your lives as you spiral into worry and paranoia—or argue until dawn. A word to the wise: Leave the "creative fiction" out of your relationship.

But here's the beauty of your Neptune in Gemini: The two of you can heal through dialogue! When you learn to speak up, ask questions and engage in healthy conflict negotiation, you grow both as individuals AND a pair. But don't think you have to figure this out on your own. Talk therapy, interactive coaching, and mindset-shifting workshops can give you the tools you need to master this!

Ψ

Create your own Supercouple Chart at **SUPERCOUPLE.COM**

SUPERCOUPLE NEPTUNE

CANCER ✳ ♋

OR THE 4TH HOUSE

Our idea of a fantasy may involve:

- Building our dream home together
- Raising a picture-perfect family

Bless this nest! With dreamy Supercouple Neptune in this domestic position, you two can turn any space into a sacred oasis. And you'll do it with the flair of a Broadway set design team: lights, backdrops, music, visuals! And of course, feng shui. Since every object is sentimental to you both, it's easy for clutter to collect. Working with a professional organizer can be life changing for your relationship. And if neither of you has the housekeeping gene, periodic visits from a cleaning service can spare you some epic battles.

Wherever you fall on the decorating spectrum, you feel "at home" around one another. There's a natural pull to blend your families or create one of your own. Whether with kids or fur babies, you two will grow closer when you have someone to nurture.

Setting boundaries with relatives can be an issue, however. Cancer's family-oriented influence on sacrificial Neptune can leave you both feeling guilty for turning away a struggling loved one. While you'd never leave anyone out in the cold, a shared goal is to empower people to "do for self" rather than enabling them to be dependent on you. That goes for the both of you, too! When one of you is uncomfortable or off-balance, the other can physically feel it. Easy though! If you subvert your needs in an effort to be helpful, you two will wind up weakened. Sometimes, saying "no" is the kindest thing.

Since Cancer rules the stomach, you may both "stuff down" unpleasant feelings with food, drink or other unhealthy escapes like zoning out TV or engaging in an emotional affair. Take extra care to nurture yourselves with healthy habits and a balanced diet. (Let food be thy medicine!) As the two of you retire from compulsive caretaking, you can both learn to give back in a way that feeds your relationship the clean fuel it needs.

Create your own Supercouple Chart at **SUPERCOUPLE.COM**

SUPERCOUPLE NEPTUNE
LEO

OR THE 5TH HOUSE

> **Our idea of a fantasy may involve:**
>
> - Glamorous nights on the town
> - Being a famous Supercouple

Lights, camera, glamour! With fantasy-weaver Neptune in theatrical Leo, the spotlight loves you two. One of Neptune's tours through Leo, from 1914 to 1929, brought us the Golden Age of Hollywood. Your idea of the perfect date may involve dressing up like movie stars and acting out a decadent fantasy that could require a studio budget to pull off. (Save the receipts!)

Fact is, no-limits Neptune already struggles with "real world" responsibilities. But add hedonistic Leo to the mix and things could get a little out of control. Willpower is scarce for Neptune in Leo Supercouples—especially in the face of luxury temptations like shopping on the Champs-Élysées or settling down for a decadent five-star meal with wine pairings. And too much time hanging out with the jet set can be your undoing! No, you never want the party to end, but (sigh), that's part of the problem here.

Although you two may learn some harsh lessons about the dangers of excess, the road to recovery could set you both on a spiritual path. That's when the truly enlightening phase of your union begins. Your connection may always be susceptible to peer pressure; however, so be mindful of the company you keep. Replace the "eat, drink and make merry" bandits with a high-vibe soul squad.

Bring on the words of affirmation! Praise is a love language for partners with Neptune in Leo. There's a tendency to hoist each other onto a pedestal, but no one can live in that idealized light 24/7. Feelings of disappointment are common, and emotional waves can be extreme, going from high highs to dramatic crashes. Buckle yourself up for the emotional roller coaster rides that can give you both whiplash.

Despite the dramatic narrative arcs of your love story, the two of you never stop inspiring people when you shine your lights. As you grow and learn, you become powerful leaders, paving the way for others to heal without shame. Step up and testify! Your lived experiences might even be the inspiration for an actual, scripted movie one day.

Ψ

Create your own Supercouple Chart at **SUPERCOUPLE.COM**

SUPERCOUPLE NEPTUNE
VIRGO ✳ ♍

OR THE 6TH HOUSE

Our idea of a fantasy may involve:

- Sharing a serene and healthy lifestyle
- Enjoying natural wonders and "the little things"

What's the glue for a couple with Supercouple Neptune in Virgo? The spirit of humble service. With soothsayer Neptune in this helpful position, you'll drop everything to be there for one another. The rest of the world, too! Whether you're fostering children or digging wells on a voluntourism trip, this relationship brings a zeal for supporting the world's underserved populations.

Neptune toured Virgo from 1928 to 1943, a period that included The Great Depression and World War II. Resources were scant and people had to lean on each other, but one could argue that this was an era when the human spirit was shining. There was no escape into luxury during that time, so people had to find magic in the simple things. As Anne Frank wrote in her diary in 1924, "Think of all the beauty still left around you and be happy."

For you two, nature is a chapel that will always lift your spirits. Get outdoors together often! You'll love growing your own food and preserving the beauty of the land that you live on. "Getting away from it all" might just look like becoming homesteaders for both of you. Earth-based wisdom is the "woo" that calls couples with Neptune in Virgo, the sign of natural wonders.

As for the woo-woo side of this planet? That's not so easy for you to embrace with pragmatic Virgo in the mix. The reason? Neptune is in "detriment" in Virgo—the sign opposite its home turf of Pisces, making its energy harder to incorporate. Neptune is dreamy and idealistic, while Virgo is precise and rational. At best, this connection brings a gift for balancing fantasy and reality. At worst, together you may wind up with a raging case of analysis paralysis as you two try to "logic" your way out of subconscious urges. One of your great lessons together is to give up worrying about what the neighbors will think. Some rules were made to be broken!

That said, sticking to a routine as a couple can be both a struggle and your saving grace. Ideally, the two of you won't have a rigid schedule, since together you're sensitive to stress. As responsible as you are, this Supercouple Neptune may give you both a tendency to "space out" and forget about things like paying the bills, making doctor's appointments, showing up for plans. And trying to commit it all to memory leads to shared anxiety. Keep your lives simple, but set up systems for tracking all the things. The simple act of writing appointments on a calendar will bring massive relief.

Create your own Supercouple Chart at **SUPERCOUPLE.COM**

SUPERCOUPLE NEPTUNE
LIBRA ✳ ♎

OR THE 7TH HOUSE

Our idea of a fantasy may involve:

- Having the picture-perfect wedding day
- Decadent nights of cultural activities

Hopelessly devoted to you! When Supercouple Neptune drops anchor in Libra's partnership port, love IS the drug. Your relationship may feel like an addiction some days, because, yes, you're THAT into each other. Under this decadent placement, you live to spoil one another. Lavish Libra is all about vintage champagne, elegant dinners, bright bouquets hand-delivered weekly.

Generally speaking, this Composite Neptune position makes you a magnetic and enchanting pair. When you both are in the zone, this relationship is a force of nature. Libra is the sign of beauty and luxury, and when you're lit up by this connection, the two of you are a sight for sore eyes. And you'll play it up with your refined sensibilities, from your fashionable outfits to your lilting fragrances. Warning: This relationship can get expensive, especially since Neptune isn't great with any sort of boundaries, including financial ones.

Ψ

Neptune was in Libra from 1942 to 1957, the era of the Baby Boom. As the world emerged from war and a depression, life could be beautiful again. Fittingly, marriage and birth rates skyrocketed. That urge to merge was no-doubt powered by romance-junkie Neptune in the sign of committed relationships. It was time to leave all that unpleasantness behind and get swept up in the spirit of Eros. If you were both born during these years, you may live and breathe romantic idealism.

But with all things Libra, the zodiac's sign of the Scales, you must find a healthy balance between "me" and "we." With sacrificial Neptune here, you'd be willing to give up everything for your dynamic duo. But is that REALLY the best thing for the two of you? Without ample autonomy, relationships can flatline. Trouble is, Neptune in Libra can turn your couple bubble into a foggy maze that feels impossible to get out of—and downright claustrophobic after a while. (Picture those Stepford Wives popping their "little helpers.") To avert this disaster, give each other permission and support to pursue independent interests.

The other way this balancing act can play out is that you polarize to opposite extremes. This can happen if one of you is feeling under-appreciated and resentment kicks in. Rather than waging a cold war, challenge yourselves to face the conflict head on—and BEFORE it escalates into a battle royale. Chances are you simply need to practice asking for support. Give up the people-pleasing tendencies of Neptune in Libra and dare to rock the boat with a direct request. It's a lot easier than playing the damsel or dude in distress!

Create your own Supercouple Chart at **SUPERCOUPLE.COM**

SUPERCOUPLE NEPTUNE
SCORPIO ✳ ♏
OR THE 8TH HOUSE

Our idea of a fantasy may involve:

- Erotic exploration and spiritual chemistry
- Merging assets to create greater security

How close can you get? With boundary-dissolving Neptune in sexy Scorpio, that depends on the day. One moment, you'll want all barriers to disappear, as if your bodies could meld into one. The next? You will race to opposite corners, gasping for air! Scorpio energy is intense and hot to the touch, which means sometimes it's far too smoking for you two to handle. Your connection may benefit from a syncopated rhythm where you spend bouts of time together AND apart.

For what it's worth, the Free Love Era occurred while Neptune was touring the Scorpion's realm from 1957-1970. With a rallying cry of "love the one you're with," this social movement invited Neptune's fluidity into the world's ideas about intimacy—and who was allowed to experience it proudly and openly.

Supercouple Neptune in Scorpio is definitely a liberating force in your lives. Sex can be a transcendent experience that leads you on a tantric trail to ecstasy! How could it not be with spiritual Neptune in the zodiac sign associated with erotic pleasure? There's no limit to what the two of you will explore. If it turns you on, it's worth a try. But here's the rub: Since your intimate exchanges are so all-encompassing, you can get so swept up in them that other parts of your life start to suffer from neglect. Though we can't say we blame you, this is a surefire way to burn out your connection.

Another way this boundlessness plays out for couples with Neptune in Scorpio? You may hoist one another onto pedestals, even becoming addicted to their attention or approval. But imbalanced power dynamics can get tricky if you don't know when to turn them on and off. It's one thing to be a "dom" or "sub" with consent in the bedroom. But if you're expected to play that role in areas of life where you're craving equality, there will be trouble in paradise.

Scorpio rules investments and shared resources, and you two may be miraculous magnets for wealth. Be warned, however, that money can get funny with hazy Supercouple Neptune here. Learn to be upfront around joint finances, even drafting contracts like prenups. Scorpio is the sign of vengeance, and while we hope things will work out forever, you don't want to wind up in years of courtroom drama because you "believed in the power of love." Spell out all fiscal maters to the letter rather than moving forward on faith alone—or you'll have to hope for the best!

Create your own Supercouple Chart at **SUPERCOUPLE.COM**

SUPERCOUPLE NEPTUNE
SAGITTARIUS ✴ ↗

OR THE 9TH HOUSE

Our idea of a fantasy may involve:

- Escaping on magical vacations
- Learning more about each other's cultures
- Starting an impact-driven business together
- Taking couples workshops with master teachers

Have Airstream, will travel! With nomadic Supercouple Neptune in sojourning Sagittarius, you two may struggle to stay in one place for too long. Traveling frees your souls and unleashes your imaginations. Whether you're backpacking through Asia, spending a year as surf instructors, or just going on a long drive to a festival, your getaways are a travel blogger's dream. Putting down roots can be grounding, as long as you don't pin yourselves down completely. If housing costs eat into your travel fund, you won't be happy glampers!

But are these journeys an escape or straight-up escapism? Composite Neptune here can turn you into a pair of rolling stones who gather no moss and burn through cash. Not that this will stop you. Without a second thought, you may leap into questionable experiences and chase after fantasies—like say, buying a 100-year-old farmhouse without an inspection or investing in a food truck without any prior cooking experience.

Fortunately for you both, Sagittarius (the zodiac's gambler) is the luckiest sign. The power of positive thinking gets you far! When you put your heads together, you can manifest anything. While you'll land on your four feet, it won't be without its share of avoidable and expensive mistakes. With dreamy Neptune in this entrepreneurial position, you may start many businesses together. Over time, you'll learn to pace yourselves, scaling back the lofty goals—or saving them for your Phase 3.

No matter your GPS coordinates, this Supercouple Neptune makes you worldly ambassadors. Boundaries...what are those? Beyond adapting easily to your environment, you two interlopers are often "adopted" into cultural groups outside your personal heritages. No matter where you go, inclusivity is the rule of the day. Bringing people together across ethnic divisions is a gift that you'll bless the world with.

Sagittarius is a wise, philosophical sign and Neptune is the planet of spirituality. Organized religion may feel too limiting for you as a couple. Even if you are part of a faith or group, you'll be open to exploring ideas from religions around the globe. You may participate in ceremonies and rituals from many backgrounds, showing up for Buddhist chanting one night, then lighting Shabbat candles the next.

Neptune was in independent, mutable Sagittarius when many Gen X-ers were born (1970 to 1984), so it's not surprising that this generation is known for its self-reliance and flexibility.

This group witnessed the most rapid transformation in technology of any generation to date, moving from an analog youth to a wired adult existence. These miraculous developments are only part of the reason Gen X is known for being open-minded—a quality Neptune in Sagittarius Supercouples should always lean into. After all, you NEVER know how things will work until you try, right?

SUPERCOUPLE NEPTUNE
CAPRICORN ✳ ♑
OR THE 10TH HOUSE

Our idea of a fantasy may involve:

- Being seen as a power couple
- Mastering the traditional principles of love and romance

Soulful, creative Supercouple Neptune isn't naturally at home in this driven, ambitious placement. But once you learn to combine these dissonant forces, you can strike quite the powerful chord! Much of Neptune's influence may be channeled toward some very ambitious goals. Driven by the energy of this connection, you may feel called to do something meaningful that heals the world in a large-scale or public way. Changing the system from within is not an impossible dream here.

But are you trying to keep up with the Joneses? Neptune struggles with limits in every zodiac sign. With Supercouple Neptune in Capricorn, you may feel such a strong pressure to achieve that you overdo it and exhaust yourselves. Yes, you two CAN build an empire, but running it by yourselves is another story. (Check that sacrificial Neptunian urge!) As your lives together expand, you may need to bring in outside support to manage it all: lawyers, estate keepers, or even a fierce assistant who can say no (or yes) on your behalf. Others in the fog of Neptune's energy may resist the structures required to succeed—or even go through periods of feeling lost about the direction you're heading together.

Creative Neptune here can mean success through artistic pursuits: dance, film, music and art, perhaps even achieving celebrity status as a healer, faith leader or spiritual adviser. Feeling "good enough," however, may be a struggle in periods of your relationship. Capricorn is associated with perfectionism. Self-deprecating Neptune can give you a raging case of imposter syndrome when you're in this connection, yet no good ever comes from comparing and despairing.

Capricorn is the sign that governs the economy, governmental systems and family legacies. True healing takes place once you two stop seeking societal validation and step into your role as authorities. People will follow your lead—a responsibility that should be taken seriously by you both. Your shared leadership can attract resources that don't just feed your families but provide sustainable options for your entire community.

Millennials (and some Gen Z) born between 1984 and 1998 have Neptune in earth sign Capricorn in their birth charts. These generations carry a heavy cross around keeping the environment sustainable for human life and fixing the economy so that it doesn't continue to polarize the rich and the poor. No small mission, but this empathic Supercouple Neptune makes you both concerned with systems that are far bigger than yourselves. Music, the arts and spirituality—this planet's domain—will figure in to your strategies.

Create your own Supercouple Chart at **SUPERCOUPLE.COM**

SUPERCOUPLE NEPTUNE

AQUARIUS ✳ ♒

OR THE 11TH HOUSE

Our idea of a fantasy may involve:

- Building a shared community
- Going on mindfulness and spiritual retreats

Ascend! Supercouple Neptune in high-minded Aquarius brings your relationship into an elevated state of consciousness. With the planet of compassion in the zodiac sign of the humanitarian, how could it not? The focus of your union is far bigger than "just" the two of you. Together, you may direct a good deal of your attention toward activism, community service and setting up cooperative systems so that all the people you love have the resources that they need. If any couple could thrive in a communal living situation, it's you two! The more isn't just the merrier; it's the mightier for Composite Neptune in Aquarius.

Mind and spirit are innately entwined in this relationship. You'll love exploring metaphysical subjects together. Astrology falls under the reign of Aquarius, so it's no surprise you're reading this now! From meditations to medicine ceremonies, both of you may be drawn to anything that activates the pineal gland or "third eye chakra," which is where Aquarius reigns. Or you'll develop your healing gifts via intellectual pathways or in group settings like transformational seminars and mindset trainings.

Neptune orbited through Aquarius from 1998 to 2012, when mindfulness practices went mainstream. Yoga studios became the new gyms. We gained understanding about the connection between food and mood, giving rise to organic grocers and the growing popularity of veganism. People born between 1998 and 2012—late Gen Z and early Generation Alpha—have Neptune in Aquarius in their natal charts and were raised with the virtual reality of the Internet. With Supercouple Neptune in sci-fi sign Aquarius, you're both wired for life in the metaverse, where molecules and pixels collide.

The ever-seeking and idealistic spirit of your connection may feel out of sync with mainstream society, but that's fine by you. Both of you are here to reinvent the rules about how we humans take care of one another. And it's hardly one size fits all! People born with Neptune in Aquarius have adopted a list of 78 (and growing) gender pronouns.

By the same token, you two can fall under the spell of groupthink as Neptune dissolves boundaries in communal Aquarius. Choose your inner circle wisely! When both of you join a group, you contribute with compassion and want everyone to feel included. But the underdogs aren't always willing to be team players and the narcissists don't always deserve the level of empathy you deploy. Make sure that you aren't going into denial about the impact people have on the collective whole.

With the right crew, you can thrive in artistic and spiritual collaborations. Hello, supergroup! Double down on your discernment though. In your desire to bond with "your people," the two of you can get swept up in cult-like experiences—fringe groups masquerading as activists or healing circles that financially benefit a narcissistic leader. Ultimately, a shared lesson of your Composite Neptune in Aquarius is this: true "divine belonging" is an inside job. You two fit in nowhere and everywhere—and that is the gift of this relationship!

Create your own Supercouple Chart at SUPERCOUPLE.COM

SUPERCOUPLE NEPTUNE
PISCES ✳ ♓

OR THE 12TH HOUSE

Our idea of a fantasy may involve:

- Sharing and building dreams
- Transcending the physical and material plane through love and spirituality

---

Is this real life or just fantasy? Or maybe it's all just a bohemian rhapsody for couples with numinous Supercouple Neptune in dreamy Pisces. Being grounded in your bodies means dealing with the harsh facts of human life. Um, where's the fun in that? It's not that you're cynical or jaded, but the urge to escape into the imaginative realm is too strong to ignore. As a result, your time together doesn't require being in the same room. Your relationship may begin through DMs, video chats, even appearing in each other's lucid dreams.

In 2012, Neptune returned to its home sign of Pisces for the first time since 1862. If you were born between 2012 and 2025, you have natal Neptune in Pisces in your chart, which also means your entire existence on this planet includes AI and VR as your reality. So why WOULD you limit yourself to the sentient experience when you picked up your mother's iPad and started traveling through time and space when you were, oh, three?

Regardless of how embodied you are as a couple, this fluid formation gives your relationship an otherworldly, old soul quality. Like a pair of weary sages, you just can't buy into all the fuss happening here in this dimension. Shiny gold stars from schoolwork, professional prestige, keeping up with the Joneses...huh? Your relationship's yardstick for success is measured through the love, service and generosity the two of you spread throughout the world.

With this Neptune Supercouple position, together you could abdicate your worldly possessions for a higher purpose—at least for a period of time. This relationship could take you to the far reaches of the world to work with underserved populations or to learn sacred healing arts from shamans deep in the jungle. You'll certainly be there for each other too! With the limitless empathy Neptune in Pisces stirs up, you can get lost in each other's worlds. Your relationship's clock is set to liminal Kairos time, and anyone who tries to rush the two of you into their chronology is on a fool's errand.

Both Neptune and Pisces struggle with limits. Creating boundaries is a challenge—and a necessary lesson for you here. Without proper parameters, you can easily burn out or become codependently entangled in each other's issues. There may be struggles with addictions, from recreational drugs to people-pleasing. To bring your relationship into its highest state, you must both do your individual healing work. It's an inside job! Learn to empower each other, instead of rushing in for the save every time.

And, we hate to break it to you, but even as ascended beings, you are still bound by the rules of the material plane. For the time being, people exchange money for goods and security. Which means if you want to put food on your shared table, you will have to figure out your hustle strategy. Sadly, your deep and abiding love is not enough in that department. With Composite Neptune in Pisces, you might even team up to create a fantasy experience for people: a retreat center on a tropical beach, a local day spa with water features, a boutique with an art gallery and plant-based ice-cream counter. Let yourselves dream, then make your action plan!

Create your own Supercouple Chart at **SUPERCOUPLE.COM**

SUPERCOUPLE
Compatibility
WITH YOUR
NEPTUNE SIGN

Ψ

If our Supercouple Neptune is in a fire sign :
(ARIES, LEO OR SAGITTARIUS)

And my personal Neptune is in a fire sign
(ARIES, LEO OR SAGITTARIUS):

When it comes to boundaries, you'll run hot and cold in this relationship. One minute, you can't get close enough. The next, you're claustrophobic and racing away to reclaim a grasp on your autonomy. The illusion is that you're being overpowered. If this relationship is healthy, playing with power dynamics can be both therapeutic and sexy.

And my personal Neptune is in an earth sign
(TAURUS, VIRGO OR CAPRICORN):

Your slow and sensual bonding style might suddenly move at a faster pace here. You'll get into action around your dreamy ideas and creative plans, and may feel a lot more like a daredevil than you would on your own. Just don't lose sight of your moral compass in the process.

And my personal Neptune is in an air sign
(GEMINI, LIBRA, AQUARIUS):

Suddenly all those naughty ideas that you've only written about in your journal could become real deal scenarios in your life. Definitely choose a safe word and discuss boundaries, because you may be surprised by your own emotional reactions when you drop your guard.

And my personal Neptune is in a water sign
(CANCER, SCORPIO OR PISCES):

Pace yourself, because the excitable energy of this relationship can evaporate some of the slower-forming fantasies that you're nurturing. You know that good things come to those who wait. And you'll need to trust your instincts even when passion tries to accelerate your timeline.

If our Super Couple Neptune is in an earth sign:
(TAURUS, VIRGO, OR CAPRICORN)

And my personal Neptune is in a fire sign
(ARIES, LEO OR SAGITTARIUS):

Your spicy fantasies and wild ideas may feel a bit tempered in this relationship. However, there's a strong likelihood that you'll turn SOME of your dreams into reality. Don't resist structure, safe words, spreadsheets and anything systematic. Laying these on top of your visionary notions could be the key to pleasure and profit!

And my personal Neptune is in an earth sign
(TAURUS, VIRGO OR CAPRICORN):

Fantasy or reality? The two can meet in this relationship, hooray! That is something that comes naturally to you in your own life. But here you have a partner with whom you can play out your quixotic fantasies. Just try not to put too much structure into every fanciful notion. A little spontaneity goes a long way!

And my personal Neptune is in an air sign
(GEMINI, LIBRA, AQUARIUS):

Your normal way of fantasizing centers around thoughts and ideas. You can be a bit of a scientist when it comes to your dreams. This relationship will challenge you to be more in tune with your physical desires and material pleasures. Come down from the clouds and discover the magic of the present moment. What once seemed boring will be titillating!

 And my personal Neptune is in a water sign
(CANCER, SCORPIO OR PISCES):

You can be fluid with your fantasies, sometimes even living in the dream world or the 5D realm! This relationship can feel like a reality check at times, reminding you to also live in the 3D world and pay attention to some of the limitations that exist here and learn to work within them. You may shift from indulging and escaping to enjoying simple but sensory pleasures.

If our Supercouple Neptune is in an air sign:
(GEMINI, LIBRA, AQUARIUS)

 And my personal Neptune is in a fire sign
(ARIES, LEO OR SAGITTARIUS):

Who knew you'd ever find someone willing to go there with you? Your naughtiest fantasies suddenly become the things you can't stop talking about. Acting on them is another story, and you should be extra judicious about pulling the trigger on anything taboo here. By the same token, your pillow talk game will level up exponentially.

And my personal Neptune is in an earth sign
(TAURUS, VIRGO OR CAPRICORN):

You know what feels good in your body, but how about connecting that to your intellect and thoughts? This relationship brings a new connection to your higher mind, and is sure to incite creative strategies for manifesting the most pleasurable (and profitable) things in life.

And my personal Neptune is in an air sign
(GEMINI, LIBRA, AQUARIUS):

Ascension ahoy! Your already elevated state of consciousness rises higher in this relationship, which brings out your altruism, as well as your innate ability to tune into other people's energetic states. Just remember: we have an ego for a reason, so make sure you're also protecting yourself and not getting completely lost in the collective conscience.

And my personal Neptune is in a water sign
(CANCER, SCORPIO OR PISCES):

This won't exactly be a free-flowing relationship when it comes to your feelings and creativity. However, you will learn to be more strategic in your interpersonal dynamics, and start vocalizing boundaries in a way that supports your serenity.

If our Supercouple Neptune is in a water sign:
(CANCER, SCORPIO OR PISCES)

And my personal Neptune is in a fire sign
(ARIES, LEO OR SAGITTARIUS):

Ψ

This could be quite the sultry escape for you, finally helping you relax into the safety of fantasy exploration. But boundaries may be a little too flexible for your liking. Know thyself, and don't be afraid to say no to things that don't support your emotional growth.

And your personal Neptune is in an earth sign (TAURUS, VIRGO OR CAPRICORN):

Swept away or washed away? In the right balance, this relationship can bring together your body-based sensuality with a deep sense of emotional fulfillment. However, if you're not clear on where your limits lie, you could lose sight of your own true north. Practice the art of delayed gratification.

And my personal Neptune is in an air sign (GEMINI, LIBRA, AQUARIUS):

This relationship expands your empathy exponentially, bringing you out of your head and into your heart. It might seem weird to feel things this deeply, but once you see the connection between thoughts and feelings, you'll become a force to be reckoned with. Don't be surprised if this connection unlocks your healing gifts.

And my personal Neptune is in a water sign (CANCER, SCORPIO OR PISCES):

Trauma bonding alert! There's so much empathy here that at times, you may drown in your shared pain, or battle each other for soothing time. You'll both need outside support networks for processing all the feels. That way, you can bring your healthy, whole selves to the union.

Create your own Supercouple Chart at **SUPERCOUPLE.COM**

SUPERCOUPLE

PLUTO

our shadow

Use Your Supercouple Pluto to Understand:

- When you're projecting your issues and blaming each other
- Unconscious issues to work through as a couple
- Where you can become obsessive or addictive together
- Where you might be codependent, cruel or contemptuous
- How to handle power dynamics
- Your relationship's blind spots

WHAT'S THE SHADOW SIDE OF YOUR RELATIONSHIP? WHERE DO ISSUES OF POWER, CONTROL AND DOMINATION COME IN?

Every relationship has a blind spot—and usually several. How to find yours? Look where you point the finger of blame, get triggered or project your childhood issues onto each other. Investigate where the urge to control or fix your partner flares up. It's where you might shout, "You're acting just like my mother!" or "You sound exactly like my dad!"

In astrology, power is Pluto's domain. From trigger points to obsessions to codependence, Composite Pluto is the psychologist's notepad of your relationship. It's the real s*** that we don't want to talk about: Shame. Humiliation. Domination. Contempt. Your Supercouple Pluto reveals where dormant issues rise to haunt you until you resolve them at the core level. For most duos, this takes

Create your own Supercouple Chart at **SUPERCOUPLE.COM**

time, courage and a few dark nights of the soul. Not all of us make it through.

Let's have a Pluto mythology moment: The god of the underworld, Pluto (AKA Hades) kidnaps his niece Persephone, bringing her into his shadowy lair with the help of his brother Zeus, who also happens to be Persephone's father. (WTF)

Persephone's mom, earth goddess Demeter, is bereft and goes on strike, causing all the crops to die. To prevent starvation, Zeus strikes a bargain and allows Persephone above ground for six months of the year. From this, we get a torrid explanation of summer and winter—and a twisted origin story for our "mommy and daddy issues."

But what if these are the terms of long-term engagement? Maybe we're required to spend 50 percent of the time frolicking in bliss, and the other half submerged in the icy winter of shadow work...at least until we sort our baggage out.

Are relationships half heaven and half hell?

The Gottman Institute, one of our favorite sources of modern relationship research, identifies the "four horsemen" that break connection: contempt, defensiveness, stonewalling and criticism.

Ask yourself: Which one do you turn to when you feel hurt at the deepest level? Bonus question: Which parent are you punishing when you do?

The only way out of Composite Pluto hell is forgiveness: of ourselves and yes, of those who hurt us most. Forgiveness doesn't mean redefining someone's harmful actions as "okay." It simply means you release yourself from the toxic grip of their misdeeds so you can stop reliving that nightmare.

Pinpointing the zodiac sign and house of your Supercouple Pluto can clarify where a relationship will activate those hidden issues. Will you micromanage each other (Virgo), kill each other with passive-aggressive kindness and love bombing (Libra) or wage war through sexual manipulation and obsession (Scorpio)? Moreover: What are you hoping to gain by doing so?

As much as Pluto can torment us, it's also an astrological source of redemption. When you hit rock bottom, there's only one direction to go: Up. Shining light onto the shadows of Pluto can deliver the ultimate transformation, turning your relationship into a phoenix rising from the ashes of addiction, domination and suffering.

There's one final ask of Supercouple Pluto. We must own that, though we have been hurt and even victimized, that does not make us immune from hurting and victimizing others. Accepting this truth, and the responsibility that comes with it, brings us out of relationship hell and into the light.

Is Composite Pluto a design flaw of relationships...or the price of admission into intimacy? Since we believe the "human condition" is a training camp for the soul, we accept that life may serve up some character-building tests and hardships. When we can turn the lens of blame away from our partner and put the magnifying mirror on ourselves instead, our shared Pluto lessons are underway.

Supercouple PLUTO
IN THE ZODIAC SIGNS

In the Sign of	We get in zone together through	As a power couple we are	Our unconscious power struggle is
ARIES	Challenges and physical exertion	Trailblazers	Aggression
TAURUS	Creating financial stability and generational wealth	Pillars	Righteousness
GEMINI	Our charm and wit	A dynamic duo	Manipulation
CANCER	Being the heart and home of the family	Parental	Defensiveness
LEO	Expressing our eminence	Royals	Domination
VIRGO	Combining our logic and intellects	The "central intelligence" agency	Perfectionism
LIBRA	Working seamlessly in partnership	#CoupleGoals	Avoidance
SCORPIO	Our sexy swagger and commanding presence	Influential	Destruction
SAGITTARIUS	Taking risks and sharing wisdom	Boundless	Gambling
CAPRICORN	Building business and generational wealth	Role models	Superiority
AQUARIUS	Co-founding communities, disrupting society	Best friends	Withholding
PISCES	Art, music and soulful channels	Spiritually awakened	Guilt

FIND YOUR SUPERCOUPLE PLUTO AT
SUPERCOUPLE.COM

SUPERCOUPLE PLUTO
ARIES ✴ ♈

OR THE 1ST HOUSE

We are magnetized to each other's:

- Trailblazing leadership
- Self-confidence
- Seductive style, passion

Mysterious and magnetic, Supercouple Pluto's position in Aries gives this connection a lot of power to play with. It's up to you both to choose what image you want this relationship to project to the world: Will you disappear or captivate the crowds? When you feel like going undercover together, you're as slick as an international spy duo, literally "disappearing" into the background while you observe the scene and gather clues. But you're equally adept at commanding the room, drawing all eyes your way with your potent presences. Intuitively, together you know what to hide and what to reveal, leaving people wondering and wanting more.

Within this relationship, you're master seducers—and can even be a bit of a tease with one another. Charming and attracting each other

Create your own Supercouple Chart at **SUPERCOUPLE.COM**

is a total turn-on! If we flung open your closets, we'd likely see a lot of black numbers (Pluto's favorite hue) in sexy cuts...and maybe even some fetishwear or racy lingerie. Meow!

But Composite Pluto in this independent position can also create a push-pull dynamic that drives people over the edge. Within the energy of this connection, you two may feel repelled when the other comes too close, or you draw each other in only to drive them away. Part of your shared evolution may involve working through intimacy issues and letting people get past the self-protective shield. That pursuer-distancer dance gets exhausting!

Anger and aggression can be this relationship's Achilles heel. This Pluto placement makes you highly reactive together. When provoked or jealous, you may lash out and lose all sense of perspective. Getting in touch with your triggers is a must to prevent embarrassing and destructive outbursts. Pluto rules the unconscious; however, so when you're in this connection, you may only recognize what provokes you after an unfortunate outburst.

Channeling your prodigious energy into physical activity together is a great tool for anger management. Pluto in Aries makes you feel highly competitive when you come together. Sports that involve medals and titles will be right up your shared alley. That applies to all areas of life together. You both vie for the best and know you deserve it—and with obsessive Pluto spurring you on, you two won't stop until you've reached the top.

SUPERCOUPLE PLUTO

TAURUS ✳ ♉

OR THE 2ND HOUSE

We are magnetized to each other's:

- Resourcefulness
- Financial stability
- Traditional values
- Voices

Make it rain! With wealth-agent Pluto in this financially savvy position, this relationship is a money magnet. Together you intuitively understand how to turn any situation into a profitable opportunity. Since Pluto rules the invisible realm, you two may have a knack for making something out of nothing when you work together. What you can create on a shoestring budget or with limited resources is mind-blowing! Gut instincts may lead you to monetizable opportunities long before others have a clue. Acting quickly on your hunches could make you both industry trailblazers and the first to market.

The challenge? Supercouple Pluto here can make you a cautious couple with low appetites for risk. In this comfort-loving position,

Create your own Supercouple Chart at **SUPERCOUPLE.COM**

both of you might do best working for a steady paycheck or long-term contract, ideally with the benefits of health insurance and vacation time. When you don't have enough money in the bank, you simply can't relax in this connection.

Pluto is in detriment here, meaning it's in the opposite zodiac sign of its homebase. As such, some of Pluto's more charming and seductive qualities can be tamped down, making you a little too practical of a pair for your own good. Being realistic is fine, but if you play it too safe, you'll miss the bigger wins that you are capable of manifesting as a couple.

Taurus is associated with the throat. With seductive Pluto in this position, this relationship may be characterized by the power of your voices. You give "good phone," and there may be singing or broadcasting associated with this connection. But the charming dwarf planet also reveals where we want to win at any cost. Be careful not to make promises you can't keep...or to send unwitting superfans crashing into the rocks!

SUPERCOUPLE PLUTO
GEMINI ✳ ♊

OR THE 3RD HOUSE

We are magnetized to each other's:

- Wordplay and killer charm
- Constant evolution
- Cooperative thinking

Hello, you silver-tongued devils. With Supercouple Pluto in this communicative sign, you can woo each other with words. Few can say no to your killer charms when you come together! This Pluto placement makes you both masterful flirts, and you may have roving eyes to match. The key is to connect to people and opportunities that bring lots of variety, growth and stimulation to your connection. Stagnation is death to you two! In order to sustain this relationship, both of you may need an outside hobby that involves collecting or "treasure hunting" to keep the curious parts of your minds occupied.

Thanks to the energy of this connection, you may find success in sales or work as motivational speakers or coaches. There's power in your shared persuasion! In less enlightened moments, you two might even be accused of being manipulative. Pluto here can be a

Create your own Supercouple Chart at **SUPERCOUPLE.COM**

ticket to a one-track mind. You might just say anything to convince people or get your way. This short-term strategy will backfire on you both repeatedly if you make promises that you can't keep. As you evolve through life together, you'll stop twisting arms and instead open people's minds to new possibilities. That's when your true transformational shared gifts shine! Writing, teaching or spreading a message may figure in.

Socially, you can read any room with near-psychic precision when you're together. Shrewd Pluto helps you radar in on the "right" people in any crowd: folks who can help advance your joint agenda or connect you two to resources that might otherwise be out of your reach. Working in partnership is your shortcut to wealth and fame, so long as you sync up with people who are not just clever but who also match your tireless combined devotion.

SUPERCOUPLE PLUTO
CANCER ✴ ♋

OR THE 4TH HOUSE

We are magnetized to each other's:

- Nurturing capabilities
- Family loyalty
- Comforting energy
- Protectiveness

Privacy, please! With undercover Pluto in this Supercouple placement, your relationship may prefer to fly under the radar. If you're not both full-on introverts when you're in this connection's energy, you two are certainly introspective, needing periods of quiet time to clear your heads and engage in deep reflection. Your shared sense of security can be delicate with Composite Pluto here—and you have heightened emotional sensitivity together. This planet rules the unconscious, so childhood traumas and wounds could stick in your psyches, creating a false sense of danger in the world. Working with a therapist to "re-parent" yourselves can help you to feel safe. Over time, both of you can distinguish when you're projecting your own "shadow" emotions (like anger, sadness, or fear) onto other people (including each other) instead of courageously owning up to what you actually feel.

Your shared sense of loyalty is to the family—almost to mob boss levels at times. Whether they share your DNA or are "chosen family," the people who are in your innermost mutual circle will be treated with the utmost reverence. Highly devoted, you'd literally do anything for each other's families and friends. But if folks don't have your trust, look out. In this connection, both of you can be guarded and suspicious, and outsiders are going to have to pass through complex tests to prove their allegiance. If this unconscious tendency becomes too severe, the two of you can become isolated or stuck in an echo chamber of people who think and feel like you do. Alas, that will only short circuit your shared evolution. Make a point of getting out more often together, and to sometimes pull in people from different backgrounds and walks of life to join the group.

Since Cancer is associated with nurturing, there's a strong parental quality present in this relationship. Taking care of one another can be a huge aphrodisiac for you two. Dole this out selectively to avoid codependence. That said, Pluto rules the reproductive organs and this placement could give you both the urge to parent at a young age. With wealth-agent Pluto in this domestic zone, you could earn your fortune together through real estate investments, or simply save enough to make a fateful purchase one day. A family inheritance could also set you up for success as a couple.

SUPERCOUPLE PLUTO

LEO ✳ ♌

OR THE 5TH HOUSE

We are magnetized to each other's:

- Talent
- Regal elegance
- Charm
- Commanding leadership
- Financial success
- Larger-than-life personalities
- Starpower

With power-player Pluto nestled into regal Leo, this relationship exudes eminence. People look to you both as a power couple, even if neither of you has ever steered the ship in your life. Your shared confidence—and the killer style you inspire each other to display—make you two magnetic. Whether it's just optics or well-honed capabilities, you have a celebrity quality in this connection. When you DO take charge together or wind up in the limelight, watch your egos. Pluto in this royal court can make you thirsty for dominance or a little too controlling for your own good.

Create your own Supercouple Chart at **SUPERCOUPLE.COM**

Seduction is an art form for you both, and one that might require lights, cameras and props! With sultry Supercouple Pluto in the "Hollywood" zodiac sign, together you won't settle for any ho-hum efforts in love. Slipping into "old married couple" mode can be the death knell of this relationship. Fortunately, this Composite Pluto placement makes you passionate and playful lovers. Dreaming up next-level dates is one of this relationship's specialties, and this is a partnership where you both appreciate an over-the-top approach.

Leo is associated with the heart. When you two lead with yours together, you can't go wrong. Your loving spirits can transform an entire room! Channel your deep-diving emotions into a passion project, whether you're making art as a couple or becoming obsessive appreciators of a particular genre.

With your Supercouple Pluto in this theatrical position, both of you are not always aware of when your "shadows" have taken center stage. You two may be obsessed with getting attention and validation. When you're deep in the energy of this connection, your competitive streaks can rise to cutthroat levels. A flair for drama can reach destructive levels if you let yourselves spiral out. If one of you feels hurt or disappointed, you may get vicious. Learning to temper your fierce emotions is a key lesson in this lifetime together. Otherwise, you may strike too hard and damage your connections, something you both may live to regret.

©2022 Astrostyle. All rights reserved.

SUPERCOUPLE PLUTO
VIRGO ✳ ♍
OR THE 6TH HOUSE

> **We are magnetized to each other's:**
>
> - Mindfulness and a sense of social/spiritual consciousness
> - Practicality and "kitchen table" wisdom
> - Earthy sensuality
> - Vitality and effortless beauty
> - Resourcefulness

Is perfection possible? With this Supercouple Pluto, you'll certainly try your hardest together to find out! With the obsessive planet in this detail-driven position, nothing escapes your four exacting eyes. At best, this can make you both true masters who will work tirelessly to hone your craft. At worse, you two may be perpetually dissatisfied, never feeling like you can do, have or be enough. Unconscious forces are definitely at play. Your spiritual evolution together may involve learning the art of surrender. Sometimes you simply need to let go and accept that done is better than perfect.

PLUTO

A precise and analytical duo, you can be sticklers for the details when you're in the energy of this connection. Discovering all the finer points of your latest passions could keep you two up all hours, researching and practicing. Thankfully, Virgo is the sign of routine, so you may have an easier time than other Composite Pluto signs taking breaks to eat, sleep and handle real-world responsibilities.

With seductive Pluto in the sign of service, you two are generous in bed. Sex is a craft to be mastered and honed in this relationship. (And you probably have the toy chest or Red Room to prove it.) While power games can be sexy in some measure, be careful not to use your amorous talents to manipulate or control your mate. Just because you can, doesn't mean you should!

Spending time in nature together is transformational for this connection, and your shared values are decidedly "salt of the earth." While you each feel a need to have a sense of financial security when you're in the energy of this relationship, you tend toward modesty. You'd both rather invest in quality, sustainably sourced goods than anything flashy or trendy. Owning land together—and possibly turning into a resource through farming—may be an investment that calls to you in this lifetime.

SUPERCOUPLE PLUTO
LIBRA ✳ ♎

OR THE 7TH HOUSE

We are magnetized to each other's:

- Physical beauty
- Strong sense of style and fashion
- Dreamy romanticism
- Wealth and access to luxury
- Clear principles and a keen sense of justice

How deep is your shared love? Hang on a sec while we go grab our scuba gear! With plumb-the-depths Pluto in this partnership-powered position, it probably ranges somewhere between "wholeheartedly devoted" and "totally obsessed." This relationship may be your *raison d'etre,* and you love to give each other all of your focus! No matter the nature of your collaboration, you thrive as a power couple. Libra is the sign that rules marriage, and it won't be long before the two of you want to make this union official in a public (and government-sealed) way. However, with rosy-eyed Libra at the wheel, there's a tendency to focus on the "for better" and convince yourselves that you'll deal with the "for worse" when it arises. This blithe attitude may leave you woefully unprepared for the lean years and stormy days. Planning ahead may not feel natural for you two, but it can be the best insurance policy for your relationship's success.

With secretive Pluto in this collaborative position, you have a high code of honor to live up to. A firm privacy policy is essential for both of you to feel safe opening up to others. And no spilling state secrets unless you want to destroy your bond. At times, you two can take this "us against the world" vibe to extremes, disappearing into the couple bubble or creating a secret universe with your mate. Come out and engage with the rest of the world too—or your bond can grow too close for comfort.

In this relationship, you each may grapple with darker emotions like jealousy and possessiveness—and in some cases romance addiction—looking to your partner to fill a sense of emptiness. Having a strong support network is a crucial insurance policy for you both, ensuring that you won't put too much pressure on your primary relationships. "You Are My Everything" might be the perfect music for your wedding dance, but don't turn it into your lifelong theme song.

Vulnerability is NOT this planet's specialty. Supercouple Pluto's unconscious impact can act like a magnet, repelling you from the very person whose name you doodled in a thousand hearts. This will definitely be a balancing act, but with Libra, the sign of the scales, as your Supercouple Pluto, it's to be expected!

SUPERCOUPLE PLUTO

SCORPIO ✳ ♏

OR THE 8TH HOUSE

We are magnetized to each other's:

- Sexual energy, attentiveness
- Intensity
- Soulful interests
- Brooding and mysterious personalities
- Artistic talents—and temperaments!

Pluto is right at home in its native sign of Scorpio! This deep-diving Supercouple placement makes it hard for you both to do anything by half-measure when you're together. This relationship can be feast or famine, in fact. When you are in the throes of this connection, it's hard for you two to focus on much else. Sex is your karmic teacher and your kryptonite with Pluto the projector here. Sexual interactions can provide a high—and sometimes those are truly transformational. You may enjoy playing with power dynamics together, exploring BDSM or in some cases, acting out violent fantasies. Sex can plunge you two into the shadows, arousing jealousy, vengeance, obsession and other blinding emotions that pull you far from your logical center.

Create your own Supercouple Chart at **SUPERCOUPLE.COM**

In the energy of this connection, you may be prone to self-soothing with addictive behaviors, from drinking to emotional eating and other escapes. In extreme cases, stormy emotions can turn violent, making these relationships toxic or abusive. Complex? Absolutely. But bringing your unconscious urges—and yes, your animal instincts—to light is your shared path to your evolution, whether you become each other's life partners or a lesson that you'll never forget.

Wealth agent Pluto in Scorpio can make this relationship a money magnet! Once you two crack the code on financial strategies, you can be shrewd investors. Compounding interest and a real estate portfolio might be your path to early retirement together. Even if neither of you has a trust fund—although you might with Composite Pluto here—you two could be skillful at raising start-up cash through a bank loan, private equity or another investor.

Loss and death may be a theme in your shared transformational path in this lifetime. One of you may be the beneficiary of an inheritance or you could find each other after a devastating bout of grief. There's a feeling that you're resurrecting each other, in fact, so no matter how long the lifespan of your union, you can be certain that you've come into each other's lives for a reason.

SUPERCOUPLE PLUTO
SAGITTARIUS ✳ ♐
OR THE 9TH HOUSE

We are magnetized to each other's:

- Daring and adventurous spirits
- Optimism
- Worldliness
- Intelligent humor
- Broad-mindedness
- Social awareness
- Independent thinking (and independence in general)

What happens when secretive Pluto takes root in the zodiac sign known for being an open book? Sometimes it gives this relationship a powerful range. At other moments, you two will feel deeply conflicted. How much to share and how much to hide? That is the question with Supercouple Pluto in Sagittarius...and you'll both ponder it like Plato and Aristotle, thanks to this philosophical placement.

Fate has appointed this connection to be about seeking life's great mysteries. Paradoxically, the search for higher truths can plunge you two deep into the shadows. Together you traffic in polarities, knowing that there can be no darkness without light, no love without heartbreak, no joy without despair. As such, when you're in the energy of this

Create your own Supercouple Chart at **SUPERCOUPLE.COM**

relationship, you distrust anything that seems "too easy" or superficial. You'd rather learn things experientially (and the hard way!), traveling the world together and exploring a subject from every possible angle.

While you two value authenticity, you may struggle with transparency and vulnerability. Together you're more interested in sussing out other people's stories than revealing your own. Both of you can be highly strategic about how much you share, which can keep one another at arm's length. This Composite Pluto placement can cause you both to come across as suspicious—and a little bit superstitious. But that's only part of the story! Behind the prickly outer shell that can rise up in this connection lies a couple of sensitive hearts. Together you have an ability to see people's highest, truest potential. Once you lean into Pluto's alchemical powers, you may find paths as motivational speakers or coaches or teachers. Sagittarius is associated with beliefs. In your case, by holding the belief of "you can do it!" can literally provide the transformational boost others need to step into their power.

In order to harness this gift together, you two must cultivate patience for the other's humanity—not to mention the rest of the world's. Accept that when you're together, you learn faster than many folks— and try to remember that even YOU have your blind spots. Chief among them may be your struggles with timing. It's not always the right moment—or the best idea—to speak your truths, especially if doing so would wound other people.

There are times as a couple when you can be idealists (or full-on ideologues) who espouse a perspective to the point of zealotry. While you like to think of yourselves as open-minded, you both can be highly intolerant of people who you consider small-minded, myopic or who simply don't share your views. The desire to be "right" can cause your own disagreements to wage on with each of you insisting that you know the answer. Accepting one another's independent POVs can be the key to longevity here. Sometimes it's just better to let it go!

SUPERCOUPLE PLUTO

CAPRICORN ✳ ♑

OR THE 10TH HOUSE

We are magnetized to each other's:

- Success
- Status
- Power
- Wealth
- Access to elite opportunities
- Resourcefulness
- An ability to provide for others
- Natural beauty

In achievement-obsessed Capricorn, Pluto imbues this Supercouple relationship with a goal-getting spirit. When you set your four eyes on a benchmark, you two will hustle tirelessly to accomplish it. Given this planet's penchant for extremes, you may disappear from the public to produce your shared vision. When you emerge, the results are spellbinding! People regularly remark at your amazing ability to pull things off.

You may be a classic power couple, rising through the ranks with each other's support. In this strategic union, "it's all about who you know," and as a pair, you are magnets for magnates. Charming the power players will quickly earn you an invite into their elite circles—

and a shortcut to the C Suite. And there's no denying that you love being there together!

Having the planetary wealth agent positioned in Capricorn intensifies your competitive streaks. When together, you're both in it to win it! Whether you express that desire to be number one outwardly or secretly push yourselves to be the best, your shared drive is unmatched. But don't get carried away or you may get a reputation as supervillains. As you evolve, you'll learn to redefine "success" as both an individual gain and a collective victory.

In this relationship, there is no shortage of big bold ideas, and it doesn't take much persuading to get the other's support. People may buy into your plans based on the sheer force of your combined personalities. Since Capricorn is associated with corporate entities, banks and governments, you could be quite the savvy fundraisers. Whether you're investors or environmentalists, you know how to work with "old money" types to bring about the new order. Together, you could find success as influencers, getting behind a sponsored product and taking your sales skills to the bank.

Capricorn energy can skew perfectionist. As you push one another to new heights, you may simultaneously struggle with insecurity and imposter syndrome. Yet no good ever comes from "comparing and despairing." Your shared healing takes place once you stop looking to others for validation and decide to be the authorities of your own lives.

That doesn't mean you should slip off the radar as an army of two. Build a shared a community of supporters who bolster your confidence. This can help you stay purpose-driven should you get the urge to sabotage your well-deserved success. And as you'll quickly discover, there's strength in numbers.

SUPERCOUPLE PLUTO
AQUARIUS ✳ ♒

OR THE 11TH HOUSE

We are magnetized to each other's:

- Unconventional thinking
- Disruption of the status quo
- Team spirit
- Community efforts

Private, esoteric Pluto isn't exactly at ease in this communal, logical placement. But once you two learn to balance your disparate energies, you'll become a force of nature together. Like sexy spies and sci-fi creatures rolled into one duo, you can make yourselves completely inconspicuous OR stop people dead in their tracks as if they've spotted a unicorn. Powerfully expressed, this Composite Pluto placement makes this relationship one of fearless disruption and change!

As you evolve together, you come to embrace this connection's uniqueness and see it as a gift. That said, finding a "soul squad" is

definitely key to your happiness. Pluto in Aquarius can swing
you as a couple toward socialism or populism, as you find your
flow with this "power to the people" energy. You two may feel at
home in a progressive group that has a mission around equity and
revolutionary change. Self-development classes, humanitarian
organizations, or even political campaigns may be where you find
your shared community. In fact, as you both gain confidence, you
may discover that empowering people together is one of your
transformational gifts as a duo.

With Composite Pluto in this high-minded position, your
relationship may include a study of organizational and behavioral
psychology. Astrology also falls under this domain, and you two
have a knack for memorizing people's entire charts! Pluto here
could lead you both to careers in team building or as consultants
who help companies restructure with equity, diversity and
inclusivity as their core values. Since Aquarius is associated
with the Internet, you could become powerful voices for change
through your social media feeds and webinars.

While Pluto is known for being possessive and jealous, Aquarius is
all about co-ownership and community. When it comes to money
and love, you two can ping-pong between poles. Team investing
could be your shared path to prosperity, whether you're raising
capital through crowdfunding or pooling savings to purchase
rental properties. (You might even team up with a group to
develop a viral app.) With Pluto in this detached position, you
could revolutionize your joint relationship to money altogether
by creating a barter system for goods and services with a group of
like-minded individuals.

Sex and seduction can be quite the experimental voyage for both of you in this connection. If you had it your way, who knows? But Pluto is still Pluto, craving one-to-one intimacy and primary partnership. Even in this open-minded position, together you're probably what sexpert Dan Savage calls "monogamish." What attracts each of you most in this connection is intellect and the rush of "sapiosexual" connectivity that brings a meeting of minds, then bodies and souls.

Create your own Supercouple Chart at **SUPERCOUPLE.COM**

SUPERCOUPLE PLUTO
PISCES ✳ ♓

OR THE 12TH HOUSE

We are magnetized to each other's:

- Spirituality
- Fantasy-weaving
- Boundless creativity and compassion

No crystal ball required! With psychic Pluto in this esoteric Supercouple position, this relationship tunes you in to the enigmas of our vast universe. From algorithms to mysticism, understanding complex codes is one of your shared fascinations. When you come together, you have a high-speed connection to the invisible realm, and this can unfold in fascinating ways. If you're in tune with your Composite Pluto's psychic powers, this relationship may include the gifts of channeling, mediumship or animal communication. You two may also be drawn to other forms of fantasy generation, such as working with film, VR, AI, music production, dance or anything that comes to life through a coding language.

Developing a meditation practice will sharpen your gifts as seers and keep you mindful in your relationship. Quieting the "monkey mind" allows your spirit guides to clearly get through to you. But even so, you may literally need to go check out of reality because Pluto is the planet of the unconscious. Messages come to you both while you sleep. Shamanic plant medicine ceremonies could also support your illumination. One proviso: this Pluto placement can make you two prone to addictions, so tread with extreme care when it comes to going into an altered state.

In extreme cases, this placement could bring an awakening that utterly destabilizes your mental states for a period of time as you both connect to your intuitions—especially if your upbringings led you to doubt the unseen world. Surrendering the need to intellectually understand is essential to your souls' evolution together. But this can be particularly difficult for you as a pair!

Boundaries or boundlessness? In this relationship you may struggle to find balance between the two. Some deeper feelings and fears may play out in the bedroom—Pluto rules sex, after all. Choose a safe word! With nefarious Pluto here, fantasies might veer toward BDSM. Pisces is the "sub" of astrology, and the power games could be mighty hot in the bedroom as long as you both know where your limits lie.

This is not the easiest Pluto Supercouple placement—especially if either of you grew up in an abusive household or in a community where sexual shame and guilt run rampant. Here's the key to your evolution together: Understanding that you are whole, perfect and complete. There is nothing wrong with you! (So stop looking for the fly in the ointment.) Until you both accept this, you run the risk of checking out in unhealthy ways, like tech addictions and illicit substances. Finding a place where you feel safe and guilt-free is a must. You may have a lot of jumbled thoughts to confess, sure—but suppressing them will only strengthen their hold on your psyche. Be the safe space for each other to sort through those thoughts, and you'll pull each other through dark spells and into the light.

Create your own Supercouple Chart at **SUPERCOUPLE.COM**

SUPERCOUPLE
Compatibility
WITH YOUR PLUTO SIGN

If our Supercouple Pluto is in a fire sign:
(ARIES, LEO OR SAGITTARIUS)

 And my personal Pluto is in a fire sign
(ARIES, LEO OR SAGITTARIUS):

Illumination is a hallmark of this relationship, which supports you with bringing the hidden realms of life to light. While it won't be easy on your ego, you'll be amazed by how rapidly you can learn, grow and evolve in this bond.

 And my personal Pluto is in an earth sign
(TAURUS, VIRGO OR CAPRICORN):

Your need for material security may be less intense in this relationship, which thrives on a currency of creativity, passion and adventure. Expect a few uncomfortable moments as you realize ways that you may be restricted, uptight or suppressed. But honesty is the best policy here.

 And my personal Pluto is in an air sign
(GEMINI, LIBRA, AQUARIUS):

Locked up thoughts may spring free in this relationship, which can help you vocalize or even write about some esoteric concepts. You may find that one or both of you require more undivided attention than you'd normally need, but watch out for manipulation in that arena.

And my personal Pluto is in a water sign
(CANCER, SCORPIO OR PISCES):

Your inner child might play with wild abandon here, or throw a raging temper tantrum. You can't ignore your wounds, but you can take massive strides to heal them instead of drowning in the sorrow and pain.

If our Supercouple Pluto is in an earth sign:
(TAURUS, VIRGO, OR CAPRICORN)

And my personal Pluto is in a fire sign
(ARIES, LEO OR SAGITTARIUS):

You want what you want when you want it, but this relationship teaches you the art of delayed gratification. Expect lots of frustration as you strengthen your willpower and learn how to focus on long-term gains instead of your immediate desires.

And my personal Pluto is in an earth sign
(TAURUS, VIRGO OR CAPRICORN):

Your strategic skills are right at home in this relationship, which knows that good things come to those who plan and wait. However, there's a shrewdness here that could verge on manipulative if you don't develop a good vocabulary for your feelings.

And my personal Pluto is in an air sign
(GEMINI, LIBRA, AQUARIUS):

Buzzkill alert! Your irreverent approach to problem-solving might not cut it in this heavy Pluto configuration, which demands serious long-term strategies. Forget about minimizing, dealing with it tomorrow or going unconscious. Problems must be dealt with fully here, which can ultimately bring you profound peace.

And my personal Pluto is in a water sign
(CANCER, SCORPIO OR PISCES):

Get a grip! Wild and tempestuous emotions will not fly in this relationship, which demands social responsibility and conscious communication in order to reach its highest potential. While you don't have to sacrifice, you do need to learn emotional resilience and restraint.

If our Supercouple Pluto is in an air sign:
(GEMINI, LIBRA, AQUARIUS)

And my personal Pluto is in a fire sign
(ARIES, LEO OR SAGITTARIUS):

Individually, you experience animal magnetism in the form of heat, urgency and a desire for action. In this relationship, you'll need to adjust to finding that spark through words and exchanging ideas. At first, this may feel rather unsexy, but things

Create your own Supercouple Chart at **SUPERCOUPLE.COM**

like tantra, a shared meditation practice and even developing a rock-solid friendship will soon become the juiciest parts of your union.

And my personal Pluto is in an earth sign
(TAURUS, VIRGO OR CAPRICORN):

You come alive with touch, tactile objects and the promise and allure of wealth. In this relationship, the currency is more invisible: thoughts, ideas and energy exchange. You may have to create pampering rituals to get yourself in that relaxed, receptive state to appreciate this relationship's thought-provoking qualities.

And my personal Pluto is in an air sign
(GEMINI, LIBRA, AQUARIUS):

You'll feel right at home with the unspoken energy and magnetic communication style this relationship brings. It may feel at times like you're drawn into a world where just the two of you exist, as you share secrets, make inside jokes and even speak in code. Try to be mindful of this "insider's club" energy when you're with other people, so as to not alienate them.

And my personal Pluto is in a water sign
(CANCER, SCORPIO OR PISCES):

Your emotional depth is as deep and mysterious as the ocean itself, yet you may feel pulled to shallower waters. Your desire to explore trauma, healing and identity may have to be done outside this relationship. Don't treat your partner like your "processing center," but share your revelations once you've had them!

If our Supercouple Pluto is in a water sign:
(CANCER, SCORPIO OR PISCES)

And my personal Pluto is in a fire sign
(ARIES, LEO OR SAGITTARIUS):

You want to evolve and you want to do it now, but this relationship has zero tolerance for emotional bypass. Stop and drop into your feelings, and be patient with your process. While the wait won't be comfortable, it will make you stronger.

And my personal Pluto is in an earth sign
(TAURUS, VIRGO OR CAPRICORN):

How much security can you actually give yourself? This relationship may stir up some unconscious fears of scarcity disguised as "responsibility." As a result, you might restrict yourself from spiritual and emotional growth. Learn to let go of control sometimes.

And my personal Pluto is in an air sign
(GEMINI, LIBRA, AQUARIUS):

It's definitely not all fun and games in this relationship. In fact, you may feel like you're being audited quite often. It's not easy to be accountable for every thought and word, but being more mindful in these arenas can actually help you forge more honest and intimate relationships.

And my personal Pluto is in a water sign
(CANCER, SCORPIO OR PISCES):

Codependent no more? The line between support and enabling gets blurry fast here. It might even take an outside resource like a therapist or coach to point out those unconscious blind spots. Caring deeply is wonderful, but the lesson is to not abandon yourself in the process.

Create your own Supercouple Chart at **SUPERCOUPLE.COM**

SUPERCOUPLE

LUNAR NODES

our karmic purpose

Use Your Supercouple Nodes to Understand:

- Karmic or past-life issues you're working through together
- Triggers that don't make sense to you but feel real
- Deep-rooted patterns to break together
- Why you're in each other's lives
- The soul purpose of your relationship
- The shared lessons you're here to learn (over and over again)
- How you can evolve on a soul level through a shared mission

---

YOUR LUNAR NODES: WHAT'S YOUR KARMIC PURPOSE AS A DUO?

Do you ever get that déjà vu feeling, like you've met before... somewhere, perhaps in another lifetime? The Supercouple Lunar Nodes (AKA the North and South Node) could be playing their hand. These charged points in your Superchart reveal both your past-life karma and your ultimate soul purpose together.

Heavy-duty? Well yeah. You didn't expect a light-and-breezy answer to a deep, philosophical question like, "Why has this person appeared in my life?" or "What the heck are we meant to accomplish together?"

The Nodes reveal your deepest shadows and your highest illumination. The North Node gives you a map to where you'll grow

Create your own Supercouple Chart at **SUPERCOUPLE.COM**

together, evolve spiritually and receive tests of will that help you both develop new dimensions of your character.

When you fight or trigger each other, the Composite South Node reveals ways that you two may be working through unresolved conflict from prior lifetimes. You could glimpse where you may have been siblings, each other's parents, BFFs or mortal enemies.

The Lunar Nodes are always in opposite signs, showing the "hero's journey" of your relationship. They reveal where you're coming from (Composite South Node) to where you're headed (Composite North Node). It's a road you'll travel over and over again as you seek personal and spiritual mastery.

Didn't realize you signed up for this when you fell in love? Surprise!

We once read a Superchart for a woman who was irrationally afraid of being abandoned by her current partner. It was something she'd never felt before, and there was no trace of this pattern in her stable, nuclear family of origin. We pinpointed a Cancer South Node in the blended chart's eighth house (which can show death and extreme tragedy). From this we surmised that she could have been her partner's mother in a past lifetime, perhaps sending him off to war or grieving his devastating loss to illness.

We have no scientific proof of past lives, though we're happy to report that many researchers are working on that. So for now, we suggest looking at the Lunar Nodes as archetypes and allegories, fictional tales with a lesson that strikes a transformational chord.

It didn't matter to our client whether she actually had been her partner's mom in ancient Egypt or feudal Europe. Simply visualizing this metaphor performed a deep soul healing for her. She was able to see that she was reacting toward her boyfriend's perfectly normal departures (for work or to grab a beer with his buddies) as though he was never going to come back home again.

He responded to her freakouts with his own version of Cancerian traits: emotionally withdrawing into his shell and shutting her out. This distancing occurred after he spent draining hours trying to comfort her inconsolable terrors, which were utterly confusing to both of them!

We guided this couple to their Composite North Node in Capricorn, the sign of boundaries, clear agreements and mentors. Capricorn is all about taking one incremental step at a time toward a shared goal.

The two agreed that, for 90 days, her boyfriend would text her when he arrived at his destination and when he was heading home. If a plan changed, he would communicate that as well. She agreed to work with a professional coach who was also a licensed therapist, someone she could ping for a reality check when fears and feelings flooded her. We also did a private guided grief ritual with her to mourn the "son" she lost in another lifetime. Did it feel a little weird and silly to simulate? Of course. But she reported that it indeed took the "charge" out of those worrisome thoughts and soon, the karmic grip began to fade.

Through this process, this couple built new neural pathways for their relationship. The Supercouple Nodes gave them a go-to GPS, alerting them with clear warning signs when they were slipping back into Cancerian codependence. They could also reach for Capricorn tools that grounded them in the here-and-now and stopped them both from spiraling into a nightmare. Their relationship feels steady and rewarding when they bring this awareness to it. Spiritual closure works.

Supercouple LUNAR NODES
IN THE ZODIAC SIGNS

North Node In the Sign of	Is Teaching Us the Magic of	We're Moving Away From (South Node)	We're Moving Toward (North Node)
ARIES	Selfhood	Dependence (Libra)	Autonomy
TAURUS	Simplicity	Secrecy (Scorpio)	Stability
GEMINI	Curiosity	Exaggeration (Sagittarius)	Facts
CANCER	Family	Head (Capricorn)	Heart
LEO	Luxury	Anonymity (Aquarius)	Pride
VIRGO	Logic	Fantasy (Pisces)	Reality
LIBRA	Companionship	Selfishness (Aries)	Partnership
SCORPIO	Power	Materialism (Taurus)	Mysticism
SAGITTARIUS	Worldliness	Intellect (Gemini)	Wisdom
CAPRICORN	Systems	Personal & Private (Cancer)	Professional & Public
AQUARIUS	Community	Entitlement (Leo)	Teamwork
PISCES	Spirituality	Thinking (Virgo)	Feeling

FIND YOUR SUPERCOUPLE LUNAR NODES AT **SUPERCOUPLE.COM**

SUPERCOUPLE NORTH NODE
ARIES ✳ ♈ OR 1ST HOUSE
& **LIBRA** SOUTH NODE OR 7TH HOUSE

Release:

- Taking the comfortable path
- Avoiding challenges and conflicts
- Compromising too quickly
- Being halves of a whole
- Passive-aggression
- Overindulging

Embrace:

- Supporting each other's goals
- Being comfortable when apart
- The rewards of risk
- Expressing anger in an open and healthy manner
- Using "I language" instead of "we"

Hello, past-life partner? Libra is the sign of committed relationships and marriage. With your Supercouple South Node here, you two share some serious soul history. From your very first interactions, an uncanny ease flows between you; there's a spark of excitement and familiarity. We've heard this from couples who have a Supercouple Libra South Node (and felt it ourselves!): The minute you see each other, you just KNOW that you've met before.

Romance often takes off at a galloping pace in this Supercouple Node placement, but it doesn't stop at shared plates of pasta and rose petals strewn across the bed. The click is so strong that you'll start talking "serious relationship" in record time. That's how magnetic this past-life pull can be! With a Composite Libra South Node, you've found a qualified candidate for the role of "your other half." In the dynamic balancing act of your relationship, you'll pick up where the other leaves off. The Jerry Maguire syndrome is real: You really do complete each other.

If you're both off the market when you "reunite," get ready to face an excruciatingly difficult choice. You won't be able to stop thinking about each other. In some cases, you may leave other relationships in order to be together. (Or privately consider it as you lie awake with your bodies on fire for each other's touch, night after night.) So powerful is this pull that you might even have to stop communicating at some point, so you don't go from past-life heartthrobs to present-life home wreckers.

But wait! Your relationship comes with a major plot twist: A Composite North Node in independent, self-sufficient Aries. As magical as it is to meet someone who fills in all your blanks (and vice versa), that is not your shared destiny this time around. If you are indeed to be together, you must empower the other to stretch and grow! Rather than being two halves of a whole, carve out your own powerful paths. In the process, you'll have to face down insecurities around "differentiating" and learn what it means to TRULY stand for each other's happiness.

While it's incredibly easy to fall into patterns of dependency, those will be the death knell of your relationship. Aries is the warrior sign, tough and capable. The more you slip into knight-and-distressed-damsel roles, the harder this relationship will be. Being there for one another looks different this time around—and it's something you two have never experienced before. If your idea of a perfect marriage is spending every waking moment together, you'd better look elsewhere. The Supercouple Aries North Node has zero tolerance for codependence or stagnation.

If fate blesses your bond, it's not going to follow a classic script. Sure, there will be romance! You two can't help but spoil each other and get all gushy in the other's presence. But there may also be times of prolonged separation, incompatible schedules and general difficulties with aligning your individual interests and priorities. If you can give one another space to breathe—and lots of room to pursue "greatness" as you each define it—life together can be a beautiful adventure where you learn more about yourselves than you ever bargained for.

Create your own Supercouple Chart at **SUPERCOUPLE**.COM

SUPERCOUPLE NORTH NODE
TAURUS ✳ ♉ OR 2ND HOUSE
& SCORPIO SOUTH NODE OR 8TH HOUSE

Release:

- Seducing and manipulating to get your way
- Using sex as a weapon
- Secrecy, the "us against the world" mentality
- Testing each other's loyalty

Embrace:

- Simplicity
- Truth
- Grounding yourselves with daily habits and routines
- Living in the moment
- Pure human connection
- Straightforward communication
- Affection and touch

Passionate power couple or gloves-off power struggle? That depends on the day. With Supercouple Scorpio as your South Node, your souls have a long and complex history together. After all, this is the zodiac sign that rules sex, secrets, reproduction, death and rebirth. No surprise, your relationship burns with the intensity of a thousand suns!

From the moment you lock eyes, you feel the magnetic charge. Attract. Repel. Attract. Repel. You might start out as competitors or straight-up rivals! But as they say, there's a thin line between love and hate. And with the Composite South Node—your past-life marker—in Scorpio, you've danced together near that boundary before.

In truth, you may have quite a score to settle with each other from a prior lifetime. Every soul has moved through a range of incarnations, so please don't get hung up on this! Whether or not your souls shared a violent or criminal history, you're here for an entirely DIFFERENT purpose this go 'round. And it's meant to be peaceful.

Some Composite South Node in Scorpio couples have an "us against the world" mentality. If you battled evil together in prior lifetimes, it would make sense, given this zodiac position. But you have different dragons to slay as a duo this time around. If you get fixated on people being "out to get you," your twin trust issues may unconsciously attract more betrayals.

How to break this cycle? Enter the Composite Taurus North Node. This grounded earth sign energy pulls you two out of Scorpio's dungeon and plants your four feet on terra firma. Make the rule of K.I.S.S. your standard operating procedure as a couple: Keep It Simple, Sweetheart.

The tendency to read between the lines, assume malicious intent, and fling accusations? That's what you two are here to outgrow. When you catch yourselves speculating, flip the switch ASAP and shift your internal monologue into a fact-finding dialogue. In most cases, your imaginations are spiraling to worse catastrophes than what the present-day situation is serving up. Ask straightforward questions! It's the path to peace for Supercouples with their Composite North Node in Taurus.

Another important growing edge for you two? Allowing yourselves to enjoy comfort and luxury. In prior incarnations, you had to be resourceful, using the Scorpionic gift of turning trash into treasure to create beauty. The secretive nature of your bond may have forced you to squirrel away your funds, never fully enjoying them in the open.

Message from your Composite Taurus North Node: You CAN and should enjoy luxury without apology in this lifetime. While the two of you may be masterful upcyclers, it's not a crime to buy new—especially if you let earthy Taurus guide you to sustainable, environmentally conscious brands! And with the savvy investment skills you two bring in from your karmic past, funding these decadent splurges shouldn't be a problem.

Not for nothing, Scorpio is the sex sign! And for the two of you, this Supercouple South Node brings a baseline of erotic chemistry that other couples dream of experiencing. When your souls are on fire, you can get lost in the bliss of your lovemaking. However, don't sleep on that Composite Taurus North Node. (Except post-coitally on silky, Pima cotton sheets, that is.) This sensual earth sign is all about the full-body experience: touch, taste, scent, music, visuals. The spiritual connection you enjoyed in past lives is far more embodied this go-round. So set up the scene and don't forget the frills!

Life is also a lot less dramatic once you two realize that the Scorpionic desires for control and possession have no place in a true love relationship. Grant each other the right to be whole individuals who come together by choice! At first, this dialed-back intensity might actually feel "boring." Don't run away. Once you burn off that mythical belief that it's gotta be tormented in order to be hot, you stand to discover an equally fulfilling brand of sex magic—one that you can be FULLY present to enjoy.

SUPERCOUPLE NORTH NODE
GEMINI ✳ ♊ OR 3RD HOUSE
& **SAGITTARIUS** SOUTH NODE OR 9TH HOUSE

Release:

- Ungrounded wanderlust
- Fixating on the future
- Righteous zealotry
- Biting off more than you can chew
- Being overly self-reliant
- Arrogance
- Hedonism and greed
- Overwhelming yourselves with too many options

Embrace:

- Cooperation
- The power of "now"
- Playful exploration
- Doing one thing at a time
- Dialogue and active listening skills
- Engaging in local activity and hobbies together

Greetings, intrepid travelers! Care to set down your bags and stick around for a while? Staying put is the karmic challenge for couples with a Supercouple South Node in worldly, adventurous Sagittarius. In past lives,

Create your own Supercouple Chart at **SUPERCOUPLE.COM**

you shared many odysseys, perhaps as roving religious nomads, seafaring spice merchants or hitchhiking beatniks with flowers in your hair. And when you come together in this lifetime, your desire to explore the planet accelerates.

New passport stamps are practically guaranteed. You might, in fact, start dating in a long-distance configuration—and frankly, that suits you both just fine. Being tourists in each other's hometowns is guaranteed fun! But that's not the only perk. Sagittarius is one of the most indie-spirited signs of the zodiac. With this Supercouple South Node, a decent amount of "absence" CAN make your hearts grow fonder, provided you keep in regular touch via phone, text and video chat.

Because nomadic Sagittarius is your Composite South Node, it represents what comes easily to you as a pair. The two of you might feel more at home in the international terminal of an airport than your own love nest! But don't get TOO comfortable in those 180-degree flatbed seats. Those voyages across the goddess' green earth are the bonus of your relationship, NOT its higher purpose. With locally zoned Gemini as your Composite North Node, the real adventure begins when you find your ideal community and settle in there.

Notice we said settle in, not settle DOWN. Even when you're circulating through a smaller radius, the two of you are destined to be an active pair. Like Sagittarius, Gemini is a mutable sign, keeping you two in perpetual motion. The trick is to "think globally, act locally." When you stay in one place for a while, you'll make a profound impact on the area. Pour your considerable energy into creating a community that's interesting enough to make you two WANT to stick around. You're the couple that builds playgrounds, organizes block parties and books noteworthy bands to perform concerts in the park.

Since Sagittarius is the zodiac's lawmaker (lesser known fact about the sign), your Composite South Node might be a springboard that launches you both into local politics, fundraising for candidates or even running for the school board or city council. With the worldly perspective you bring to the table, diversity, equity and inclusivity initiatives will be hot topics that the two of you support.

On a personal note, how's your communication as a couple? The philosophical Composite Sagittarius South Node makes it easy for the two of you to pontificate broadly, but as a result, you could gloss over personal data. News alert! Questions like, "How was your day?" are not actually trite if you answer honestly and engage with each other's response. Your Composite Gemini North Node is here to teach the two the art of finding magic in the seemingly mundane. Inquisitive Gemini is a bit like an investigative journalist, here to find the who-what-when-where-how of every situation. Add some active listening prompts to your dialogues like, "Say a little more about that" or "Can you expand on that a bit?"

The mirroring technique is a particularly salient practice for your Composite Gemini North Node. Before you respond to each other's commentary, stop to reflect back what the other just said. For example, "It sounds like you're saying you'd like to spend more time together in the evenings. Am I understanding you correctly?"

Simplistic as this may sound, you two are here to learn what Eckhart Tolle famously calls "the power of now." Your current reality is rich with possibility, but so easy to overlook when you have intrepid, future-focused Sagittarius as your Composite South Node. With your Composite North Node in Gemini, you'll crack open your relationship's highest purpose when you pair your worldly explorations with daily habits that make every moment feel like an adventure. Would you like your morning coffee as a pour-over or espresso drink, dear?

Create your own Supercouple Chart at **SUPERCOUPLE.COM**

SUPERCOUPLE NORTH NODE

CANCER ✳ ♋ OR 4TH HOUSE

& **CAPRICORN** SOUTH NODE OR 10TH HOUSE

Release:

- Elitism
- Defining yourselves by your worldly accomplishments
- Being too competitive
- Drive for status
- Cool and unemotional detachment
- Materialistic values

Embrace:

- Emotional sensitivity
- Family time
- Compassion for each other
- Creating a home base
- Nurturing
- Self-care
- Connecting from the heart
- Being more inclusive than exclusive

They say that long-term relationships take hard work and determination. If that's the case, you two have arrived with sleeves rolled up, eager to dive in! With a Supercouple South Node in goal-getting Capricorn, anything worth having is worth hustling for. Your souls have shared many lifetimes being large and in charge together, perhaps city-planning for ancient empires or overseeing royal treasuries. Thanks to this success-driven Supercouple South Node, you are positioned well to create security and long-term wealth in this lifetime, too. You'll naturally support each other's loftiest ambitions, popping up as a power couple and managing every mission like a boss duo.

Teaming up as business partners is a stellar use of your natural abilities as a couple, but guess what? It's not actually the core purpose of your relationship. With nurturing, domestic Cancer as your Composite North Node, your shared destiny will be unveiled through emotional exploration rather than external validation. Less achieving, more feeling: Are you ready to open your hearts?

Probably not, if we're being totally honest. Cool, strategic detachment? You two have that dialed in. Naming and claiming your feelings? Squirm! Navigating the seas of Cancer's emotion ocean could begin as a choppy ride. Before both of you can reach smooth sailing, you may feel like passengers on a tiny craft getting tossed around in a tropical storm. No, this is not the kind of "moving and shaking" you VIPs have experienced together in the past. But let the profoundly sentimental energy of Cancer wash over you, and you'll be in for a heart-opening journey.

One of the major lessons of your Composite Cancer North Node is this: The best things in life are not actually things. That wasn't the case for your prior Capricorn-directed incarnations, however. Early in your relationship, you may feel a compulsion to keep up with the Joneses, flashing luxury labels and joining all the "right" organizations. Fortunately, you'll both bore quickly of that game.

Create your own Supercouple Chart at SUPERCOUPLE.COM

It's not that you WON'T have a comfortable life together—Cancer demands that as much as Capricorn. But you'll probably have a simpler life, finding joy in all manner of nesting activities: preparing nightly dinners, renovating the kitchen, planning family vacations. Charity truly begins in the home for the two of you! This will come as a welcome relief after lifetimes in the status-conscious "society" of Capricorn. At last! You can focus on your innermost circle of loved ones, instead of scattering your energy far and wide. There's a sense that you're coming home to one another. Speaking of homes, building one together may be the single-most important thing you do as a pair.

The Cancer-Capricorn axis is all about family, and it's possible you two were relatives in prior incarnations. A fatherly energy flows between you, which can give you the urge to protect and provide for one another. This is a beautiful basis for your relationship as long as you don't get caught up in a "life coach" dynamic. Sometimes, the best advice is the kind that you don't offer. (At least not until it's solicited.)

Make sure you're adding Cancer's archetypical motherly energy into the equation! With this Composite North Node, it's wise to use a softer, sweeter touch instead of pummeling each other with tough love. Become the shoulders for the other to lean on—and yes, cry on, too. As you'll learn many times over in this relationship, few things are more healing—or exhilarating—than a long, tender hug in one another's arms.

SUPERCOUPLE NORTH NODE
LEO  OR 5TH HOUSE
& **AQUARIUS** SOUTH NODE OR 11TH HOUSE

Release:

- Allowing friends to weigh in on your relationship
- Emotional detachment
- Being overly intellectual
- "Head over heart"
- Not showing your feelings
- Too much nomadic living with no roots
- Rejection of material and sensual pleasure

Embrace:

- Unbridled self-expression
- Indulging in luxury
- Leading by example
- Following your hearts
- Tuning into your desires and sensuality
- Spoiling each other
- Open displays of affection

Ready to work the buddy system? Let's go! The friend zone is a familiar place for couples with Supercouple South Node in Aquarius, the sign of universal love. Consider it a blessing! Many would argue

Create your own Supercouple Chart at **SUPERCOUPLE.COM**

that there's no stronger foundation for a long-term relationship than being "in like" with each other. And if that's the case, you two are textbook BFFs with benefits.

Quirky Aquarius is the zodiac's rebel. With this past-life signature anchoring your relationship, your souls have had loftier matters on your minds than chasing rainbows and unicorns. (Not that Aquarius doesn't appreciate those, too.) In prior incarnations you may have teamed up as revolutionaries and activists. Perhaps you even co-existed in a fringe society where you had to disguise your identities from the divergent mainstream. Whatever the case, you felt like a duo of outsiders—a vibe that carries over into this lifetime. As a result, you don't just accept each other's "weird" side—you celebrate it! Couples with Composite South Node in Aquarius often feel blessed to meet each other for this very reason. However it can be a double-edged sword. On the one hand, what a relief to NOT have to put on airs! But a tendency to develop an "us against the world" mentality can cause you both to isolate—which is so NOT the purpose of your relationship.

Another way your Aquarius South Node can play out is like this: The two of you become community leaders, organizing a micro society of people who share your forward-thinking ideals. (Just make sure you don't accidentally start a cult together, okay?) Wherever you focus your combined energy, you're sure to be a popular pair.

News alert: You don't have to fit in with people in order to "belong." But that might not be immediately obvious to you both. Cue the Composite Leo North Node! With this showstopping, individualistic zodiac sign directing your shared destiny, you are being pushed onto the world stage like a pair of dynamic co-stars. And if you REALLY want to make the most of this Supercouple North Node, you'll outfit yourselves in the flashiest costumes possible. You two are here to command attention, not fade into the background. In prior incarnations, you had to cut a low profile in order to blend in with your community. This time around, you can actually live differently, being loud, proud and free. It might take a moment for both of you to realize that the world is not out to condemn you. No one said moving into your Composite North Node was a cakewalk. Turning your relationship into performance art WILL be a process.

Another essential growth hurdle to cross? Learning how to romance each other. With decadent Leo as your Composite North Node, this Romeo and Juliet stuff is all new to the two of you. Intellectual Aquarius is the land of sapiosexuals, where turn-ons come from exchanging ideas. But slowly, you must stretch into the terrain of candlelight dinners, warming massage oil and those damn rose petals. Cynical though you both may be, don't knock the multi-sensory date until you try it. Light the votives, turn on the sexy playlist, pick out special lingerie. Plan dress-up dates to see live music then have drinks at a rotating skybar on the top floor of a hotel. Take pictures of yourselves—lots and lots of pictures. This playful, provocative Leonine behavior will awaken your pleasure receptors and bring some long-awaited joy into your lives.

Maybe this seems superficial—especially to a couple who has spent so many incarnations standing up for the underserved members of society. No one's saying you can't canvas, campaign and create social change this go-round. But maybe, just maybe, you could do that without so much suffering? You two have earned the right to enjoy some of life's luxuries together. So follow the compass of your Composite Leo North Node, and let yourselves indulge in the finer things!

SUPERCOUPLE NORTH NODE

VIRGO ✳ ♍ OR 6TH HOUSE

& **PISCES** SOUTH NODE OR 12TH HOUSE

Release:

- Getting lost in fantasy
- Not setting boundaries
- Making too many sacrifices
- Codependence and enabling
- Getting lost in your daydreams and unrealistic fantasies
- Self-medicating with addictive substances

Embrace:

- Solving problems with facts and data
- Financial structure
- Grounding routines
- Setting clear boundaries
- Healthy living
- Discipline
- Processing your emotions without substances or other escapes
- Recovery from addiction

Talk about living the dream! With fantasy weaver Pisces as your Supercouple South Node, your time together may begin like a fairy tale, with all the sweep-you-off-your feet intensity that your inner Disney prince(ss) could hope for. It won't take much prompting for the two of you to float away on Aladdin's carpet—or tumble down a rabbit hole into Alice's Wonderland. It's such a sweet escape from the harsh reality of the "real world."

Or is it? In the early stages of your relationship, we'd say, yes, absolutely. The Composite South Node in Pisces supercharges your honeymoon phase with high-stakes romance. Because of the boundless nature of this watery zodiac sign, you may feel as if you've melted into each other. And faster than a rushing river, you'll become integral parts of each other's lives. You'll meet (and naturally, charm) BFFs and family, cry on each other's shoulders, and form an instant support network. You'll revel in great works of art, dance all night to music and indulge in profound pleasures of the flesh. It's as if you were both just waiting to find each other in order to finally...relax.

The reason for this ease? With Pisces, the 12th and final sign of the zodiac, anchoring your bond, your souls have shared MANY journeys together. You won't simply recognize each other, you'll tune in to one another on every level. So close is your connection, in fact, that you're perfectly content to slip off in a "just the two of us" bubble and rarely emerge.

Sounds like the answer to your romantic prayers, right? Sure, but hang on, lovers. The closeness of your bond can become a slippery slope. Compassion can easily turn into codependence as you attempt to "rescue" each other from feeling any pain. Since Pisces is the sign of escapism, some couples with this Composite South Node may find themselves in the throes of addiction—to food, drink, drugs, or other unhealthy vices. Over time, you may pull each other deeper into a spiral of depravity—until someone intervenes.

Enter your Composite Virgo North Node. With this grounded,

Create your own Supercouple Chart at **SUPERCOUPLE.COM**

disciplined earth sign guiding your shared destiny, the two of you are here to learn limits in this incarnation. Excessive hedonism will be your undoing as a pair...unless you make that U-Turn into a healthier lifestyle. Whether you wind up as regulars on the yoga retreat circuit or die-hard 12 Steppers is anyone's guess. But you'll both discover a vast inner power once you learn the art of delayed gratification. Who knew that pushing through boot camp trainings could be so rewarding?

Over time, the two of you will redefine "living our best lives" into something far sweeter and simpler than you originally imagined. It's not that you WON'T tap into that Pisces pleasure pool, but you may redefine what sparks joy. Passing out after sex on the beach and a champagne bender? Nah. How about deeply interconnected lovemaking in a deep woods bungalow followed by a vegan breakfast and adaptogen-infused morning coffee?

In past lives, you may have been healers together; perhaps you made great sacrifices to literally rescue the people that you loved. With your Composite North Node in Virgo, your relationship will still be service-oriented, but in a much more measured way. Surprise! You don't have to give up all your worldly possessions in order to do good. In fact, this time around, the two of you are here to create a sense of material stability. What you once considered boring might be the glue that holds the two of you together: simple daily routines, following a budget so there's money saved up for a major trip each year. Life doesn't have to be such a roller coaster ride in order to remain interesting!

There's no denying the esoteric energy that a Composite Pisces South Node brings, and you can rest in the certainty of your telepathic connection. With keenly analytical Virgo as your North Node, however, you need to balance out those intuitive hits with solid facts. Once you strike that balance between fantasy and reality, your relationship's highest purpose will emerge.

SUPERCOUPLE NORTH NODE
LIBRA ✳ ♎ OR 7TH HOUSE
& **ARIES** SOUTH NODE OR 1ST HOUSE

Release:

- The "me first" mentality
- Aggression
- Fighting
- Too much self-reliance
- Selfishness
- Acting without considering each other's feelings
- Bulldozing
- Hotheadedness
- Rushing
- Impatience

Embrace:

- The power of partnership
- The "peaceful warrior" within
- Cooperation
- Compromise
- Commitment
- Generosity
- Patience
- Making sacrifices for the good of the relationship

Create your own Supercouple Chart at **SUPERCOUPLE.COM**

Well, hello, stranger. With your Composite South Node in Aries, the zodiac's first sign, your souls don't have much history together. Hell, you might be starting with a blank slate. Lucky you! We're not joking. As exciting as it sounds to say, "We've met in another lifetime," there's so much baggage that comes with sharing a karmic past. And that can make everything feel SO heavy.

With the brand-new energy of Composite South Node in Aries setting the tempo, you get a fresh start together this go-round. Even if you DID coexist in other incarnations, you've likely completed prior soul contracts. The cycle begins anew! Now, you can ask yourselves: What love story do we want to co-author? And will it be sci-fi, fantasy lit, manga or...?

With fire sign Aries at the base of your union, the heat, passion and attraction are immediate. But don't expect to become an overnight Supercouple. Aries is playful, trailblazing and innovative—and most of all, it's a highly independent zodiac sign! Sharing this Composite South Node leaves you with a riddle to resolve: How can we blend our lives without sacrificing our individuality?

Good question, right? It's a huge deal for you two. Fears of engulfment can balloon in this relationship. Will you lose yourselves under the "domination" of the other's strong personality? Get burned in a conflagration of desire? Let's all take a breath here, okay? The Composite Aries South Node is "avoidant attachment style" issues in action. Pull back a bit and you'll realize that yeah, you're probably overreacting.

Fortunately, your destiny-driven Composite North Node is in Libra, the sign of committed, long-term relationships. The universe is pulling for togetherness for the two of you! You'll just have to get through some clumsy "dance lessons" before you can tango like pros. Please don't get hung up on winning the metaphoric DWTS "mirrorball trophy." (Aries IS competitive like that.) Syncing your steps will be a lifelong practice. And once you embrace the process, you'll find the most delicious groove.

Here's a samba you can start with: Choose your battles! Since Aries is the zodiac's warrior sign, fighting instincts are strong for this Composite South Node. It's too easy to fly off the handle at the slightest whiff of a criticism—or come at each other with your defenses (and dukes) up. You won't have trouble vocalizing opinions here. Trouble is, you may jockey to be "right" instead of leaning into the Libran art of compromise. While the makeup sex is bound to be epic, we don't recommend picking fights as foreplay. Sooner or later, you'll just wind up burning bridges for good.

Bottom line: You are here to teach each other how to share, compromise and cooperate. That's the primary reason the universe brought you together. Supporting one another doesn't have to mean sacrificing your needs. Libra is represented by the Scales, and this Composite North Node makes every moment you share a balancing act.

Don't merely embrace your differences. Celebrate them! The opposing forces you bring to the table can coalesce into a harmonious sense of wholeness neither of you could experience on your own.

Create your own Supercouple Chart at **SUPERCOUPLE.COM**

SUPERCOUPLE NORTH NODE

SCORPIO ✳ ♏ OR 8TH HOUSE

& **TAURUS** SOUTH NODE OR 2ND HOUSE

Release:

- Attachment to luxury
- Earthly appetites and overindulgence
- Being too practical
- Sticking with what you know
- Hiding in a comfort zone
- Not speaking up for your beliefs

Embrace:

- Spiritual connection
- Allowing for mystery
- Combining your finances
- Exploring your erotic natures and shadow sides

Well isn't this comfortable? As easy familiarity flows between couples with grounded Taurus as their Supercouple South Node. With little effort, routines click into place, bringing you both a greater sense of stability. Excitement? You're going to have to work on that part. But first, take a moment to appreciate the breathing room your relationship opens up. Inhale. Exhale. Repeat.

Rooted Taurus is the first of the zodiac's three earth signs—and you two have planted seeds together in many past incarnations. Perhaps you were pioneering spouses, raising a family in the sweet, simple spirit of love. With this traditional placement, you may have shared an austere lifetime where rigid rules interfered with your full expression of your sexuality. (That's Scorpio's domain...more on that in a minute.)

Since Taurus is not an inherently couple-y sign, your prior configuration wasn't necessarily a romantic one (although we're not ruling that out). In some manner, you worked toward a common goal of meeting basic needs: food, shelter, clothing. Survival instincts are strong for Composite Taurus South Node couples, and you are masters of manifestation when you team up!

Hopefully you are enjoying some well-deserved luxury in this lifetime. Taurus is ruled by beauty-loving Venus, and if you save your pennies, you can (and should!) treat yourselves to silky sheets, eye-catching art, copper-bottomed cookware and relaxing vacations when there are funds to spare. Whether you buy everything brand new or score a deal on secondhand goods matters not! Consider it your baseline duty to help each other live an elegant life with whatever means you have available.

But that's not where the REAL juice of this relationship lies. Directly across the zodiac wheel, your Composite North Node in Scorpio sizzles with spiritual and erotic potential. Your shared mission, should you choose to accept it, is far sexier than scouring eBay for china plates to add to your Royal Limoges Nymphea Paradis Bleu collection. (Again, no judgments...)

Create your own Supercouple Chart at **SUPERCOUPLE.COM**

The Composite Scorpio North Node wants a bond that contains multitudes, entwining your minds, bodies and souls for all of eternity. That's a whole lot of intensity, we're not going to lie. It's also a deep well of magic to draw from. Our prediction? Neither of you will ever feel 100% ready to dip your bucket into those waters. There's just so much mystery surrounding anything "Scorpio" that you have to push forward on faith alone, understanding that there will be stormy nights on those seas as well as marvelously placid ones.

Guess what? You two signed up for this. After so many lifetimes of comfortable but controlled existence, you are ready to escape from those restrictive confines. Forging ahead toward your Composite North Node in Scorpio means breaking free from traditions. It also means touching taboos from your past incarnations. We're talking sex, plant medicine, rock and roll—and if you put your clever heads together, breaking into a new wealth bracket.

To activate this Composite North Node, here's a simple rule to follow: choose the magical over the mundane. How can you amplify the sexiness in all that you do? Does it make your heart race a little faster? Now we're getting somewhere. Together, you can and should push yourselves past your edges.

Know that this will be a process. With every two steps you take forward, fears may arise, sending you scurrying for shelter. Give yourselves permission to be vulnerable as you evolve. Scorpio is an incredibly private sign, and the two of you may need to go to your separate corners in between "field research" so you can reconnect to your own centers. Since you are essentially doing shadow work together (Scorpio's realm), you WILL have to accept each other for better and for worse.

The sum of your superpowers is greater than your individual parts! So don't ice each other out if you see something you don't particularly love. One of the keys to your bond is sharing buried feelings as you bring secrets to light. Put down your journals and talk through the swirling thoughts in your heads. It's actually a privilege to witness the other's transformation—and offer one another unconditional love. Since Scorpio rules the esoteric, exploring mysticism is a huge part of your connection. Don't be surprised if you share supernatural experiences as you get closer to your partner. That's the miracle of the Composite Scorpio North Node!

SUPERCOUPLE NORTH NODE
SAGITTARIUS  OR 9TH HOUSE
& **GEMINI** SOUTH NODE OR 3RD HOUSE

Release:

- Compromising at the expense of individuality
- People pleasing and manipulating the truth
- Being overly dependent on each other
- Staying too close to home
- Scattering your energy in too many directions

Embrace:

- Traveling the world
- Authenticity and honesty
- Leaving your comfort zone
- Allowing for autonomy
- Taking risks
- Supporting one another's independent dreams

Hello, soul twins! Couples who have their Supercouple South Node in Gemini share a special synergy. In past lifetimes, you've likely been siblings or actual twins. Maybe you were peers who worked together closely. As a result of your close-knit pasts, you cooperate easily in this lifetime, as if you've always been a single unit. Together, you're the epitome of a dynamic duo.

Cerebral Gemini is the zodiac's communicator, and with this Composite South Node, no subject is off limits for you two! You'll dissect any topic like scientific researchers, analyzing, strategizing and unlocking the code of the universe. There's a huge wealth of cognitive capital in this relationship. Because of that, you two could team up to write a best-selling book, co-host a podcast or dispense advice on a talk show.

Heady as your bond may be, you're also a totally playful pair. Mobile Gemini keeps you two on the move with a steady stream of social engagements. From barbecues to concerts to weekend road trips, it's hard to find an open slot of whitespace on your shared calendar. Warning: This addiction to "busyness" may become a pitfall for your partnership, in fact. It's fine to let the good times roll, but how about pulling over for a rest stop in between a few of those engagements?

In each other, you've found a best friend with benefits, and how sweet it is. But how about THIS for a twist? Your Gemini-ruled doppelgänger dynamic is actually the opposite of your destiny as a pair. With freedom-loving Sagittarius as your Composite North Node, you are here to break the "twinning" tendency. Rather than being two halves of a whole who "complete" one another, your soul mission is to support your partner's evolution to wholeness.

Cue the sad trombone. It's a tiny bit crushing to pull away from the person who mirrors you so perfectly. But if you don't carve out a few separate spaces, your dynamics will invariably get complicated. Your bond may devolve into bickering, codependence and resentment. If one of you sacrifices your dreams in order to keep the relationship

Create your own Supercouple Chart at **SUPERCOUPLE.COM**

alive, look out! The battle for dominance can get vicious. Let this linger on for too long, and the uglier traits of Gemini may emerge: backstabbing, betrayal, infidelity—oh my!

Fortunately, this low-vibe drama CAN be avoided. But it's going to take some conscious efforts to emerge from your couple bubble and pursue your individual life paths. Make no mistake: Doing so will feel like a risk to your joined-at-the-hip relationship template. Lucky for you two, Sagittarius is the zodiac's gambler. Once you begin pushing each other into liberated terrain, your relationship blossoms in untold ways. Growth and expansion is the name of the game for both of you in this lifetime, so you might as well embrace it. And don't forget, you can always process the feelings that arise with your famous all-night, philosophical conversations. (Wine, weed and psychedelics optional.)

And don't misunderstand us. By "independent," we don't mean "separate". There may be times, however, that life leads you to different zip codes. Long-distance spells can be challenging for any couple, but for the two of you, they are like a karmic test. There's only one thing to do: Embrace them, should they arise. Time apart provides the perfect training ground for your worldly Composite Sagittarius North Node. Utilize these periods to ramp up the pursuit of your individual interests. Sign up for the painting class, learn Spanish or how to code apps. Besides that, visiting each other in new cities can be exciting and romantic!

And guess what? As you pursue the parallel adventures of your Composite Sagittarius North Node, something magical happens. Your Composite Gemini South Node draws you back together to share what you learn with one another. Over time, you might even discover overlaps that allow your newfound skills to dovetail beautifully. Since Sagittarius is the sign of the traveler and the teacher, it's anyone's guess where this will take you. Perhaps the two of you will team up as retreat leaders who bring people on a journey to remote areas for experiential learning.

No matter your GPS coordinates, here's one of the greatest challenges you'll face: telling each other the truth instead of manipulating the uncomfortable facts. The Composite Gemini South Node makes you masters of doublespeak, which probably springs from a good intention, like not wanting to hurt one another's feelings. But wise Sagittarius is the zodiac's most authentic sign. This Composite North Node wants you both to open up ALL the way! Sure, you may push each other's buttons (or trample on egos) as you master the art of diplomacy. Mastering authentic communication is a marathon, not a sprint. Keep on keeping on, and you two could experience the rare gift of being fully seen and witnessed by another human.

SUPERCOUPLE NORTH NODE

CAPRICORN ✳ ♑ OR 10TH HOUSE

& **CANCER** SOUTH NODE OR 4TH HOUSE

Release:

- Caretaking and codependence
- Spending too much time at home
- Indulging with food and drink
- Holding in your emotions
- Letting moods dominate the relationship

Embrace:

- Emotional restraint
- Setting goals and reaching them
- Proactive leadership
- Achieving status and success together
- Family bonds

Welcome home! With nurturing, domestic Cancer as your Supercouple South Node, this relationship is chicken soup for your souls. Finally! You can relax, knowing that you're with someone who truly cares about your feelings. That level of emotional validation feels like the warmest hug in the world. So why don't you stay awhile? The Cancer Composite South Node plants deep, permanent roots. Even if you swore you'd never settle down, surprise! It won't be long before you're making appointments with realtors and figuring out whether to style your love nest in boho-chic or Japandi.

With familial Cancer ruling your past-life connection, you have surely lived together under many roofs—from a thatched hut to the stone turret of a gothic castle. But in what relational configuration, exactly? Since Cancer is associated with the archetypal mother (and feminine energy in general), it's possible you've been moms, sisters or daughters to each other in prior incarnations. Even as romantic partners, that soul signature shows up in the caretaking energy that flows naturally between you. You may fuss over each other, worrying, scolding and even veering into codependent terrain by trying to "rescue" one another from making a grave mistake. And yes, there will always be food on the table. With epicurean Cancer as your relationship's anchor point, sharing meals may be your favorite ritual.

Before you slip into a food coma, however, let's talk about your Composite North Node in Capricorn. Across the zodiac wheel from the Crab, the disciplined Sea Goat blows the whistle on some of those indulgent tendencies. Are you ready for the challenge? Dust those cookie crumbs off your laps and get your butts off the couch! When your Composite Capricorn North Node comes a-calling, it puts the two of you in cosmic boot camp. Time to ditch the safe and familiar route and embark on the challenging road to growth.

Capricorn is the sign of achievement, status and public recognition. While no one would begrudge you the beautiful home life that you share, if your space has turned into a fortress, there will be

Create your own Supercouple Chart at **SUPERCOUPLE**.COM

trouble in paradise. Inevitably, you'll both wind up feeling stuck and unhappy—and the inflammation and extra pounds don't help matters one bit. Your shared destiny involves building something together that impacts the world OUTSIDE your home. Sure, you might develop plans from your kitchen table, but ultimately, you will need to go interact with other humans besides each other. Your path to success involves pushing yourselves OUT of your comfort zones, even if you return to that bliss bubble to relax after a hard day's work.

Another way your Composite Capricorn North Node may play out? You will become each other's greatest champions, spurring each other on to achieve great things. Reluctant though you may be to adopt this moniker, you two are destined to become a power couple.

Start building up your endurance. Your evolution from private partners to public figures will be a marathon, not a sprint. Both of you would rather slip away from the rest of the world—or at least avoid the "harshness" of the material realm and all its status-based rules. PS: That's not a bad thing! The heart-centered warmth of your Composite Cancer South Node is a brilliant springboard into the cool and rational realm of your Capricorn North Node. The two of you may start a business together, for example, that's grounded in ethical practices, sustainability and a family-like company culture. People gravitate to whatever nest you bless, whether it's your humble abode or your cozy office space. (With kombucha on tap, a living room area and pinball machines, naturally.)

Because of this external-world focus, children may or may not be part of your destiny in this lifetime. While you'll definitely birth SOMETHING, it could just as easily be a game-changing creative project or online venture as an actual kid. You may help each other heal ancestral traumas and break intergenerational patterns that have been holding your families back for years.

On the subject of kids, let's talk about your inner children. One pitfall of the Composite Cancer South Node is that your shared sensitivity can spiral into charged emotions in the blink of an eye. Trigger alerts? Set them to Code Red. Should one of you feel slighted or attacked, out come the Crab claws ready to do damage in the name of "self defense."

We don't say this lightly: Reactivity can be the undoing of your relationship. Here's where you must head for the high elevations of the Capricorn Goat standing at the peak of the mountain. Yes, you may need to take regular cool-down breaks before you can calmly discuss certain topics without someone screaming or bursting into tears. More than most couples, you'll need to create systems for managing the flood of feelings when they arise. But adopt this mantra and you'll ascend to the heights of your Composite Capricorn North Node: Rise above.

Create your own Supercouple Chart at **SUPERCOUPLE.COM**

SUPERCOUPLE NORTH NODE
AQUARIUS ✳ ♒ OR 11TH HOUSE
& **LEO** SOUTH NODE OR 5TH HOUSE

Release:

- Attention-seeking
- Creating drama for "excitement"
- Focusing too much on the external
- Entitlement
- Being overly protective or loyal to a fault
- Vanity
- Over-the-top emotional responses

Embrace:

- Building a community
- Activism
- Creating a lifestyle based on values and principles
- Living by your own rules, experimentation

If life imitates art, with the Supercouple South Node in Leo, your relationship might be as charged with dynamic tension as a Shakespearean balcony scene. Romeo, meet Juliet. (Yes, again.) This past life signature brings all the trappings of young love, sweeping you both into a cresting wave of emotion from the moment you lock eyes. In the early days of your relationship, the two of you might act like giggling teenagers in the throes of a first crush. There will be lots of canoodling, PDA and selfies of you both at various luxury outposts. Friends, however, will NOT enjoy spending time with you two during this cycle of your relationship. (So awkward!) They might even ban you from mentioning the other's name more than twenty times over brunch. (Oops!)

What can you say? Leo is one of the zodiac's fiercest romantics. Both of you were destined to fall hard for one another. The beautiful part of this Composite South Node is how easily it allows you two to keep the magic alive—long after the so-called honeymoon phase is supposed to fade. You're the couple who lives to spoil each other with tailor-made gifts and over-the-top experiences! You'll dress up special and flirt with one another into your sunset years. "She was the prettiest gal I ever laid eyes on, and she still is to this day." Swoon!

Since Leo is the sign of fertility, this Composite South Node makes you a naturally creative pair. The two of you may have a brood of children or be prolific in other ways, co-creating works of art or business ventures. If you weren't literally royalty in past lives, you may have lived in the upper echelons of society. The spirit of abundance flows through all that you do together—and oh, how glamorous it is!

But let us warn you about overindulging in Leo's royal dowry. This CAN indeed be too much of a good thing if you don't balance it out with the high-minded humanitarianism of your Composite Aquarius North Node. In past lives, you were part of the "special people's club," and made no bones about it. In this lifetime, any abuse of privilege is like swigging that vial of poison that took down the scions of Montague and Capulet.

You two are here to share your Leo-ruled wealth in the interest of Aquarian activities, like building community and singing the praises of "one love" equality. In the process, you might have to give up a few VIP perks. Membership to a country club? Maybe, maybe not. But how about joining an activist organization too? With Aquarius as your Composite North Node, your peak experiences may involve protesting unjust laws or serving meals to the homeless. This idealistic Aquarian dharma work is the secret to your fulfillment as a pair.

In fact, don't be surprised if your relationship goes from superficial to metaphysical at an accelerated clip. Resort vacations may soon hold less appeal than yoga retreats and medicine ceremonies. Push the envelope romantically, too! While your Composite Leo South Node makes you masters of romance, there's far more breadth to your connection than candlelight dinners and candygrams. Experimental Aquarius rules the higher mind, and with this air sign as your Composite North Node, tantric breathwork could soon give way to all sorts of full-chakra explorations. You two MIGHT even opt into a non-traditional relationship structure, such as an open marriage or living in separate residences.

But we'll let you ease into that, should you choose. With the foundation of your Composite Leo South Node, there will be hell to pay if you don't make the other one feel like your number one. Showering each other with attention will always be a must, even when the two of you are interacting with family or outside groups. Affection is equally essential for your passionate pairing. And once you bring in the intellectual stimulation of your Aquarius North Node, yours could be a legendary love affair that has the makings of an epic script!

SUPERCOUPLE NORTH NODE
PISCES ✳ ♓ OR 12TH HOUSE
& **VIRGO** SOUTH NODE OR 6TH HOUSE

Release:

- Nagging and worrying about each other
- Being rigid in your routines
- Using head over heart
- Giving unsolicited advice

Embrace:

- Tapping into imagination and intuition
- Developing faith in the universe
- Surrendering to pleasure
- Romance for romance's sake
- Holding space for each other's emotions
- Compassion

Call it practical magic or simply "meant to be": Your Supercouple South Node in no-nonsense Virgo makes you quite the sensible pair. With your four feet anchored on solid ground, you are masters of

Create your own Supercouple Chart at **SUPERCOUPLE.COM**

the material realm. There's literally nothing you can't manifest when you combine your visionary powers with your joint ability to bring a plan to fruition. But here's the thing: You're not a "wanting" couple. With Virgo's minimalist ethos directing your past-life energy, a kiss is just a K.I.S.S. for the two of you. And by K.I.S.S. we mean, Keep It Simple, Sweetheart!

At your best, you're a no-drama duo who has better things to do with your time than spiral out over other people's stupidity. The two of you may become role models for your families and communities, living an ethical lifestyle that is rooted in the value of integrity. Since Virgo is the sign of natural health, wellness may be a huge part of your connection. You may grow your own food (in organic soil, of course), adopt a back-to-earth or vegan lifestyle and regularly train together for half-marathons. Nature-based activities keep you centered. There's nothing quite like a healing hike or camping trip to get you back on the same page when you've been squabbling.

Since Virgo is the sign of service, volunteering can be a major bonding activity. You're an eternally helpful pair! Neighbors rely on you to host the block party, petition the co-op board or otherwise call out any behavior that is deemed "unacceptable." Even your vacations may revolve around giving back, like building houses for underserved communities or doing a day of cooking at a shelter. Yes, there's something quite wholesome going on in this relationship. And you have the framed family photos to prove it!

With all due respect to your merit-badge-winning lifestyle, you two could use some naughtiness in your lives! With free-flowing Pisces as your Composite North Node, you're actually here to release some of those rules and rigidity. You have such a solid foundation together that it's actually fine to cut loose without worrying that your entire worlds will fall apart. An even better plan? Turn your mundane routines into sacred rituals. For example, rather than reading side-by-side in bed, how about listening to a podcast together? Or, to be more Piscean, doing a tantric meditation or listening to a sultry playlist while you give each other massages?

More than most couples, you'll need a little nudging to talk about your fantasies and turn-ons. But once that dam is opened, look out! This boundless Composite North Node may send you further out to sea than most people dare tread. Use the Virgoan structure of your Composite South Node to set regular date nights on the calendar and block time each year (or more often, ideally) for vacations. Pisces is the sign of escape, and you two are at your best when you're away from the nagging duties of home. Even going out to dinner at a decadent restaurant opens up your pleasure centers and gets you in the mood to loosen up your boundaries, the gift of dreamweaver Pisces.

Analytical Virgo loves kitchen table wisdom and has a solution for every problem. As a result, this Composite South Node may create an unhealthy dynamic of playing life coach for one another. Power struggles may emerge with one of you overfunctioning while the other slacks off—or both of you nagging and worrying as a way of expressing your love. NOT sexy! Pisces is the sign of compassion and empathy. To truly tap the highest expression of your relationship, guess what? Rather than fixing each other, all you have to do is hold space. (Yes, it really is that "easy.") Give hugs instead of lectures. Instead of jumping in with, "let me tell you how to handle that," ask questions like, "Tell me a little more about that?" A softer, sweeter touch will bring out the best in you both.

At points throughout your relationship, you may have to make sacrifices for each other. One of you may be dealing with grief or healing from a health crisis—and the other won't hesitate to jump in with support. As beautiful as this dynamic may be, it can also veer into codependence if you're not careful. Supporting one another with information is great, but there are times when you must surrender and trust the other to walk their path without interference. With Pisces ruling the invisible realm, this Composite North Node relies on faith as its beacon. You simply can't see what's ahead all the time—and it might be mystical, supernatural or otherworldly.

SUPERCOUPLE

Compatibility

WITH YOUR
LUNAR NODES

Create your own Supercouple Chart at **SUPERCOUPLE.COM**

If our Supercouple North Node is in a fire Sign: (ARIES, LEO OR SAGITTARIUS)

And my personal North Node is in a fire sign (ARIES, LEO OR SAGITTARIUS):

Your creative drive gets a supersized burst of energy in this relationship, which supports you in bringing your big ideas into form. You will also be doubly challenged to rethink your highly engaged interpersonal strategy and learn to be less of a "we" and more of a self-defined "me."

And my personal North Node is in an earth sign (TAURUS, VIRGO OR CAPRICORN):

It's easy to feel "oversensitive" in this relationship, which relies more on logic than feelings. Don't underestimate the emotional intelligence that you bring to this bond. Your deep connection with your internal workings is a crucial compass that will help you both navigate the external world with foresight and care.

And my personal North Node is in an air sign (GEMINI, LIBRA, AQUARIUS):

Talk about a role reversal! This relationship flips your natural tendency to be independent on its head, making it a little awkward to figure out when to move closer and when to pull away. Include your partner in your activities while also encouraging them to be self-sufficient. Keep your "me time" sacred, but don't create a fortress around yourself. It's definitely a balancing act!

And my personal North Node is in a water sign
(CANCER, SCORPIO OR PISCES):

Kiss your stubborn side goodbye! Like a gale wind, this relationship sweeps you into an fantastic voyage of new ideas, travel and creative exploration. Do keep at least one foot on solid earth, which is the anchor for your personal South Node. You'll have to be "the responsible one" in this connection—perhaps more often than you deem fair—and say no to risks that are actually foolish gambles.

If our Supercouple North Node is in an earth sign: (TAURUS, VIRGO, OR CAPRICORN)

 And my personal North Node is in a fire sign
(ARIES, LEO OR SAGITTARIUS):

Where do you think you're going? Your self-directed compass spins in a wholly unanticipated direction as this relationship unfolds. Instead of chasing shiny things, you want to settle down and build a lasting legacy. But DO hang on to your sense of adventure. Otherwise, you could wind up rebelling against the very structures you worked hard to create.

 And my personal North Node is in an earth sign
(TAURUS, VIRGO OR CAPRICORN):

This family-friendly relationship will be an easy fit with your existing lifestyle. Here, you find plenty of support for your complex emotions and your ambitious material world pursuits. Settling down is a sweet reward!

And my personal North Node is in an air sign
(GEMINI, LIBRA, AQUARIUS):

Your passionate nature could set new depth records in this
relationship—IF you're willing to stick around and explore all
the emotions that arise. But you'll have to fight hard against
a "grass is always greener" mindset. Put structures in place
for dealing with difficult moments. Since you're here to learn
how to communicate together, working with a counselor (or
another third party) can keep things lovingly productive rather
than angry and destructive.

 And my personal North Node is in a water sign
(CANCER, SCORPIO OR PISCES):

In many ways this relationship is totally on-brand for
you—except you're doing things backwards here since the
relationship is moving from water to earth (the opposite of
your personal nodes). Your natural planning abilities will be
a powerful beacon for the two of you. Emotionally, however,
you're going to feel out of your depth. The intensity of this
connection can be a shock to your system, forcing you to
confront your own walls and hopefully bring them down in the
name of your own evolution. Just expect to be triggered and
flooded fairly often along the way.

If our Supercouple North Node is in an air sign: (GEMINI, LIBRA, AQUARIUS)

 And my personal North Node is in a fire sign (ARIES, LEO OR SAGITTARIUS):

This relationship's goals may move in the opposite direction of your personal destiny. You're here to embrace a greater sense of independence. Meanwhile, your connection is pulling for more sharing and communal coexistence. This can be a tricky paradox to navigate! Fight against people-pleasing tendencies and take a stand for your autonomy. Determine what's "mine" and what's "ours," and stick to your guns.

 And my personal North Node is in an earth sign (TAURUS, VIRGO OR CAPRICORN):

Caution: turbulence ahead. The fiery foundation of this relationship could set off your alarm bells, especially if it moves too quickly into unknown territory. You may find yourself slamming the brakes, even when you're on the verge of progress. However, if you can both pace developments, your connection can help you evolve into a far more adventurous soul.

 And my personal North Node is in an air sign (GEMINI, LIBRA, AQUARIUS):

You're right at home in the fire-to-air progression of this relationship, which follows the same trajectory as your personal path. Expect nonstop adventures and room to explore your independent pursuits. To avoid being like two ships passing in the night, however, develop a shared social group and find activities that you enjoy doing together on a regular basis.

And my personal North Node is in a water sign
(CANCER, SCORPIO OR PISCES):

Buckle up, Buttercup. This relationship's direction is a major disruption to your slow-and-steady groove. You thought you had your life all planned out, then bam! Your connection has you galloping off on a fantastic voyage that was NOT on your itinerary. While you may welcome the excitement, it can also be ungrounding. At some point, you'll have to drop anchor—for sanity's sake!

If our Supercouple North Node is in a water sign: (CANCER, SCORPIO OR PISCES)

 And my personal North Node is in a fire sign
(ARIES, LEO OR SAGITTARIUS):

Welcome to the sensitivity training you didn't realize you needed. Normally, you defer to easy life hacks to solve problems, but not here! This connection requires you to slow down and dissect everyone's feelings. The protracted processing will try your patience; however, and may not be your cup of tea. Your gift here? Supplying levity and humor to your bond.

 And your personal North Node is in an earth sign
(TAURUS, VIRGO OR CAPRICORN):

Flip the script! In your personal life, you begin with your feelings and strategize the best plan of action from there. This relationship demands the opposite: starting with a structured goal sheet of milestones and benchmarks of success. How do you feel about it? You can discuss AFTER the work is done. This approach can be disorienting, causing you to suppress your emotions. But try not to! Your heightened sensitivity is what brings your relationship into balance. It's all about learning how to express your concerns proactively, not reactively.

And my personal North Node is in an air sign (GEMINI, LIBRA, AQUARIUS):

Are you ready to settle down a little? If not, you might find yourself perpetually frustrated in this relationship, which could clip your wings. You need to move around freely and independently, but the responsibilities of this connection could interfere with that. The key to success may lie in bringing in third-party support (babysitters, housekeepers, etc) to open up more free time in your schedule. Just don't forget to invite your partner to join you on your adventures every now and again!

And my personal North Node is in a water sign (CANCER, SCORPIO OR PISCES):

Talk about being in the flow! This relationship runs along the same karmic current as you do personally. Here, you've found a person who understands your desire to plan, live practically and achieve material world comfort. But what about your feelings? It's a little too easy to avoid tapping into your emotional intelligence here, so make sure you are actively making space to expand your empathy with (and toward) one another.

Final Thoughts...

Love in the Aquarian Era

Why modern love needs new a relationship system—and how astrology serves that need

Have relationships outlasted their original purpose?

Some 6,500 years ago, when humans transitioned from nomadic hunter-gatherers to settled farmers, we began pairing off into official couples. Agricultural developments created a surplus of food, which meant healthier people, a booming population and the rise of a trade economy. Suddenly, people owned property, lived longer lives and created generational wealth. If everyone was sleeping with everyone else, who would be the heir to the bounty? A need to draw boundaries around lineage emerged.

This relationship model made sense in the Agrarian Age. But in the current-day Aquarian Age? Not so much. We are living in a time where technology reigns. The rules of living get updated to a new version regularly, like the system software on our devices. Love is running on a wholly different framework where we stay together by choice, not by necessity.

Today, people have endless entry points to help them get into a relationship. There are books and podcasts to help people source for soulmates, dissect compatibility and seduce a lover. We spend $4.2 billion a year on dating apps, flicking through options with the same FOMO-fied mentality that we use to order lunch on Grubhub.

We get engaged, sometimes because we want to, other times because all our friends have and we don't want to be left out. Nearly half of Millennials are married and 80% of Gen Z show an appetite for the institution. Whether it's out of comfort, convenience or true desire, most people aim to settle down with one person. To have kids. Buy homes. Repeat until the nest is empty.

But are we truly happy with the results? The average U.S. marriage lasts only 8.2 years. Since the early 1990s, the divorce rate has doubled for adults over the age of 50 and tripled for the 65-plus set. So much for the fear of growing old alone. It seems we're more scared of spending our golden years unhappy.

With so many choices and so little relevant guidance, it's no surprise the micro-tears of day-to-day life add up to an intractable rupture. And you'll find just as many experts to help navigate divorce, infidelity and breakups when it's time to "move on" or "let go" and "start over."

But what about that placid, seemingly uneventful time after the honeymoon phase; the flat stretch of countryside without all the highs and lows?

You know, the actual relationship itself?

There aren't nearly so many resources (or very much sympathy) for people who tread this middle ground. You've arrived at the holy grail of coupledom, so what do you have to worry about? Turns out, a lot. As anyone who has made it past the seven-month mark can attest, "new relationship energy" will invariably fade. From there, navigating the day-to-day reality of relationships can be subtle and stark. The novelty has worn off and the temptation to look elsewhere for the "high" kicks in. Before we know it, we're on cruise control, defaulting back to habits learned from our families of origin.

But we are here to deliver some hopeful news. Autopiloting through your "real relationship" isn't the only option! Nor is handing your inner children the wheel and allowing them to drive your partnership off a cliff. In that spirit, we wrote *Supercouple*. We wanted to give the modern population a guidebook, a "cosmic care and feeding manual" for their relationships.

Staying together, should you choose that route, is a delicate and nuanced web of emotional, psychological and (yes) astrological factors, woven together like fine lace. They can't be pulled apart without unraveling the whole piece.

We know this intimately, not only from the romantic relationships and marriages in our personal history, but also from being born identical twins. We came into this world as a pair and have shared everything from a crib to a piggybank to our business, Astrostyle, since we took our first breaths.

Recently, we spent two years developing and debuting the first astrology reality dating show, *Cosmic Love*, a full-fledged streaming series released on Amazon Prime Video in August 2022. In this *Bachelor*-meets-astrology "social experiment," twenty Gen Z singles spent a month in a stylishly appointed Malibu mansion, hoping to find their astrologically "perfect" partner via our celestial matchmaking.

Would the stars deliver a better success rate than Tinder or a tequila-soaked hookup?

Admittedly, the "selection pool" was limited due to reality TV standards. The cast members who made the cut were physically fit, genetically blessed twenty-somethings who had the law of supply and demand on their side, at least when it came to dating and sex. But we took on the challenge because this experiment was too good to pass up.

We pored over countless casting tapes, calculated charts and wrote scripts that translated the 5,000-year-old language of the stars into a simple format that mainstream viewers could grasp. We did our best to present the power of astrology, planet by planet, without watering it down.

One of the key deciding factors for matchmaking was the Composite Chart. When the final couples were determined, we knew that it might take a moment for this blended astrological magic to kick in. But we trusted in the power of the stars and watched it play out on the video monitors.

We knew the Superchart would be the kicker for Capricorn Maria and Leo Chris R., whose Composite Sun landed in couple-centric Libra along with a stellium of Composite Scorpio planets in their seventh house of marriage. The two stylish East Coast castmates eyed each other from a distance, but they didn't mingle much in the beginning. Once they learned we had matched them, however, it was on! Their chemistry was exothermic. After passionate kissing and pillow talk about family (hello, Composite Taurus Rising), they inevitably made it to the reality TV altar, with us as their wedding officiants.

Create your own Supercouple Chart at **SUPERCOUPLE.COM**

The "experiment" of *Cosmic Love* reinforced a rising trend: People want companionship, but when it comes to fitting a long-term relationship into their busy, individualized lives, they are often at a loss. And that is where *Supercouple* can be an endlessly useful tool!

This book is a slow-jam version of what we would have taught the romantic hopefuls of *Cosmic Love* if we had more time with them.

We submit to you *Supercouple*, a hopeful note in the rising chorus of "new thought" relationship resources. Our wish is that this work will provide an intriguing path back to yourself and each other, ingredients you can substitute for the refined and unhealthy ones to remix the old romantic recipe.

We may never solve the mystery of love, but we *can* take some of the confusion out of it, offering you tools you can try anytime you feel a strain coming on. Regardless of how long your commitment lasts, there is so much to learn from the experience.

Lean into love,

Ophira + Tali Edut

OPHIRA + TALI
THE ASTROTWINS

THE ASTROTWINS

Identical twin sisters Ophira and Tali Edut, known as the AstroTwins, are professional astrologers who reach millions worldwide. As the official astrologers for *ELLE* magazine and the matchmakers on Amazon Prime Video's *Cosmic Love* they bring the stars down to earth with their empowering approach to horoscopes.

Bestselling authors, they've written a collection of books, including *Love Zodiac* and *Momstrology* (their #1 Amazon parenting guide) and their own brand imprint annual horoscope guides.

With a mission to "empower astrology lovers how to create lives of passion and purpose using the stars as a guide," the AstroTwins have created a suite of courses applying astrology to love, career and home design. Their membership program, Astropreneurs, teaches aspiring and current business owners how to tap into their unique astrological strengths to build careers they love.

HOROSCOPES FOR YOUR BEST LIFE
astrostyle.com | @astrotwins

MORE RELATIONSHIP BOOKS BY THE ASTROTWINS

How to Get Along with Anyone (*Yes, Even That Person)

Any two zodiac signs CAN be compatible, as long as they understand what makes the other one tick. The AstroTwins simplify the secrets of synastry—the 7 unique energies encoded in the distance between your signs. Take your relationships from difficult to dynamic and start bringing out your best.

The AstroTwins' Love Zodiac (AKA Manstrology)

What does a Gemini mean when he says "I'll call you?" Is that Scorpio in love with you because you met his mom...or is this just another test? Our essential guide to the men of every zodiac sign decodes the dudes in your life. For anyone dating a male-identified person, or just looking to better connect with men, Love Zodiac is the "bible" you can't live without!

Momstrology

Parenting DOES come with instructions! This ultimate guide to raising your kids AND flourishing as a mom takes you through every season of parenthood, from birth to toddler to school years and leaving the nest. A favorite baby shower gift, featured by *Good Morning America* and a #1 Amazon bestseller.

START READING NOW AT **ASTROSTYLE.COM/BOOKS**

Made in the USA
Coppell, TX
29 May 2023

17466504R00295